D1450949

# The African Bourgeoisie

Sponsored by the Joint Committee on African Studies of the American Council of Learned Societies and the Social Science Research Council

# The
# African Bourgeoisie
## Capitalist Development
## in Nigeria,
## Kenya,
## and the Ivory Coast

edited by
# Paul M. Lubeck

Lynne Rienner Publishers • Boulder, Colorado

To the memory and accomplishments of
Walter Rodney and Ruth First

Published in the United States of America in 1987 by
Lynne Rienner Publishers, Inc.
948 North Street, Boulder, Colorado 80302

Library of Congress Cataloging-in-Publication Data

The African bourgeoisie.

   Includes bibliographies and index.
   1. Capitalism--Nigeria--History. 2. Capitalism--
Kenya--History. 3. Capitalism--Ivory coast--History.
4. Capitalists and financiers--Nigeria--History.
5. Capitalists and financiers--Kenya--History.
6. Capitalists and financiers--Ivory Coast--History.
I. Lubeck, Paul M.
HC1055.Z9C33  1986          332'.096          86-17778
ISBN 0-931477-86-7 (lib. bdg.)

Printed and bound in the United States of America

The paper used in this publication meets the requirements of the
American National Standard for Permanence of Paper for Printed
Library Materials Z39.48-1984.   ∞

# Contents

# Tables

# Acknowledgments

This book developed from research first presented at the Dakar Conference on the African Bourgeoisie in December 1980, sponsored by the Joint Committee on African Studies of the American Council of Learned Societies and the Social Science Research Council, the Council for Economic and Social Research in Africa, and the Environment and National Development in Africa Program (ENDA). As local hosts of the conference, A.S. Bujra, Jacques Bugnicourt, and Liberty Mahlanga were especially generous with their time, resources, and staff; the editor and the Joint Committee on African Studies are extremely grateful for their kindness and advice. The support of Peter Anyang' Nyong'o was critical to the success of the conference. The Western and Eastern Africa Regional Offices of the Ford Foundation provided financial support so the conference could be held in an African city. The support of Goran Hyden and Robert Drysdale and their staffs at the regional offices is deeply appreciated.

Martha Gephart of the Social Science Research Council deserves praise for guiding the project to publication. Sue Warga and Lily Heom, staff members of the Social Science Research Council, also deserve recognition for their dedicated efforts. Here at Santa Cruz, Wendy Fassett, Kay Mohlman, Brian Folk, and Dana Priest assisted in the editing and preparation for publication. Robert Price of the University of California, Berkeley, was invaluable as a critic and evaluator of the book, and Allen Isaacman and Jane Guyer contributed analyses that improved the book immensely.

Others provided assistance, ideas, and valuable criticism. Michael Cowen, Bjorn Beckman, Michael Chege, Wally Goldfrank, Bill Friedland, Stan Trapido, A. Founou, and Samir

Amin contributed in diverse ways to the ideas contained in this book. Robert Alford and the working group on the state here at Santa Cruz, together with the Joint Committee on African Studies, provided critical support. The financial support of the Academic Senate Research Committee of UCSC is also gratefully acknowledged.

Finally, Lynne Rienner and her staff are to be complimented for their advice, patience, and editorial assistance.

*Paul M. Lubeck*

# Part I

## Issues, Theories, and Method

*Paul M. Lubeck*

# The African Bourgeoisie: Debates, Methods, and Units of Analysis

Since the onset of the transition to national independence after World War II, both theorists and policy makers have debated the capacity and potential of indigenous African classes for extending and deepening capitalist economic development. By centering analysis on the historical experience of indigenous capitalist classes, the authors of this book attempt to advance the debate by assessing the role of indigenous accumulating classes and the state in the transition to capitalism in Black Africa's three most developed states: Nigeria, Kenya, and the Ivory Coast.

For most social scientists, the critical debate has focused on the degree of autonomy possible for indigenous accumulators under the external structural constraints imposed by the capitalist world economy and state system. Indeed, for many African political economists, the orthodox view now holds that *external* factors determine the nature, potential, and contemporary crisis of African capitalism. Recently the orthodox view has been challenged.[1] To be sure, it is not that critics of the external determination thesis dismiss the importance of external factors such as world market cycles, declining terms of trade between industrial and underdeveloped economies, monopoly rents charged by multinational corporations, or political and military intervention to support their dependent local allies. Rather, critics argue that the situation is far less determined than a world-systemic, macroexternal view postulates. That is, *internal* microlevel factors, such as capitalist class formation, conflict within and between classes, efficient resource allocation, following market signals instead of unrealistic state planning, and allowing indigenous accumulators to produce without intervention from rent-seeking state

3

elites, explain the success and extent of indigenous capitalist development. Theorists arguing for the primacy of internal factors insist that microlevel analysis is appropriate because Africans control their own territory and state institutions. Therefore, at the level of intellectual practice, rather than attempting to reform the international economic system (i.e., NIEO), one should analyze the problems of advancing the technical forces of production, developing the home market and creating popular, yet disciplined, class coalitions around the national state.

If one examines the economic and social history of African states during the period of relatively high economic growth extending from the early 1950s to the late 1970s, when the world economy plummeted into deep depression, a clear process of economic *differentiation* has occurred among African states. It is this conjuncture--1950-1980--that forms the framework for this study. During the period of high post-war growth, three states differentiated themselves from the typical African experience by their comparatively high rates of economic growth, by their rates of private agricultural and industrial investment, by their public investment in infrastructure and basic industries, and by their relative increases in agricultural productivity. For all these reasons, Nigeria, Kenya, and the Ivory Coast were selected as prime examples of successful and unambiguously capitalist states different from the African norm.

At this point, the appropriate methodological question is, how representative are these three states for generalizing about capitalist development in Africa? This study argues that, although each possesses a distinct history, each represents a more generalized process of capitalist development. Nigeria, for example, reflects the experience of resource-rich, agriculturally diverse and highly populated states that aspire to exercise regional hegemony. Despite its recent problems, Nigeria compares favorably with Zaire, a potentially rich state with staggering social, political, and economic problems. Whereas Nigeria represents the large regional power led by petroleum exports, Kenya represents the smaller agricultural exporting state that has evolved from white-settler agriculture to African control of that rich and productive agricultural sector. Contemporary Zimbabwe, for example, parallels Kenya in statistical measures and historical experiences. The Ivory Coast, the final case, typifies francophone states that have maintained close economic ties with France and remained within the franc monetary zone, such as Cameroon and Senegal. Because the

Ivory Coast has avoided any economic nationalist policies, unlike Nigeria and (to a lesser degree) Kenya, foreign investment
and confidence remains high as does the postwar rate of economic growth.  The complexity of capitalism in Africa generates states whose experience remains outside these three; but
none have been successful in creating an indigenous bourgeoisie nor in advancing the technical level of capital accumulation in industry and agriculture.  Finally, as the most economically advanced state within its region, each aspires to political and economic hegemony within its sphere of influence.
For Nigeria, it takes the form of the Economic Community of
West African States; for Kenya it was and may again be the
East African Community; and for the Ivory Coast, it is the
Entente Council of West African States.

## Why the Indigenous Bourgeoisie?

The argument for focusing analysis on the indigenous bourgeoisie rests upon the role that capitalist classes play in the
social division of labor and in the process of capitalist accumulation.  In addition, they play a crucial role either within
the state apparatus or in formulating state policy.  Finally, at a
theoretical level, it is important to understand the way in
which capitalist classes figure into most theorists' explanations
for either dynamic and accumulating or stagnating and dependent forms of African capitalism.  Indeed, the capacity of
capitalist classes to direct state policy toward their gaining access to land and capital, toward limiting the role of foreign
capital, and toward nurturing indigenous capitalist investments
by facilitating institutions of labor control and supplying technical services are seminal issues for explaining successful capitalist development.
    Most important, much of the theorizing between depen-
dency/world-systems theorists (external determination) and
more orthodox Marxist and even neoclassical theorists (internal
determination) rests on the activities of indigenous capitalists.
This is because each theoretical perspective presumes that the
bourgeoisie will pursue a mutually exclusive strategy of capital
accumulation, which is characterized by a distinct set of class
alliances, a relationship to the state and to the international
economy.  Focusing attention on the activities of the African
bourgeoisie not only allows one to assess theories purporting to
explain their behavior, but also encourages empirical research
so as to specify ambiguous areas of theory and empirical gen-

eralization. Despite their uneven development and heterogeneous composition across sectors, regions, and states, aggregating indigenous accumulators under the rubric of the African bourgeoisie creates a valuable conceptual tool that links micro- and macrolevel theorizing. For the African bourgeoisie is interwoven into the state and international economy while, at the same time, inextricably linked to the social relations and cultural practices of indigenous society.

## Defining and Situating Africa's Accumulating Classes

Though historically deep-rooted and a major source of African capital accumulation, merchant capital by itself can resolve neither the central debate nor the problem of indigenous control over capitalist production, upon which the future of indigenous capitalism ultimately rests. Instead, the problematic of the African bourgeoisie depends upon its ability to organize agriculture, industry, and modern services (finance, transportation, and technical consultation) with the objective of expanding capitalist production into noncapitalist areas, and to innovate by advancing the technical components of the means of production and *locating* capital accumulation within boundaries of their respective states. It is the production of commodities for a market through the employment of wage labor that specifies the problematic for African capitalist and for this study. Of course, insofar as state technocrats manage and plan commodity production for a market, or figure critically in accumulating or allocating state financial resources, they too may be defined as state capitalists who fall under the rubric of the African bourgeoisie.

The inclusion of state bureaucrats in the African bourgeoisie raises a theoretically important question concerning the divisions among the capitalist classes. Since a distinguishing feature of capitalism is uneven development across national regions, ethnic groups, and even among capital accumulators, theorists have attempted to account for distinct locations, affiliations, and activities of capitalist classes by referring to divisions within a class as either *class fractions* or *class segments*.[2] Whatever language is employed, the key point is to recognize the *autonomy* of a particular form of accumulation under a system where distinct forms of capital are potentially or actually in competition with each other. More specifically, private industrialists are in competition with state bureaucrats in an embryonic African economy over the limits of state capitalist activities; there is a contradiction between the profits of agricultural capitalists who produce foodstuffs and industrialist capitalists who wish to lower the cost of wage goods. Small-scale capitalists are always threatened by more efficient or more monopolistic large-scale capital, be they foreign or indigenous nationals.

The process of capitalist development and the formation of capitalist classes in Africa has been extremely uneven, often joined and articulated with the precapitalist social relations and strata from which they emerged. To appreciate the uniqueness of the African bourgeoisie, it is essential to grasp the significance of *intermediate forms* of capital accumulating activities carried out by independent producers, chiefs, and merchant capitalists, especially during the colonial era when many were excluded from more productive activities.[3] Indeed, what is exciting about the study of African capitalism and the formation of the African bourgeoisie is the way in which indigenous institutions were mobilized for accumulation and, conversely, how these practices have transformed the accumulation process itself. Swainson, for example, cites Cowen's pathbreaking research, which illustrates how a nascent petite bourgeoisie "straddled" wage labor and household production in order to accumulate from colonial Kenya's expanding internal market.[4] Groff's account shows how traditional labor services owed to chiefs by junior lineage members among Akan speakers of West Africa served as a foundation for a rise of a planter class in the Ivory Coast. And Watts' examination of Muslim aristocrats and their alliances with Hausa merchants illustrates how precapitalist institutions and class structures were used to squeeze capital from the Northern Nigerian peasantry.

## Indigenous Accumulation: External versus Internal Determination

Until recently, variants of dependency theory (e.g., dependent development or world-systems theory), which argue for external determination, reigned among political economists as the orthodox explanation for African underdevelopment and a comparatively backward bourgeoisie. Indeed, external determination remains the dominant perspective among Africa's nationalist, radical, and progressive theorists. Because this view is one pole of the central debate in this study, one should review its assumptions and explanations for the contemporary situation. Since Kitching's essay trenchantly critiques the major theorists, only the essential concepts and arguments need be outlined here.

Arguments for external determination derive from Latin American dependency theory and the subsequent revisions by Amin, Wallerstein and Cardoso.[5] This perspective argues that capitalism was always an international system characterized by exchange between technically advanced and backward states through a world market. The technical and military superiority of center states resulted in the domination, exploitation, and distortion (i.e., underdevelopment) of peripheral states and regions of the world economy. The unit of analysis is states or regions, not social classes. The explanatory factor is the process of *unequal exchange* during alternating upturns and downturns in world market cycles. Through the process of unequal exchange, economic surplus is extracted from the periphery through plunder, repatriation of superprofits, deteriorating terms of trade, monopoly rents for the utilization of the center's technologies, as well as trade and tariff policies that deny the periphery control over internal markets or access to those of the center. Most importantly, unequal exchange denies peripheral states the *economic surplus* necessary for autonomous national development and, by extension, an autonomous national bourgeoisie. Hence, the structure of the capitalist world economy blocks the periphery from obtaining the benefits of capitalism.

According to dependency theorists, political domination by the center over the periphery complements unequal exchange and thus contributes to underdevelopment. Imperialist intervention in potentially dynamic societies undermines progressive or nationalist class coalitions, which are assumed to be capable of capitalist transformation if only they had avoided imperialism. The center states often support backward, sometimes feudal, ruling classes who remain docile clients within the dependent class alliance. World economic and regulatory institutions such as the International Monetary Fund and the World Bank are perceived as agents of the center states and thus pursue the interests of their mentors. Together, center states, international firms, and world regulatory agencies encourage dependency, block autonomous national development, protect their export markets, advocate inappropriate technologies and loans, and thus corrupt local elites. When these policies fail to control recalcitrant peripheral governments, the center states seek to destabilize their economies or, ultimately, to overthrow governments by covert or overt military intervention.  It is noteworthy, as Oculi's chapter indicates, that this radical perspective conflates the political and economic by fusing states and international firms and by downplaying rivalries among states and among international firms.

The combination of economic and political factors does more than eliminate sources of surplus, create dependence on external technologies, and create blockages to growth and investment.  According to dependency theory, participation in the capitalist world economy distorts a dependent state's social structure so that the fundamental cleavage is not class-based but sectoral.  Class fractions allied with the international economy lack the consciousness of an autocentered national bourgeoisie because their investments are oriented toward accumulation in the center, servicing linkages with the world economy or producing low value-added raw material exports for the world market.  Hence, the peripheral bourgeoisie invests profits abroad (e.g., capital flight), avoids high-risk, productive investments locally, and participates at the social and cultural level in the consumption patterns of the internationalized sector.  If the indigenous bourgeoisie is technically backward, allied with foreign capital and incapable of extending indigenous accumulation into precapitalist spheres and the domain of foreign capital, this perspective also dismisses the state bourgeoisie as impotent.  According to Langdon, the latter is in a symbiotic and dependent relationship with international capital.  Neither the indigenous bourgeoisie nor a state-centered capitalist coalition is capable of overcoming the blockages and underdevelopment of the periphery.  Hence, stagnation is inevitable:  capitalism must be rejected in favor of a socialist development strategy.

Theorists predicting stagnation, blocked industrialization, and the impotence of a bourgeois-state technocratic alliance had great difficulty explaining the expansion and structural transformation of peripheral economies during the late 1960s and 1970s.  Regional giants--Brazil, India and Mexico--were achieving high rates of economic growth by combining raw material exports, labor-intensive manufactured goods both for internal consumption and export, as well as the production of intermediate goods (e.g., autos, appliances, and machinery) for internal and export markets.[6]  In East Asia, the "gang of four" (South Korea, Taiwan, Hong Kong and Singapore) were achieving high rates of growth through an export-oriented industrialization strategy.  For example, per capita GNP in South Korea grew from $70 (1960) to $2,281 (1979).[7]  Further, the growth rate of manufacturing in Latin America was 360 percent higher than that of the United States during 1969-1976.[8] Between 1966 and 1974 the productivity of labor increased by 91 percent in Brazil compared to only 17 percent in the United States.[9] Sophisticated state intervention in these cases indicated that the peripheral state elites could articulate an alliance of state, local, and foreign capital which, in certain instances, introduced land reform, eliminated backward interest groups, and created a hegemonic national developmentalist ideology--albeit at the cost of labor exploitation, increased income inequality, and extensive human rights abuses.

The economic dynamism and economic nationalism (e.g., OPEC) of the periphery stimulated a rethinking of the African situation and generated a challenge to the hegemony of dependency theory. While more sophisticated versions of dependency theory emerged, e.g., Wallerstein's semiperiphery and Cardoso's dependent development, which is the approach taken by Biersteker in this volume, the revived Marxist explanation for African capitalism acknowledged changes in the world economy, but focused on internal factors. And, further, it offered a critique of the methodology, assumptions, and generalizations advanced rather uncritically by dependency theorists. Since Kitching articulates the arguments for the primacy of internal determination so clearly, here one need only review essential elements of the Marxist argument and methodological critique of dependency theory.

Accordingly, the three nations of interest in this work are in *transition* to capitalism, a social process that is defined as a contradictory set of social relations involving production, exchange, consumption, and reproduction via political force. The distinguishing feature is commodity production: a capitalist produces by employing wage labor, which necessarily creates the incentive to innovate technically in order to reduce costs and raise profit levels. Competition between capitals, be they foreign or indigenous, drives the capitalist mode to penetrate, undermine, and articulate in contradictory ways with precapitalist modes. The process of capitalist expansion is uneven, contradictory, and destructive of precapitalist values, social solidarities and venerable institutions. It generates crises as new sources of growth, territorial expansion, or technologies are exhausted; it generates social misery as artisans and independent peasants are displaced, often illegally, by new capitalist production processes. During the transition to capitalism, social misery for displaced producers is nearly universal and not evidence for the failure or blocking of capitalist development. Viewed dialectically, however, displaced independent producers flowing into urban centers provide an available and cheap labor supply, as well as a market for wage goods produced by new capitalist industries. The transition to capitalism is a long-term historical process that spans several generations.

The anarchy of capitalist production, the destruction of the former social order, and the disruption of traditional and national institutions means that the transition to capitalism is inherently contradictory and thus characterized by political instability and vicious class struggles between winners and losers. Widespread administrative corruption, the seizure of public resources, and the erosion of institutionalized mechanisms of social control signals the onset of the primitive accumulation of capital--a phase that generates an objective need for the bourgeoisie to exercise internal class, as well as general social, discipline, or else risk a class-threatening social upheaval (e.g., social and political reform). Any analysis of the transition must focus on the interdependence of classes and the dialectical relationship between dominant and subordinate classes.

Just as classes are dialectically related, so too are center and peripheral states; neither relationship, however unequal, is unidirectional in terms of leverage and benefits, but rather part of an interdependent totality whose microlevel processes and linkages to macrolevel concepts such as the state and world economy must be specified and analyzed empirically. Thus, the dominance and penetration of international capital is acknowledged but, at the same time, the dialectical method argues that: "External causes are the condition of change and internal causes are the basis of change, and the external causes become operative through internal causes."[10]

The Marxist perspective argues that when one evaluates the African bourgeoisie, one must apply the *appropriate standard of comparison* and avoid ahistorical comparisons with idealized images of dynamic, disciplined, uncorrupted national bourgeoisies allegedly typical of the transition to capitalism in the center states. In fact, there is no correct or universally applicable model for predicting a successful transition to capitalism during a concrete historical conjuncture; rather, the particular combination of social forces depends upon the character of the precapitalist social formation, the conditions of the historical conjuncture, the nature of the world economy and state system, and the dialectical interplay of subjective and objective forces in a particular society. Marxist theorists emphasize that it is common for neophyte capitalist classes to demand protection for their investments in the face of foreign competition, to avoid risky ventures if more secure ones are available, to strike corrupt political bargains with local elites or international firms in their class interest and, if possible, to protect their liquid assets from rent-seeking state elites and state confiscation.

Much of the debate on Kenyan capitalism focuses on the relationship between indigenous and international capital, which is appropriate as long as one bears in mind the growing strength and technical capacity of indigenous capital since independence.[11] The emphasis on the accumulating capacity of indigenous capital should not obscure the unity and mutual interest of "capital in general." Notwithstanding nationalist rhetoric, both indigenous and international capital are allied against barriers to private capitalist accumulation such as relatively autonomous state bureaucrats who favor state industries, "uncaptured" independent peasants who resist capitalist penetration and, of course, populist and socialist political movements. The point is that, as capitalists, indigenous and international capital are both in competition and alliance with each other at different times over different issues.

Because it is less than three decades since Africa's political independence, Marxists argue that it is naive not to expect indigenous capital to engage in joint ventures with international capital. How else are they to acquire the technology and organizational expertise to deepen the level of indigenous accumulation? Again, the degree of internationalization of capital among firms in the center suggests that the era of an autonomous national bourgeoisie has passed and a new, highly integrated mode of global accumulation is beginning, aided by new microelectronic technologies and financial institutions. The seminal question is not where the indigenous accumulators acquire capital, technology, and organizational expertise but rather, how do their investments transform the peripheral society and alter the balance of class forces?

## The Relationship of the State to the Indigenous Bourgeoisie

The transformative potential of the African state is also a subject of debate. Dependency theorists see it as a "neocolonial" organ of international capital controlled by corrupt, imperialist agents. Marxists do not deny the corruption of the African state, but insist that it possesses a degree of relative autonomy, which allows it to avoid serving the dominant interest of international capital. This autonomy enables the state to form a nationalist class alliance to advance indigenous accumulation in important ways: (1) by restricting participation in the market to nationals through indigenization of industry policies; (2) by protecting and subsidizing indigenous investments; and, (3) where private capital refuses, by investing in basic industries necessary for private indigenous accumulation (steel, petroleum refining, and engineering) and industrial infrastructure in order to modernize the technical means and scale of production. In his autocritique of his previous dependency position, Colin Leys argues for the transformative potential of the state-indigenous bourgeois alliance when he describes the Kenyan "state as the register of the leading edge of indigenous capital in its assault on those barriers."[12] In this volume, Swainson and Forrest argue that during periods of intense nationalism, state intervention, directed by the alliance between indigenous bureaucrats and capitalists, has benefited indigenous ownership, intensified local accumulation and, to a limited degree, increased control over capitalist enterprises in Kenya and Nigeria.

In the face of Africa's greatest social and economic crisis in modern times, both liberal and Marxist theorists have demanded that policy makers reconsider whether weak and incompetent state bureaucratic intervention into the market has contributed to the current crisis. At issue here is whether interventions such as marketing boards, small-scale farming schemes, and price-control agencies do more harm than good by limiting the scope and opportunities for indigenous accumulation. Equally important, the record of state agencies in achieving planned, collective accumulation is almost universally abysmal. Whatever the good intentions of the original planners, any cost-benefit analysis of extensive state intervention suggests that the tendency toward rent-taking is very high; that the state is often too weak and poorly integrated to perform the oversight and internal discipline functions necessary for state-led accumulation; and, that the uncertainty and irrationality of immature state intervention, such as capital-intensive agricultural projects, has frightened away indigenous or even foreign investments.[13]

Since the African state has always been involved in the process of accumulation, it is unlikely to withdraw completely, no matter how forcefully "privatization" policies are demanded by international capital and the center states. The crucial question concerns the capacity of the indigenous bourgeois-state bureaucratic alliance to inculcate discipline, motivation, and a sense of national purpose in the state apparatus and in society in general. This involves cultural issues and probably requires fundamental ruptures with traditional institutions, forms of material distribution, and existing forms of status reproduction. Perhaps only the threat of Hobbesian social anarchy, which apparently is approaching in metropolitan Lagos, will provide the stimulant for the creation of a nationalist movement capable of resolving the crisis. Since Nigeria, Kenya, and the Ivory Coast are unequivocally capitalist states and no left alternative is yet visible, any nationalist transformation depends upon the capacity of the indigenous bourgeoisie to form productive class coalitions.

By arguing that significant internal change is impossible without socialist revolution or transformation of the international economy, the dependency/world-systems position has been accused of extreme pessimism. Yet, in face of declining raw material prices and increasing international penetration of national economies globally, one is pressed to offer a strategy that creates a class coalition where the indigenous bourgeoisie might break with the dependent capitalist class alliance and play a transformative role in Africa's three capitalist states. One strategy worthy of serious consideration has been advanced for Latin America by Alain de Janvry.[14]

Following Amin's model that identifies the dependent class alliance as one where the bourgeoisie produces and markets export and luxury goods, de Janvry envisions the formation of a popular-national class coalition where the indigenous bourgeoisie will produce and market goods that are produced and consumed internally by wage and salaried workers (e.g., food, textiles, soap). Thus, the internally oriented bourgeoisie possesses an *objective* interest in wage-led rather than externally determined demand for its products. Any productivity increases in this sector tend to accrue to indigenous capital, or to raise local wage rates (hence demand) or to lower the cost of goods consumed by wage and salaried workers. If continued, the *productivity increases* will extend workers' consumption into new commodities that were once considered luxury goods (motorcycles, housing materials, and small appliances), which in turn will provide new areas of investment for the indigenous bourgeoisie. It is a class alliance that creates an *objective* link between indigenous capital and labor and one that is also linked to the progressive features of capitalist development: i.e., the development of the productive forces and the advancement of the number, concentration and technical knowledge of the working classes. If the class coalition described by de Janvry came into power, then the power of a

relatively autonomous state could mobilize popular consciousness as a *subjective* social force in the form of nationalism and
anti-imperialism so as to reinforce the *objective* basis of the
popular-nationalist strategy. Practically, the depth of the crisis
obligates progressives to evaluate internal strategies as popular
democratic projects and avoid academic pessimism.

## Situating Indigenous Capitalists in Three African States

After the next chapter by Gavin Kitching, the papers in this
volume are organized under four themes: (1) African capitalist
classes in historical perspective; (2) the agrarian origins of
African capitalist classes; (3) the role of the state in African
capitalism; and (4) the transition to industrial capitalism. With
these theoretical and methodological points in mind, the following sketches situate the African bourgeoisie in each state--
Nigeria, Kenya, and the Ivory Coast--by reviewing the relevant historical, statistical, institutional, and political information necessary for grasping the rise of the indigenous bourgeoisie in each state.

### Nigeria: "The Brazil of Africa"?

Its entrepreneurial traditions and population (80-100 million, growing at 3.5 percent per annum) make Nigeria unique
in Africa.[15] Its natural resources include petroleum, natural
gas, tin, iron ore, coal, and uranium, which are complemented
by wide climatic variation. The latter enables Nigerians to
produce tropical crops (cocoa, coffee, palm products, and tu-
bers), savanna cereals (maize, rice, sorghum, and wheat), tem-
perate crops in the eastern highlands (tea, fruits, and vegetables), and livestock in the northern plains. During the precolonial period, the ecological division between north and
south created the material base for a Muslim, prebendal feu-
dalism and the lineage kingdoms or clan societies in the north
and south respectively. The south was gradually incorporated
into the capitalist world economy via the slave and palm oil
trade, but neither mining nor white settlers intruded during
the colonial period (1861-1960). Instead, international firms
and indigenous merchant capitalists exported the products of
peasant households (groundnuts, cocoa, cotton, and palm products) to the world market. A weak federal state collapsed in
the wake of regional rivalries into a civil war (1966-1970), but

the civil war experience produced much indigenous accumulation and a centralized federal state.

After joining OPEC in 1971, the shape of Nigerian capitalism was driven by the twin forces of economic nationalism and petroleum rents that reached $24 billion in 1980 (compared to total foreign exchange earnings of $1 billion in 1970).[16] A centralized federal state initiated a qualitatively distinct period of capitalist development. It was one where the state controlled and distributed capital, where indigenous capitalists expanded by investing in commerce, housing, construction, and manufacturing, and where a fledgling capitalist state strove to penetrate the mosaic of civil society in diverse ways: by distributing contacts, by constructing industrial infrastructure and industries, by intervening directly into the peasant-household sector, and at the cultural level, by expanding public education, rather chaotically, from universities to universal primary education.

During the "boom," petroleum accounted for about 95 percent of foreign exchange earnings and for between 65 and 75 percent of all government revenues. Petroleum rents distorted any balance that previously existed by creating a dependence that spelled a "crash" when prices fell, by generating inflation that discouraged peasant production and increased rural-urban migration, and by encouraging intervention by the state in economic sectors and circuits that it was organizationally and technically incapable of performing adequately.

Although the Nigerian state generated massive corruption, irrational industrial and agricultural projects and capital flight overseas, the petroleum boom (1974-1982) initiated a deepening of capitalist social relations of production and an unprecedented expansion of the indigenous bourgeoisie. Under the leadership of the economic nationalist, Murtala Mohammed, the state nationalized and now owns about 75 percent of Nigeria's petroleum producers; it has initiated an integrated iron and steel industry consisting of a gas reduction plant at Aladja, an enormous complex at Ajaokuta (estimated cost, $7 billion), several foundries and many dispersed wire, rod, and rolling mills. Two 100,000 barrels/day refineries, a national petroleum pipeline distribution system, a natural gas-fed fertilizer plant and, subject to funding, a planned fourth refinery, with a petrochemical complex and natural gas collection system from Warri to Lagos, indicate the scale of state investment in hydrocarbon-based intermediate industries. Eventually, Nigerian state investments will deepen indigenous accumulation.

Manufacturing is dominated by multinationals; it is dependent on raw material imports (e.g., 65 percent in 1984); it lacks linkages to basic industries, an engineering sector or intermediate metal and electrical industries (e.g., textiles, beverages, cigarettes, soaps and detergents accounted for 60 percent of manufacturing output in 1984). Automobiles, trucks, tractors, and motorcycles are assembled but with few local inputs. Also significant are the massive state investments in transportation and communications infrastructure:  seaports, roads, airports, telephone and rail improvements.

The increase in food imports (about $3 billion in 1980), the end of agricultural exports (groundnuts, palm products, and cotton), as well as increased demand by manufacturers for raw materials encouraged the state to intervene into the agrarian and peasant sector. Although not yet fully enforced in southern states which practice communal land tenure systems, a 1978 decree "modernized" land tenure so that unoccupied land can be more easily reallocated to indigenous and international capital. Eleven federal river basin authorities, managing capital-intensive irrigation and dam systems, have taken control of some of Nigeria's richest peasant land--but not without peasant resistance (e.g., see Oculi on Bakalori). The World Bank has joined the federal and state governments in establishing integrated rural development projects, which inevitably promote commercial farming and "kulakization" of the peasantry. Agricultural banks also have funded generalized commercial farming and poultry production, most of which is owned and managed by local capitalists. Unlike manufacturing, where indigenous capital is present but not strong, the free-fall of oil prices and the end of foreign exchange for agricultural imports have stimulated indigenous capitalist investment in the agrarian sector.

Both Biersteker and Forrest's papers describe how indigenization and state subsidies nurtured indigenous capital into a position of *financial* if not technical control over many manufacturing and agricultural enterprises. Despite the widespread looting and capital flight during the petroleum boom, the state and private bourgeoisie came of age and became political forces, especially within the National Party, during the brief period of civilian politics (1979-1983).

Policy changes since the collapse of the civilian government illustrate how the crisis generated by the falling demand and price for petroleum force changes in the indigenous investments and for indigenous accumulation (e.g., Nigeria's foreign exchange earnings dropped from $24 billion to $10 billion from 1980 to 1983). Nationalism forced both military governments headed by Buhari and Babangida to refuse the IMF's terms for settling its estimated $22.5 billion external debt. But, bowing to capitalist rationality, Babangida has implemented most of the IMF's terms, such as devaluation, halving the petroleum subsidy, and privatizing state industry. The shortage of foreign exchange for imported raw materials has stimulated investment (e.g., backward linkages) in agriculture by international and indigenous capitalists. Food imports have declined, and local food production has increased; textile manufacturers are planning an outgrower system to supply local cotton; beverage firms are planning to produce corn sweeteners and beer ingredients. The crisis generates social misery but, for the first time, some corrupt officials are being held accountable and jailed; a bloated and nonproductive state bureaucracy is being pruned, and there was even an effort to create a culture of social discipline (e.g., "War Against Indiscipline"), albeit in the face of continuing institutional decay and declining living standards. In the present conjuncture, the drive to "privatize" industries and inculcate market discipline by center states through international agencies such as the World Bank and even the United Nations, creates opportunities for indigenous capital to invest in directly productive enterprises, since demand for housing and trade has stagnated. Here one searches for the class coalition and the policy that will force productive investment by indigenous capitalists, since international center states, banks, and firms are reluctant to invest until an IMF agreement is reached with Nigeria.

### Kenya: From White Settler to Black Capitalism

The contrast of Kenya's white settler colonialism with Nigeria's experience of "indirect rule" explains the comparative success of Kenyan agrarian capitalism.[17] White settler agriculture meant that indigenous precapitalist institutions were dislodged; land was a commodity from the outset; and wage labor was thrust upon Africans who were forced onto the reserves. White farms were large: they averaged over 2,400 acres per occupier in 1932. By 1953, 4,000 settlers occupied 7.3 million acres.[18] The colonial state's infrastructural investments benefited the Europeans; settlers had obtained state protection for their production by denying Africans the right to grow high value crops like coffee and tea. Kenyan industry and agro-processes also flourished because of colonial Kenya's role as industrial and commercial center for the British protectorates of Uganda and Tanganyika.

White settler capitalism was founded upon the primitive accumulation of African land and labor. Politically, it employed the state to preserve monopolies, subsidize transport costs, and institutionalized government support for a dynamic and technically advanced capitalist agriculture. In spite of the privileges enjoyed by white settlers, Cowen's research shows how an indigenous capitalist class was spawned in the interstices between the white highlands and the native reserves. By subsisting at a lower level of material reproduction, by utilizing household labor and thereby "straddling" wage labor and household production, Cowen documents how African entrepreneurs initiated the production and distribution of banned products such as tea.[19] From this beginning, indigenous accumulators expanded into trade and, after independence, entered industry, as well as gaining privileged political access to large farms in the white highlands. Viewed dialectically, therefore, the brutal intrusion of white settler agriculture undermined many precapitalist institutions and practices that otherwise would have resisted the penetration of capitalist relations of production. Therefore, after the successful anti-imperialist Mau Mau insurrection, an indigenous bourgeoisie inherited a productive base in capitalist agriculture with large units of production and a disciplined state bureaucracy, as the quality of Kenyan statistical data bears witness.

The Kenyatta regime (1963-1978) used state power to advance the scale and extend the activities of indigenous accumulators. Seizure of state lands and semiforced takeover of expatriate farms or businesses are taken as examples of indigenous primitive accumulation by Leys. Later, he argues, this capital was used to purchase foreign-owned coffee estates so that by the end of 1977, 57.3 percent of total coffee hectarage (i.e., nearly 1,800 hectares) had come under the control of indigenous capitalists.[20] Even in the lands allocated to cooperative and peasant smallholders there is evidence of peasant differentiation and land concentration that suggests the emergence of capitalism. Although the question of peasant differentiation is sharply debated, Njonjo's survey of Kiambu and Nakuru documents increased land concentration: "91 percent of the owners held only 21 percent of the land and each had less than three acres, whereas 5 percent of the owners, those with over twenty acres, controlled 79 percent of the land." Those owning over 100 acres, amounting to 2 percent of the owners, held 69 percent of the land.[21] There can be no doubt that indigenous accumulation has grown enormously in the areas of agriculture, wholesale and retail trade, construction and housing, hotels and tourism.

Although still possessing the most advanced manufacturing sector in the region, Kenya's early advantage was hampered by the breakup of the East African Community and the subsequent loss of the Ugandan, Tanzanian, and other East African markets. Manufacturing accounted for 15.8 percent of GDP in 1983 but its growth had slowed to around 3 percent in 1983, down from an annual average of 9.5 percent from 1965-1979.[22] Industries included textiles, food processing, soda ash, paper products, cement, petroleum products, electrical equipment, and three motor vehicle assembly plants. Again, Swainson's contribution in this volume emphasizes the rapid entry into manufacturing by indigenous capital while Langdon focuses on the limits to indigenous expansion. But even the skeptic Kaplinsky acknowledges that "the indigenous capitalist class has managed to carve out a slice of the benefits arising from accumulation in large-scale industry."[23] Furthermore, 25 percent of private commercial banks are now owned by indigenous capitalists.[24] Unlike Nigeria, Kenya's manufacturing sector is limited by the size of its internal market and its regressive income distribution profile. Since 60 to 70 percent of its inputs are imported, foreign exchange constrains industries from operating anywhere near capacity. Recent government policies call for emphasis on export-oriented industries, a strategy that may be aided by improved relations with Tanzania and the end of the civil strife in Uganda.

Optimists point out that Kenya's agricultural production doubled from 1960-1980, marked by a GDP annual growth rate of over 6 percent. But, as an agricultural exporting state without petroleum or minerals, such glowing statistics may mask many serious problems. Kenya's population (15.5 million) is growing at over 4 percent annually, the world's highest. With 85 percent of the population located in rural areas, landlessness is becoming a serious problem because once marginal lands are nearly fully cultivated. In addition, game preserves, so necessary for foreign exchange earnings, constrain the expansion of peasant agriculture. Given the fact that 82.6 percent of Kenya's land is classified as having "low potential" or "unsuitable" for agriculture, it is doubtful whether export agriculture can continue to grow as it has for the past two decades.[25] Foreign exchange necessary for industrial development is already constrained; typically, the total value of coffee exports, Kenya's most important export, pays for

11.  On the Kenyan debate, see C. Leys, Underdevelopment in Kenya (Berkeley:  University of California Press, 1975), and "Capital Accumulation, Class Formation and Dependency," The Socialist Register (London:  Merlin Press, 1978); R. Kaplinsky, "Capitalist Accumulation in the Periphery: Kenya," in M. Fransman, Industry and Accumulation in Africa (London:  Heinemann, 1982); B. Beckman, "Imperialism and Capitalist Transformation:  A Critique of the Kenyan Debate," Review of African Political Economy 19, 48-62.

12.  Leys, "Accumulation...", op. cit., 253.

13.  For the application of this perspective, see G. Andrae and B. Beckman, The Wheat Trap (London: Zed Press, 1985).

14.  de Janvry, op. cit., chapter 1.

15.  For an overview of Nigeria, see Review of African Political Economy no. 13 (1979) edited by G. Williams; S. Schatz, Nigerian Capitalism (Berkeley: University of California, 1977); T. Forrest, "Recent Developments in Nigerian Industrialization" in Fransman, op. cit.; O. Oyediran, Nigerian Government and Politics under Military Rule (New York:  St. Martin's Press, 1979); M. Watts, Silent Violence (Berkeley:  University of California Press, 1983); H. Bienen and V. Diejomaoh, eds., The Political Economy of Income Distribution in Nigeria (New York: Holmes and Meier, 1981); Andrae and Beckman, op. cit.; T. Falola and J. Ihonvbere, The Rise and Fall of Nigeria's Second Republic (London:  Zed Press, 1985).

16.  Unless otherwise stated, all statistics presented in this section are taken from World Bank, World Development Reports, 1980-1985 (New York:  Oxford University Press, 1981).  All statistics relating to Nigeria are estimates except possibly the debt, foreign trade, and oil revenue figures.  To relieve the reader of any chagrin, I recommend the caveat from The Economist (12 January 1984): "This is the first survey published by The Economist in which every single number is probably wrong.  There is no accurate information about Nigeria. Nobody knows within a margin of error of about one-third, how many people the country contains, where they live, or how much they produce."

17.  On Kenyan development, see Leys, Underdevelopment... op. cit., A. King, An Economic History of Kenya and Uganda (Nairobi:  EAPH, 1975); R. Kaplinsky, Readings on the Multinational Corporation in Kenya (Nairobi: Oxford University Press, 1978); N. Swainson, The Development of Corporate Capitalism in Kenya (Berkeley:  University of California, 1980).

18.  C. Leys, Underdevelopment... op. cit., 29-30.

19.  M. Cowen, "The British State, State Enterprise and an Indigenous Bourgeoisie in Kenya after 1945," (unpublished manuscript, London, 1981).

20.  Leys, "Accumulation...", op. cit., 254.

21.  A. Njonjo, "The Kenyan Peasantry:  A Reassessment," Review of African Political Economy no. 20 (April-June 1981): 39.

22.  Statistics for manufacturing, growth and sectoral distribution for all three states have been culled from The World Development Reports, op. cit., African Contemporary Record 1983/84 (New York:  Africana Publishers, 1985),

Africa South of the Sahara (London: Europa Publications, 1986).

23. Kaplinsky, op. cit., 218.

24. African Business, November 1985, 19.

25. W. House and T. Killick, "Social Justice and Development Policy in Kenya's Rural Economy," in D. Ghai and S. Radwan, eds., Agrarian Policies and Rural Poverty in Africa (Geneva: ILO, 1983), 31-33.

26. For the Ivory Coast, see B. den Tuinder, The Ivory Coast:  The Challenge of Success (Baltimore:  Johns Hopkins, 1978); B. Campbell, "Ivory Coast" in J. Dunn, West African States (Cambridge:  Cambridge University Press, 1978); H. Marcussen and J. Torp, The Internationalisation of Capital (London: Zed, 1982); T. Bassett, Food, Peasantry and the State in the Northern Ivory Coast, (Ph.D. diss., University of California, Berkeley, 1984); E. Lee, "Export-led Development: The Ivory Coast," in Ghai and Radwan, op. cit.

27. The industrial statistics are from Torp and Marcussen, op. cit., 97-103, and Fraternité Matin, no. 81, Abidjan.

28. Bassett, op. cit.

29. On the impact of the crisis, see West Africa, 7 January 1985.  On the rise of economic nationalism, see West Africa, 28 October 1985.

Gavin Kitching

# 2 The Role of a National Bourgeoisie in the Current Phase of Capitalist Development: Some Reflections

A chapter that focuses on the concept of the "national bourgeoisie" in Africa can easily become an exercise in sterile and
formal taxonomy. A conventional approach, and one by which
I was initially tempted, is to start with a history of the concept, beginning with its use in Comintern debates from the
second congress onward. One might then proceed to some
formal list of characteristics that a "national bourgeoisie" may
be supposed to possess and then compare those with such candidates for the title as exist in black Africa today and particularly in Kenya, the Ivory Coast, and Nigeria.

On reflection, however, it seemed to me that such an approach would risk relegating primary concerns to a secondary
or incidental level. For historical materialism is largely unin-
terested in who or what the "national bourgeoisie" *are*; it is far
more concerned with what they *do*, and in fact it is impossible
to define the national bourgeoisie, even formally, without
some reference to its *activity*, its role or function. Thus, for
example, the position around which this book is based defines
the national bourgeoisie as "an alliance of entrepreneurial capitalists, state bureaucrats, and technocrats who collectively
pursue an economic development strategy that increases national control of agricultural and industrial production." From
the second congress onward, the Comintern essentially defined
the national bourgeoisie in "colonial," "semicolonial," and
"dependent" countries (the latter term has been around a lot
longer than is often assumed) as that class or alliance of classes
which would carry through a "bourgeois-democratic" revolution.[1] The content of the "bourgeois-democratic" revolution
was seen to vary somewhat from case to case but nearly always
involved the destruction of "feudal" forms of politics and

27

agrarian structures and an anti-imperialist struggle for national liberation. With the destruction of juridical imperialism, the concept of the national bourgeoisie has metamorphosed, the prime function or role of that class now being to direct a process of national capitalist development. This is my phrase, but as Bernstein has noted there is a "plethora of neologism,"[2] a whole variety of labels in both the bourgeois and Marxist literatures to designate a similar concept--"autocentric development," "independent industrialization," "economic independence." Whatever the name and whatever the concept (the latter is to be examined here), we know that a national bourgeoisie reveals itself as such by producing it, by nurturing it. And if there is no "it," i.e., no "independent" or "autocentric" capitalist development going on, but only "dependent development," "unequal development," "peripheral" capitalist development, or the "development of underdevelopment," then we know that if there is a bourgeoisie in the place where such things are occurring, it isn't a "national" bourgeoisie, but merely "comprador," or "lumpen," or "petite," or "managerial bureaucratic." If all this seems a little frivolous, it is important to notice how everpresent is the danger of formalism and arid taxonomy, and how often in recent years development theory has fallen foul of such dangers. If we are to avoid them, we must be careful to distinguish a concept from a word, the description and analysis of substantive process from the attachment of labels. In the current conjecture, Marxists would do well to cultivate a certain liberalism, even a catholicity or promiscuity, about names. It would be a useful antidote to a potentially damaging formalist trend.

So, if the national bourgeoisie is that class or alliance of classes which produces "independent," "national" capitalist development, we must first decide whether the latter concept is capable of clear formulation and empirical validation. In short, what is "independent," "autocentric" capitalist development? More important, is there some characteristic or set of characteristics that must always be present if capitalism is to transform the forces and relations of production in a social formation and thus raise the living standards of both the bourgeoisie and other classes within the social formation? I shall treat this latter question as a historical one. That is to say, I will look at a variety of countries currently regarded as unambiguously part of the advanced capitalist world, and I shall endeavor to see whether such invariant characteristics were present during their development. That, however, will be a task for the third part of this paper. The second part, which

Let us suppose, then, that in most underdevelopment theory dependence on the capitalist periphery is deemed unacceptable primarily because it maintains, or provides no means of ending, the continued poverty and marginalization of the mass of the population. The prime characteristic of dependence would then be the "marginalization" of the masses of which Amin speaks, itself the social counterpart of the economic "dislocation," or coexistence of different modes of production and consumption internally, with the petty commodity producers both in agriculture and outside subordinated by the demands of primitive accumulation by the world system. But let us now switch paradigms and quote at length from a conventional bourgeois economic history of Japan:

> While unemployment in manufacturing (including building) rose from 4.7 million in 1914 to 5.9 million in 1930, the numbers employed in transport and communications, commerce, administrative, professional and personal service rose from 5.5 million to 8.5 million in the same period.  In some degree this great increase was a necessary accompaniment of economic progress, for, as is well known, as countries advance in wealth, an increased proportion of their manpower is absorbed in the tertiary trades.  But in Japan's case it would be incorrect to regard the scale of growth as a measure of economic prosperity.  One must also observe that some part of that growth was to be explained by the fact that opportunities for employment in the new capital-intensive industries were insufficient to provide occupation for the large annual additions to the labour force.  Much of the increase in this period, therefore, found its way into the small-scale industries or the service trades where productivity was low.  Striking contrasts between the incomes of those employed in the modern sector of the economy and the small-scale sector appeared.  In subsequent years these contrasts, and the conflicts they provoked, were to occupy a leading place among Japan's economic and social problems.[18]

Now, change paradigms again and strip this account of the rather glib certitude which comes from being able to write about Japan in the 1920s from the prosperous perspective of the 1970s, and what does one have?  Surely a classical case of "dislocation," "marginalization," etc. à la Amin.  And yet Japanese capitalism was able to advance beyond this stage; it took, among other things, a U.S. invasion and an enforced land reform to help in the process, but it happened.  How do we know that it cannot happen in Kenya, or Senegal, or the Ivory Coast?[19]

Thomas, at least, is aware of this kind of argument, acknowledges it and tries to meet it. It is worth quoting his argument at some length.

> We have focused on the small underdeveloped economies because they
> represent the vast majority of states in the present world order and
> because the establishment of capitalist relations of production does not
> seem capable of providing a framework for the development of their
> productive forces--although we would accept the possibility that in
> theory capitalism can succeed in the isolated cases of the large
> economies, such as Mexico, Brazil, India, in developing indigenous
> productive forces to the point where widespread poverty will be ruled
> out. In particular, this development may occur through the initiation
> of relatively advanced forms of industrialization. Such a condition does
> not, of course, indicate a preference on our part for capitalism, but
> merely acknowledges that the historical evidence is not sufficiently
> conclusive at this stage for us to rule out absolutely and unequivocally
> the possibility of 'capitalist successes,' such as Japan. Other people
> have shared this uncertainty . . . [he refers to Sutcliffe] . . . . The main
> reason for our not precluding such development is that in the large
> underdeveloped economy which is generating an increasingly large
> demand for capital goods, market incentives may be sufficient to
> stimulate the necessary investments to create an adequate range of
> Department 1 branches of production. If such development occurs, we
> see it as taking place with the active support of the state machinery . . .
> . It is because technico-material conditions favour the development of
> the productive forces that state capitalist relations may generate a sort
> of development, without a revolution in social relations of production,
> which will take the society beyond capitalism. <u>In the small
> underdeveloped economy, however, the social cost to the population at
> large of undertaking a transformation along these lines (particularly
> where the benefits are to be appropriated by a capitalist class) is
> prohibitive.</u> [Emphasis added][20]

So it is smallness that prohibits. And yet, Norway, Sweden, Finland, and Denmark were (are) small countries. Sweden had about four million people in 1870, when its economic
development really got underway; Denmark, Norway, and
Finland had about 1.8 million each. In 1914, Sweden still had
only 5.5 million people, Denmark and Norway still fewer than
three million and Finland just over that figure. New Zealand,
in population terms at least, was even smaller, with fewer than
700,000 people in 1890, a little over a million by the onset of
the First World War and still far fewer than two million at the
onset of the Second World War.[21] Nor would one have been
much impressed with the natural resource endowment, espe-

cially not in the Nordic countries, if one had been assessing that in 1870. The agriculture and land use pattern was heavily constrained by long, severe winters, and communications were very poor (except to a certain extent by sea) in all four countries; the latter factor operated as a major constraint also in Denmark, where agricultural conditions were better.    Apart from that, there was a great deal of wood in Sweden, Norway and Finland, but no coal.    And yet now, Sweden, Norway, Finland, and New Zealand rank respectively third, fourth, fourteenth, and twentieth in the world by the conventional index of national prosperity--per capita income.[22]

Of course, this kind of bald comparison must be qualified as soon as it is made.  All five of these countries based their initial economic development on the supply of agricultural raw materials and food to other parts of the world capitalist system; and all of them enjoyed their most rapid rates of growth in a period (circa 1890 to 1914) when demand for their exports (notably wood, paper, meat and dairy products) was growing rapidly through rapid expansion and rising incomes in the larger European capitalist economies.  This was reflected in a strongly positive trend in the terms of trade for all five countries in the period from 1860 to the First World War, a marked contrast to the experience of most primary producers in the period since the Second World War.[23]    Moreover, the background conditions within these countries were somewhat different from those of small peripheral capitalist economies today--notably in agrarian structures and in the degree of development of commodity relations both in agriculture and in petty commodity production prior to the nineteenth century. Against this, however, it should be noted that all of these countries manifest in varying degrees the same pattern of industrialization, in that rising agricultural incomes from exports (in a situation where, even at the turn of the century, all of the Scandinavian countries had around 50 percent or more of their populations engaged in agriculture)[24] produced a buoyant domestic demand both for producer goods (for agriculture) and mass-consumer durables.    Meanwhile, foreign investment (mainly indirect) provided the bulk of infrastructural development, though not without producing severe balance-of-payments difficulties at various periods.[25]

In general, therefore, the pattern of industrialization in these small countries was "backwards," from simple consumer durables (especially textiles) through agricultural inputs and finishing processes (stimulating light engineering and the chemical industry in particular) to heavy "producer goods" industries, the latter generally coming latest in sequence.[26]  It is also notable that even before the First World War, as agricultural employment fell proportionately, employment in services, commerce, and administration generally rose faster than employment in manufacturing.[27]  In all cases except Denmark, these countries avoided the need for heavy pressure on domestic consumption in the interests of capital formation (the "prohibitive social costs" in small countries mentioned by Thomas) by foreign borrowing and capital investment, made possible by buoyant exports, low interest rates at a period of unprecedented mobility of capital and, in the case of New Zealand, by a "gold rush" in the 1860s.[28]

That such a pattern of capitalist development for small countries has occurred in the past does not, of course, necessitate that it will occur in the future.  As already noted, some of the parameters of the world system that made such a pattern possible have shifted, notably the structure of foreign investment.  Nonetheless, such cases do suffice to suggest that smallness in itself--geographic or demographic--is not an insuperable barrier to capitalist industrialization, nor indeed is an unpromising endowment of natural resources (the ultimate example here being perhaps Switzerland).

Finally, we may turn to the issue of technological dependence.  In Amin's recent work, certainly, this has now assumed the status of the major factor in the dependence of the capitalist periphery.  Historically, of course, dependence on non-national capital for technology has been a feature of capitalist development since its inception.  There was a period in the early to mid-nineteenth century when the whole of Europe was dependent upon British-made textile machinery, steam engines, and (to a lesser degree) iron and steel technology; and, indeed, Europe and America imported British engineers in quite large numbers both to install and to maintain industrial plants.  Some of these men subsequently became independent capitalists in France, Germany, and even Russia.[29]  The better known case of Japan essentially repeated the same two-stage pattern at a slightly later period, i.e., an initial stage in which technology and indeed engineers had to be imported from Britain and Europe (the early Meiji period),[30] with a second stage in which an indigenous technological capacity was developed, first simply to copy and adapt imported European technology, and ultimately to develop an indigenous research and development capacity.[31]

It is, however, arguable that a qualitatively new stage has been reached in technological development since the Second

World War, in which repetition of the European or even the Japanese pattern in impossible. The argument here is that in the initial industrial revolution, based on textiles and steam technology, neither the capital costs nor the scientific/engineering expertise required was beyond economies that had previously had a strong merchant capitalism and (more important, in this context) widespread artisanal skills in petty commodity production.[32] Even in the somewhat later Japanese case, it was possible to adapt old skills to new purposes (e.g., gun manufacture to bicycle repair and construction),[33] while at the same time a major state-directed effort in scientific and technical education was sufficient to allow Japanese industrial capital to master the industrial technology of the pre-1939 period.[34] Now, however, the capital costs of research and development are so enormous, and the concentrations of scientific and engineering expertise required are so great, that major new developments in productive technology (e.g., the microelectronic revolution) have become concentrated in the largest multinational corporations, closely supported by massive state and military funding. In such a situation, we have the conversion of quantity to quality. Peripheral capitalist economies are *too* far behind and would never be able, even if they had states or national bourgeoisies committed to the attempt, to develop an indigenous technological capacity or, at any rate, one which would allow effective competition in corporately dominated world markets.

To this kind of argument, a number of replies are, I think, possible. First of all, blanket assertions about the degree of capital intensity and scientific and engineering expertise required in capitalist industrialization should be treated with some caution; in particular, it is important not to be blinded by the brilliant light of microelectronics. As Thomas himself suggests, it is possible, certainly with protected internal markets, to set up a range of "basic industries" using plants and equipment that are both less capital-intensive and less technologically sophisticated than that available at the frontiers of productive development.[35] Indeed, multinational corporations frequently make use of such "secondhand" equipment for production in smaller markets.[36]

But second and rather more important, one must ask how much, from a world capitalist perspective rather than a nationalist perspective, an indigenous "independent" research and development capacity actually matters. For, if the application of a new, highly productive technology raises the productivity of labor power in a certain part of the world capitalist system, then market growth in that part of the world system may provide growth opportunities in other parts of the system. Moreover, in the era of the multinational corporation, technological developments spread rapidly (through subsidiaries) as soon as a proven capacity to increase labor productivity is demonstrated, and states may take advantage of multinational competition for markets to ensure that such spread is as speedy as possible. In short, in such a situation, loss of a competitive research and development capacity (as in large sections of United Kingdom national capital) may deliver larger and larger shares of the domestic market to "nonnational" multinationals, without necessarily entailing a secular decline of the productivity of the labor power in that social formation.

A much more central argument in the technological dependency thesis stresses the mismatch of the technology imported, often under the control of multinationals, and domestic factor endowment. Most importantly, the incapacity of capital-intensive industrialization to generate employment in a situation of rapid population and labor force growth is stressed. To begin with, however, as we have seen in the case of Japan, such a situation is not new and may be a feature of a certain stage of capitalist development. In the second place, it is clear that employment generation in the current phase of capitalist development (and indeed for some time past) has not located primarily in the industrial sector, but in transport, commerce, personal and other services, and administration. If this is the case, then the essential task for a national bourgeoisie is to ensure a degree of productivity growth in agriculture and/or industry sufficient to allow rapid employment growth in these tertiary sectors (such growth to be generated by both taxation and consumer demand from proletarians, whose real wages are rising).[37]

This part of the chapter has based itself on a rather shabby intellectual trick: a characteristic of "dependence" or peripherality is selected (predominance of production for export, reliance on foreign investment in capital formation, technological dependence, internal economic "dislocation," smallness), and then, in a lightning "Cooks tour" of Western economic history, a discrepant example is found and the proposition is duly knocked down. This hardly suffices in itself to render concepts of "dependence" or "peripherality" meaningless, because it may well be that internal capitalist development can be arrested or stunted for long periods (as in Latin America), not by a single characteristic but by a particular interlocking combination of characteristics both internal and external, economic and sociopolitical, which together generate a total situation of dependence and underdevelopment. I myself have little doubt that this is true, and that such a multifaceted concept can do much to explain particular periods in the history of Latin America and elsewhere.[38] But, even then, through slow shifts in both the national and international situation, such structural blockages to capitalist development can be broken through, either partially or totally, as they have been in Mexico, for example, or more recently in Brazil. So, theoretically, from the point of view of the science of historical materialism, the moral of the story appears to be clear. If, logically, a particular variant or pattern of capitalist development is possible or, rather, if there is no logical necessity that precludes it, then one is ill-advised to assert its impossibility. In particular, there is simply no theoretical or historical warrant for assertions such as that quoted from Thomas (variations of which can also be found in Baran, Amin, and Frank), that in peripheral capitalist economies there is now "no alternative" available save underdevelopment or socialism. Such assertions may have a place (and a rightful one) in political speeches or polemical tracts designed for particular political conjunctures, but they have no place in Marxist science. In that science, the relationship between theory and history is central, and in that relationship, theory defines the limits of the logically possible, while history reveals the selection of phenomena from the logically possible which have been actualized. For reasons that I shall touch on in the conclusion to this paper, a principal weakness of recent Marxist writing on capitalist development and underdevelopment has been to underestimate the variety of forms and sequences of capitalist development that *have* been actualized in the course of the necessarily uneven development of the world system. Such an underestimation leads to an unduly pessimistic and foreclosing estimation of the possibilities for continued capitalist development in peripheral capitalist economies.

## Conclusions

The final part of this chapter draws together and reiterates some of the points made earlier, but it also goes beyond them to consider some of the more fundamental theoretical and political implications that have been implicit in the preceding analysis but now need to be made explicit. The conclusions fall under six headings.

## The Need for Periodization

This first point can be dealt with rather briefly, since it has already been made explicitly. There is a clear need for a much more exact periodization of the stages and sequences of capitalist development, both in the center and at the periphery. Indeed, there is a need to periodize both the "center" and the "periphery" themselves, since it is clear that particular capitalist economies, in the course of their development, have moved from peripheral status in the world system, and indeed some (Brazil, Mexico, Korea, Greece, Spain, Portugal) may be making that transition in our own era. In the case of the study of peripheral capitalist economies in particular (the central concern of this volume), there is a need to replace the comparative statics of underdevelopment theory with long-period historical/theoretical analyses of the sequences and forms of capitalist penetration, both in the colonial and postcolonial periods. In such work, the distinction, deriving from *Capital* and recently elaborated by Kay, between the patterns of hegemony of merchant and industrial capital is a helpful starting point, but it is no more than that.[39] For, if not more exactly elaborated, the concept of "merchant capital" lacks analytical sharpness. Empirically, the central question is about the precise circumstances and conditions in which merchant capital will enter production within its field of dominance or will, at least, present no obstacle to the penetration of industrial capital into that field. Some recent Marxist work on Canadian history presents an interesting case study in this respect, which may be very illuminating, when contrasted with nineteenth century Latin American history, to further define both different forms and types of merchant capital and differences made by its alliances with other classes within the state structure.[40]

## The Importance of Prerequisites

Commencing systematic study of the history of development in the presently advanced capitalist economy, I have been struck by the apparent importance in their industrialization of two prerequisites created in earlier periods. These are, first, the spread of commodity relations and increases in productivity in agriculture (often produced in part by "agrarian reforms" designed to weaken a feudal landlord class) and, second, the broad spread of certain sorts of artisanal skills (particularly in textiles and engineering), through the ubiquity of merchant-dominated petty commodity production. Such observations are hardly new. Brenner and Kemp, among Marxists, have recently drawn attention to the first,[41] and a number of bourgeois authors have treated the second, under the heading of "protoindustrialization."[42] The need for a more exact periodization of the uneven development of the world capitalist system, along with the apparent importance of at least two prerequisites dating from the preindustrial period, confirms for me the importance to historical materialism of Wallerstein's work.[43] However, although important in principle and of great interest empirically, his project seems vitiated to some extent by the crucial weakness in his theoretical premises noted by Brenner.[44]

## The Implicit Hegemony of the United Kingdom Model

As well as the problems created for underdevelopment theory by its penchant for comparative statics (a vice, one might suggest, carried over by Marxist economists in particular from their neoclassical pasts!), the implicit hegemony exercised over much modern Marxist and neo-Marxist writing by the United Kingdom model, or more exactly, the United Kingdom model as theorized and generalized in Marx's *Capital*, also poses difficulties. This hegemony is all the more pernicious because, being deeply interred in theory, it is only half recognized. It seems especially odd that, whereas Marxist writers have stressed the special impetus to capitalist industrialization in Britain deriving from colonial exploitation and have also analyzed the necessarily unique advantages of being the first fully developed capitalist economy in the world, neither empirical nor theoretical work in historical materialism has sought to locate the parameters of this uniqueness more exactly by comparative work on the development of other advanced capitalist economies *without* such advantages.[45] As has already been suggested, from the perspective of small economies on the contemporary periphery, the history of small advanced capitalist economies without great natural resource endowments (Norway, Sweden, Denmark, Japan, Finland, Switzerland, New Zealand) may be of particular relevance.

*The Concept of the "Progressiveness" of Capitalism*

In Lenin's debate with Vorontsov and Danielson, disagreement over the meaning to be attached to the concept of the "progressiveness" of capitalism was central.[46]    Vorontsov in particular held to a conception of progressiveness which has been repeatedly echoed in underdevelopment theory.  Here is his argument as summarized by Walicki:

> The disadvantages of competing with more developed countries were seen by Vorontsov as unremovable obstacles in the way of the capitalist development of Russia.  Russian capitalism, he argued, has no external markets, and, at the same time, cannot produce for the internal market since its own development, by bringing to ruin peasants and artisans, restricts more and more the purchasing power of the population.  Thus capitalist large-scale industry in Russia, having a ready-made modern technology but devoid of markets, can develop <u>intensively</u> i.e., by increasing the productivity and (by the same token) the exploitation of labour, being unable at the same time, to develop <u>extensively</u> i.e., to give employment to the increasingly growing number of workers; it can create small islands of modern production which would be able to satisfy the wants of the upper classes, but it cannot become a prevailing, nation-wide form of production; it can exploit the masses and bring to ruin many independent small producers, but it is unable to give them employment and thus become for them, a school of the higher 'socialised' methods of work.  In Western Europe capitalism was historically necessary and progressive as a form of 'socialisation of labour'; in Russia, and in the backward countries in general, it can be only a form of exploitation, a 'usurper', an abortive enterprise, and illegitimate child of history.[47]

To this Lenin replied:

> We . . . have . . . to sum up on the question which . . . has come to be known as the 'mission' of capitalism, i.e., of its historical role in the economic development of Russia.  Recognition of the progressiveness of this role is quite compatible . . . with the full recognition of the negative and dark sides of capitalism, with the full recognition of the profound and all-round social contradictions which are inevitably inherent in capitalism, and which reveal the historically transient character of this economic regime.  It is the Narodniks--who exert every effort to show that an admission of the historically progressive nature of capitalism means an apology for capitalism--who are at fault in underrating . . . the most profound contradictions of Russian capitalism by glossing over the differentiation of the peasantry, the capitalist character of the evolution of our agriculture, and the rise of a class of rural and industrial allotment--holding wage-labourers, by

glossing over the complete predominance of the lowest and worst forms
of capitalism in the celebrated 'handicraft' industries.

The progressive role of capitalism may be summed up in two brief
propositions; increase in the productive forces of social labour, and the
socialisation of that labour; but both these facts manifest themselves in
extremely diverse processes in different branches of the national
economy.[48]

The terms of the debate have changed somewhat, but not,
I think, the essential issues and propositions. Nowadays, in a
curious elision of Marxist and liberal notions, evidence to the
effect that within the capitalist periphery interpersonal and
interregional income disparities are growing or unemployment
is increasing, or that shanty towns and slums are swelling, is
adduced as evidence of the "bankruptcy" of capitalism and of
the necessity for socialism. But capitalist development has
*never* occurred without such phenomena, which are, as Lenin
says, "quite compatible" with the continued progressiveness of
capitalism expressed in the continued absolute increase of labor productivity (and, one may add, continued absolute increases in real per capita income). Such certainly has been the
case in Kenya from the 1930s to the present day, with "social
contradictions" growing in severity in the last two decades,
along with an acceleration of economic growth.[49]

I believe that the continued viability of historical materialism as a science depends upon restating and maintaining this
hard-edged concept of capitalism's progressiveness, a progressiveness expressed centrally and solely in its capacity to develop the forces of production and with them the productivity
of human labor.[50] Of course, capitalist development does not
bring equality or social justice or even (in its primary accumulation periods) the general satisfaction of "basic needs." If
one thought that it did, one would presumably not be a social-
ist--a reflection which brings me to the fifth conclusion.

## The Transition to Socialism

In a great deal of underdevelopment theory, socialism (often
coming in a purple passage a line or two before the final full
stop) is evoked as the sole means of attaining the "genuine,"
"real" development of which capitalism has been demonstrated
incapable. Such also was the view of the Russian Social
Revolutionaries. It must be clear from what has been said
above that, at least as a general proposition about the capitalist
periphery, I reject this view. The classical view, as I under-

stand it, is that the possibilities for revolutionary action against
capitalism are given by the contradictions that it produces in
the course of its growth within any social formation, *and that
such contradictions may be particularly acute in periods of very
rapid capitalist development of the forces and relations of production.* Of course, such revolutionary opportunities may not
lead on to socialism; they may take populist or religious forms,
as most recently in Iran.[51] The possibilities for specifically
socialist revolutions depend upon a host of other variables and
especially upon particular sociopolitical conditions. This view
is not merely the classical Marxist view of the conditions of
socialist transformation within capitalism; it also seems to me
to be eminently sensible and in broad accord with historical
observation.

But in the context of small peripheral capitalist economies
(with which we are particularly concerned in Africa), it does
seem that something more needs to be said. For it seems rea-
sonably clear that in these cases the economic and social costs
of "independent," "national" industrialization, whether via capitalism *or* socialism, are likely to be considerable. In the case
of socialist development from a low material base, some very
hard issues need to be squarely faced, and they are seldom
faced in underdevelopment theory. Briefly put, the central
problem revolves around the necessity to restrict personal
consumption markedly in the initial period of capital formation ("primitive socialist accumulation" as Preobrazhensky
termed it) and the political consequences that are likely to
flow from this imperative.[52] Even Thomas's brave book does
not, it seems to me, face this issue adequately. It is, of
course, true that unlike the USSR in the 1920s and 1930s,
small socialist states in the period of primitive accumulation
*may* obtain some aid from other socialist states (as, for example, in the case of Cuba) but, leaving all else aside, this may
itself place boundaries on national self-determination as acute
as those placed by capitalist imperialism.

In the case of the "national capitalist road" in small states,
much the same issues arise, although, in this case, primitive
accumulation may be made less "visible" and politically explosive because of the mystificatory mediation of market forces.
But, in any event, without access or with only limited access
to multinational capital and technology, surplus value appropriation is likely to have to take an extensive ("absolute") form,
rather than an intensive ("relative") form, with the usual consequences for the real incomes and degree of exploitation of
both workers and peasants.[53] In the socialist case, one must

also face longer term issues, notably the degree of understanding and sympathy for the socialist ideal that is likely to remain with peasants and workers after several generations of exposure to an authoritarian regime engaged in primitive accumulation, and the difficulties of introducing socialist democracy "later" into a political system which has ossified into authoritarian forms.  I do not suggest that the likelihood of these kinds of future should be agonized over before socialist revolution is commenced.  In any case, as Trotsky observed, real revolutionary situations do not allow the luxury of that kind of moral agonizing.  But, unlike in 1917, these kinds of dangers (then only glimpsed) are now known to exist and to be difficult to avoid in any strategy of "socialism in one country," and it does at least behoove Marxist theorists (who *are* allowed the luxury of this kind of reflection) to bear them in mind before glibly adducing "socialism," without definition, as the "only available" road to "real" development.

## The Role of the State in Capitalist Development

Even a preliminary comparative appraisal of capitalist development reveals, as Gerschenkron stresses, that each successive capitalist development effort involved a larger and larger degree of state involvement.[54]  That involvement was multidimensional and varied somewhat from case to case, but in nearly all cases it included (1) the provision of infrastructure, especially power and communications (usually using capital borrowed abroad); (2) the mobilization of the indigenous surplus through support for and, in some cases, organization of a banking system; (3) improvements and expansion of the existing mass education systems--or the introduction of such a system--with, in the cases of Germany and Japan in particular, a stress on technical and scientific education; (4) controlled importation of foreign capital and expertise where local sources were inadequate or nonexistent; and (5) support for or, in the Japanese case, virtual creation of an indigenous financial and industrial bourgeoisie.  This often involved tariff protection, although not always (for example, in Japan or in the Scandinavian countries), but it did involve placing state contacts with indigenous capital and supporting its export efforts by subsidies of one form or another.[55]

The class base of such states has varied, and there is neither time nor opportunity to elaborate upon that issue here, but again the important point to note is that such strategies never involved the total exclusion of foreign capital and *did* involve, at particular periods, significant degrees of "dependence" of the types outlined in the third part of this chapter and often adduced as proof of permanent blockages to capitalist development (in the present-day periphery).

In the current conjecture, such national capitalist strategies are more difficult to pursue, and in particular (as noted), the switch from a predominance of indirect to direct (multinational) investment in the structure of foreign investment makes state control over foreign capital (and over overseas trade and financial flows) more difficult to attain. More difficult, but not impossible. I believe, for example, that Swainson's recent study of Kenya shows clearly that significant pressure can be exerted on multinational capital in the interests of sections of a local ruling class with interests that, by no means, simply echo those of the multinationals.[56] In this context, then, a "national bourgeoisie" is that class or part of a class which, in the pursuit of its own interests, uses state power in a manner which speeds up the process of building the forces of production locally. Depending upon particular conjunctures, this may be done in alliance with multinational capital or in competition with it. The situation may even vary from industry to industry or sector to sector. In any event, in the current phase of world capitalist development, a "national bourgeoisie" is *not* a class that endeavors to exert total control over domestic industrial production or to pursue capital accumulation purely by exploitation of its own working class and peasantry.

We can proceed a little further than this purely negative characterization. We can say that Marxists and others involved in analyzing peripheral capitalist development must now consider the possibility of a future coexistence, which a certain reading of history had suggested was precluded. That is, we must begin to consider the possibility that a genuinely transformatory capitalist development (i.e., a development that succeeds in the medium-to-long term in massively raising productivity and the general income level) *may be possible without the need of a national bourgeoisie.* Such a development may occur in certain circumstances, under the hegemony of international capital and in alliance with dominant sections of a local ruling class (an alliance not without its contradictions and tensions). At the same time, that very development would expand and transform peripheral ruling classes and, indeed, the general class structure in such social formations. This continual transformation would require, in turn, periodic and possibly highly problematic and stressful "renegotiations" of this alliance, renegotiations that might include a progressively more important role for local capital in some sectors.

It is this coexistence--of "genuine" development on the periphery with the continued hegemony of international capital--that both liberal and radical theorists of development have seen as *necessarily* precluded, a preclusion which I have argued rests on a partial misreading of history and (in the case of much dependency theory) on an implicit nationalism. But to argue for a frank recognition of this coexistence as a theoretical and actual possibility is not simply to invert the dependency position and argue (as has Warren, for example) for its inevitability.[57] On the contrary, a number of important obstacles stand in the way of the actualization of this possibility. In the African context in particular, two stand out: (1) the creation of an indigenous technical cadre able, as the Japanese were able, both to assess and control the forms of technology imported and, more important, to adapt them to local conditions, as well as to develop some local research and development capacity (see Biersteker's contribution to this volume for a discussion of the problem in Nigeria); and (2) the creation of a "social discipline" within peripheral capitalist economies that is conducive to effective extraction of surplus value and rapid capital accumulation (by both national and international capital).

Both of these "tasks" involve the role of the state quite centrally; more precisely, they involve the material interests and the ideological role of the local class fractions who control that state. In all states with which this volume is concerned, there seems to be a persistent orientation among large sections of local ruling classes toward both conspicuous consumption on their own account and the encouragement of such behavior among broader strata of the state and private bourgeoisie as a whole. In short, while paradoxically a national bourgeoisie may not be a necessary prerequisite of capitalist development in some parts of the periphery, the presence and hegemony of what we have historically regarded as "bourgeois ideology" (especially its Smithian elements of "discipline, thrift, and prudence") may well be. And here we must remember that historically the bourgeoisie was successful in inculcating these elements of its ideology, not only among its own ranks, but among significant strata of the petite bourgeoisie and the industrial proletariat as well.[58] In fact, this is what one means when speaking of ideological hegemony.

Thus we may pose a question that may be no empty paradox but a crucial issue for the future of Kenya, Nigeria, and the Ivory Coast. Can one have the hegemony of bourgeois ideology without a national bourgeoisie? Or, to put it another way, what sources and forms of ideology can be used to *substitute* partially or wholly for this traditional role of the bourgeoisie? In Japan, certain elements drawn from a feudal past were deliberately reified by the state education system and put to new use in factory and office. Yet there appears to be no such historical legacy in Africa to play a similar "disciplining" role. On the contrary, historically a certain form of "consumptionism" has been integrally associated with wealth and power. Solving this problem, and thus remaining a "good," "stable" risk for international and national capital, may be a crucial factor in the future of these three states, especially in a situation where world-wide recession has made international competition for such capital more severe, while reducing its availability.

## Notes

1. "The use of the term 'dependent countries' [in the Comintern Program of 1928; G. Kitching] was probably adopted because of the suggestion of Ricardo Parades, a delegate representing the Communist and Socialist parties of Ecuador. Pointing to the variation in the degree of dependence of Latin American countries upon imperialist states, he suggested that a new subcategory to be known as 'dependent' countries should be set up." Kermit E. McKenzie, Comintern and World Revolution, 1928-1943: The Shaping of Doctrine (New York: Columbia University Press, 1964), 81.

2. H. Bernstein, "Sociology of Underdevelopment vs. Sociology of Development?" in D. Lehmann, Development Theory: Four Critical Studies (Totowa, N.J.: Biblio Distributors, 1979).

3. The three works to be referred to are: Bob Sutcliffe, "Imperialism and Industrialisation in the Third World" in R. Owen and B. Sutcliffe, eds., Studies in the Theory of Imperialism (New York: Longman, 1972); Samir Amin, Unequal Development: An Essay on the Social Formations of Peripheral Capitalism, translated by Brian Pearce (Sussex: Harvester, 1976); Clive Thomas, Dependence and Transformation: The Economics of the Transition to Socialism (New York: Monthly Review Press, 1974).

4. Sutcliffe, op. cit., 176.

5. Ibid., 176.

6. Ibid., 176-177.

7. Amin, op. cit., 72-74.

8. Ibid., 75.

# Part 2
# African
# Capitalist Classes in
# Historical Perspective

All the chapters in this section analyze the emergence of capitalist classes during formal colonialism. It is not the case that precolonial merchant capital was absent or unresponsive to opportunities offered by the colonial economy, as Watts's paper on Hausa merchants illustrates. Rather, the colonial state represented an unprecedented authoritarian intrusion into indigenous civil society--one that redefined political and economic privileges among social strata and, to various degrees, introduced technologies, legal instruments, and economic institutions necessary for colonial capitalism. Whether African societies would have evolved toward industrial capitalism without imperial intervention is impossible to ascertain. But, as Kitching argues, the nationalist position that assumes that imperialism blocked and underdeveloped African societies, which would have evolved into prosperous, dynamic societies, is an act of the historical imagination. Indeed, the autonomous transition from precapitalist to capitalist modes of production is exceedingly rare in world history. Colonial society, therefore, must be seen as the incubator of the African bourgeoisie.

Wherever precapitalist merchant capital and ruling classes could be utilized for the production of the commodities destined for the world economy, colonial policy took advantage of the role of precapitalist institutions, be they Islamic brotherhoods in Senegal or *sarauta*-merchant capitalist networks in Northern Nigeria. Watts's view is inspired by Rey's thesis that the first phase of capitalist penetration is characterized by the strengthening of precapitalist institutions and by a class alliance between indigenous political elites and colonial administrators. While the railway transformed transportation, the constraints of this class alliance blocked any dynamic of innovative capitalist development in the region. Merchant capital, usury and authoritarian repression of the peasantry were institutionalized until the collapse of Nigeria's first republic. But the class alliance between aristocratic Muslim office-holders and merchant capitalists from commoner origins nurtured so carefully during the colonial period has produced a regional bourgeoisie in Nigeria--one that dominated domestic politics during Nigeria's second republic (1979-1983).

The Kenyan pattern exhibits a radically different pattern of indigenous class formation. Swainson summarizes the origins of Kenya's indigenous bourgeoisie: it "straddled" wage labor and household production, invested in education and mobilized nationalist consciousness in order to obtain access to the home market and to utilize state support for its efforts at accumulation. Seen in dialog with the paper by Langdon, she shows how indigenous control extended into industry. Again, Swainson's argument is not that international capital's hegemony has given way to national capital, but rather that the new era of international capital must allow for indigenous accumulation to occur, or else risk losing stability within the system as a whole. To focus solely on the "backwardness" of indigenous capital misses the necessary intellectual project of contemporary capitalism: to theorize the dynamics and structure of metanational capitalism.

In the case of the Ivory Coast, French colonial policy encouraged the registration of private property by Africans--in contrast to the Nigerian experience. Groff's contribution describes how obstacles to capitalist agriculture were overcome among the Juablin, an Akan-speaking group bordering Ghana. Since one of the contested issues in the Ivorian case is the relationship of the planter class to the state, it is important to grasp just how this planter class emerged, and especially how precapitalist institutions articulated with emerging capitalist processes. Most clearly, Groff's contribution documents the way in which extended family heads accumulated by privatizing family land through registration and by utilizing traditional labor services from kinship groups so as to advance private commodity production. Groff's chapter underscores the significance of intermediate forms and the diverse ways in which an accumulating class emerged during Africa's colonial era.

*Paul M. Lubeck*

Michael J. Watts

# 3 Peasantry, Merchant Capital, and the Colonial State: Class in Northern Nigeria, 1900-1945

> As flowers turn toward the sun, by dint of a secret heliotropism, the past strives toward that sun which is rising in the sky of history. A historical materialist must be aware of this most inconspicuous of all transformations.
>
> Walter Benjamin[1]

The economic downturn of the 1870s marked the end of Britain's domination of world production and trade. Prices, profits, and trade fell drastically, and unemployment deepened as Britain faced competition and protectionist legislation from newer, more robust European states. The response of British capital was, not unexpectedly, an aggressive search for untapped markets, in tandem with a drive to produce regular, cheap and abundant supplies of industrial raw materials, or what David Landes has referred to as "second industrial revolution." Several other European powers sought, for essentially similar reasons, to preserve and extend their own commercial hegemony by carving out spheres of geopolitical influence, largely through treaties of protection, which were the forerunners of formal colonial rule. Mercantile competition and the threat of reduced merchant profits not only provoked a confrontation between West African and European merchant capitals--and threatened the shaky commercial alliance that had been constructed during the nineteenth century--but also reaffirmed the necessity of formal control to maintain markets and supplies and to guarantee investments in cheap bulk transport and profitable trading networks. The development of Chamberlain's national state, then, spoke to an imperial occupation. As Lugard wrote of northern Nigeria in 1901, "Trade cannot be established on a satisfactory basis until the northern

Hausa states are included in the provinces of the protectorate rendered safe for all small traders."[2]

During the nineteenth century, these Hausa states were the constituent units of the Sokoto Caliphate, which occupied much of what is now northern Nigeria and south-central Niger Republic. It was the largest, most populous, and probably most complex of sub-Saharan African states. However, beginning with the fall of Adamawa in 1901 and terminating with the collapse of the powerful central emirates of Kano and Sokoto in 1903, the caliphate proved to be a brittle opposition to the massively superior British colonial armed forces. The imperial regiments were, in fact, never seriously threatened. The conquest brought to a close almost a century of social, economic, and political development that had opened in 1796 with the *jihadi* overthrow of the local theocratic system of government. By 1809, the *jihad* had welded together roughly thirty emirates presided over by the caliph resident in Sokoto. The nineteenth century saw a progressive centralization of the state apparatuses, a huge extension of the agricultural frontier assisted by the importation of captive labor from the Nigerian middle belt, a deliberate policy of settlement and agrarian investment, and a considerable expansion of commodity production that included cotton, indigo, and artisanal items, not least the justly famous Kano textiles. At the turn of the century, the caliphate was an agrarian bureaucracy of continental significance, consisting of perhaps ten million free peasant producers, a significant but not dominant farm slave population, a largely urban-based officeholding class (*masu sarauta*), and an influential group of merchant capitalists who, although subservient to state managers, had an important role in large-scale craft and estate-based agrarian commodity production.

And so it was that in the aftermath of the chaotic territorial scramble of the 1890 s, the proclamation of the Protectorate of Northern Nigeria was finally made in January 1901. Yet, as the Union Jack was hoisted over Lokoja, not only was British knowledge of the North imprecise, but the exact form and extent of colonial responsibility was ambiguous if not contradictory. Shackled by limitations on manpower and finance, the British opened up Hausaland to the world market at the same time that it shielded the North from some aspects of it. In due course, the cowry currency was replaced by a European specie. Emirate taxation was simplified, systematized, and incorporated into an embracing system of revenue and assessment, slavery was tardily abolished, and the colonial state organized both voluntary and forced recruitment of labor for construction and porterage. The colonial courts quickly extended their jurisdiction to include the activities of the firms and their agents, thus facilitating the extension of commerce into the interior proper. European companies were free to combine at will, while the conservative fiscal and currency policy of the banks served the firms whose merchant monopoly militated against new investment activities. Surplus money capital was repatriated to Great Britain with the profits of the firms and large portions of government salaries. In other respects, the colonial state pursued a conservative economic strategy; it inhibited the development of the forces of production, particularly in agriculture, by using state sanctions to promote commodity production based on household labor. Plantation agriculture was effectively blocked and made subservient to household forms of production based largely on domestic labor. Large agrarian capital was not given the opportunity to develop at the expense of a peasant economy which, as Governor Clifford put it in 1922, was a "natural growth . . . self-supporting and cheap."[3] All this was clearly intended to preserve the hegemony of the traditional aristocracy upon which colonial rule and political stability ultimately rested.

Northern Nigeria is generally seen, of course, as the laboratory of indirect rule. Class alliances were forged with Muslim officeholders from the Sokoto Caliphate who were converted into colonial bureaucrats. The political-economic architecture of the North rested on the foundation stones laid by millions of free peasants--in contradistinction to other forms of capitalist organization--who provided labor, export commodities, staple foodstuffs, and taxes to a revenue-conscious colonial state often tottering on the brink of fiscal crisis. Merchants--both European and indigenous--provided the crucial intermediary functions linking rural producers to the colonial state and, ultimately, to the world market. Northern Nigeria was, then, an archetypical "trade economy" dominated by smallholder agriculture and mercantile forces.[4] In class terms, indirect rule and its trade-based political economy greatly expanded the dominance of a local prebendal ruling class, opened avenues of accumulation for Hausa merchant capitalists (who increasingly came to intercede in Native Administration [NA] politics by the 1930s), but harnessed the surpluses of peasants who were both exploited and disenfranchised. Even in the closely settled commodity producing zones, such as Kano, and the peripheral labor reserve districts, such as northern Sokoto, household production--what Marx called pygmy property--rather than wage labor predominated. In short, there was much on the Hausa plains that resembled a Bonapartist state.

In this chapter, I shall situate this model on the larger terrain of the development of capitalism and the dynamics of class formation in northern Nigeria between conquest and the beginning of the independence movements of the early 1950s. While one can talk of the hegemony of the colonial project in northern Nigeria, in no sense does this imply a crude dependency, or that the northern Nigerian political economy can be mechanically read off from the map of capital logic. Indeed, a great weakness of dependency theory is its reference to a monolithic external agency in the form of British capital, an ideal model of capitalist development measured by the universalization of wage labor, and an assumption of a clearcut hegemony within the boundaries of the state. However, the colonial state in Africa was both weak and strong; that is to say, it is precisely control and domination that was at stake.[5] This is a reflection of the conflicts and struggles between and within fractions of capital, and of the contradictions, often of a conjunctural sort, engendered in the course of the capitalist development in Africa. Following Kitching, I argue that capitalist development in northern Nigeria was episodic and unstable, and that its particular trajectory associated with the proliferation of commodity production (rather than "unilinear proletarianization") must be seen conjuncturally.[6] In this view, the colonial state was a site of intense struggle between various actors and the question of hegemony, and the form of political economy itself, was at the outset of imperial rule far from overdetermined. One must then recognize the complex determinations in colonial capitalist development and the capacity of Africans themselves to shape the agency of British capital in its imperialist phase.

Colonial capital could not simply shape or take hold of the Sokoto Caliphate as it wished and, to this extent, political alliances and coalitions were necessary. Indirect rule was not, however, simply colonialism on the cheap. The colonial state struggled to perform two contradictory tasks.[7] The first was to decide a strategy in which commodity production could be undertaken for metropolitan capital; the second was to secure political stability congruent with, and capable of guaranteeing, the particular regime of accumulation. However, the social structure of accumulation that prevailed in northern Nigeria--commodity production based on household forms of production--was as much about conflict within the metropole and the power of local class structure as it was about a single-minded imperial mission. Indeed, Lugard's initial scheme to convert officeholders into landlords using former slaves as wage labor was actually defeated--a defeat marked by the passage of the Northern Nigeria Lands Committee (NNLC) mandate in 1907. This mandate nationalized land, blocked agrarian capitalism, and sealed the smallholder path--a sort of American road, to use Lenin's lexicon--of colonial development. The defeat of Lugard's radical plan--the creation of agrarian capital *de novo*--did not, however, obviate the need to seal a class alliance with Hausa-Fulani elites and make use of a much-celebrated search for industrial commodities, and the former to run the colonial bureaucracy. The outcome of the Lands Committee project was to vastly expand commodity production by leaving the rural sector somewhat intact, but at the expense of fiscal leakage and a considerable devolution of political power.

The rising merchant classes and the now-hegemonic Muslim elite running the NAs, however, made uncomfortable bedfellows for the imperial interests which the colonial state purportedly represented. Hausa buying agents often stood in intense competition with the European companies; rapacious merchants, a corrupt elite, and tax collectors threatened the political diffidence among the peasantry that so concerned nervous political officers; heavy taxes to cover the colonial state's wage bill often dampened the import trade; and the proliferation of household production and the intermittent development of wage labor naturally limited the development of the domestic market, and hence trade itself.

The colonial state, then, first grew out of intracapitalist struggle and defeat, as much as success or the demands of British industrial interests. Second, it faced the impossible task of balancing a multitude of conflicting interests, in the hope of maintaining its accumulation strategy and political stability. In this context, hegemony within the colony was far from clear, although it was the peasantry that often bore the burden of the contradictory demands of the colonial administration. The particular structure of accumulation that emerged in northern Nigeria contained two central processes relevant for class formation. The first was the absence of a clear-cut pattern of agrarian differentiation or of a polarization between capital and wage labor. While a "kulak" stratum matured in the interstices of the commodity economy, it was the proliferation and deepening of household-based commodity production, rather than the development of markets in land and labor, that distinguished the northern rural political economy. The second class-formation process was the nationalization of land, which transformed the state itself into a, and perhaps *the*, channel of accumulation; by extension, access to the state was a critical factor in shaping class formation itself. The colonial state thus became a *theatre of accumulation* and a site of intense struggle over peasant surpluses. By the 1950s, the confluence of an influential merchant oligarchy and the traditional aristocracy--a bureaucrat-merchant alliance, as Tahir calls it[8]--marked the emergence of a nascent bourgeois class which, amidst the turmoil of nationalist politics and emerging regional government, exploited, by fair means and foul, the state as a source of capital to fund its tentative incursions into industrial production proper.

## Precolonial Class Formation and Accumulation: The Sokoto Caliphate

By the end of the fifteenth century, Hausaland had already become "fully integrated into the commercial and ideological nexus which linked the Western Sudan societies together [and into] . . . the wider Islamic world."[9]  The three-hundred-year period up to the *jihad* in 1795 involved two major developments. First, the network of towns, villages, and hamlets encompassing immigrant communities of heterogeneous origin was welded into a political community under a class of officeholders (*sarakuna*). Second, expanded commodity production, migration, and longdistance trade integrated the Hausa kingdoms, in varying degrees, into the *bilad-al-Sudan*. Both developments were predicated on central governmental functions, an important consequence of which was the expanded position that Islam came to occupy in social life. The Islamization of Hausa society seems to have been coterminous with the rise of the city in the fourteenth century and the proselytizing efforts of a community of Malian traders and clerics. By the sixteenth and seventeenth centuries, Islam had been adopted by a significant proportion of the urban commoners (*talakawa*), as well as throughout those densely settled and ethnically diverse rural areas subject to immigration. In providing the basis for social cohesion and a code for personal conduct, Islam was especially relevant to those embedded in emerging commodity relations, since it provided an appropriate juridical framework for the proliferation of exchanges, trade, and craft production.

Islam gradually penetrated the *sarauta* system and produced a Muslim intelligentsia capable of providing leadership among rural and urban *talakawa* distinct from the office-holders.[10] If there were instances of Muslim kings who lent political support to both Islam and the clerics, the latter, as a class, were unequivocably distanced from the loci of authority. The eighteenth-century efflorescence of state power and the birth of something like an Islamic theocracy were ultimately, however, built on a rickety, not to say contradictory, foundation. For, while the citizenry was largely Muslim in terms of values, conduct, and identity, the rulers--while nominally Islamized--sustained their authority from a dynastic context welded to the pre-Islamic spirit pantheon. An increasingly influential Muslim intelligentsia had no institutional function in a government that was overseen by a cadre of slaves and eunuchs.

By the close of the eighteenth century, the contradictions between the ideals of Islamic piety and the reality of dynastic practice and sacerdotal kingship, and between an urban elite and a rural peasantry sharpened considerably. The tension between social cohesion and political authority was expressed in the fundamental split between the *cikin gida*, the palace clique, and the *cikin fada*, the influential Islamized commoner class.[11] The eighteenth century had, in any case, seen massive political disruption with the collapse of the Kebbi cities and the leveling of the Zamfara kingdom. In this atmosphere of great political insecurity, the escalation of intercity conflict was critical, for it necessitated increased taxation, the growth of military conscription, and presumably much agrocommercial dislocation. It was amidst this enmity and discord that the preachings of the *mallamai*, and especially of the reformist intelligentsia centered on Usman Dan Fodio, offered an appropriate avenue for the expression of political protest.

The social blueprint held by the Muslim intelligentsia was, of course, quite unlike the paradigm of society held by the former Hausa kings. Fodio, above all else, aspired to establish a community of believers under the aegis of the Muslim state and nourished by the security of *shari'a* rule. The *jihad* projected a new social order: the king was to be replaced by an emir--a first among equals--whose legitimacy rested on personal piety toward Allah, in whom all authority was ultimately vested. Political process was relatively unbureaucratic; it was designed to limit the excesses of palace-centered *sarauta* rule and to redress the hypocrisy of a nominally Muslim kingship sustained in some measure by local religious belief. The architecture of the new emirate system was explicitly detailed in Fodio's exegesis on the Kano constitution, the *Diya'al-hukkam*, which was modified, adapted and reformed by the Shehu's successors. As Last points out, there was a sense in which the political and intellectual history of the nineteenth century was an extended exercise in the implementation and reform of the original blueprint.[12]    The political consequence of this grandiose social design was the birth of a huge Muslim community, the Sokoto Caliphate, covering some 150,000 square miles.

The central institution of the new emirate system was the sultan or caliph (*amir-al-muminin*) resident at Sokoto, whose authority derived from his investiture by the entire Muslim community as supreme ruler. Within the political community of the caliphate, the constituent units or cells were the emirates; unlike the earlier kingdoms, they were not sovereign but were subject to the discretionary powers of the sultan, who devolved power to his representatives, the emirs, who had direct jurisdiction over their territorial domains. The emir, as an official of the sultan, was vested with specific powers--most notably, the performance of religious duties, tax collection, and material improvement--whose appointment or dismissal was the sole prerogative of the *amir-al-muminin*. The execution of emirate functions was undertaken by elected administrators who were solely functionaries of the emirate government. The territory was thus held in quasi-vassal status with respect to Sokoto authority, which was, in fact, physically represented in the provinces by a caliphate office-holder, usually the vizier. In contrast to the previous *sarauta* system, which was administered through a bureaucracy of slaves, eunuchs, and freemen, the emirate was characterized by a discrete and clear-cut aristocratic component. In practice, the aristocracy consisted of families or lineages (often with genealogical connections to the sultan) who drew their wealth from peri-urban estates given as territorial grants by the caliph.

The *jihad* of the early 1800's established a Muslim emirate aristocracy who ruled, through Islamic law, over a community of free or servile peasants (*talakawa*). The emirs allocated land in the form of fiefs to office-holding nobles and slaves who were agents for the collection of tax. The officeholders and the emirs controlled state power, intervened in the production system and presided over a relatively wealthy urban merchant class. The state extracted surpluses from the *talakawa* as *corvée* labor, rents in king (*zakkat*), and money taxes. Central fiscal policy, certainly in Kano Emirate, created incentives for immigration, effected tariff controls, and encouraged commodity production. There is every indication that, during the nineteenth century, the emirates prospered, the state apparatuses became more centralized, and Islamic learning and jurisprudence increased. As a prosperous formation, ideologically knitted together through Islamic law and culture, the ruling-class domination was never seriously threatened. As a totality, the caliphate was neither integrated into a single division of labor nor was it a peripheral dependency of North Africa. Contact with the Muslim diaspora was diffuse and informal through peripatetic scholars, the *hajj*, and the Islamic brotherhoods. The *jihadi* ideology was, in this sense, the basis for internal state building, yet also the cultural link to a more universalistic Muslim community.[13]

The basic unit of production in the caliphate was the household (*gandu*), embracing sons, clients, and slaves in an extended domestic structure. The household head organized agricultural and craft production, as well as the distribution of the product, and paid taxes. Such household groups, then, possessed the means of production, provided labor, and disposed of at least part of their collective product. This was, however, far from a natural economy in the Luxemburgian sense. Peasant surpluses were appropriated by the state as rents in money, kind, and labor, and households entered into commodity production for local and regional markets, although on balance, to paraphrase Braudel, peasants were simply pressing their noses against the shopwindow of the market.[14] Some agricultural enterprises did mark themselves off, however, from the millions of commoner farming families. As Tahir has shown, some of the large merchant-*ulema* estates were huge patrimonial systems producing grain, in particular, on what one might call plantations, using both slave and wage labor.[15] The agricultural aspect of such enterprises was, however, often subservient to other complementary arenas of manufacture--textiles and leather, for example--and long distance trade in commodities such as kola. As I shall point out later, it was precisely these wealthy merchant families who, through the facilitation of the *sarauta* class, moved quickly into the export and grain trades, either independently or as agents for the European firms, following the postconquest commodity boom of the early twentieth century.

In spite of the strategic significance of peasant surpluses in the material basis of the caliphate, it is also relevant for this discussion to reiterate Lukac's general insight on how insecurely the precapitalist state was grounded in society. In practical terms, Hausa peasants were partially insulated from overly aggressive state predation by technological and administrative weaknesses intrinsic to caliphal society, and by the ability of rural producers to regulate elite demands. Poor communications, limited military supremacy, the absence of any standing army, the shortage of bureaucratic manpower in the districts, and the absence of any systematic revenue system effectively equipped the peasantry with some autonomy. In Hyden's terms, peasants were not easily "captured"; the state was relatively "soft."[16]  In any case, dynastic politics were city- or palace-centered, and the office-holders only rarely resided in the countryside. Much of the administration lay in the hands of village heads and the myriad agents and clients who stood to benefit by maintaining good working relations with those from whom they collected revenues. The diffuse pattern of caliphal authority, cemented through caternary systems of clientage, lent a low degree of integration to the social system. Petty oppression could be met by changing patrons, which constituted a politically significant act in such patrimonial bureaucracies, or by flight to other less populated districts. In this sense, the moral economy of the peasantry provided a buffer for rural households, and Scott is right to note the symbolic, cultural, and geographic separation of the center from the periphery, of the partial autonomy of the Little Tradition.[17]

## The Construction of Indirect Rule:
## Class Collaboration and Smallholder Agriculture

The character of the colonial state in northern Nigeria, which played a critical role in the restructuring of African production, was far more complex than would be reflected in the clinical efficiency with which conquest was effected. The centrality of the state apparatus in the political economy of the colony is, however, often seen as a mere reflection of the needs of European capital. But to the extent that one conceptualizes the state as determined by structural needs of the center expressed through the dual purposes of accumulation and political domination, such an analysis

> cannot in itself account for why particular crops were introduced in particular colonies or, more importantly, explain the variant forms of colonial production that developed in different areas, e.g., peasant commodity production, corporate plantation production, settler estate

agriculture. Nor is it sufficient to explain the variant forms and differing trajectories of development of colonial state apparatuses in particular colonies.[18]

In northern Nigeria, the state must be situated within the specific historical circumstances and the contradictory forces associated with the articulation of global capitalism and indigenous, noncapitalist forms of production. This approach to the state recognizes that the demands of capitalist accumulation and reproduction, on the one hand, and of state control and legitimacy, on the other, may be mutually contradictory.[19] Insofar as the colonial state in Nigeria straddled two levels of articulation--between metropole and colony, and between capitalist and indigenous forms of production--it condenses within it these conflicting interests.

These conflicts were present from the very moment of colonial conquest, represented within European capital itself. If the progressive sphere of British capitalism, and Lugard specifically, saw investment as an immediate necessity to capture the latent resource potential of the Hausa, this was not the case at the British treasury, which provided funds for both the conquest and the subsequent administration. The colonial project could, in short, be justified only through self-finance and general parsimony. Shackled by the poverty of a miniscule grant-in-aid sufficient to support only a diminutive cadre of political officers, the colonial state was straitjacketed in terms of the manner in which development might be undertaken. In practice, this meant few European bureaucrats, no significant standing army, and economic change under the auspices of private entrepreneurial initiative in conjunction with indigenous resources. To satisfy the demands of political stability and fiscal self-reliance, indirect rule emerged not as a sophisticated or mystical creation but simply as a practical necessity. A class alliance was forged with cooperative members of the ruling emirate aristocracies, guarantees were given to the sanctity of Islam, Christian missionaries were tightly controlled, and merchant monopolies facilitated the expansion of commodity production and exchange and simultaneously provided the wherewithal for colonial revenue collection in the form of direct taxation of rural producers. The colonial mandate, then, bore a striking resemblance to the groundwork laid by Goldie in the late nineteenth century in establishing the Royal Niger Company's commercial domination over northern Nigeria.

Clearly the British recognized their reliance upon the caliphal ruling class to seal imperial rule and, in abstaining

from any interference with Islamic religious principles, they
"allowed the ruling class to define virtually all the prerogatives
of their class."[20]  In the case of domestic and farm slavery in
Hausaland, the juxtaposition of imperial ideology with the
practicalities of indirect rule presented glaring contradictions
on an issue that had purportedly been a major moral justification of the conquest itself.  The 1901 Proclamation of Slavery
prohibited slave raiding, abolished the legal status of slavery,
and declared that all individuals subsequently born of slave
parents would be free.  Yet Lugard, in his 1906 *Political
Memoranda*, made no attempt to disguise his solicitude for the
slave-owning class, which "it was the object of the government
to preserve and strengthen."[21]  As part of the alliance with the
emirate aristocracy, Lugard had hoped to prevent fugitive
slaves from occupying land, in an attempt to temporarily preserve the relation of master and slave, and to "prevent the estates of the upper class from going out of cultivation." [22]

Imperial survival, then, became closely bound to the welfare of the sultan, the emirs, and traditional *masu sarauta*.  To
the extent that the institution of slavery shored up the authority of the indigenous ruling class, the immediate abolition of
human servitude constituted a direct threat to the survival of
the local agents of imperial rule.  Since Lugard recognized,
however, that slavery would eventually--and in practice did--
die a slow death, the legitimacy of the Hausa-Fulani was to be
maintained by its transformation into a landlord class organi-
cally linked to an ex-slave, farm-laboring class.  The Lugardian project to produce at a single stroke a landlord system of
agriculture stands in stark contrast to the later technology of
gradualism and indirect rule encapsulated in the *Dual Mandate*
and, of course, to the actuality of a household-based system of
commodity production.  In holding that slavery was pervasive,
if not dominant, in the caliphate formation, Lugard wrote that

> Government, by the very act of introducing security for life and prop-
> erty, and by throwing open fertile land to cultivation, adds to the dif-
> ficulty of the problem it has to solve, namely, the creation of a laboring
> class to till the lands of the ruling classes . . . .[23]

The genesis of a wage-laboring class, Lugard believed, could
be lent the weight of the British courts, which would ensure
that the nascent landlord class obtained "free labor" by contract
and thus enforceable by law.  The fulcrum about which the
new system turned was direct taxation of producers and the
recognition of the *right of private property in land*.  Rapid or
premature desertion by slaves could be prevented, then, "by

not permitting fugitive farm slaves to occupy land to which they had no title,"[24] while payment of taxes and rents simultaneously provided revenues for landlords and the necessary coercion "to form a class willing to work for wages."[25]

The Lugardian vision was complete; a bureaucratized Islamic theocracy presided over by a traditional caliphate aristocracy assuming newfound legitimacy as wage-paying landlords--and all this dressed up in the rhetoric of indirect rule. By 1910, however, Lugard's radical project to create agrarian capitalism *de novo* was crushed by what is arguably the single most important piece of legislation in the history of colonial northern Nigeria. The Northern Nigerian Lands Committee (NNLC) comprehensively defeated Lugard's model of colonial political economy; it marked, in fact, the ascendancy of a Liberal "single tax" philosophy and of a struggle among factions of British capital in which anti-industrial sentiments--what Barrington Moore calls "catonism"[26]--struck a victory for mercantile interests.

The Lugardian schema, in fact, never materialized for the very good reason that it was undercut by the likes of Girouard, Temple, and Palmer who, to use Charles Temple's words, saw "the primary interests of Europeans in Nigeria was trade." After Lugard's departure to Hong Kong in 1906 following the Liberal defeat of the Conservative Party, the new cadre of political officers, while recognizing the need for class collaboration in Nigeria, envisioned a quite different and more conservative imperial strategy. The triumph of the smallholder strategy needs to be situated on the broader canvas of E.D. Morel's Congo campaign, the Liberal Party's antipathy toward affairs in South Africa, and the deleterious consequences of Britain's furtherance of proprietary land rights in India. In each case, the effects of rapacious and fickle industrial and finance capital were seen to have generated social misery and political insecurity at the expense of peasant proprietorship. British merchants, conversely, who saw themselves as "friends of the natives," wanted to "buy from and sell to independent smallholders not agricultural wage workers who had already handed over a share of their surplus . . . to [agrarian capital]."[27] The Lands Committee found the perfect foil for their intentions in the form of Henry George, an influential American libertarian economist who saw a fundamental contradiction between capitalist and worker *qua* class and the landlord. His fixation with the unearned income that accrued to the landlord class led him to promote state control of both land and rents, which would ordinarily have lined the pockets of private landowners. As a moralist, George was disturbed by progress in the face of continuing material poverty, a contradiction that could be bridged by "social and political rationalism" similar to the project of the French physiocrats. Such a rationalism was, in practice, the vehicle for a type of petit bourgeois individualism--allowing the small producer to produce efficiently, free of monopolistic or elite interests--which loosely upheld "common property" but, in actuality, wished to control large-scale capitalist interests while preserving the hegemony of an English form of mercantilism.[28] George's influential views provided a perfect justification for the Temple-Girouard schema, namely the nationalization of land in the protectorate and the transformation of emirate elites into a salaried bureaucracy which, as Gowers, the governor of Kano Province, put it, "creates a body of chiefs whose interests are closely bound up with the Government."[29]

The hegemony of merchant capital is contained in the proceedings of the Northern Nigeria Lands Committee, which met in London in 1908-1909. In his preparatory documents circulated to all northern administrative residents, Girouard strove to show first that caliphal assessment had degenerated into a poll tax and second, by invoking the case of Lower Burma, that a precedent existed for the codification of Henry George's ideas. Shenton[30] and Lennihan,[31] in particular, have documented Girouard's careful manipulation of both Liberal sentiment and of Baden-Powell's work on the Burman Land Act of 1876 to justify a full revenue assessment in Nigeria as a basis for taxing peasants as de facto tenants of the state. The Lands Committee was, according to Wedgewood, nothing short of a "conspiracy" to push through Girouard's loosely collectivist economic rent agenda.[32] The carefully selected principal witness in the hearings was Charles Temple, who had earlier argued to Lugard that land belongs to the community and not to the individual; he was ably supported by the resident of Zaria, Charles Orr and by the legal talents of H.R. Palmer, acting resident in Katsina. All three waved the flag of land "nationalization", clinging desperately to the idea, in spite of evidence to the contrary, that a "fee simple" or freehold tenure did not exist, and had never existed, in the emirates.[33] What was at stake in the testimony, however, was a tussle between "enlightened commercial imperialism" and the "shady financiers" and industrialists of monopoly capitalism.

So, amidst a good deal of confusion and contradictory evidence, the "socialistic" principles of the Lands Committee and Girouard's economic theory of land tenure had won out.

Having established that neither leases in perpetuity nor a landlord class existed in the North, Girouard's coda saw no need to introduce a system of tenure--proprietary rights--on which modern nations were spending "untold millions," trying to serve the "full rental value of the land."[34] Since the Muslim community owned land prior to conquest, the whole of the North--occupied or unoccupied--became subject to government control:

> The indigenous occupier has no legal right to security of possession; he cannot sell or mortgage the land . . . nor does he transmit indefensible title to his heirs.[35]

The colonial state naturally held the right to dispossession, principally for nonpayment of tax or voluntary sale without consent. At a single stroke, the Lands Committee dealt a mortal blow to Lugard's projected landlord class and his radical *junker* vision of agrarian capitalism in Nigeria.

I have dwelled on the land revenue issue at some length because the Lands Committee marks a watershed in the political economy of northern Nigeria and set the parameters for subsequent social and economic development. Of course, the proclamations of Girouard and the Lands Committee restricting land sale did not entirely limit farm transactions and the commoditization of land, but it acted as a brake on large-scale dispossession. The ethic of smallholder production proved to be powerful and resilient, and Lever's United Africa Company (UAC), to use one example, was consistently refused support for his oil palm plantation schemes over the period 1907 to 1925. In the classic populist statement by Governor Clifford in 1920:

> As . . . agricultural industries in tropical countries which are . . . in the hands of the native peasantry (a) have a firmer root than similar enterprises when owned and managed by Europeans, because they are natural growth, not artificial creations, and are self-supporting, as regards labor, while European plantations can only be maintained by some system of organized immigration or by some form of compulsory labor; (b) are incomparably the cheapest instruments for the production of agricultural produce on a large scale that have yet been devised; and (c) are capable of rapidity of expansion and a progressive increase of output that beggar every record of the past.[36]

Lever's UAC moved heavily into the produce trade, of course, which it dominated in Nigeria after 1929, but plantations never contributed significantly to local output.

Within the first decade, colonial *economic* interests in northern Nigeria were achieved through the preservation of the already existing *political* prerogatives of the *sarauta* class. Unlike the south where, according to Laitin, the colonial state "found it useful to resuscitate the declining fortunes of the kings of the Yoruba ancestral cities,"[37] the imperial powers found in the north the hegemonic *ulema* class intact; although it suffered from the meddlings of British colonial officers concerned with the moral character, honesty, and outlook of *individual* members, it had secured its class (i.e., *collective* continuity). The hegemonic position of the new *comprador* aristocracy was further deepened by the growth of Islamic influence which colonial rule affected. The Islamic reaction to conquest by Christian "infidels" served to deepen Muslim influence in the emirates. Equally, the cultivation of the precolonial administration and the further centralization of the state actually supported Islamic institutions, particularly in the absence of a white settler community and a significant missionary vanguard. Indeed, colonial bureaucratization favored the position of emirs and, through them, elements of the traditional aristocracy who were presented with the new administrative offices to bestow on clients. In the Weberian sense, the rationalization of the bureaucracy involved no leveling, for the prerogatives of the Muslim ruling class were preserved intact. The rise of a *comprador* Muslim elite was symptomatic of the removal of traditional constraints on centralized emirate power. The emirs, supported by the expanded military and communications apparatus of the colonial state and legitimated by a revivified Islamic ideology, could retain and even extend their domination over the *talakawa*. As Abdullahi put it, the colonial epoch in the North was above all a reflection of the seemingly endless capacity of the Hausa-Fulani elites to accommodate and contain the minimal British political officers without weakening its grasp on the peasantry.[38]

### The Merchant Capitalist and the Colonial State

The centrality of the colonial state as an agent for the consolidation of European trade interests and the conduit for the appropriation of rural surpluses set the stage for all subsequent development in northern Nigeria. De facto nationalization of land and the emancipation of a large slave population did not contribute to the genesis of the wage-laboring class; rather, it blocked the development of a plantation sector or a landlord class financed by European capital and underwrote the expansion of agrarian petty commodity production based largely on household labor.   As a consequence, merchant capital was guaranteed a hegemonic role in the northern Nigeria economy. The dynamics of commercial capital are complex but not necessarily revolutionary at the point of production.   European merchant houses battened themselves onto the preexisting indigenous Hausa-Fulani and Tripolitanian merchant networks, which long predated imperial rule.   This unholy and fragile alliance, supervised by the colonial state, was often mediated by the influential caliphate elites.

Merchant capital, or what Marx referred to as ancient or "antediluvian" capital, is intrinsic to a variety of social formations, but especially within the Muslim diaspora.   Nowhere is the correspondence between Islam and trade better highlighted than in the central Sudan in the nineteenth century,[39] especially in the long-distance merchant houses of the *ulema*-merchant networks illuminated by Tahir.[40]   The traffic in commodities showed clearly that the preconditions for the expanded role of European trade--namely money and commodities--were already present and flourishing in the Sokoto caliphate.   The British did introduce a more generalized specie (which Palmer believed was in widespread circulation by 1908) to replace the increasingly impractical cowry currency, but the prevalence of the commodity form, a buoyant craft sector, and the regularity of exchange behavior obviously struck a positive note among the early commercial intelligence officials.   In particular, it was the cotton textile sector that stirred the passions of the European trade community.   Yet, despite the early enthusiasm of Churchill, Hesketh Bell, and the British Cotton Growers Association (BCGA), the active promotion of cotton cultivated by the government, and the extension of the railway in 1907, the projected cotton boom sponsored by foreign capital was never to materialize.

To break into the existing commodity production system, the BCGA was forced to offer competitive lint prices in a robust rural textile industry that produced both for domestic consumption and for export throughout the desert edge.   Intent on high profitability through commercial exclusion, the BCGA was granted monopoly buying rights in 1905 by the colonial office and set to work using other merchant companies, including Levantine firms, as buying agents on a fixed price commission basis.[41]   But the effort to curtail speculation, competitive buying and price fluctuations ultimately failed to transform the Hausa plains into a "New South."   A major reason for the failure is contained in Governor Bell's lament that local cotton lint prices were at least 20 percent higher than the fixed price offered by the commercial firms. The price that rural producers could demand from Hausa spinners and weavers in a highly integrated regional textile sector peripheral to the global commodity market was, in fact, well above the prevailing world price.

With the arrival of the railway in Kano in 1912, and with it the first flush of expatriate trading companies--totaling eighteen by December 1913--cotton prospects were especially bleak. Ironically, as the Niger Company, John Holt, London and Kano, and the like erected buildings in the township, the railhead was deluged not with cotton lint but with groundnuts. What began as an experiment was rapidly seized upon by rural producers as a means to procure tax payment. The "groundnut revolution" proceeded apace, recovering quickly from the temporary setback of the 1913 drought and further boosted by the wartime British oil demand after 1916. Like the abortive cotton trade, groundnut purchasing assumed an oligopolistic quality, particularly in the decade of struggles and mergers up to 1929, which culminated in that year with the formation of the United Africa Company. In the course of the emergence of the trading combines, the structure of middleman operations changed as the European firms made use of the influx of Levantine and Arab capital from 1917 on. To be sure, large numbers of Hausa merchants were employed as European agents, and the opportunities for accumulation, particularly among the remote buying stations far from either railhead or motorable roads, were considerable. But, as Hogendorn observed, the dominant influence of the Hausa middleman of the early period was gradually usurped by Levantine traders like Saul Raccah.[42]

By the end of the First World War, merchant capital had consolidated itself as the dominant bloc in northern Nigeria. The European firms came to regulate and control the conditions of export crop commodity production and exchange without transforming the forms of actual production. As the Genoveses put it, the extension of commerce usually led to "the chaining down of labor and not at all to the separation of labor from the means of production".[43] Trade operations and the deepening of the world market moved hand in hand nonetheless; peasant income acquired through advances or crop sale furthered what Birdwhistle called "the creation of new wants"[44]--consumer goods, which, as they became items of necessary consumption, gradually disqualified indigenous craft production. The evacuation of agricultural commodities was then paralleled by the simultaneous influx of incentive goods: European cotton goods, soap, kerosene, high grade salt, cigarettes, metalware, and bicycles. The entire import-export trade, including the financial superstructure that supported it, was a vast corporate oligopoly. Throughout British West Africa, in fact, one company alone controlled 40 percent of external commerce, while a cluster of banking operations--dominated by Elder Demster's Bank of British West Africa--established itself as the supplier of specie and financiers for the firm's advance system. By 1945, a cartel of six major firms--known collectively as the Association of West Africa Merchants--had come to dominate Nigeria's produce trade (see Table 3.1). This oligopoly was itself presided over by the UAC, a subsidiary of the Unilever combine. Prior to 1939, the firms, in collusion with the colonial state, attempted to set prices and market commodities through involuntary compliance and sanctions. But internal policing was inevitably trouble-some, and cutthroat competition in the countryside, especially between Syrians and the UAC, frequently led to litigation and physical violence.

Interposed between the corporate interests themselves, on the one hand, and the peasant producers, on the other, there developed a myriad of intermediary agents, brokers, traders, and middlemen. The evolution of this enormous commercial edifice provided salaried district and village heads, bureau-crats, and local merchant capital generally with opportunities to benefit from both the volatile terms of trade and to spread a lucrative but usurious credit system. Well in advance of the harvest, commercial agents were advanced considerable sums by European firms, sums which were, in turn, lent directly to

TABLE 3.1: Firms' Share of Produce Trade in Nigeria, circa 1945

|  | Groundnuts | Cotton |
|---|---|---|
| Percent of the 3 largest firms | 58 | 79 |
| Percent of the 5 largest firms | 76 | 96 |
| Percent of the 1937 "syndicate" | 90 | 100 |

Source: P. Bauer, West African Trade (Cambridge: Cambridge University Press, 1953), 312-313.

the producer, who pledged his crop to an agent in return for cash borrowed to cover tax or other social obligations. Baldwin's *Groundnut Marketing Survey*[45] in the mid-1950s estimated that there were 960 such middlemen directly accredited to the firms, 2,000-2,500 agents delivering the middlemen, and 3,500-4,500 buyers' boys. In a nutshell, the most successful traders--Dantata, Danbappa, Gashash, Ringim, Wada--stood at the apex of a vast hierarchy of credit and clientage, which rested firmly on the shoulders of low-level rural agents and middlemen. The merchant class, whose development was stifled but not entirely blocked by the dominant position of European capital, lived in the interstices of a colonial economy constituted by petty commodity producers committed to export and, increasingly, food production.

The various interests dependent upon the production and supply of commodities--most notably metropolitan capital, the trading firms, local merchant capital, and the colonial state--could not depend, without problems, on the apparently errant and agriculturally backward Hausa peasantry for the supply of export commodities. The state had obviously intervened directly in the positive supply response through taxation and the support of monopolistic pricing and marketing arrangements. Merchant capital, however, which organizes the circulation of commodities, generally acquires profit through the market mechanisms and particularly through a process of unequal exchange. Yet the necessity to regulate what was cultivated, and in what quantity, demanded intervention by the firms at the level of the conditions of production. Whereas the organization of production remained in the hands of household producers, commodity relations increasingly shaped the form of the household economy. The regulation of production was fashioned in two admittedly blunt ways: first, through the colonial bylaws, extension schemes, fertilizer programs, and quality control legislation that tied rural producers to specific forms of agricultural production; and second, by a type of policing the countryside, namely the advance crop-mortgaging system, which bound producers to buyers through webs of credit and indebtedness. These efforts to discipline smallholders, to "capture peasants" in the face of the relative autonomy of their labor process, was only marginally successful and seemed to work best during economic depressions! But the activities of merchant capital, especially under conditions of limited development of the forces of production, erratic rainfall, and the periodic fluctuations in the terms of trade, constituted a constant threat to the simple reproduction of households, many of whom faced hardship and famine. What is of particular significance here, however, is the role of NA bureaucrats and emirate elites as *agents of commodity relations*. Working in conjunction with traders and colonial officers, the Hausa-Fulani office-holder bureaucrats were critical for the successful operation of the firms and the expansion of the mercantile economy. In this regard, there was an obvious, but often tense, complicity of interests among the *masu sarauta*, the large Hausa traders, and the firms.

It is clear from the work of Hogendorn[46] that the foundations of the trading firm-buying agent edifice were already consolidated by the first decade of colonial rule, initially through the skins trade and, more significantly after 1912, by the groundnut operations. The European firms were clearly not in touch with potential export commodity growers and had little choice but to work through both the indigenous merchant-*ulema* networks and their agents in the countryside, as well as the influential local-level bureaucrats, particularly the district, hamlet, and village heads. By propaganda, by advances of salt and cloth, and doubtless by a measure of political "persuasion" on the part of the village patrons and elites, groundnut production spread rapidly.

The subsequent development of the produce trade created multiple commercial opportunities for intermediaries, agents, and middlemen who were active in the sale and purchase of export commodities. A complex hierarchical edifice of traders emerged, linked through ties of credit and clientage. The fortunes of the commercial actors naturally vacillated in response to prevailing global economic conditions but, by the early 1920s, the colonial pattern of trade in cotton and groundnuts was firmly in place. On the one hand, there were the European firms themselves--UAC, CFAO, the London and Kano, and others--who alternated between intense competition among themselves, in an effort to capture a large share of the produce market, and restrictive pricing or purchase agreements to divide the spoils. The firms generally operated through canteens, which functioned as buying and assemblage points in the Provinces, run in most cases by Ibo and Yoruba commercial clients (*angulum kanti*). The canteen system flourished in the interwar years and provided expanded buying opportunities for Hausa merchants who could establish trade diasporas in the more remote and isolated districts. The Levantine and Arab merchants constituted a second, but not entirely independent, buying network. After 1917-1918, the Lebanese in particular gained favor with the European firms and often acted as middlemen in the groundnut trade, using Hausa agents for local-level purchases. As licensed buying agents, the Levantine merchants came to dominate the groundnut trade until the 1950s; their influence and accumulation was partly at the expense of Hausa middlemen, pushing them into the lower orders of the buying networks, but also spawned large Lebanese trading companies that competed directly with the European firms.

Finally, there were the Hausa merchants themselves who acted sometimes as independent middlemen, sometimes as agents for the Yoruba, Ibo, Lebanese, and Syrian clerks, and occasionally as autonomous "corporations" of which the Dantata empire is perhaps the model. The Hausa merchants expanded their role in the produce trade after World War II, and by the 1950s Alhassan alone is reputed to have financed 60 percent of all licensed buying agencies (LBAs) through free cash credit. The development of an influential and powerful indigenous merchant capitalist class clearly built upon and evolved through the precolonial merchant-*ulema* networks and their connections with the caliphate aristocracy. During colonial rule, however, these networks further diversified, in part as a response to discrimination in the export produce trade, and pursued other lines of accumulation in imports (cloth, salt), kola, transportation, grain, and property development.

On balance, although Hausa merchants did not initially occupy apical positions in the produce trade pyramid, they were active and influential in the local buying operations and constituted important commercial diasporas in themselves. A typical groundnut merchant hierarchy in Kano in the interwar period probably consisted of at least four levels. First, there were the relatively autonomous merchants who operated their own networks yet were business associates (*abokin ciniki*) of an urban patron who frequently advanced cash, goods, and imported wares to them. Second, there were primary clients who operated on a smaller commercial scale and with much less autonomy within the merchant network. Third were the agents who were, in practice, middle-level wholesalers. And fourth was a phalanx of lower-level traders, the rural speculators (*madugai*), balance men (*yan balas*), and rural agents (*attajirai*) who took small cash and cloth advances from the merchant patron and distributed credit, as a corollary to buying activities, through village- and hamlet-level networks. A hierarchy of this sort, embracing various categories of business patronage and client behavior, might have a geographical range covering virtually every growing area and buying center in the province. It was not solely that village and district heads ensured the profitability and success of local-level buying operations but that there was, in many cases, a straddling between political office and commercial accumulation. By the 1920s, the Zaria resident observed that the Sokoto and Katsina cotton trade was, in this de facto sense, in the hands of the emir.[47]

As in many other parts of the Muslim world, the extension of merchant capital in colonial Nigeria went hand in hand with usury or interest-bearing capital. It is precisely through this form that merchant influence extends beyond the realm of circulation into production proper. The existence of credit-based crop purchase in northern Nigeria certainly dates back to the beginnings of the groundnut trade in Kano, where salt and cloth were advanced to rural producers by buying agents to secure harvest sale.[48]

Cash advances progressively succeeded this early cloth-and-salt system, although the latter was apparently still predominant in Katsina in the 1940s. Interest rates and the future system showed some variability, however, between provinces, and also between commodities: that is, between cotton and groundnuts. In either case, advances need to be seen as part of a much broader trend associated with what Berman calls "destruction of the cycle of simple reproduction"[49] and with the increasing insecurity among some segments of the northern household economy. Where producers enter into commodity production through merchant middlemen who give advances to secure crop sale, it is inevitable that households should turn to these same agents (especially in the face of food shortage or social expenses) for productive or consumptive loans. The loans--either in cash or kind--can be paid either by presale of corn or export crops at predetermined but undervalued prices, or with heavy interest in cash or commodity form, the value of the latter being determined at the time of delivery.

The extent of advance by trading firms was quite extraordinary, in view of the absence of legally binding credit relations. In the early 1930s, an average firm engaged in groundnut purchases was advancing on the order of £N30,000 per season, of which as much as £N18,000 might be made available to the larger Syrian merchants. This capital was then used for local-level Hausa--so-called *dan baranda*--middlemen, village and district heads, and wealthy villagers who attempted to secure the crop as it was raised. The quantities of money advanced to local agents obviously varied considerably, but in the late 1930s A.D.O. Hall estimated that a large groundnut *dan baranda* might receive £N800 per season. The resident of Sokoto alleged several years earlier that district heads engaged in the cotton trade regularly received advances in excess of £N1000.[50]  A crop mortgage system had emerged in the fertile *laka* cotton districts of southern Katsina by the early 1920s; each clerk (*fuloti*) of the firms, who received a commission of 12/6d. per ton of cotton purchased, advanced to five to ten of his *yan baranda*, who were also paid on a commission basis. The *fuloti* opened prior to the official buying season (which usually began 1 December), perhaps in October, during which time food and tax requirements had to be met. The *dan baranda* could make use of the preharvest hunger for cash by making loans to secure the cotton crop in the face of competition from other agents. Should the crop fail, the *dan baranda* and the clerk had the security of interest on the cash loan. The *dan baranda* had a monopoly until the loan was paid off, and the middlemen took advantage of this dependency, since "the farmer sells 15/- or £N1's worth of cotton before he is told that he has repaid [the] 10/-debt."[51]   In Katsina emirate, the emir had ruled that under Muslim law loans could not be made on the security of standing crops, but the provincial resident reported in the 1940s that

> lenders now make loans without mention of security [in order] to bring action for recovery . . . . However they seldom resort to the Courts . . . in fact the majority of them . . . prefer that a portion [of the loan] is outstanding so as to retain hold over the borrower.[52]

Advances continued unabated.  In 1949, 80 percent of UAC's purchases were financed by capital loaned to middlemen[53] and, in 1956, Baldwin's survey of firms established that 94% of export crop purchases were procured by advances.

A shift in credit relations occurred after 1945 due to the changes in produce marketing.  The wartime creation of state monopolies--groundnut and cotton marketing boards--had the effect of displacing European firms and their clerks from their comfortable position in the countryside.  Competition between buyers fell accordingly, and the state produce boards were not compelled to provide LBAs with advances to procure commodities prior to harvest.  While the crop mortgaging system had seen its heyday, Hausa merchants now came to dominate the produce trade as licensed buying agencies--interposed between state and rural producers and rapidly displacing Lebanese and Syrian competitors.  The LBAs could compensate for the loss of the traditional advance system by utilizing their local merchant connections to fulfill the general demand for credit among the rural poor. The structural conditions that encouraged widespread borrowing were spelled out in a six-teen-village study of Bornu and Bauchi provinces in the 1950s, which indicated that 38 percent and 19 percent of farmers in-terviewed had exhausted domestic grain reserves prior to the commencement of the farming season.[54] By July these figures had risen to 90 percent and 94 percent, respectively. Under such circumstances, households turned to local farmer/traders as sources of loans to cover immediate liquidity requirements. Those who, by virtue of their poverty and low credit worthi-ness, could not raise loans "seek work on the farms of better off farmers to earn money to buy food, leaving their own fields [untended]."[55] Vigo's work pointed strongly to the new commercial hegemony of Hausa buying agents, who used *local capital* rather than the advances of the European firms:

> Moneylenders have agents in villages or districts in which they operate. Usually they have a confederate working with them. Agents living in villages operate through a number of leading farmers called 'madugus.' They are kept informed of the movements of moneylenders to whom they are attached . . . . Moneylender agents often reside in the same village or area as their clients .. and therefore know about the state of their crops and their ability to pay at harvest. These agents with the help of harvest heads as well as [madugus] are responsible for repay-ment of loans. For this service they may have their own loans interest free . . . .[56]

Gradually, then, local merchant capital came to occupy an expanded and politically significant position in the political economy of northern Nigeria. Although in the early phase, Hausa merchants only gained access to the European firms through the traditional aristocracy, they emerged by the 1940s as a class of powerful merchant capitalists. Working through the Sufi brotherhoods, the merchants such as Dantata, Gashash, and Danbappa straddled the public and private sec-tors. To the extent that the state acted as a major theatre of accumulation, merchants both cultivated connections with the traditional aristocracy (indeed, they were sometimes one and the same), and also entered directly into NA politics. By the 1930s, wealthy urban merchants who stood at the fountainhead of rurally based trade networks had emerged as a powerful class in their own right, in some cases challenging the author-ity of the *sarauta* and in others joining hands with them as a powerful nascent bourgeois class.[57] In the 1940s, it was this amalgam of politicians, businessmen, and merchants who formed the first mercantile lobby, the Kano Traders General

Conference. They meet regularly on NA premises, were encouraged by traditional rulers such as the Madawaki of Kano and, in 1953, became the Amalgamated Northern Merchants Union, the spearhead of northern merchant nationalism.[58] It was precisely this new alliance of the progressive bureaucrat and the merchant capitalist that Tahir sees as the axis of postwar (1945) northern politics;[59] it was also this very class that in the 1950s made use of the state--particularly the surpluses accumulated through the marketing boards--as they moved into industrial, especially textile, production. The period after 1950 was, of course, one of massive corruption and the emergence of strong regional and ethnic sentiments that fed into the progressive claims of the nascent Hausa bourgeoisie. The Kano Citizens Trading Company, established in 1950 and subsequently heavily funded by the Northern Regional Development Board, is simply one important example of how the bureaucrat-merchant oligarchy drank deeply at the state well, draining financial surpluses quickly through the "kill and share" ethic of northern politics.[60] This was the beginning of the venal and corrupt use of state resources for private accumulation and of the public-private "straddling" that has become the hallmark of Nigerian political economy and class development.

## Commodity Production and Rural Differentiation

The Land and Native Rights Proclamation of 1910 was an attempt to shield northern Nigerian society from the corrosive effects of non-Muslim communities, whether they were white settlers, Ibo middlemen, or Yoruba agents. While Clifford gradually undermined this policy of sheltering in the North in the postwar period, the colonial administration nonetheless strove to preserve the authority and the legitimacy of emirate aristocracies upon which colonial hegemony ultimately depended. The necessity of forging a class alliance with the *masu sarauta* did not mean that the caliphal elites were frozen *in situ*. On the contrary, the British meddled constantly in emirate and dynastic politics, deposing emirs and high-ranking palace officials with great regularity, dispatching emirs to Ilorin, reestablishing the Hausa line in Daura, dismantling palace cliques, and pushing the preconquest district heads (*hakimi*) into the countryside. Yet the *sarauta* as a class was maintained. In rallying around the cause of peace, order, and stability, the Hausa-Fulani elites were simultaneously bound to the British and given a stake in colonial stability.[61] Although the traditional basis of society and its ideological platform was retained by the British, the military supremacy of the colonial state, however, changed the nature of aristocratic legitimacy; the support of the state apparatus enormously expanded the power of the new rural administrators with respect to the peasantry.[62] The obvious avenue for this exploitation was taxation, but as I described earlier, other opportunities presented themselves, not least commercial agentships; village and hamlet heads quickly became local-level representatives in the groundnut and cotton buying networks. The fact that their salaries remained low in relation to expected ruling class obligations--the village head salary was £N2-0-0 in 1917 but was actually reduced in the 1930s--naturally pushed district and village heads toward extortion, embezzlement of taxes, and increased commercial trafficking. As a result, districts and village areas were, as a touring officer noted of Dankama, "run like private estates,"[63] and there was necessarily considerable leakage of state surpluses through political office.

An inventory of the manner in which officeholders mobilized surpluses is hardly necessary in view of the large literature on political corruption, administrative malpractice, and venality during the colonial period. The avenues for extortion were multiple since most administrative and fiscal dicta were enacted by the rural bureaucrats; illicit grain requisition, underpayment for NA grain levies, illegal forced labor, and tithes were commonplace. Smith estimated that, in Zaria, systematic underpayment of grain to requisitioned peasants produced, in one season, roughly £N800 for one district head.[64] The preservation of precolonial officeholding estates, which Lugard saw as a necessary corollary to buttressing Hausa-Fulani privilege, also supported obligatory unpaid village labor on *sarauta* farms.[65] Tax extortion was, of course, endemic and appeared in almost every annual report, as one might anticipate in view of the imperial power's preoccupation with revenue and self-financing. District heads often collected taxes in advance (*kudin falle*) to provide the capital for their market speculations, especially buying grain in bulk at harvest to be resold during the following wet season when prices had doubled. In 1912, district officer Webster estimated that the *dagaci* were levying 30 percent more on *zakkat* and *kudin kassa* taxes since receipts were rarely given to each individual taxpayer. The lump-sum assessment system actually compounded the likelihood of tax embezzlement because the computation of the household levy lay in the hands of the village oligarchy. Corruption and exploitation were the inevitable externalities of the imperial obsession with revenue, on the one hand, and its class collaboration, on the other.

This is not to imply that the administration did not intervene in tax embezzlement issues. Indeed, the first two decades of colonial rule are positively flooded with cases of deposed *hakimi* and village heads who overstepped the license that British political officers had granted. In a two-month period in 1910, twenty-eight officials were deposed in Katsina Province;[66] in 1931, in Zaria, forty-one village heads "proved unequal to the responsibilities of tax collection."[67]  These depositions did less to regulate the political muscle of the rural oligarchy than highlight the outer limits of colonial power. First, the elites developed systematic devices to shield themselves from complaints or investigation; second, the mass depositions provided ample opportunity for the emirs to consolidate their political hegemony in the countryside. Emir Dikko of Katsina carefully used the tax issue to place his clients at strategic points in the villages.  In 1917, forty-eight of the salaried village heads were nonnatives of their towns, being relations or servants of the emir, relations of the district heads (who were inevitably closely tied to the ruling lineage), or former tax collectors (*jekadas*). The suggestion that indirect rule proved to be a form of bureaucratic authoritarianism is not too far from the mark.

The emergence of a powerful political class in the countryside (often with direct ties to mercantile activities) is suggestive of the important consequences of both commodity production and colonial rule for rural inequality.  The most prolific theorist of Hausaland has, however, adamantly adhered to the fundamental classlessness of Hausaland based on the absence of a wagelaboring class and the strength of intergenerational leveling mechanisms.[68]   Even though Hill identified marked inequality in Hausa communities, she strives to show how interhousehold inequalities are nonsystematic, i.e., are not reproduced structurally.  Her Chayanovian model of peasant economy actually sees the colonial period as a period of "withdrawal" from the countryside, a sort of changeless change characterized by lateral adjustment and internal circulation of the village-level aristocracy.  Hill's own work suggests, nonetheless, that economic mobility is, in her words, "sticky" and that there are indeed systematic relations of inequality between different economic strata.  In this sense, one should not highlight the persistence of certain archaic social forms and the absence of a wage-laboring class at the expense of the corrosive effects of commodity production. In regard to the latter, colonialism meant that "disparities [among peasants were] no longer based on social structure . . . but [arose] and spread from the manipulation of goods and money."[69]

The peasantry were, in fact, dissolved and reconstituted as petty commodity producers. An understanding of this transformation must recognize how capital provided the dynamic for the new relations of production in the countryside, and specifically creates niches for petty commodity production based largely on household labor. The character of this process of commoditization has been alluded to already in the discussion of merchant capital. Here I simply want to draw attention to (1) the increasing commoditization of land and (2) the quantitative aspects of household differentiation, both of which highlight the intensification of petty commodity production. In the first instance, the sale of farms increased significantly in spite of the Lands Proclamation.[70] Rowling's study in 1946 showed that, of eighteen case histories at Dawaki near Kano, eleven involved outright sale.[71] In addition, Rowling documented the proliferation of other land transactions, notably pledging (*jingina*), lease (*aro, kudin goro*), and sharecropping (*kashi mu raba*). In many cases, of course, the hiring out or in of land in whatever form was rarely reported to village heads, since Muslim ideology poses obvious practical limitations on such transactions. Language can further obfuscate these land dealings: *aro*, for instance, may mean loan, although the nature of the exchange can be, in practice, direct rental. The undeniable fact, however, is the emergence of farm land as a rentable commodity and of a class of agriculturalists who derived income, whether in cash or labor power, from such dealings.

This commodification proceeded slowly and unevenly, of course, particularly in view of the abolition of the legal right to own property in land. The latter acted as a brake upon large-scale land accumulation, certainly, but land transactions --in spite of the NNLC--laid the basis for expanded inequalities in rural communities and the gradual emergence of a petit bourgeois class in the countryside.

The most fundamental quantitative measures of landholding and income differences between households in the colonial period are difficult to gauge in spite of survey assessments at the village level. The most accessible statistics pertain to landholding: in 1937 two communities studied for revenue purposes in the heavily populated and highly commercialized Kano close-settled zone showed that 35 percent of all holdings were less than four acres while 33 percent were in excess of seven acres per farm household. A much clearer picture emerges from a study by Morrison in Dawaki-ta-Kudu district in 1947.[72] Dawaki village had a mean household holding of roughly six acres; 25.9 percent of all households held fewer than three acres apiece, while 27 percent of households owned over 50 percent of all farmland.[73] Seventeen percent of all households held less than one acre of land, and 13.1 percent were landless, presumably renting in or borrowing land. In light of the critical role of household labor, it is perhaps worth noting that 50 percent of all households consisted of five or fewer individuals, while 27 percent consisted of ten or more. Morrison also estimated that between 1937 and 1947, the percentage of holdings in the fewer-than-three-acres category had increased in the three communities studied by 1.7 percent; the proportion in the over-six-acres group, conversely, had fallen by 2 percent.

The differentiation issue is given further clarity in Smith's budgetary data collected in 1949 in Zaria emirate (Table 3.2).[74] Unfortunately, the smallness of the sample size severely limits a detailed examination of household stratification but, by recomputing some of Smith's household data, a striking juxtaposition of economic extremes is brought into focus. The households have been ranked by gross income per adult male; the difference in mean incomes and farm acreages between rich and poor households varies by a factor of almost 4. That is to say, the rich peasants own roughly three to four times as much farmland and generate four times as much gross income per adult male as the poor families. Whereas the community as a whole is grain deficient, poor farmers are clearly purchasing more as a percentage of domestic foodstuffs grown on family farms than are their wealthy brethren. Cotton and groundnuts were both significant income sources, although the rich households produced almost four times more by value; 18 percent of the cultivated area was devoted to export commodities among the wealthy peasantry as opposed to 30 percent of the farm area among the poor. Perhaps most significant, however, is the extent of commoditization in the nonagricultural sphere-- principally crafts and trade--and the contributions these activities make to household reproduction. Among both rich and poor peasantry, the value of off-farm income was between seven and twenty times greater than that of agricultural export commodities.

The Hausa case shows dramatically how central was off-farm employment for household reproduction. However, since

TABLE 3.2: Household Inequality and Differentiation: Zaria,[a] circa 1949

| Gross Income | Income per adult male (£N)[b] | Percent cash income | Acres | Cotton/groundnut production (£N) | Trade profit (£N) | Craft profit (£N) | Gifts in (£N) | Gifts out (£N) | Tax | Women's Profit | Staple food purchased | Purchased staples as percent of grown |
|---|---|---|---|---|---|---|---|---|---|---|---|---|
| Rich | | | | | | | | | | | | |
| | 114-15-2 | 70.6 | 6.3 | 10-10-0 | -- | -- | 8-9-0 | 4-11-0 | 14-8 | 35-8-0 | 13-4-0 | 50 |
| | 78-10-0 | 70.4 | 7.8 | 5-9-0 | 102-10-0 | -- | 3-19-0 | -- | 1-10-0 | 32-8-0 | 8-15-0 | 25 |
| | 69-2-0 | 25.9 | 3.8 | 5-3-0 | -- | 10-11-0 | 5-12-1 | -- | 1-1-0 | 12-10-0 | 3-11-0 | 10 |
| | 66-1-0 | 40.7 | 8.7 | 4-14-0 | 48-9-0 | -- | 5-0-9 | -- | 2-13-6 | 18-7-0 | 7-14-0 | 16 |
| Average | 81-15-0 | 51.9 | 6.6 | 6-10-0 | 37-15-0 | 2-15-0 | 5-15-0 | 1-3-0 | 1-8-0 | 24-17-0 | 8-5-0 | 25.25 |
| Poor | | | | | | | | | | | | |
| | 15-6-0 | 22.8 | 3.0 | -- | 6-4-0 | 0-16-6 | -- | -- | 11-5 | 21-0-0 | 5-10-0 | 33 |
| | 27-4-0 | 47.2 | 2.1 | 3-18-0 | 15-7-0 | 3-10-0 | -- | -- | 7-0 | 9-3-0 | 2-19-0 | 20 |
| | 21-17-0 | 52.8 | 1.2 | 1-0-6 | -- | 9-7-0 | -- | -- | 7-0 | 7-12-0 | 2-2-0 | 30 |
| | 17-2-0 | 67.4 | 1.2 | -- | -- | 19-17-0 | 10-8 | -- | -- | 10-6-0 | 8-3-0 | 250 |
| Average | 20-5-0 | 47.0 | 1.87 | 1-5-0 | 5-7-0 | 8-7-6 | 4-2 | -- | 6-5 | 12-0-0 | 4-15-0 | 83 |

[a] Refers to an old market town on a trade route and road.

[b] Refers to gross annual income per adult male; the other craft, trade incomes and so on refer to household incomes.

Source: M.G. Smith, The Economy of Hausa Communities in Zaria, Colonial Research Series 16, London: HMSO, 1955.

rich households clearly monopolized the lucrative merchant/trade occupations and the poor families were saddled with high-turnover but low-return crafts such as mat weaving and the provision of community services (praise singers, barbers), the off-farm sector was markedly segmented. Lucrative petty commodity production is congruent with the concept of "kulak," that is, an all-around agent of commodity relations functioning as a moneylender, transporter and credit facilitator, and a renter of land and machinery. The craft economy, however, provided alternative avenues to the sale of labor power among the rural poor, in spite of the fact that 25 percent of all household heads did not practice any "industrial" trade. The relatively low incidence of farm labor in areas subject to intense merchant activity was not necessarily universal, but is interesting that even by 1947, in Dawaki-ta-Kudu district in Kano Province, Morrison estimated that only 10 percent of households regularly hired in labor. The undeveloped nature of wage laboring was not unrelated to the relative attractiveness of mercantile operations, which rests on *dependency* not *dispossession* (i.e., proletarianization). As Bernstein observed, the higher rate of return in trade versus reinvestment in production "can help account for the limited formation of agrarian capital and the limited differentiation of units of production simultaneously with the extension (and intensification) of commodity relations."[75]

In some respects, any attempt to estimate the extent of wage laboring is bedevilled by the shame that surrounds the act of working in another man's farm; furthermore, the high incidence of indebtedness almost certainly indicates that repayments were not infrequently made in labor power. Hence Morrison's survey in 1947, which noted the widespread use of *gayya* (collective farm labor), may be rather deceptive. Neither should this cloud the generality of dry season migration (*cin rani*) for the purpose of wage laboring. Prothero's survey, for instance, estimated in 1957 a quarter of a million migrants passing through Sokoto Province alone in search of work.[76]

In many respects, the changing relations of production among household producers affirms Lenin's insight that differentiation among the "American roads" is a slow process and that capital takes hold of agriculture in complex and unexpected ways. Hausa peasants increasingly entered into commodity production, and a rising proportion of socially necessary labor time was expended on the production of exchange values. The rise of wage laboring, indebtedness, and of land transactions reflected this process of increased commoditization. Such developments were, nonetheless, uneven in time and space and were coincident with complex immediate forms of social organization governing access to and control of resources. In this context, rural differentiation is best conceptualized not as a pyramid of wide, layered strata but "as a finely graded spectrum from richest to poorest with the intertwined criteria of size of off-farm income and size of landholding as the twin axes around which differentiation revolved."[77] I have suggested, however, that although there was an expansion of petty commodity production based on a middle peasantry, a wealthy rural petit bourgeois class emerged, often heavily involved in local trade and with organic links to urban merchants and local government officials alike. These stood in sharp contrast to those indebted rural producers who regularly sold their labor power, migrated, scavenged on the sidelines of the commodity economy, especially in the close-settled zones like Kano, and struggled on lilliputian holdings.

In sum, there are four critical points that emerge from this brief discussion of agrarian class formation and merchant capitalism. First, the hegemony of merchant interests in northern Nigeria was, at best, an ambiguously progressive force in the countryside; its corrosive effects on social structure did not entail a proletarianization of propertied commodity producers. Indeed, as Harris shows in his study of south India,[78] the logic of mercantile operations was not dispossession in the classic Leninist sense but the perpetuation and reproduction of dependent relations between household producers and merchants, a dependency that was the touchstone of mercantile accumulation. Second, the expansion of household commodity production, the limited specialization of farming families, and the uneven development of socioeconomic differentiation among rural producers all constrained the domestic market for manufactures. The smallholder strategy, then, supported by an alliance of fractions of metropolitan capital and powerful local northern class interests, placed restrictions on what Kitching calls "the universalization of capitalist relations of production." Third, the complex and contradictory effects of commodity production on household producers did not generate a neat class stratification in Hausaland but, instead, complex intermediate forms of production and social organization. In addition, there was a great deal of straddling between various forms of income earning: for example, between wage labor and craft production, political office and merchant activities, agricultural production and access to state resources. As a result, there was no clear-cut pattern of either agrarian capitalism or a generalized rural proletariat. Fourth, the surpluses mobilized by the colonial state and the accumulation strategies of merchants all ultimately rested on noncapitalist forms of production: namely, the labors of petty commodity producers or peasants. Their surpluses fed the state and its clients (through taxes) and merchants (through unequal exchange and usury). To the extent that office-holders, local and foreign merchants, the mining companies, and the colonial state all had their own, often contradictory, interests in peasant production, it was inevitable that the burdens that peasants shouldered were frequently excessive. For this reason, the short-term reproduction of large sections of the peasantry was a sort of lottery and, on occasion, in the face of drought and the equally pernicious vicissitudes of the market, their very survival was at stake. The series of famines between 1901 and 1960 pay testimony both to the terrible weight carried by commodity-producing households, and the contradictory nature of colonialism itself, which quite literally killed many thousands of those upon whom the entire imperial project depended.[79]

## Conclusion

[In] the agrarian question and the agrarian crisis, the heart of the matter is not simply the removal of obstacles to the advance of agricultural technique, but what way these obstacles are to be removed. What class is to effect this removal, and by what methods?

Lenin[80]

I have tried to suggest that the obstacles to which Lenin refers were not removed in the course of colonial rule, and that the designs of Lugard to promote a radical conversion of a Muslim aristocracy into a landlord class using wage labor was aborted by a conjunctural alliance of Liberal, mercantile, and anticapitalist interests. The parsimony of the British treasury and the strength of a preexisting Muslim status-honor group in the caliphate ensured that the populist strategy of Girouard and Temple would be attached to a class alliance with indigenous elites (what came to be called "indirect rule"). The specific outcome of these struggles and political realities was a merchant-dominated strategy in which land nationalization converted the colonial state into a theatre of accumulation. Class formation in northern Nigeria was therefore forged within the crucible of this colonial project that emerged in the first decade of the century.

I have emphasized in particular the expanded power of the Hausa-Fulani bureaucrats, a caliphal aristocracy who preserved and deepened their class prerogatives, and the rise of an influential merchant class--often from the ashes of precolonial trading families, who operated diversified trade networks in the interstices of the colonial economy. In practice, there was considerable straddling between these two constituencies and, by the 1940s, a bureaucrat-merchant alliance had appeared that marked a conscious effort by a nascent bourgeois class to use the state for its own ends.

I have, of course, not dealt with the obvious partiality of this concern with a *northern* bourgeois class; in other words, the Northern Region was itself part of a highly regionalized Nigerian colony. One of the consequences of imperial rule in Nigeria was to deepen regional and ethnic identification. Class formation in the North was heavily crosscut with strong religious and ethnic forces. In the move toward independence, of course, these regional class differences were further deepened by the struggle for national control; what was true for the colonial state--namely, its conflicting internal interests--was as true for the fledgling Nigerian state at independence. Even though the North was finally able to secure some sort of national hegemony, it was both fragile and volatile. The very forces that had shaped the emergence of an increasingly conscious Muslim, Hausa-Fulani bourgeois class in the North also acted to fragment and cleave a national ruling bloc capable of holding a newly independent Nigeria together.

## Notes

All citations in the text referring to NAK refer to archival materials deposited in the Nigerian National Archives at Kaduna.

1. Benjamin, W. Illuminations (New York: Schocken, 1969), 255.

2. F. Lugard, cited in F. Okediji, An Economic History of the Hausa-Fulani Emirates (Ph.D. diss., Indiana University, 1972,) 52.

3. Cited in Buell, The Native Problem in Africa (New York: MacMillan, 1928), 772.

4. See for example G. Hopkins, An Economic History of West Africa (London: Longmans, 1973).

5. B. Berman, "Structure and Process in the Bureaucratic States of Africa," Development and Change, no. 15 (1984): 161-202.

94     Michael J. Watts

6.  G. Kitching, "Politics, Method and Evidence in the Kenya Debate," in H. Bernstein and B. Campbell, eds., Contradictions of Accumulation in Africa (Beverly Hills, Calif.: Sage, 1985), 139.

7.  See B. Berman and J. Lonsdale, "Crisis of Accumulation," Canadian Journal of African Studies, no. 14 (1980): 37-54.

8.  I. Tahir, Scholars, Sufis, Saints and Capitalists in Kano 1904-1974 (Ph.D. diss., Cambridge University, 1974).

9.  R. Adeleye, Power and Diplomacy and Northern Nigeria 1804-1906 (New York: Humanities Press, 1971), 492.

10.  See Y.B. Usman, The Transformation of Katsina circa 1796-1903 (Ph.D. diss., Ahmadu Bello University, 1974).

11.  R. Shenton, The Development of Capitalism in Northern Nigeria (Toronto: University of Toronto Press, 1986), 1-10.

12.  M. Last, "The Sokoto Caliphate and Bornu 1820-1880," postgraduate seminar paper, Bayero University, Kano, 1978.

13.  P. Lubeck, "Islam and Resistance in Northern Nigeria," in W. Goldfrank, ed., The World System of Capitalism (London: Sage, 1979), 200.

14.  F. Braudel, Afterthoughts on Material Civilization and Capitalism (Baltimore: Johns Hopkins University Press, 1977), 19.

15.  Tahir, op. cit.

16.  G. Hyden, Beyond Ujamaa in Tanzania (Berkeley: University of California Press, 1980).

17.  J. Scott, "Hegemony and Peasantry," in Politics and Society, no. 7 (1977): 267-296.

18.  Berman and Lonsdale, op. cit., 42.

19.  See M. Watts, Silent Violence: Food, Famine, and Peasantry in Northern Nigeria (Berkeley: University of California Press, 1983), for an elaboration of this point.

20.  Lubeck, op. cit., 199.

21.  F. Lugard, Political Memoranda (London: Waterlow, 1906), 221.

22.  Lugard, op. cit., 138.

23.  Lugard, op. cit., 136.

24.  Lugard, op. cit., 142.

25.  Lugard, op. cit., 138.

26.  Barrington Moore, Social Origins of Dictatorship and Democracy (Boston: Beacon, 1966), 491-496.

27.  L. Lennihan, "Rights in Men and Rights in Land," Slavery and Abolition, no. 3 (1982), 131. See also Shenton, op. cit., 22-49.

28.  W. Lissner, "On the Centenary of Poverty and Progress," American Journal of Economics and Sociology, no. 38 (1979), 1-16.

29.  Cited in G. Tomlinson and G. Lethem, History of Islamic Propaganda in Nigeria (London: Waterlow, 1927), 9.

30.  Shenton, op. cit., 22-50.

31.  Lennihan, op. cit., 121-131.

32.  J. Wedgewood, Memoirs of a Fighting Life (London: Hutchinson,

1940).

33. C. Temple, Native Races and Their Rulers (London: Cass, 1918), 138-139.

34. NAK SNP 6 C 162/1907, 68.

35. Report of the Northern Nigerian Lands Committee, London, HMSO Cd. 5101-5102, 1910, 68.

36. Clifford, op. cit.

37. D. Laitin, "Hegemony and Religious Conflict," in P. Evans, D. Rueschemeyer and T. Skocpol, eds., Bring the State Back In (Cambridge: Cambridge University Press, 1985): 285-316.

38. M. Abdullahi, The Modernization of Elites in Northwestern State, Nigeria (Ph.D. diss., University of Chicago, 1977), 79.

39. P. Lovejoy, Caravans of Kola (Zaria: Ahmadu Bello University Press, 1980).

40. Tahir, op. cit.

41. NAK SNP 7 1521/1905.

42. J. Hogendorn, Nigerian Groundnut Exports (Zaria: Ahmadu Bello University Press, 1978), 141.

43. E. and E. Genovese, Fruits of Merchant Capital (Oxford: Oxford University Press, 1980), 8.

44. NAK SNP 7/8 1765/1907.

45. J. Baldwin, Groundnut Marketing Survey (Kaduna: Ministry of Agriculture, 1956), 26.

46. Hogendorn, op. cit., 141.

47. NAK SNP 386/1918.

48. Hogendorn, op. cit., 78-79.

49. Berman, op. cit., 169.

50. NAK Kadminagric 19735.

51. NAK Katprof 234.

52. NAK SNP 17 1864.

53. Hogendorn, op. cit., 143.

54. NAK MSWC 1358.

55. NAK MSWC 1358/S.5A.

56. NAK MSWC 1358/S.5, vol. 1, 35-36.

57. I. Bashir, The Politics of Industrialization in Kano (Ph.D. diss., Boston University, 1983).

58. See Bashir, "The Political Economy of an Oligarchy," Boston University African Studies Center Working Paper no. 89, 1984.

59. Tahir, op. cit.

60. Tahir, op. cit.

61. I. Okonjo, British Administration in Nigeria 1900-1950 (New York: Nok, 1974), 36.

62. See Watts, op. cit.

63. NAK Katprof 1, no. 4 1926/79.

64. M. Smith, "Historical and Cultural Conditions of Political Corruption among the Hausa," Comparative Studies in Society and History, no. 6 (1964): 164-194.

65. NAK Sokprof 368/1911.

66. NAK Katprof 1/1 1865/1910.

67. NAK Zariaprof 7/1, 125/1931.

68. See Polly Hill, Rural Hausa: A Village and a Setting (Cambridge: Cambridge University Press, 1972).

69. C. Raynault, "Circulation monétaire et evolution des structures socio-économiques chez les hausa du Niger," Africa, no. 47 (1977): 168

70. A. Frischmann, The Spatial Growth and Residential Location Pattern of Kano (Ph.D. diss., Northwestern University, 1977).

71. G. Rowling, Report on Land Tenure, Kano Province (Kaduna: Government Printer, 1949).

72. NAK Kanoprof 5/1 6551/S.1.

73. NAK Kanoprof 5/1 655/S/1.

74. M.G. Smith, The Economy of Hausa Communities in Zaria, Colonial Research Series no. 16, London, HMSO, 1955.

75. H. Bernstein, "African Peasantries: A Theoretical Framework," Journal of Peasant Studies, no. 6 (1979): 432.

76. R. Prothero, Migrant Labor from Sokoto Province (Kaduna: Government Printer, 1957).

77. G. Kitching, Class and Economic Change in Kenya: The Makings of an African Petit Bourgeoisie 1905-1970 (New Haven: Yale University Press, 1980), 154.

78. J. Harriss, Capitalism and Peasantry (New Delhi: Oxford University Press, 1981).

79. Watts, op. cit., 187-372.

80. V. Lenin, Collected Works (Moscow: Foreign Languages Publishing House, vol. 15, 1893), 136.

David H. Groff

# 4 When the Knees Began Wearing the Hat: Commercial Agriculture and Social Transformation in Assikasso, the Ivory Coast, 1880-1940

In the late nineteenth and early twentieth centuries, commercial agriculture was one of the principal mechanisms by
which African peoples became integrated into the world
capitalist system. In West Africa, in particular, a varying
combination of market forces and colonial administrative blan-
dishments converted large numbers of indigenous cultivators
into export-oriented cash crop producers. This process of incorporation was especially important in the Ivory Coast, where
it gave rise to a category of relatively large African producers
usually referred to in the literature as "planters."[1] By most
accounts, these "planters" have played a central role in the
history of the modern Ivory Coast not only because of their
economic achievements but also because of their leadership of
the Ivorian nationalist movement.[2]

Much of the discussion of the planters concerns their relationship to the present-day Ivorian ruling class. Some observers have argued that the larger planters constitute a class
of rural capitalists,[3] a "véritable bourgeoisie de planteurs," as
one writer put it.[4] As such, so the argument goes, they form
the principal social basis of the Ivorian ruling class, thereby
lending it a bourgeois coloration. In this view, the present
Ivorian state can best be understood as an instrument of class
rule by an African planter bourgeoisie.

Other observers reject this view of the Ivorian ruling class
and its relationship to the planters. Michael Cohen, for example, has argued that while the ruling class may have originated
among the planters, it is today an essentially urban-based
group deriving its power primarily from political and bureaucratic office-holding.[5] Jean-Pierre Chauveau and Jacques
Richard also deny the link between the planters and the ruling

class and portray the latter as primarily a political-bureaucratic formation.[6] In the view of these writers, the planters should be regarded as an exploited peasantry rather than a rural bourgeoisie. For them, the bourgeois character of the Ivorian ruling class comes not from its origins among the planters but rather from its function as an intermediary between international capital and the direct producers of the Ivory Coast.[7]

This debate over the class character of the current Ivorian regime remains tentative and exploratory, as other contributions to this volume suggest. Nevertheless, it raises critical questions that must eventually be answered if we are to arrive at a solid understanding of the Ivorian political economy. Is the contemporary Ivorian state with its "liberal" economic policy primarily a reflection of the interests and aspirations of the African planters? If so, which planters, and how have they been able to gain economic power and translate it into political power under conditions of economic dependency? Or is it more accurate to portray the Ivorian state as an essentially "Bonapartist" formation manned by a political-bureaucratic elite bent on managing the claims of the planter and other Ivorian classes in the interest of a neocolonial form of capital accumulation? Definitive answers to these general questions are impossible, given the current state of our knowledge. The task of analysis at this stage must, perforce, remain a more modest one. To understand the broader history of the Ivorian political economy, we must begin by analyzing the origins and class character of indigenous Ivorian commercial agriculture, the principal engine of economic growth in the country. This essay seeks to make a contribution to such an analysis by providing a detailed case study of the development of export-oriented cash crop production in one region of the Ivory Coast in the formative period prior to World War Two.

## Indigenous Rural Capitalism in West Africa

Any analysis of indigenous commercial agriculture in the Ivory Coast must situate itself within the context of the continuing debate over whether or not the colonial era gave rise to a form of African agrarian capitalism. A key issue in this debate is how best to view the role of West African cash crop producers. One leading school of thought, best represented by Polly Hill, Sara Berry, and Jan Hogendorn, regards West African cash crop producers as rural capitalists and stresses their initiatives in creating and sustaining the colonial economy.[8]

Following Weber, these writers define capitalism as an orientation toward economic activity, characterized by the rational (that is, systematic and calculating) pursuit of economic gain by primarily economic means. Accordingly, when they find among selected groups of African market-oriented producers a propensity to calculate, save, and invest, they declare them capitalists.

By documenting cases of African economic achievement, this school has done an admirable job of correcting the older, colonialist view of Africans as economically passive. However, in their zeal to demonstrate that Africans frequently initiated economic change, these writers have tended to underemphasize or, in some cases, to ignore altogether the broader political-economic context in which African innovators were obliged to operate. Their studies generally neglect the effects not only of imperialism and colonial rule but also of the larger institutional structures of the indigenous African social formations themselves. In addition, their methodological focus on individual economic behavior, coupled with their reliance on rather rigid concepts of class, has led them to downplay the importance of class formation among African cash crop producers.

Marxist, dependency and world-system theorists, on the other hand, have stressed the centrality of the colonial context, which for them constitutes the fundamental determinant of African underdevelopment.[9] For these writers, the basic fact of life in colonial Africa was economic dependency, a condition that virtually ruled out the possibility of indigenous African capitalism. While these writers have recognized the importance of initiatives taken by African cash crop producers, they have tended to analyze such initiatives primarily in terms of their general relationship to the world capitalist system. Viewed from this global perspective, cash crop farmers appear less as capitalists and more as yet another group of exploited inhabitants of the periphery. Such an approach provides a useful account of the external constraints under which African producers labored, but it tends to overlook the specific ways in which these producers responded to the market conditions arising under colonialism. Because it remains at a "macro" level of analysis, this approach downplays not only the measure of freedom African cash crop producers exercised but also the diverse ways in which they exercised it.

Clearly, if we are to advance our understanding of the nature and limits of capitalist development in Africa, we must adopt an approach combining elements of the "macro" analysis of the "development of underdevelopment" school with rigorous analyses of specific groups of cash crop producers. Discussion of the elements of such an approach has proceeded rapidly, if unevenly, in recent years within the broader theoretical debate over the transition to capitalism. The problem of the transition to capitalism is a complex and challenging one. In this chapter, I do not presume to enter in a direct and formal way into the thicket of debate surrounding this problem. Instead, I propose to describe and analyze a specific historical case of transition, that of the Anyi cocoa and coffee producers of Assikasso, an area in the southeastern Ivory Coast. My analysis of this case owes much to the work of Alan Richards and to that of Chauveau and Richard.[10] Like these writers, I will emphasize the specific ways in which forces emanating from the world capitalist system interacted with local conditions to produce a form of commodity production that was neither capitalist nor precapitalist in the commonly accepted Marxian meanings of these terms. The resulting process of rural class formation both encouraged and limited the broader process of capitalist transformation in the Ivory Coast as a whole.

The argument I advance in this paper may be summarized as follows. In the period from circa 1880 to 1940, the Anyi-Juablin of Assikasso moved from a situation of relative autonomy within the regional political economy of what is now the eastern Ivory Coast and western Ghana to a position of colonial dependency within the French Empire. In so doing, they became increasingly involved in the world capitalist system, first as suppliers of gold and natural rubber, eventually as cash crop producers of cocoa and coffee. By the 1930s, they had become major participants in the Ivory Coast's export sector. The Juablin's increasing involvement in commodity production under conditions of colonial domination affected the Juablin social formation in contradictory ways. On the one hand, it weakened older relations of production and the forms of authority associated with them and gave rise to new capitalist relationships and behavior patterns. On the other hand, it preserved and restructured certain precapitalist institutions, most notably the land tenure system and the domestic group, and created a new form of labor recruitment that was neither capitalist nor precapitalist. This contradictory process of dissolution-preservation-creation permitted the Juablin to increase rapidly their production of agricultural commodities, but it also threw up formidable obstacles to their transition to full capitalist development.

## The Anyi-Juablin Social Formation, circa 1880-1897

The Anyi-Juablin are an Akan people, one of the six groups of Anyi inhabiting the forest region of the southeastern Ivory Coast. Their ancestors migrated into this region sometime in the eighteenth century from what is now southwestern Ghana. Prior to their incorporation into the French Empire in the 1890s, the Juablin formed a small kingdom known as Assikasso. According to the first colonial census, taken in 1904, they numbered some 3,200 grouped into thirty-seven villages and bush camps scattered over an area of approximately 1,600 square kilometers.[11]  Before the arrival of the French, the Juablin had been loosely allied with their neighbors to the north, the Abron of Gyaman, and nominally tributary to Asante.[12]  These political ties do not seem to have weighed very heavily on the Juablin, who, for all practical purposes, were self-governing in the precolonial era.

The portrait of precolonial Juablin society presented in this section inevitably represents a kind of ideal type.[13]  It abstracts from the multifaceted historical reality those elements most pertinent to our task of analyzing the Juablin's uneven transition to capitalism. Commercial agriculture, the principal engine of capitalist development among the Juablin, emerged within the context of the Juablin's preexisting system of production and exchange.  The social relations of production governing this system thus became our principal object of analysis, since it was precisely at the level of the relations of production that the Juablin experienced the most dramatic changes in the years following their adoption of export-oriented cash crop production.

To understand the Juablin's precapitalist relations of production, we must begin with the single most salient feature of their precolonial social formation:  the hierarchical structure. Morphologically, Juablin society consisted of four levels of sociopolitical organization, each of which centered on an authority figure.  In ascending order of magnitude, these were the domestic group, the extended residential unit or *aulo*, the village, and the kingdom.  The life chances of the individual depended heavily on his relations with the authority figures in each of these organizational units.  In the words of a common Anyi proverb, "If there is a head, the knees must not wear the hat."  The hierarchical pattern of sociopolitical relationships reflected in this proverb governed the relations of production underlying the Juablin economy.

The key sociopolitical units in terms of their role in production and exchange were the domestic group and the extended residential unit. It was within these units that the principal forms of labor mobilization took place. In the period prior to the emergence of commercial agriculture, the Juablin divided their labor time among eight types of productive activity: agriculture, gold mining, natural rubber processing, hunting, fishing, gathering, animal husbandry, and artisanal industry. In addition, they engaged in long-distance trade relations with both the coastal European trading posts and the northern Muslim entrepôts of Kong and Bondoukou. The crucial factor in virtually all these activities was human labor power. In Assikasso, as in most of nineteenth-century Africa, human muscle power was the primary source of productive energy. The Juablin's tools (hoes, machetes, axes, knives, and pickaxes) were relatively simple, representing little more than extensions of the human arm. The relative simplicity of this technology, coupled with an abundance of arable land, made labor power the critical factor of production. Under such conditions, control over labor power became the principal basis of wealth and power, and such control was exercised mainly within the domestic group and extended residential unit.

With the partial exception of artisanal industry, an activity little developed in Assikasso and heavily dependent on outsiders, all the Juablin's productive activities took place primarily within the context of either the domestic group or the *aulo*.[14] Accordingly, the relations of production governing these activities were defined by the ties in kinship, affinity, and personal dependency upon which these units were based. Therefore, in order to understand the institutional framework within which Juablin commercial agriculture later developed, we must take a closer look at these two units and the relationship between them.

**The Domestic Group: The Locus of Agricultural Production**

The Juablin domestic group consisted of a man, his wives, their children and other dependents (including slaves), and pawns.[15] This unit formed the primary social context for agriculture, hunting, and gathering, the Juablin's principal subsistence activities. In agriculture, the members of a domestic group worked together under the control and supervision of the domestic group head, who appropriated and redistributed the foodstuffs produced. A clearcut sexual division of labor governed the course of the agricultural cycle for yams and plantains, the Juablin's staple crops. The men and boys prepared the fields and joined in the harvest; the women did the planting, cultivating and most of the harvesting. Hunting and gathering, the Juablin's other subsistence activities, could be carried out by individuals or small groups made up of persons from several domestic groups, but all game and gathered foodstuffs were returned to the domestic group heads for redistribution. In food production and certain domestic activities such as house building, the Juablin sometimes resorted to various forms of interdomestic group cooperation, but these were always arranged and controlled by the heads of the particular domestic groups involved in them. Thus the relations of production governing subsistence production reflected the superordinate-subordinate relationship between the domestic group head and the rest of the members of the group.

In theory, the goal of agricultural production was autosubsistence, and present-day Juablin express fierce pride in the capacity of their forebears to provide for their basic nutritional needs. Nevertheless, because production varied from group to group and from year to year, some local exchange in foodstuffs took place. These local food sales increased substantially in the 1890s as a result of the natural rubber boom and the attendant growth in the number of trading caravans passing through Assikasso. The social effects of this trade in foodstuffs are difficult to assess given the absence of data. The benefits derived from it seem to have been confined to the relatively small number of domestic groups living along the caravan routes. Yet the very existence of this trade, whatever its scale, foreshadowed the role subsequently assumed by Juablin domestic groups in the production and sale of cash crops.

## The Aulo: The Locus of Production for Exchange

However dominant its role in agriculture and subsistence production in general, the domestic group cannot be considered the most important sociopolitical grouping in precolonial Assikasso. A more important unit in terms of its contribution to overall production and reproduction was the extended residential unit or, to use the Anyi term, the *aulo*. Consisting of several kin or fictive kin-related domestic groups united under the authority of a male elder called an *aulo kpagne* (pl. *aulo nkpagnemo*), the *aulo* served as the principal unit for collective political and judicial action, and functioned as the main producer of commodities and the sole vehicle for the accumulation of wealth. It was this institution, moreover, which felt most acutely the erosive effects of commercial agriculture during the colonial period.

Because the Juablin, like other Akan peoples, combine matrilineal descent with patrilineal residence, *aulo* membership could be based on either maternal or paternal ties. The core of every *aulo* consisted of an *aulo kpagne* and several of his matrilineal kinsmen including his uterine brothers, his unmarried, widowed or divorced sisters, the latters' infant children, and also sometimes his nephews by uterine sisters living in other residential units. To this core group were added, with wives of the *aulo kpagne* and his brothers' wives, their unmarried daughters, their sons who had not received an inheritance, their sons' wives and dependents, and their own slaves and pawns. This corporate group was bound together not only by common residence and allegiance to an *aulo kpagne* but also by common ritual observance and participation in certain collective economic activities, most notably gold mining, rubber processing and long-distance trading expeditions.[16]

To understand the *aulo* as an institution, we must examine the role of the *aulo kpagne*, for all aspects of *aulo* life revolved around him. These redoubtable men functioned as the political leaders, judicial mediators, land chiefs, ritual leaders and economic organizers of precolonial Assikasso. Each *aulo kpagne* succeeded to his position by virtue of his genealogical rank within a particular matrilineage (Anyi: *abusua*) and his own leadership abilities.[17] Upon his succession, each *aulo kpagne* assumed control of his *aulo*'s treasury of *dja* and trusteeship over the section of Juablin land worked by his subjects. In addition, he became the principal arbiter of disputes among his subjects and their representative within the broader Juablin judicial system. These three functions--land chief, guardian of the *aulo* treasury, and judicial mediator--formed the principal basis of his power and authority. Each provided him with both material resources and political legitimacy.

As land chief, an *aulo kpagne* was expected to administer *aulo* lands so as to enable his subjects to provide for their own subsistence. The Juablin land tenure system, like that of many other African peoples, was based on a combination of communal ownership and individual usufructuary rights. Theoretically, overall control of Juablin lands was vested in the king or *famien*. In practice this meant that the king could establish farms anywhere in Assikasso and could confer usufruct on strangers wishing to settle in the Juablin domain. Although Juablin kings occasionally exercised these prerogatives in the precolonial era, in general they delegated responsibility for land distribution to village headmen, who in turn passed it on to their *aulo nkpagnemo*. As a practical matter, this responsibility obliged each *aulo kpagne* to provide his subjects with the farm land they needed, an obligation easily fulfilled in precolonial Assikasso, where low population density and the predominantly noncommercial orientation of agriculture made land plentiful.[18]

If the *aulo kpagne*'s role as land chief did not give him direct control over the agricultural production of his subjects, it nevertheless provided him with certain immediate, concrete benefits. In the first place, it served to justify his claim to regular labor services from his subjects. During the most intense phases of the agricultural cycle, the phases devoted to field preparation and harvesting, each *aulo kpagne* received, on average, one day of labor per week from each of his male subjects.[19] Since the village headmen and the king were also residential heads, they also received these labor services. But they, by virtue of their wider responsibilities within the Juablin social formation, could also call on the services of men from the larger units under their authority. Thus each village headman received labor from the residential units of his village, and the king mobilized workers from throughout his kingdom. Through this system of labor services, the *aulo nkpagnemo*, village headmen and king (whom I shall henceforth refer to collectively as the "officeholders") extracted a form of surplus labor from their subjects. As some analysts have noted, the use of these labor services for the production of cash crops during the colonial era gave the officeholders a marked advantage over other producers and enabled them to become the largest planters in Assikasso.[20] But in the precolonial era, it mainly served to enhance their ability to maintain large domestic groups.

The *aulo nkpagnemo* and other officeholders also derived other benefits from their function as land chiefs. If the Juablin regarded agricultural produce as the property of the domestic groups, they viewed other products of the lands as the rightful property of the officeholders. The most significant of these products were gold and natural rubber. The role of gold in Akan societies is well known.[21] Like other Akan, the Juablin used gold as a general purpose currency. In particular they used it as a means of paying judicial fines, or

buying imported goods from Europeans on the coast and from
Muslim traders in the north, and of storing and displaying
wealth. In the 1880s, gold was the main commodity linking
the Juablin with the world capitalist system. They obtained
most of their gold by pit mining, a process requiring relatively
large amounts of labor.[22] The labor requirements of gold production, coupled with gold's status as a natural product of the
land and hence the property of the *aulo kpagne*, made the *aulo*
the organizational basis of Juablin gold mining. The *aulo
kpagne* organized the mining teams and appropriated the gold
they produced. He used this gold to increase the size of his
*aulo*'s treasury, to pay off the judicial fines of his subjects and
to mount trading expeditions.

Rubber production followed a broadly similar pattern.
This line of productive activity began in Assikasso in the
1890s at the initiative of Africans from the Gold Coast and its
hinterland.[23] Initially, these Africans (known in Anyi as *poy-
ofwe*: people of rubber) produced most of the rubber exported
from Assikasso. But they did so under the patronage of the
Juablin officeholders, who extracted a rent payment amounting
to one-third of the output.[24] When the Juablin themselves began producing rubber in the mid-1890s, they did so within the
context of their residential units because rubber, like gold, was
a natural product of the land requiring relatively large
amounts of labor that could best be mobilized on the basis of
*aulo* ties.

Control over gold and rubber gave the *aulo nkpagnemo*
control over long-distance trade. In the late nineteenth and
early twentieth centuries, the Juablin conducted what Claude
Meillassoux has called "trade by expedition," that is, trade that
was limited in its objectives, closely integrated with production and carried out by the producers themselves.[25] Its purpose was to provide the Juablin with European imports such as
firearms, cloth, and gin and certain savanna commodities like
shea butter, iron, and slaves. The *aulo nkpagnemo* organized
expeditions to obtain these goods, which they then appropriated and redistributed within their residential units. Juablin
officeholders were especially eager to purchase slaves as a
means of increasing the size of their residential units; this, under the conditions prevailing in late nineteenth-century
Assikasso, was tantamount to increasing their wealth and
power.[26]

Thus, the officeholders based much of their power and
authority directly or indirectly on their role as custodians of
the Juablin's land. But they also based their position on their

control over their *aulo* treasuries and on their function in the Juablin judicial process.    In fact, these two functions were closely intertwined.    The accumulated wealth of the *aulo* treasury, consisting mostly of gold dust and jewelry, provided the *aulo kpagne* with a means of paying his subjects' fines and thereby defending the integrity of his *aulo*.    Under Juablin customary law, disputes between members of different residential units were settled in village courts or in the court of the *famien*.    In the judicial process, emphasis was placed on reconciling the disputants and compensating the one judged to have been wronged.    The underlying principle was the collective responsibility of the *aulo* for the actions of its individual members.    The payment of fines, the normal mode of compensation, thus involved the transfer of gold from one *aulo* to another.    Any *aulo kpagne* who could not pay the fine established by the court would be required to place one of his subjects in pawnship in the aggrieved *aulo* until he could come up with the necessary amount of gold.    By assuming the task of adjudicating his subjects' disputes, the *aulo kpagne* thus sought to defend the accumulated wealth of his *aulo*, not only in the sense of its accumulated gold reserves but also in the sense of its human resources.    The Juablin judicial system itself functioned both as a means of legitimating the authority of the officeholders and as a mechanism of circulating wealth among them, thereby helping to differentiate their residential units on the basis of wealth.

An examination of the Juablin judicial system and the role of the officeholders within it can provide insights into the dynamics of the Juablin social formation and the kind of tensions that arose within it.    Social stratification in precolonial Assikasso was based largely on the degree of one's control over labor and the nature of one's role within the judicial system. The dominant stratum consisted of the officeholders, who appropriated the labor of their subjects and adjudicated their disputes.    Conversely, the subordinate groups--junior men, women, children, and slaves--consisted of persons who worked under the direction of others and depended on their *aulo nkpagnemo* to defend their interests in court.    Within this scheme, the nonofficeholding domestic group heads formed an intermediate stratum.    They appropriated the labor of their subjects, but also supplied labor to their *aulo nkpagnemo*, village headmen, and the king.    At the same time, they represented their subjects within their residential units, but depended on their *aulo nkpagnemo* to defend them and their subjects in Juablin courts.    Although the system provided the subordinate groups with certain avenues of social ascent, it did so in a manner designed to maintain the overall pattern of officeholder dominance. Accordingly, systemic tensions manifested themselves primarily in acts of insubordination against the officeholders.

Given the present study's preoccupation with the social effects of agricultural change in the colonial period, the most noteworthy tensions were those between the officeholders, on the one hand, and between the domestic group heads and the young men aspiring to become domestic group heads, on the other. The latter group's acts of "insubordination" took the form of refusals to contribute fully to *aulo* work projects, generalized disobedience to the commands of the *aulo nkpagnemo*, attempts to secede from the *aulo*, sorcery, and acts of poisoning against *aulo nkpagnemo*. To deal with such acts, an *aulo kpagne* could invoke the assistance of the *famien* and his entourage. Herein lies the main significance of the rudimentary Juablin state apparatus. It functioned to maintain the prevailing pattern of social relations in Assikasso, a pattern based on the dominance of the officeholders. At the request of an *aulo kpagne*, the *famien* and his royal executioners, the *adumfoo*, could take disciplinary action against young men deemed offensive. Minor offenders could be beaten or forced to perform extra labor. Sorcerers and men guilty of poisoning or other acts of murder could be executed.[27]

The incidence of such punishments and the acts giving rise to them is impossible to determine on the basis of existing evidence. Late nineteenth-century Assikasso, as portrayed by present-day informants and early colonial documents, does not appear to have been a particularly stressful or violent society. But neither does it appear to have been tension-free, and one of the principal loci of social tension was the relationship between officeholders and the junior men subordinate to them. The tensions inherent in this relationship eventually conditioned the process of social change ignited by colonial rule and the development of commercial agriculture in the 1920s and 1930s.

## French Colonial Rule and the Juablin Social Formation

The hierarchical pattern of social relations described in the previous section provided a coherent framework within which the nineteenth-century Juablin lived out their lives. As such, it constitutes a sociological baseline against which the changes of the twentieth century can be assessed. Under the impact of colonial rule and commercial agriculture, the Juablin social formation underwent a pervasive process of restructuring. In particular, the Juablin's precapitalist relations of production based on the institution of the *aulo* gradually weakened and eventually gave way to a new, more capitalist form of productive organization. This process of change resulted from the pressures created, on the one hand, by the administrative policies of the colonial state and, on the other, by the effects of the Juablin's adoption of cash crop production. Chronologically, the pressures from the colonial state preceded the effects of commercial agriculture. But both factors worked together to propel the Juablin along the path of capitalist development.

The incorporation of Assikasso into the French empire was, in its initial stages at least, primarily a political process.[28] The French had been attracted to Assikasso largely because of its strategic location astride the two main caravan routes running through the southeastern Ivory Coast. They needed to control Assikasso in order to secure the commercial hinterland of their posts at Assinie and Grand Bassam.[29] Thus, while they certainly wished to channel Juablin trading caravans away from British factories on the Gold Coast and toward their own establishments, their main objective was to take control of the Juablin and mobilize their resources for the task of creating the administrative and communications infrastructure of colonial rule. To this end, the colonizers implemented a number of specific policies that collectively had the effect of undermining the Juablin's traditional pattern of social relations.

The first of these policies, the incorporation of the Juablin king and village headmen into the colonial administration, undermined traditional authority patterns among the Juablin. Once the French established their control over Assikasso by brutally suppressing Juablin resistance and executing the Juablin *famien* who led it, they set about the task of converting the Juablin's traditional authorities into agents of colonial rule. The king and village headmen became, in effect, the lowest ranking line officers of the French administration. In this capacity they collected taxes, recruited labor for the administration's work projects, and performed whatever other tasks were required of them by their new overlords. If they failed to fulfill these tasks, they were subjected to imprisonment or even deposition.[30] The clearcut subordination of their traditional authorities was not lost on the Juablin people, and it was not long before the old leadership institutions began losing their legitimacy.[31]

The French also undermined Juablin authority patterns through judicial policy. In an effort to reform what they considered barbaric judicial procedures, the colonizers outlawed certain traditional legal practices, such as the swearing of oaths, and set limits on the fines that could be levied by Juablin officeholders. In addition, the French arrogated to themselves jurisdiction over criminal cases and created "native tribunals" to handle civil cases. Juablin officeholders participated in these tribunals, but only under the close supervision of the local French administrator. These measures had the effect of weakening the judicial function of the officeholders, thus reducing their ability to fulfill their traditional role as guarantor of the Juablin social order.

Two other French policies, the head tax and the regime of forced labor, served to mobilize Juablin resources for the support of the colonial state. In so doing, they underscored symbolically, as well as materially, the Juablin's status as a colonized people. Implementation of these two policies compelled the Juablin to help create the administrative and transportation infrastructure needed to facilitate the expansion of cocoa and coffee production in the 1920s and 1930s. The head tax can also be said to have contributed indirectly to the Juablin's decision to take up cash crop production in the first place. First imposed in 1901, this tax fell on every man, woman, and child over ten years of age.[32]  Initially set at 2.5 francs per taxable individual, its rate in Assikasso rose steadily throughout the period covered in this study.[33]  Since the Juablin were already export commodity producers when the tax was first imposed, the necessity of paying it every year did not force them into the money economy. But it did serve to reinforce their commitment to market-oriented production by increasing the amount of cash income each domestic group needed in order to survive. When the bottom dropped out of the world market for natural rubber in 1912-1913, the necessity of paying the head tax made the Juablin more receptive to the idea of becoming cocoa producers.

The regime of forced labor also had certain corrosive effects on the Juablin social formation. This policy, requiring all African adult males except chiefs to provide the administration with twelve days of unpaid labor per year,[34] created intense resentment among the Juablin, resentment which caused some of them to seek refuge across the border in the Gold Coast where forced labor was much less common.[35]

Since labor recruitment, like tax collection, became the responsibility of the *famien* and other officeholders, there grew up among many Juablin a tendency to conflate the French system of forced labor with the traditional system of labor services. This tendency became more pronounced in the 1920s, when the administration gave explicit support to the *famien*'s use of labor services to build up his personal cocoa and coffee plantations.[36] As a consequence, some of the popular resentment against forced labor inevitably became directed against the older system of labor services and the officeholders who benefited from it. In this way, the legitimacy of the traditional hierarchy declined still further.

The final French policy with major consequences for the Juablin social formation was the abolition of domestic slavery. The reasons behind the French decision to implement this policy in 1906 have been treated elsewhere and need not concern us here.[37] What matters for our purposes is the effect this policy had on the Juablin's relations of production. In precolonial Assikasso, the institution of slavery had functioned primarily as a means of expanding the labor force of the domestic group and the the *aulo*. Slaves were incorporated into these units as individuals and underwent an intensive process of assimilation.[38] Both the importation of slaves and the process by which they were incorporated into Juablin society were controlled by the officeholders. By importing slaves and redistributing them among his subjects, an *aulo kpagne* not only expanded his following, but also strengthened his control over the domestic group heads under his command. For domestic group heads, the possibility of obtaining slaves served as a powerful incentive for loyalty to their *aulo nkpagnemo*. By removing this possibility, the French further weakened the power of the Juablin officeholders. At the same time, abolition destroyed the Juablin's principal mechanism for recruiting labor from outside their group. When the French announced their policy of ending slavery, many Juablin slaves left their masters and returned to their regions of origin.[39] In the short run, this exodus meant the loss of a significant portion of the Juablin's labor force. In the longer run, it meant that new mechanisms of labor recruitment would have to be devised if Assikasso was to develop as a cash crop-producing region. The emergence in the 1920s of the migrant labor system was to provide such a mechanism.

The policies described above were all implemented in the period prior to the emergence of cash crop production in Assikasso. Their explicit purpose was to ensure French control over the country and harness Juablin resources for the colonial project. In this, the policies proved largely successful. By the end of the first decade of the present century, Assikasso was firmly in the French orbit. But the policies also had other, unintended consequences, which the colonizers only gradually came to recognize. By weakening the Juablin's traditional authority structures and destroying their principal means of recruiting outside labor, the French colonial state created the preconditions for the transformation of Juablin relations of production under the impact of commercial agriculture.

## The Expansion of Commercial Agriculture in Assikasso, 1912-1940

The Juablin's adoption of cocoa cultivation in the years 1912-1920 can best be viewed as the result of the interaction of three factors: the effects of the decline and eventual collapse of the rubber industry; local Juablin experiments with cocoa planting in response to the rubber crisis; and the pressures exerted on the Juablin by the colonial administration through its program of forced cultivation.[40]

As indicated earlier, exports of natural rubber had, since the 1890s, formed the Juablin's principal link with the world capitalist system. By 1908, however, the market for rubber was becoming increasingly unstable, as new sources of higher-quality plantation rubber opened up in southeast Asia. The upshot was a crisis in the Ivorian rubber industry, a crisis that reached its climax in 1912-1913 when the French import-export houses suspended their purchases. It was this crisis that led a few Juablin officeholders to begin experimenting with cocoa, a crop they had first encountered during their travels in the neighboring Gold Coast.[41] Such experiments mark the beginning of cocoa cultivation in Assikasso but, by themselves, do not account for the rapid adoption of the crop by virtually all Juablin domestic groups in the period 1912-1920. The rapidity with which cocoa cultivation spread in Assikasso and elsewhere in the southeastern Ivory Coast was largely a function of the colonial administration's program of forced cultivation, a program that compelled, often with great brutality, the entire population to take up cocoa as a cash crop.[42] This effort by the administration, coupled with improved prices and marketing conditions in the coastal factories, made cash crop production the source of the Juablin's export commodities.

By 1920, commercial agriculture had become firmly established in Assikasso. Cocoa remained the principal Juablin cash crop throughout the 1920s and 1930s, but from the mid-1920s on, coffee also became important, largely as a result of French promotional efforts and the Juablin's desire to diversify their sources of cash income. Exports of both commodities increased steadily throughout this period, as the figures represented in table 4.1 indicate. These figures represent exports of cocoa and coffee from the *cercle* of Indénié as a whole and therefore do not give a precise indication of the levels of production in Assikasso.[43] Nevertheless, they provide a good general idea of the upward progression in the level of Juablin participation in cash crop production and marketing.

What factors account for the steady expansion of cash crop production among the Juablin in the period 1920-1940? An answer to this question can best be found through an examination of the interaction of two sets of forces, one external to the Juablin social formation, the other largely internal. In the former group are those forces emanating from the political economy fashioned by Western imperialism: price fluctuations in the world markets for cocoa and coffee, the marketing practices of European import-export companies, and the road-building and agricultural extension activities of the colonial administration. The main forces internal to the Juablin social formation were the organizational structure of the production process for cocoa and coffee, and the emerging pattern of labor relations.

### External Factors: The Role of World Markets and the Colonial State

World market forces, as mediated by the pricing practices of the import-export houses, strongly conditioned the Juablin's pattern of participation in commercial agriculture. Much of the impetus for the steady increase in cash crop production in the 1920s can be traced to the rising prices experienced during this period. Average prices paid in Abengourou, the main marketing center in the *cercle* of Indénié, rose from 1.2 francs per kilogram of cocoa in the period 1912-1922 to 5.2 francs in 1928-1929.[44] Average prices declined only in 1920-1921 and 1926-1927, the latter the one marketing season to show an actual drop in cocoa exports from the *cercle*. The relative stagnation of cocoa production in the mid- and late 1930s reflects the effects of the Great Depression and the efforts of the im-

TABLE 4.1:  Cocoa and Coffee Production in the Cercle of Indénié, 1919-1938

| Marketing Season | Cocoa (in metric tons) | Coffee (in metric tons) |
|---|---|---|
| 1919-1920 | 250 | |
| 1920-1921 | 376 | |
| 1921-1922 | 800 | |
| 1922-1923 | 1,110 | |
| 1923-1924 | 2,125 | |
| 1924-1925 | 3,200 | |
| 1925-1926 | 3,500 | |
| 1926-1927 | 3,488 | 3.5 |
| 1927-1928 | 4,000 | 6 |
| 1928-1929 | 5,400 | 16 |
| 1929-1930 | 7,500 | 18 |
| 1930-1931 | 7,800 | 48 |
| 1931-1932 | 9,000 | 50 |
| 1932-1933 | 10,000 | 60 |
| 1933-1934 | 11,000 | 100 |
| 1934-1935 | 11,000 | 145 |
| 1935-1936 | 12,500 | 171 |
| 1936-1937 | 17,000 | 300 |
| 1937-1938 | 17,000 | 350 |

Sources:  Colonie de la Côte d'Ivoire, Service de l'agriculture, Rapport annuel, 1921, ANCI III-4-159; Cercle de l'Indénié, Service de l'agriculture, Rapports, 1926-1927 and 1932, ANCI XI-43-426; Service de l'agriculture, secteur de l'Indénié, Rapports trimestriels, 1936, Thomas, agent, ANCI XI-42-313; Cercle d'Abengourou, Service de l'agriculture, Rapport annuel 1938, E. Bally, agent, ANCI X-9-187; Cercle de l'Indénié, Rapport agricole et zootechnique, 1931, ANCI IV-26-68; and Cercle de l'Indénié, Rapport économique, 4ème trimestre, 1933, ANCI VI-16-238.

port-export houses to maintain their profit levels by forming buyers' cartels.  The production increases in 1935-1936 and 1936-1937 occurred during the only major price rally during the decade.  On the other hand, the consistently upward trend in coffee output in the 1930s was a function of the relatively high average prices paid in the heavily protected French coffee market.[45]

However, the expansion of cash crop production among the Juablin was not simply a function of price fluctuations.  It also reflected greater market accessibility resulting from improvements in transportation and marketing facilities. In the late 1910s and early 1920s, the Juablin marketed their cocoa in the same way they had marketed their rubber; they head-carried it to market centers near the coast. As cocoa plantations expanded, their labor requirements began to conflict with those of porterage. The more labor time devoted to porterage, the less that could be employed in the creation and maintenance of plantations.[46] The colonial administration and the export-import houses were acutely aware of this problem and took steps to resolve it. The administration, for its part, accelerated its program of road building and, by 1925, had created a network of motor roads linking the regions of N'Dényé and Assikasso to the administrative/market center of Abengourou and, via Abengourou, to Agboville, a major stop on the Abidjan-Niger railway.[47] The completion of this network enabled the export-import firms, heretofore confined largely to the coast and its immediate hinterland, to establish branch trading posts in the *cercle* of Indénié. In late 1919, CFAO established a facility in Abengourou; by 1922, it had been joined by four other leading firms. The following year, these companies began sending their agents to Agnibilekrou to buy Juablin cocoa. These moves simplified marketing throughout the region and effectively ended the old system of "commerce by expedition."

Besides constructing motor routes to drain off Juablin cocoa and coffee, the colonial state also contributed to the expansion of cash-cropping in Assikasso by providing technical assistance to producers. Although understaffed and meagerly financed, the colonial agriculture service nonetheless helped increase Juablin cash crop production by furnishing planters with improved varieties of seed and information on better ways to maintain their trees and prepare their crops for market. The service's major achievement in the region was to introduce coffee as a second export crop.

## Internal Factors: Changes in the Juablin's Social Relations of Production

The external factors described in the preceding paragraphs served to stimulate and facilitate the expansion of cash-cropping in Assikasso. Yet these factors alone do not explain how this expansion occurred. In reality, of course, it was the African planters of the *cercle* of Indénié and their laborers who actually produced the steadily increasing quantities of cocoa and coffee depicted in table 4.1. If these rising production figures represent a local African response to world market forces and colonial administrative initiatives, they also reflect the material outcome of a new process of production rooted in the local African social formations. The creation of this new process of production involved a reorganization of the existing forces of production and a gradual reformulation of the relations of production governing export-oriented productive activity. In turn, these changes, in conjunction with the political and judicial effects of colonial rule, significantly modified the Juablin social formation and gave rise to a new system of local power and prestige.

The most salient feature of cash crop production in Assikasso is that it took place primarily at the level of the domestic group. Unlike gold mining and rubber production, the Juablin's previous forms of export-oriented production, cash-cropping was an agricultural activity. As such, it was by definition a prerogative of the domestic group. Nothing in the Juablin tradition impeded the emergence of the domestic group as the new social basis of the export commodity production. Accordingly, with the shift from rubber processing to cocoa cultivation, control over export-oriented production passed from the *aulo nkpagnemo* to the domestic group heads. For a time, the *aulo nkpagnemo* continued to control the marketing of cocoa through their role as organizers of trading expeditions. But with the establishment of European export-import houses in Assikasso, this role also declined. To be sure, the continued operation of the traditional system of labor services enabled the *aulo nkpagnemo* to draw on the labor of their *aulo* subjects to build up their own domestic groups' plantations. But this was not the same as exercising structural control over the entire process of producing and marketing export commodities. By the mid-1920s, such control lay in the hands of the domestic group heads.

Initially, the advent of cocoa and coffee cultivation did not bring any major changes in the Juablin agricultural production process, since the requirements of the new crops could easily be accommodated within the old system. Juablin cultivators merely interplanted their cocoa and coffee seedlings with their normal set of food crops. By the end of the usual four-year food crop cycle, the young trees were well established and producing their first crops. Beyond the fourth year, however, the maintenance requirements of the trees placed unprecedented demands on the Juablin domestic group. To develop properly, cocoa and coffee trees must be free from underbrush and weeds; coffee trees also require regular pruning to achieve maximum productivity. These requirements, plus those associated with the harvesting and preparation of the cocoa and coffee beans, necessitated the mobilization of significant amounts of labor. In 1934, the French agricultural agent in Abengourou estimated that the average Anyi domestic group could only maintain about five hectares of cocoa and coffee trees without recourse to nonfamilial labor.[48] Therefore, as a domestic group extended its plantations from year to year, accumulating ever larger numbers of the long-lived trees, it soon ran up against limits imposed by its own numbers. Thus the basic characteristics of cocoa and coffee production tended to give rise to labor shortages.

The Juablin's options in dealing with such shortages were limited. The old method of expanding the size of domestic groups by purchasing slaves was no longer possible. Officeholders could rely to some extent on labor services, but this option was not available to most Juablin producers. Traditional forms of agricultural interaid were of some use but, by the mid-1920s, the overall demand for labor exceeded its local supply.[49] No amount of interdomestic group cooperation could alter this basic fact. The growing inability of Juablin cash crop producers to meet their labor requirements thus gave rise to the need for some new means of mobilizing labor. What arose to meet this need was the system of migrant labor.

Much has been written about this system whose origin lies in the uneven pattern of colonial development in West Africa.[50] For Africans living in regions lacking the capacity to produce the kinds of commodities demanded by the capitalist world market, there was only one reliable way to earn the cash needed to pay taxes and buy imported consumer goods: the sale of labor power in regions more highly favored by the colonial economy. The flow of migrants into the *cercle* of Indénié began as early as the late 1910s.[51] Most of these early migrants came from the neighboring *cercles* of N'Zi Comoé and Bondoukou, where cash crop production had not yet begun in earnest. Most migrants came on their own, but some were recruited by Anyi planters.[52] By the mid 1920s, migrant labor had become a mainstay of the Juablin agricultural economy; in 1927, according to administration estimates, between four and five thousand migrants were working in the *cercle* of Indénié.[53]

The development of the migrant labor system transformed the relations of production of Juablin agriculture. Whereas under the old subsistence system, tasks had been assigned and carried out on the basis of ties of social dependency, much of the work of the production process now fell under a regime of contractual obligations governed by market principles. From a structural point of view, the development of what amounted to a rudimentary labor market marked a new, portentious stage in the development of commercial agriculture in Assikasso. Now, for the first time, Juablin cultivators began to function as capitalist employers.

In the 1920s and 1930s, three types of labor contract predominated in Assikasso: a short-term, task-oriented contract; a time contract; and a form of sharecropping known locally as *abusan*. The short-term contract served as a means of mobilizing labor for tasks associated with the initial establishment of a cocoa or coffee plantation. This form of contract involved an agreement on the part of the Juablin cultivator to pay the laborer a negotiated sum of money in exchange for the performance of certain specified tasks, usually field clearance or maintenance of a new plantation during its first few, unproductive years. The level of pay received by laborers under such task-oriented contracts varied according to local conditions of labor supply and demand. Thus the short-term contract was, in effect, a form of wage labor, and its widespread usage suggests the degree to which capitalist relations of production had begun to develop in Assikasso during the 1920s and 1930s.

The second type of contract, the time contract, was also a form of wage labor. It involved an agreement on the part of the laborer to work for a set period of time, usually between one and six months, performing whatever tasks the Juablin planter assigned him. In compensation for his labor, the migrant received a monthly wage as well as food and lodging.[54]

However important the short-term and time contracts were as a means of meeting immediate labor needs, it was the third form of labor contract, *abusan*, that became the true foundation of Juablin commercial agriculture. *Abusan*, from the Asante term for division in thirds, was (and remains) a form of sharecropping.[55] Its main feature was an agreement whereby a laborer promised to take over responsibility for a plantation for a set period of time, usually a year. During this period, the laborer performed all tasks necessary for the maintenance of the plantation and the harvesting and preparation of its product. In addition, he was usually expected to work a few days each year on the food farms of his Anyi employer. In exchange for these services, the planter provided the laborer with food, lodging, and medical care and allowed him to keep the proceeds from the sale of one-third of the crop he harvested. As more and more plantations came into production in Assikasso during the 1920s, it was this form of labor contract that came to dominate relations between Juablin planters and their migrant workers.

In summary, the rise of commercial agriculture after 1912 brought profound changes in the material and social conditions underlying the Juablin's system of export-oriented production. Within the Juablin social formation, the locus of commodity production shifted from the *aulo* to the domestic group. The old system of commodity production, in which the office-holders had organized the production process and appropriated its fruits, rapidly disappeared. In its place arose a new system in which each domestic group head became, in effect, an independent commodity producer. With the development of the migrant labor system, many domestic group heads also became employers of extrafamilial labor. Increasingly, the market impinged upon the Juablin's kinship-based relations of production.

At the same time, the shift from natural rubber to cocoa and coffee production had the effect of intensifying the Juablin's involvement in the world capitalist system. The processing of rubber, a natural product of the land, had only marginally altered the basic pattern of resource allocation in Assikasso. To be sure, the rise of rubber processing had diverted labor away from gold mining, but it had had little or no effect on land use. Cocoa and coffee production, on the other hand, required that the Juablin not only reallocate their labor but also change their pattern of land use. Henceforth they would convert more and more of their land into long-term cocoa and coffee plantations. In so doing, they would become more tightly enmeshed in the world market than they had ever been before.

## The Social Consequences of Commercial Agriculture in Assikasso, 1920-1940

The rapid expansion of commercial agriculture described in the preceding section transformed the structure and dynamics of the Juablin social formation. As a result of their ever-increasing involvement in cash crop production under conditions of colonial domination, the Juablin saw their old patriarchal pattern of social relations gradually disintegrate and a new, more individualistic pattern rise in its place. In 1975, one of my informants, the old headman of the village of Damé, described this process:

> Before, there was a headman in Damé who was also an aulo kpagne.
> Now every young man who enriches himself calls himself aulo kpagne.
> All that has been brought by the whites. It was their fault.[56]

This acerbic observation points not only to the relative diminution of the officeholders' authority, but also to the decline of the *aulo*'s socioeconomic importance within Juablin society and to the emergence of the domestic group as the key unit of Juablin socioeconomic organization. In this and the following sections, I shall analyze the reasons for this transformation, with a view to determining to what extent it contributed to a process of capitalist class formation in Assikasso in the period before 1940.

As I have already suggested, the decline of the *aulo* was the result of three interrelated processes of change: the shift in the locus of export-oriented production precipitated by the rise of commercial agriculture; the changes in marketing practices brought about by improvements in transportation and the establishment of local branches of the import-export companies; and the weakening of traditional authority structures by their incorporation into the colonial state. The first two of these processes destroyed the *aulo*'s old position as the principal unit of export-oriented production and exchange. The third undermined its legitimacy as an institution. All three operating together created a situation in which domestic group heads gained a greater measure of economic and social independence than they had ever had before. They, rather than the officeholders, now controlled the export sector of the Juablin economy.

What is most striking about this transformation is the apparent ease with which it occurred. Clearly, the processes described above provide much of the explanation for this development. Yet they don't explain the domestic group heads' apparent readiness to exploit the new opportunities opened up by commercial agriculture to liberate themselves from the officeholders. This readiness would appear to have been a function of the long-standing tensions between the domestic group heads and their *aulo nkpagnemo*. Although it is difficult to document, it seems plausible to suggest that the domestic group heads saw commercial agriculture as a means of accelerating their personal ascent within the Juablin status system. Perhaps this is what the headman of Damé meant when he asserted, "Now every young man who enriches himself calls himself *aulo kpagne*."?

It is noteworthy that the economic basis of this social transformation lay less in the workings of the world market than in the effects of the relations of production governing commercial agriculture in Assikasso. The Juablin had participated in the world market economy for a long time. However, prior to their adoption of commercial agriculture, their links with the world market had strengthened the *aulo* as an institution and reinforced the dominant social position of the officeholders. The production processes of gold and natural rubber, the commodities the Juablin had previously sold to the Europeans, had been under the firm control of the officeholders. Cocoa and coffee, however, were agricultural commodities, governed by the same organizational principles as other forms of agricultural production. Thus these commodities became the property of the domestic groups, and the domestic group heads became the main recipients of cash income. The emergence of the domestic group as the key unit of export-oriented production neatly illustrates the way in which the development of commercial agriculture in Assikasso involved elements of both continuity and change in the Juablin social formation. The new activities of cocoa and coffee cultivation fit easily into the old pattern of agricultural production but in so doing, subverted the broader pattern of Juablin social relations and created a new basis for social stratification.

In systemic terms, the decline of the *aulo*, and the rise of the domestic group resulted in a dissociation of wealth from high traditional social status. Heretofore, the Juablin had conceived of wealth in terms of people, gold, and imported goods. Wealth in these terms had been largely the prerogative of the officeholders. With the rise of commercial agriculture, wealth became associated with cash crop plantations and the cash incomes they generated. Wealth in this new sense could no longer be controlled by the old ruling group. To be sure, the officeholders as individuals suffered no economic decline; indeed, their continued access to traditional labor services, the last vestiges of the *aulo*-based economy, enabled most of them to become large planters. But their wealth as planters belonged to them as domestic group heads, not as *aulo nkpagnemo*, and the progressive realization of this fact by other Juablin led eventually to the end of labor services as an institution. A major effect of commercial agriculture as practiced in Assikasso was to diffuse wealth more widely throughout

Juablin society by making the domestic group rather than the *aulo* the principal unit of accumulation.

This diffusion of wealth among Juablin domestic groups may be seen in the pattern of plantation-holding that prevailed in Assikasso by the end of the 1930s. By this time, Juablin cash crop producers had become differentiated into three groups: (1) those possessing plantations of fewer than five hectares and relying almost exclusively on familial labor; (2) those with five to ten hectares and an average of two migrant workers; and (3) those controlling ten or more hectares and

TABLE 4.2: Land Holding in Assikasso, 1940

| Village | Total No. of Cultivators | Small Cultivators[a] | Middle Planters[b] | Large Planters[c] |
|---|---|---|---|---|
| Agnanfoutou | 46 | 25 | 7 | 14 |
| Agnibilekrou | 87 | 58 | 13 | 16 |
| Akobouassué | 52 | 32 | 7 | 13 |
| Amoriakro | 78 | 49 | 16 | 13 |
| Assikasso | 37 | 33 | 2 | 2 |
| Assuame | 40 | 28 | 10 | 2 |
| Attobro | 12 | 7 | 3 | 2 |
| Ayenou | 59 | 31 | 15 | 13 |
| Brindoukrou | 24 | 15 | 6 | 3 |
| Damé | 96 | 36 | 17 | 43 |
| Kongodia | 51 | 34 | 7 | 10 |
| Kotocosso | 53 | 33 | 9 | 11 |
| Manzanoua | 23 | 9 | 8 | 6 |
| N'Djorekrou | 58 | 36 | 9 | 13 |
| Nianda | 65 | 29 | 15 | 21 |
| Tenguelan | 136 | 103 | 18 | 15 |
| Yebouakrou | 83 | 37 | 11 | 35 |
| Totals | 1,000 | 595 | 173 | 232 |

Source: Service de l'agriculture, Cercle d'Abengourou, Subdivision d'Agnibilekrou (Fiches Cadastrales, 1957).

[a] 1 - 5 hectares of land in cocoa and coffee plantations.
[b] 6 - 10 hectares in cocoa and coffee plantations.
[c] Over 10 hectares in cocoa and coffee plantations.

TABLE 4.3:  Big Planters in Assikasso, 1940

| Village | Number of planters with 10-20 hectares | Number of planters with 20-50 hectares | Number of planters with 50 hectares |
|---------|---------|---------|---------|
| Agnanfoutou | 6 | 6 | 2 |
| Agnibilekrou | 14 | 1 | 1 |
| Akobouassué | 12 | 1 | 0 |
| Amoriakro | 9 | 4 | 0 |
| Assikasso | 2 | 0 | 0 |
| Assuame | 2 | 0 | 0 |
| Attobro | 2 | 1 | 0 |
| Ayenou | 13 | 0 | 0 |
| Brindoukrou | 3 | 0 | 0 |
| Damé | 30 | 12 | 1 |
| Kongodia | 7 | 2 | 1 |
| Kotocosso | 7 | 4 | 0 |
| Manzanoua | 4 | 2 | 0 |
| N'Djorekrou | 9 | 4 | 0 |
| Nianda | 18 | 3 | 0 |
| Tenguelan | 11 | 4 | 0 |
| Yebouakrou | 17 | 13 | 4 |
| Totals | 166 | 57 | 9 |

Source:  Service de l'agriculture, Cercle d'Abengourou, subdivision d'Agnibilekrou (Fiches Cadastrales, 1957).

relying heavily on migrants. Data derived from a cadastral survey carried out in 1957 enable us to show how the cultivators from seventeen of the twenty-one Juablin villages were distributed among these groups.[57]   Out of 1,000 individuals with cocoa and coffee plantations created before 1940, 595 or 60 percent were in the first group, 173 or 17 percent were in the second group, and 232 or 23 percent were in the third. This latter group was itself highly differentiated. Of its members, 166 held between ten and twenty hectares, fifty-seven held between twenty and fifty hectares, and nine individuals had over fifty hectares. While it is likely that most of the very largest planters were traditional officeholders, it is also clear that the vast majority of planters with more than ten hectares were simple domestic group heads.[58]

## Assessing Capitalist Development in Assikasso

If commercial agriculture created a new basis for wealth and social status among the Juablin, can it also be said to have given rise to the development of capitalism in Assikasso? If we mean by "capitalism" what Marx meant by it, that is, a system of commodity production based on a market-mediated relationship between one class that owns the means of production and another that has only its labor power to sell, then it seems apparent that capitalism had, at best, only begun to develop in Assikasso prior to 1940. To be sure, the Juablin had by this date become more fully involved in commodity production than ever before, and their production system had become heavily dependent on a form of quasi-wage labor. In these respects, their plantation economy contained capitalist elements. However, the crucial indicator of capitalism, the capital-labor relationship, had not yet developed to an appreciable extent. Neither a full-fledged capitalist class nor a proletariat had clearly emerged within the Juablin social formation. What had emerged was, on the one hand, an internally differentiated group of Juablin cash crop producers, some of whose members were becoming increasingly capitalistic, and, on the other hand, a non-Juablin group of migrant workers, none of whom had become fully proletarianized. Thus, while the local plantation economy of Assikasso manifested certain tendencies in the direction of capitalist class formation, it also contained certain obstacles to full-blown capitalist development.

To sustain this argument, we must be clear about what constitutes "tendencies" and "obstacles" to capitalist development. The capitalist, as an ideal type, is an economic actor who saves, invests and thereby expands production and productivity. In so doing, he manifests a form of market rationality which, among other things, leads him to treat labor primarily as a cost of production. For such rationality to operate smoothly, labor power must be a commodity. More generally, capitalist development, in the Marxian sense of the term, involves the emergence of capitalists and workers as more or less self-conscious classes. Forces fostering any of these conditions may be regarded as "tendencies" toward capitalism. Conversely, forces impeding the emergence of such conditions should be seen as "obstacles" to capitalist development. What "tendencies" and "obstacles," defined in this way, emerged among the Juablin in the 1920s and 1930s?

In the matter of saving and investing, the available evidence clearly indicates that many Juablin domestic group heads were manifesting capitalist tendencies in this period. The cadastral survey shows a steady growth in the number and size of cocoa and coffee plantations throughout the 1920s and 1930s. When one considers that the varieties of cocoa and coffee trees then in use took up to seven years to come into full production, one can readily appreciate the degree to which Juablin planters were behaving like risk-taking, time-discounting capitalists.[59] To establish their first plantations and sustain themselves and their families until the first harvests came in, producers resorted to a variety of financial ploys. Some informants reported that they used the proceeds from such activities as hunting, petty trade, and palm wine production to meet their expenses. A few said they relied on gifts or loans from their fathers or *aulo nkpagnemo*. Whatever means they used, Juablin producers clearly were behaving in a capitalist manner.

What of their view of labor? Were they treating it as a cost of production? Alan Richards has argued forcefully that the tendency to treat labor in this way represents a clear indicator of emerging capitalism.[60] Among the Juablin, such a tendency was clearly operating by the late 1920s. Interestingly, it is most evident in practices associated with the *abusan* sharecropping system. According to present-day Juablin informants, it was common in the 1920s and 1930s for planters to appropriate one-tenth of the entire cocoa and coffee crop prior to making the normal division required under the *abusan* contract. From the Juablin point of view, this practice represented a kind of deferred return on the planter's initial investment in his plantations. The name for the practice in Anyi, *atotomangue*, comes from a prickly plant that grows in the forest, suggesting a belief on the part of the planter that he deserved some special compensation for the physical suffering he experienced in clearing the land and creating his plantation. From our point of view, this practice of *atotomangue* constituted a bold assertion of what amounted to the planters' rights of ownership, as well as an obvious attempt to lower labor costs. Another widespread planter practice was to manipulate the division of the crop in such a way as to secure for themselves most of the highest quality cocoa and coffee beans.[61]  Finally, the Juablin planters' tendency to view their labor expenses as a cost of production may be seen in their insistence that their laborers contribute to food production, thereby helping to meet not only the cost of their own maintenance but also that of the planters' families.

Capitalist tendencies were also evident in the land-holding practices that developed as a result of the expansion of cocoa and coffee production.  In contrast to the Juablin's food staples, cocoa and coffee were both long-term crops.  The longevity of cocoa and coffee trees (up to thirty-five years for the former, up to twenty-five years for the latter) meant that the Juablin's cash crop plantations became, in effect, permanent.  As a consequence, Juablin land tenure took on certain features of the Western model of freehold tenure, as domestic groups came to exercise long-term control over well-defined parcels of land devoted exclusively to market production.  The colonial administration sought to encourage this trend by making it possible for individual African planters to receive legal title to their plantations.[62]  By the early 1930s, a small but growing minority of Anyi planters were having their land surveyed and registered.[63]  In this way, private property in land began to develop in Assikasso.

Yet, despite the existence of such capitalist tendencies among Juablin cash crop producers, a number of important obstacles still impeded the full-blown emergence of capitalism in Assikasso.  Such obstacles existed within both the Juablin social formation and the system of labor relations binding together the Juablin planters and their migrant laborers.  On the Juablin side, the fact that most planters continued to rely on their own labor and that of their families retarded the formation of a genuine bourgeoisie.  Indeed, for the majority of Juablin cash crop producers, participation in commercial agriculture involved more a process of "peasantization" than one of *embourgeoisement*.[64]  This was clearly the case for Juablin with plantations of fewer than ten hectares.  But it was also true for those with between ten and twenty hectares, since they also relied heavily on familial labor.  Only planters with more than twenty hectares were so dependent on hired labor that they had to act more as capitalist managers than as direct producers.  These larger planters constituted the beginnings of a rural bourgeoisie in Assikasso, but even they remained enmeshed in precapitalist institutions.  Despite their growing tendency to regard their plantations as their own private property, they, like their poorer Juablin neighbors, continued to acquire land in the traditional manner and to treat food production as primarily a subsistence activity rather than a commercial one.     Markets for land and food remained relatively undeveloped in Assikasso in the pre-World War Two era.

There were also definite limits to the planters' propensity to save and invest.     Juablin investment in this period was largely confined to the simple expansion of plantations through new inputs of hired labor.     Although a few of the larger planters also invested in trucks as a means of improving their marketing situation, there were virtually no efforts to intensify production.[65]     As regards saving, it was limited by the persistent tendency on the part of Juablin domestic group heads to devote a substantial proportion of their cash incomes to ritual and other noneconomic expenditures.[66]

All these factors weakened the objective conditions for the emergence of a planter bourgeoisie among the Juablin. Under these circumstances, it is not surprising that Juablin planters continued to define themselves primarily in ethnic rather than class terms.     Indeed, their ethnic consciousness may well have intensified as a result of their relationship to their laborers.     In Assikasso, as in other peripheral areas of the world capitalist system, a social relationship possessing some class attributes came to be defined exclusively in ethnic terms.     In the minds of the Juablin, planterhood became conflated with Anyi-hood and the status of laborer became bound up with that of being a stranger African.

If the obstacles to the formation of a bourgeoisie were formidable, those impeding the development of a proletariat were even more so.     The vast majority of migrant workers maintained strong ties with their homelands, where they continued to enjoy access to land.     As many observers have noted, these were men with one foot in the precapitalist economies of their home villages and one foot in the more capitalist economy of the forest belt.[67]     Few seem to have intended to stay in Assikasso, and those who did saw themselves not as permanent wage laborers but rather as potential planters.     Such an aspiration was far from unrealistic. Although actual land sales were rare in Assikasso before 1940, the Juablin king continued the traditional practice of giving land to would-be settlers in exchange for relatively small cash payments and promises of political allegiance.[68]     Chauveau and Richard, in their study of the Oumé region of the west-central Ivory Coast, have argued that without the possibility of obtaining land for cocoa and coffee plantations, few migrants would have been willing to sell their labor power to autochthonous planters.[69] This argument is based on evidence from the postwar period in a region that has always had a larger concentration of migrant planters than Assikasso. Nonetheless, it accurately portrays the mentality of migrant workers throughout the forest belt of the Ivory Coast. Objectively such workers may have been semiproletarianized, but subjectively they were light-years away from thinking of themselves as a working class. Such was certainly the case in Assikasso prior to 1940.

Thus the transformation described and analyzed in this paper cannot simply and without qualification be characterized as the development of capitalism in Assikasso. This, of course, is hardly surprising. Transitions to capitalism have never been smooth or unambiguous. They have invariably been uneven and contradictory, involving fluid combinations of new and old elements. So it was for the Juablin. In 1940, the relations of production governing Juablin commercial agriculture, although increasingly capitalist, still bore the stamp of older precapitalist modes of socioeconomic organization. Yet, what is most striking about the case of Assikasso in the period covered in this chapter is the rapidity with which the Juablin social formation came to represent an organic blend of capitalist and precapitalist elements. The experience of the Juablin in the years ca. 1880-1940 neatly illustrates what Marx was getting at in *The German Ideology* when he wrote:

> History is nothing but the succession of the separate generations, each of which exploits the materials, the capital funds, the productive forces handed down to it by all the preceding generations, and thus, on the one hand, continues the traditional activity in completely changed circumstances and, on the other, modifies the old circumstances with a completely changed activity.

# Notes

## Abbreviations

ANCI:  Archives Nationales de la Côte d'Ivoire
ANS:  Archives Nationales du Sénégal
ANF-OM:  Archives Nationales de France, Section Outre-Mer
PRO:  Public Record Office, London

1. Use of the term "planter" to refer to African cash crop producers originated among the agents of the colonial administration. Today it is a mainstay of both scholarly and popular discourse in the Ivory Coast. Although the term lacks precision, it is difficult to avoid given its widespread usage. In this paper, I shall limit my use of "planter" to those African coffee and cocoa producers who relied on extrafamilial labor to perform some of the tasks of the agricultural production process.

2. Ruth Schachter Morgenthau, Political Parties in French-speaking West Africa (Oxford: Clarendon Press, 1964); Aristide Zolberg, One-party Government in the Ivory Coast (Princeton: Princeton University Press, 1969).

3. Samir Amin, Neocolonialism in West Africa, F. McDonagh, trans. (New York: Monthly Review Press, 1973), and Le développement du capitalisme en Côte d'Ivoire (Paris: Editions de Minuit, 1967); B. Campbell, "The Ivory Coast," ch. 4 in John Dunn, ed., West African States: Failure and Promise (Cambridge: Cambridge University Press, 1978).

4. S. Amin, 1967, op. cit., 277.

5. Michael Cohen, Urban Policy and Political Conflict in Africa:  A Study of the Ivory Coast (Chicago: The University of Chicago Press, 1974), 60.

6. J.P. Chauveau and J. Richard, "Une 'périphérie recentrée': à propos d'un système local d'économie de plantation en Côte d'Ivoire," Cahiers d'études africaines 17: 485-523.

7. Ibid., 518.

8. P. Hill, Migrant Cocoa Farmers of Southern Ghana (Cambridge: Cambridge University Press, 1963), and Studies in Rural Capitalism in West Africa (Cambridge: University Press, 1970); S. Berry, "Cocoa and Economic Development in Western Nigeria," in C. Eicher and C. Liedholm, eds., Growth and Development of the Nigerian Economy (Lansing: Michigan State University Press, 1970), 16-29, and Cocoa, Custom and Socio-economic Change in Rural Western Nigeria (Oxford: Clarendon Press, 1975); J. Hogendorn, "The Origins of the Groundnut Trade in Northern Nigeria" (Ph.D. diss., University of London, 1966), and "The Origins of the Groundnut Trade in Northern Nigeria," in C. Eicher and C. Liedholm, op. cit., 30-51.

9. S. Amin, 1973, op. cit.; E.A. Brett, Colonialism and Underdevelopment in East Africa (New York: Nok, 1973); Walter Rodney, How Europe Underdeveloped Africa (London: Bogle-l'Ouverture Publications, 1972); I. Wallerstein, The Modern World System: Capitalist Agriculture and the Origins

of the European World Economy in the 16th Century (New York: Academic Press, 1976).

10. A. Richards, "The Political Economy of Gutwirtschaft: A Comparative Analysis of East Elbian Germany, Egypt and Chile," Comparative Studies in Society and History 21: (4 October 1979), 483-518; J.P. Chauveau and J. Richard, Bodiba en Côte d'Ivoire (Abidjan: ORSTOM, 1976), and Chauveau and Richard (1977), op. cit.; J.P. Chauveau, "Agricultural Production and Social Formation: The Baule Region of Toumodi-Kokumbo in Historical Perspective," in M. Klein, ed., Peasants in Africa (Beverly Hills: Sage, 1980), 143-176.

11. Cercle d'Indénié, Poste d'Assikasso. Rapport mensuel, August 1904, ANCI IEE 43 (4).

12. E. Terray, "Relations de domination et d'exploitation dans le royaume du Gyaman," paper presented at the seminar of GRASP, 1970/71, Centre d'études africaines, Ecole pratique des hautes études, Paris; D. Groff, "The Development of Capitalism in the Ivory Coast: The Case of Assikasso, 1880-1940" (Ph.D. diss., Stanford University, 1980).

13. The reconstruction of the precolonial Juablin social formation presented in this paper is based on information from three sources: the oral testimonies of present-day Juablin informants, some of whom came of age in the 1890s, others of whom remember stories told them by their elder kinfolk about "the time before the whites came"; early colonial documents, especially the cercle monographs for Indénié on microfilm in the National Archives of the Ivory Coast (3Mi, no. 1); and accounts by British and French officials who visited Assikasso in the 1880s and 1890s, especially those by L. Binger, Rapport sur la commission de délimitation de la Côte d'Ivoire, 20 October 1892, ANF-OM: Côte d'Ivoire III 3, Captain Braulot (Rapport de mission, 1893; ANF-OM: Côte d'Ivoire III 3), J.E. Lang, Report on the Mission to Delimit the Gold Coast-Ivory Coast Frontier, 13 July 1892, PRO CO96 225; and Report on the Territory Explored by the English Commissioner for the Delimitation of the Frontier on the West of the Gold Coast Colony, 17 November 1892, (PRO CO96 229 5269).

14. D. Groff, 1980, op. cit., 148-150.

15. In using the term "domestic group" instead of "household," I follow the lead of Jack Goody, The Developmental Cycle in Domestic Groups (Cambridge: University Press, 1971), 1-14.

16. The cult of the Tano river spirit is observed at the level of the aulo.

17. For discussions of Anyi principles of descent, inheritance and succession, see F. Amon d'Aby, Croyances religieuses et coutumes juridiques des Agni de la Côte d'Ivoire (Paris: Larose, 1960), 127-136; A. Köbben, "L'Héritage chez les Agni: l'influence de l'économie de profit," Africa 24 (1954): 359-63; D. Groff, 1980, op. cit., 424-436.

18. The population figure of 3,200 may well underestimate Juablin numbers, since early colonial censuses are notoriously unreliable. However, even if the Juablin population were twice what the French estimated it to be in 1904, Assikasso, an area of roughly 1,600 square kilometers, would still have been only sparsely populated.

19. The Juablin, like other Akan, observed a seven-day week. They worked five out of the seven days and rested the other two.

20. S. Amin, 1967, op. cit.; R. Stavenhagen, Social Classes in Agrarian Societies (Garden City, N.Y.: Anchor, 1975).

21. K. Dickson, A Historical Geography of Ghana (Cambridge: University Press, 1971); I. Wilks, Asante in the Nineteenth Century (Cambridge: Cambridge University Press, 1975).

22. For detailed descriptions of pit mining operations among neighboring Akan peoples, see E. Terray, "Classes and Class Consciousness in the Abron Kingdom of Gyaman," in M. Bloch, ed., Marxist Analysis and Social Anthropology (New York: John Wiley and Sons, 1975), 85-136; and K. Dickson, op. cit.

23. The beginnings of the rubber industry in the Gold Coast hinterland are discussed in R. Dumett, "The Rubber Trade of the Gold Coast and Ashanti in the Nineteenth Century," Journal of African History 12 (1971):    79-101. Information on rubber production in Assikasso in the 1890s may be found in H.M. Hull, Report on the Rubber Industry, enclosure in Maxwell to Chamberlain, 27 May 1897 (PRO CP96 293 5269).

24. This arrangement is described in the report of A. Solichon, Adjoint des Affaires Indigènes, "La Côte d'Ivoire et ses produits," 30 April 1905 (ANCI R8, Microfilm).

25. C. Meillassoux, "Introduction," in C. Meillassoux, ed., The Development of Indigenous Trade and Markets in West Africa (London:  Oxford University Press, 1971).

26. For a detailed description of Anyi domestic slavery, see C.H. Perrot, "Les captifs dans le royaume Anyi de N'Dényé," in C. Meillassoux, ed., Esclavage en Afrique précoloniale (Paris: Maspéro, 1975), 351-388.

27. L. Tauxier, Religion, moeurs et coutumes des Agni de la Côte d'Ivoire (Paris: P. Geuthner, 1932), 83.

28. For accounts of the French penetration and conquest of Assikasso, see C. Forlacroix, "La pénétration française dans l'Indénié (1887-1901)," Annales de l'université d'Abidjan, série F (Ethnosociologie), 1 (1969): 91-135; and D. Groff, op. cit., 206-239.

29. C. Forlacroix, 1969, op. cit. 92-101.

30. In 1920, the French deposed Ahua Kouao's successor, Kabran Aisi. See Governor Antonetti, Rapport politique, Second trimester, 1923 (ANCI 2EE 9, 13).   The monthly reports of the post at Assikasso for the years 1901-1904 contain  several references to the jailing of Ahua for refusing to recruit labor.

31. As early as 1902, the chef de poste of Assikasso was reporting that "the native chiefs are poorly obeyed by their subjects." Poste d'Assikasso, Rapport mensuel, March 1902 (ANCI 1EE 43, 2).   Other references to the decline of chiefly authority may be found in the post reports of February 1903 and June 1908 (ANCI 1EE 43) and in the Lt. Governor's Political Report, Second trimester, 1919 (ANS 2G 19-7).

32. R. Anouma, "L'impôt de capitation en Côte d'Ivoire de 1901 à 1908:

modalités et implications d'un instrument de politique et d'économie coloniales," Annales de l'université d'Abidjan, série 1, 3 (1975): 121-139.

33. The rate in the cercle of Indénié rose to three francs in 1910, four francs in 1911 and five francs in 1914. The upward trend continued in the 1920s and 1930s. In discussing the head tax, one of my informants noted wryly: "The white was cunning. He began with a very small tax, but little by little he made it grow."

34. Lt. Governor Angoulvant, circular of 29 July 1910, ANCI XVII-41-22 and the Journal officiel for July 1910.

35. Allusions to such border crossings may be found in the Lt. Governor's political report for the first trimester of 1915 (ANS 2G 1510) and in the post report for May 1911 (ANCI 1EE 45, 3).

36. Lt. Governor of the Ivory Coast, Political Report for the Second Trimester, 1919 (ANS 2G 19-17).

37. J. Boutillier, "Les captifs en AOF (1903-1905)," Bulletin de IFAN 30, série B, no. 2 (1968); and C. Meillassoux, "Introduction," in C. Meillassoux, ed., Esclavage en Afrique précoloniale (Paris: Maspéro, 1975), 351-388.

38. Information on domestic slavery in Assikasso is contained in Labaye, Rapport sur la captivité dans le cercle de l'Indénié (ANCI 1M: 63, K21). For a study of domestic slavery in neighboring N'Dényé, see Perrot, op. cit.

39. One colonial source estimates that some 2,000 former slaves left the cercle of Indénié in the period 1906-1907: Renseignements coloniaux, October 1913 (ANCI X-13-250). If we assume that the number of Juablin slaves included in this figure was proportional to the Juablin percentage of the cercle's total population, then perhaps 400 individuals left Assikasso in 1906-1907.

40. In their reports, colonial administrators generally took credit for the introduction of cocoa in the southeastern Ivory Coast. Most writers have taken these reports at face value and attributed the spread of cocoa to administration initiatives. See, for example, H. Labouret, Paysans d'Afrique Occidentale (Paris: Gallimard, 1941); and G. Rougerie, "Le pays Agni du sud-est de la Côte d'Ivoire forestière," Etudes éburnéennes 6 (Abidjan, 1957): 7-211. Recently, scholars influenced by Polly Hill have questioned this interpretation. Joseph Lauer, in "Economic Innovations among the Doo of the Western Ivory Coast, 1900-1960" (Ph.D. diss., University of Wisconsin, 1973, 131) has suggested that African initiative provides a better explanation for the rapid spread of cocoa cultivation among the Anyi. My own research in Assikasso suggests that neither of these interpretations, by itself, is sufficient. Both African and colonialist initiatives lay behind the Juablin's adoption of cocoa as a cash crop.

41. Information on Juablin innovators may be found in the following documents: Post of Assikasso, monthly reports, March 1908, July 1909 (ANCI 1EE 45); the commandant de cercle's report of his inspection tour of November and December 1910 (ANCI 1EE 59, 2); the post economic and agricultural report for the fourth trimester of 1912 (ANCI XI-43-426); and the monthly report of the agricultural agent of Assikasso for January 1913 (ANCI XI-43-426).

42. For information on the French program of forced cultivation in

Assikasso, see "L'Agriculture à la Côte d'Ivoire--conférence faite devant la chambre de commerce de Grand Bassam par professeur Perrot," 11 April 1914 (ANS R16); "Le Développement de la culture du cacaoyer," JOCI, 15 March 1916; and L. Clerc, Rapport politique du cercle de l'Indénié, 3e trimestre, 1921 (ANCI 1EE 59, 1/2).

43. Qualitative evidence from local administrative documents suggests that Assikasso accounted for between one-third and one-half of the cercle's production. Dellabonin to the Director of the Agricultural Service, 6 April 1925 (ANCI XI-43-426); and cercle de l'Indénié, Service de l'agriculture, Rapports trimestriels, 1930 (ANCI XI-43-426).

44. Cercle de l'Indénié, Service de l'agriculture, Rapports 1912-1930 (ANCI XI-43-426).

45. In 1930, France consumed between 170,000 and 180,000 tons of coffee. Of this total, only some 5,000 tons came from French colonies. To increase the colonial contribution to national coffee imports, the government offered colonial producers a system of tariff rebates and bonuses. For information on this system, see: Côte d'Ivoire, Circulaire sur l'intensification de la production agricole et pastorale en Côte d'Ivoire, 4 April 1931 (ANCI VI-8-203); and Lauer, op. cit., 152-3.

46. Rapport de l'inspecteur de l'agriculture Bervas sur le cercle de l'Indénié, 30 November 1918 (ANCI XI-43-426).

47. Z. Semi-Bi, "La politique coloniale des travaux public en Côte d'Ivoire (1900-1940)," thèse de troisième cycle, University of Paris VII (1973): 190-191.

48. Audru to the Chief of the Agriculture Service of the Ivory Coast, 8 July 1934 (ANCI XI-42-313).

49. By the early 1930s, the cercle of Indénié possessed more than 21,000 hectares of cocoa and coffee plantations and an adult population estimated at less than 15,000. The former figure comes from M. Taméchon, Rapport d'inspection, cercle de l'Indénié, 6 October 1932 (ANCI IV-44/15). The population estimate comes from Lt. Governor Bourgine's Arrêté local of 29 December 1931 (ANCI IV-43/20).

50. H. Labouret, op. cit., J. Rouch, "Migrations au Ghana," Journal de la société des africanistes 26 (1956): 33-196; and Elliot Berg, "The Economics of the Migrant Labor System," in H. Kuper, ed., Urbanization and Migration in West Africa (Berkeley: University of California Press, 1965), 160-184.

51. Clerc, cercle de l'Indénié, Rapport agricole, second semester, 1919 (ANCI XI-43-426).

52. Several of the elderly Juablin planters I interviewed recounted how, as young men, they had been sent by their domestic group heads to Baule country to recruit laborers.

53. L. Fourneau, cercle de l'Indénié, Service de l'agriculture, Rapport annuel, 1927 (ANCI XI-43-426).

54. According to the local administration, the average monthly wage in 1932 was 35 francs. Cercle de l'Indénié, Rapport sur la situation agricole et zootechnique, second trimestre, 1932 (ANCI XI-43-426).

55. Stavenhagen, op. cit., 141-143.

56. Interview with Nana Kouassi Amia, Damé, 2 August 1975.

57. Service de l'agriculture, cercle d'Abengourou, subdivision d'Agnibilekrou, Fiches cadastrales, 1957. This survey may be consulted at the agriculture service's Agnibilekrou office.

58. There could not have been more than eighty Juablin officeholders in 1940. Thus it would appear that the majority of the 232 larger planters in the period were simple domestic group heads.

59. Sara Berry stresses this point in her analysis of cocoa farming in western Nigeria. See, in particular, Berry, 1975, op. cit., 71, and Berry, Sara, "Social Science Perspectives on Food in Africa," in Food in Sub-Saharan Africa, Art Hansen and Della E. McMillan, eds. (Boulder, Colo.: Lynne Rienner Publishers, 1986).

60. A. Richards, op. cit., 484.

61. According to one administrator, this practice was widespread and constituted one of the reasons for labor shortages in N'Dényé and Assikasso. Cercle d'Abengourou, Rapport politique et social, 1941 (ANCI VI-44/17),

62. Administrative encouragement of private property holding among Africans can be seen in: Lt. Governor Angoulvant's 1915 circular to cercle administrators (ANCI XI-39-407); Lt. Governor to the governor general of AOF, 5 September 1929 (ANCI IV-35-124); and the decree of 26 July 1932, Journal Officiel, 1933.

63. See Taméchon, Rapport d'inspection, cercle de l'Indénié, 6 October 1932 (ANCI IV-44/15).

64. K. Post, "'Peasantization' and Rural Political Movements in Western Africa," Archives européenes de sociologie 13 (1972): 223-254.

65. According to my informant, at least five Juablin purchased light trucks prior to 1940. Nana N'Da Kouassi, the famien from 1920 to 1933, and his successor Nana Kouao Bile both bought trucks, as did two aulo nkpagnemo and one simple domestic group head.

66. In 1941, the administrator of the cercle of Indénié (by now renamed the "Cercle of Abengourou") noted: "Dans le budget familial, les grosses dépenses sont celles commandée (sic) par les cérémonies rituelles. Là aussi, ainsi devant la coutume, le plus généreux sera le plus considéré. Ceci explique les sommes parfois importantes dissipées lors de certaines fêtes coutumières." Rapport politique et social, 1941 (ANCI VI-44/11). (Editor's translation: In the family budget, the large expenses are those commanded by ritual ceremonies. There, as is the custom, he who is most generous will be most highly considered. This explains the occasionally significant sums spent on certain traditional festivals.)

67. S. Amin, ed., Modern Migrations in West Africa (London: Oxford University Press, 1974).

68. The major center of non-Juablin planters in Assikasso prior to 1940 was the village of Siakakrou founded by a Sudanese laborer who obtained land in this manner. The 1957 cadastral survey lists seven planters in Siakakrou with plantations dating back to the 1930s.

69. Chauveau and Richard, 1977, op. cit., 510-511.

---

The study resulting in this paper was conducted in the Ivory Coast in 1974-75 under a fellowship from the Foreign Area Fellowship Program. The conclusion, opinions and other statements in this paper are those of the author and not necessarily those of the fellowship program.

# 5 Indigenous Capitalism In Postcolonial Kenya

Nicola Swainson

It is necessary to place this discussion of "Indigenous Capitalism in Postcolonial Kenya" in the context of the wider debate on industrialization in the so-called periphery. The "underdevelopment" school has maintained that the transformation of Third World economies has been immutably blocked by the dominance of "center" capitalism. In the words of Ann Phillips,

> having defined its task as that of proving the inability of capitalism to solve the problems of mankind, underdevelopment theory has limited itself to establishing that idea development cannot occur under capitalism. In pursuit of this objective it cannot perceive or fully analyze what is occurring . . . our understanding of world accumulation is obscured rather than aided by the introduction of the question, "Can capitalism promote development or does it necessarily produce underdevelopment?"[1]

It is obvious that the current phase of industrialization in the Third World cannot possibly follow the pattern of nineteenth-century Europe. It should be made clear, however, that (with the exception of Britain) the standard path of European industrialization was far from being as "autonomous" or "independent" as some underdevelopment writers would have us believe. Given the uneven nature of capitalist expansion in nineteenth-century Europe, it is not surprising to find considerable differences between countries with regard to the pattern of industrialization. The industrial process in Britain was unique in that it is probably the only case where accumulation through merchant concerns and agriculture formed the basis of a relatively independent industrial process. In Russia, on the other hand, large quantities of French finance and technology

137

were required to fuel industry, and the state played an important role in procuring these ingredients. In Germany, a special relationship emerged between the banks and industry, which was assisted by powerful state protection.[2]

From the European example, it is also evident that accumulation is not tied to rigid historical stages, and that there is no established relationship between the transformations of agrarian and manufacturing sectors. For instance, Italian industrialization proceeded in the nineteenth century without a prior revolution in agriculture (which, in many areas, retained its precapitalist forms); in Britain, on the other hand, the home market developed before the industrial transformation of the nineteenth century, due to the expansion of commodity relations through trade and commercial agriculture.[3]

A popular line of thought that has run from the Russian Narodniks through to some interpretations of underdevelopment is that backward economies fail to establish a home market for industrial products. According to the Narodniks, there was no "real" capitalism in Russia because the impoverished masses could not consume the products of industry. Lenin countered that problems of realization were not caused by market limitations but rather were related to the crises integral to capitalist *production*.[4] He noted that "the problem of the home market as a separate, self-sufficient problem not depending on that of the degree of capitalist development does not exist at all. This is why Marx's theory does not anywhere raise the problem separately . . . . The home market for capitalism is created by capitalism itself."[5] Lenin goes on to show how the very separation of the producers from their means of production serves to expand the home market for industrial and agricultural commodities, as people must buy their means of subsistence. In other words, distortions in the market place are derived from the uneven nature of capitalist production rather than the other way around.

Capitalist relations were introduced into Kenya during the colonial period, and the processes of dispossession of the peasantry and proletarianization reached a higher degree in Kenya than in any of the other East African countries. After World War Two, international productive capital came to dominate the colonial areas more thoroughly, reflecting a high degree of concentration of enterprises on a global scale. More particularly, in the 1960s, foreign investment in East Africa diversified from traditional areas (plantations and raw materials) into manufacturing. There has been a wide variety of interpretations of such changes, coming under the rubric of "dependency" theory. Writers such as Samir Amin and Gundar Frank have stressed that any development of the means of production in the so-called peripheries will be thwarted, leaving these social formations disarticulated.[6] Apart from the rather static nature of some of their formulations, dependency theorists have failed to grasp the profound differences between different "peripheral" countries. Some countries have achieved a higher degree of internal accumulation than others, largely for historical reasons. Brazil, Taiwan, South Korea, and Mexico, for example, have maintained high levels of industrial growth and are serious competitors in metropolitan markets.[7]

Indeed, the last decade has witnessed a massive *restructuring* of productive capital and a relocation of production units to the more advanced areas of the "periphery." These changes have been in response to a state of economic crisis and declining profitability in the core countries. Footloose transnational firms have interpenetrated global sites in order to maintain high rates of profit through use of cheap labor and access to markets. Imperialism in its contemporary phase is actively underdeveloping the core countries, as well as the "satellites" in the Third World.[8]

Over the past few years, there has been a vigorous debate on the nature of "development" in Kenya and the respective roles of local and foreign capital. Although this debate has unearthed some important facts, it has become tautological. Colin Leys[9] has emphasized a growth in capitalist relations of production, while Kaplinsky[10] has attacked Leys's supposed optimism about Kenya's potential for growth by pointing to a slowed rate of accumulation and foreign exchange crises. As Godfrey has pointed out, there has been much cross purpose in this debate, which stems largely from the different methodologies of the protagonists.[11] In the following discussion, some aspects of indigenous capitalism will be explored. From the outset, however, it is necessary to reject a polarization that seeks to place "dependent" and "independent" on opposite sides of the coin of "development."

Although capitalism is basically one system that continues to function irrespective of nationality, there are specificities peculiar to social formations such as Kenya's that can only be illuminated by means of a historical analysis. The concern of this paper is not to provide a comprehensive analysis of class formation in Kenya, but to stress some of the material conditions underlying the development of indigenous capitalism after independence. We will first trace the origins of the

African capitalist class before examining further the dynamics of indigenous enterprise in postcolonial Kenya.

## The Origins of Indigenous Capitalism

In the 1920s and 1930s, a new class of African capitalists was emerging, based on the links between trade, commodity production and salaried places.[12] Until 1945, the colonial state in Kenya was dominated at the political level by settler estate capital, and agricultural production was demarcated by strict racial boundaries. Thus, it was not surprising that the focus of African nationalists from the 1920s on was to remove the restrictions that surrounded land ownership and farming. The extension of commodity relations within the African reserves was subject to restriction by the colonial administration through licensing regulations, taxation, and quality controls. The aim of such restrictions was to enhance the supply of African labor to European estates while reducing the availability of labor to African farmers in the reserves. During the interwar period in particular, racial boundaries surrounding agricultural production deliberately held back the full flowering of indigenous capitalism because it was potentially competitive with settler enterprise.

Despite the extensive restrictions placed in the way of indigenous capitalism during the colonial period, a certain amount of money capital was accumulated through the production of commodities and the process of "straddling."[13] The latter term refers to the overlap of occupations, during the colonial period, which involved the channeling of money incomes from professions in the civil service into some kind of enterprise in the reserves, either trading or farming or both.

African production of cash crops greatly expanded in the period following World War Two in response to an increased demand on the world market for commodities such as tea, coffee, maize, wattle, groundnuts, etc. This rapid increase in agricultural production was encouraged and stimulated by the direction of British "development" policy after 1945. British colonial policy had shifted dramatically as a result of fundamental changes in the world economy, which involved the realignment of metropolitan economic and political power in favor of the United States. The British government, in the years following the war, adopted an interventionist economic strategy and, through financial agencies such as the Colonial Development Corporation (CDC), made a determined effort to promote colonial cash crop production.[14] This intervention of British agencies in support of large-scale production schemes had the long-term effect of undermining the economic supremacy of the settlers. The success of British agricultural policy, despite the Mau Mau revolt in the 1950s, can be illustrated by the general rise in agricultural output from the reserve areas from £1.04 million to £4.6 million between 1945 and 1955.[15]

It became increasingly obvious to the metropolitan government, after the nationalist episode of the 1950s, that an administration dominated by Europeans allowing only minimal African participation was not conducive to long-term political stability. The political dominance of settler capital had to be ended if capitalist relations were to be extended and productivity raised in both the agricultural and industrial sectors of the economy.

Moreover, the existence of a settler political monopoly and its base of economic dominance blocked expanding indigenous capitalism. During the late 1950s, therefore, the focus of nationalist demands was on the extension of political control and the removal of restrictions on African enterprise. After the war, the presence of demobilized soldiers and the availability of ready money stimulated the formation of businesses by Africans. The development of African corporate forms had been held back by the limitations imposed on borrowing by the Credit to Natives Ordinances of 1906 and 1926. The 1926 ordinance was not repealed until 1960, although after 1945 it became easier for prominent Africans to obtain exemptions from these provisions.

After World War Two, therefore, private joint stock firms were formed by Africans for the first time, and most of these companies traded in agricultural commodities. Two of the earliest examples were the Ukamba Fuel and Charcoal Supply Company and the African Growers and Produce Company. Most of the early firms were formed in the Central Province by Kikuyus, although the most significant Luo firm (its members from western Kenya) was registered in 1946 as the Luo Thrift and Trading Corporation. The latter incorporated Ramogi Press, a mouthpiece for nationalist ideas in Western Kenya. Most of these early firms were formed by an embryonic African petty bourgeoisie, most of whom were traders, farmers, teachers, and clerks. The blooming of an African merchant class continued despite the detention of many Kikuyus during the Emergency in Central Province between 1954 and 1956.

During this period, the colonial government was concerned to encourage and regulate the expansion of African merchant capital. MacWilliam has shown that African traders preferred an open system of trading, and they resented attempts by the colonial state to regulate their enterprises in the form of co-operatives.[16]    Loan schemes administered through the Local Natives Councils provided money capital for African trading and manufacturing enterprises. Leading nationalists, however, constantly attacked the restrictions placed on their enterprises by the colonial state.    Tom Mboya (then president of the Kenya Federation of Trades Unions) accused the government of discriminating against African traders in Dagoretti village in terms of building standards.    He also criticized "the difficulties placed in the way of Africans who wished to become producers as distinct from mere consumers."[17]

Despite the many restrictions on indigenous enterprise in the colonial period, by the early 1960s there had been a significant amount of surplus generated from cash crop production and trade in the reserve areas; this laid the foundation for the subsequent expansion of capitalist relations in the independence period.

## Postcolonial Kenya

After independence in 1963, political power was transferred to the nationalist party, KANU, and the Kenyan state came under the hegemony of the indigenous bourgeoisie. The dominant fractions of the African capitalist class were able to commandeer the state apparatus after 1963 and to use their power to break into areas of accumulation that had previously been monopolized by either settlers or Asians.

The transfer of European land to Africans began in 1962 with the first settlement schemes.    By 1970, more than two-thirds of the formerly European-owned mixed farm areas had been occupied by approximately 500,000 Africans.[18]    Between 1973 and 1977, the final phase of indigenous appropriation of European-held land was completed with the takeover of the remaining coffee plantations and ranches by Africans. During this time, 57.5 percent of the total number of farms in the "large farm" sector changed hands, and these transactions involved some 18,000 hectares of lands worth K£18 million (at current prices).[19]    By 1977, it was estimated that only 5 percent of the mixed farm areas within the former "white highlands" remained in expatriate hands.

After independence, the principal measures taken by the state to expand the sphere of indigenous accumulation included loans, licensing, and public investment. These methods have been used to propel indigenous capitalists into agriculture, trading and, more recently, manufacturing. Agricultural production, however, has clearly been the basis for indigenous accumulation in postcolonial Kenya, and most local investments in trading and manufacturing have been financed from agricultural surpluses. By the 1970s, local capital was expanding from farming and real estate into transportation, tourism, commerce, and small-scale manufacturing. The pronounced shift of local capital in the direction of manufacturing was assisted by the increase in revenue from the major export crop, coffee, after the hike of world market prices in 1977 and 1978.[20]

The existence of an indigenous bourgeoisie in Kenya and elsewhere in the so-called periphery has been challenged by radical theorists. The current literature on East African political economy has been strongly influenced by the "underdevelopment" writers, including Frank, Wallerstein, and Amin.[21] These authors assume that underdevelopment was the product of capitalist penetration; they also tend to assume that the dynamics of accumulation operate through the imperatives of exchange rather than production. Leys's original work on Kenya was broadly in agreement with the "dependency" school, and he portrayed the Kenyan ruling group after independence as being no more than an impotent class of intermediaries locked into the sphere of small-scale trade and dependent upon international capital. The Kenyan capitalist class, he maintained, was a weak group in terms of scale of enterprise, and it depended heavily on state monopolies for its prosperity:

> In practice, however, the shift from special assistance to protection can be seen in every field where the government tried to foster African capitalism--except those fields where it moved directly to the creation of monopoly without more ado. The effect of this was to create a new stratum of the African petty bourgeoisie ensconced within the general system of protection and monopoly in such a way as to serve and complement foreign capital, not to replace it.[22]

It is for this reason that many writers on the left have identified the metropolitan bourgeoisie as the dominant class force within the postcolonial states. Von Freyhold, for instance, in a discussion of the Tanzanian postcolonial state, declared that the dominant indigenous classes were unable to constitute themselves as a proper ruling class due to the fact they served the interests of international capital. As such, they are merely a class "governing" for the metropolitan bourgeoisie: "unless the governing class actually determines the process of economic reproduction in the country, it cannot be called a ruling class however large its formal powers may be."[23] Langdon and Godfrey, in another brand of dependency theory, have characterized the relationship between the Kenyan state and international capital as a "symbiotic" one where the state acts to integrate the interests of both, although foreign capital is inevitably the dominant partner due to its superior material strength.[24] This argument is weak in that it assumes that the state is some kind of independent force, unattached to any class interests. In these kinds of positions, classes are mechanically assumed to be appendages of economic strata, rather than the product of economic and political struggle derived from capitalist relations. The dismissal of indigenous capitalist groups in countries such as Kenya as being "neocolonial" lackeys to foreign interests is unfortunate in that it detracts attention from the political enemies of the working people. Despite being caught in the web of international capitalism, the indigenous bourgeoisie have levels of autonomy in their social formations, which would be dangerous to ignore. Certainly capitalism in Kenya is closely linked with the world economy, and elsewhere we have considered indigenous capitalism in the light of the global dominance of the multinational corporation.[25] In order to understand the dynamics of internal accumulation, it is the intention here to delve more deeply into the movement of indigenous capital from merchant to productive concerns, and to give some examples of indigenous enterprise in Kenya's nationalist phase in the early and mid-1970s.

*Africanization of the Commercial Sector, 1967-1976*

Since independence, the indigenous capitalist class has used the powers of the state to secure a predominant hold over both distribution and production in Kenya. The most important tools used to pry open the agricultural and commercial sectors since 1965 have been licensing and preferential access to credit. The most potent weapon used to Africanize the commercial sector has been the Trades Licencing Act of 1967, which excluded noncitizens from trade in rural and noncentral urban areas. It also specified goods that were to be reserved for citizen traders. At that time, these included only a few basic wage goods, such as maize, rice, and sugar, but the list was extended in the 1970s to include soap, shampoo, sweets, matches, batteries, insecticides, hardware, cement, wire, tools, etc.[26] The Kenya National Trading Corporation (KNTC) was established in 1965 with the intention of taking over the import/export trade, but it became the primary agency concerned with Africanizing the commercial sector. From 1967 onwards, the KNTC was the coordinating body for the movement of indigenous capital into trading areas formerly dominated by noncitizen firms of Asian and foreign origins. In fact, there has been considerable competition between the bourgeoisie proper and the petite bourgeoisie (mainly small traders) to gain control over the most important Asian enterprises. These traders have consistently called for the widening of access to trade and distribution of manufactured goods. Indeed, the conflicts between the traders and elements of the bourgeoisie with political power have been intense during the decade of Africanization of commerce.

Before going further into the material contradictions between different class fractions, the status of the petite bourgeoisie should be clarified. The petite bourgeoisie does not have an independent class interest, but tends to vacillate between the bourgeoisie and the proletariat, sometimes moving into the sphere of one or the other. Despite the fluidity of individuals, the petite bourgeoisie often takes on identification at any point in time. The main ideological thrust of small-scale traders in Kenya has been to challenge large-scale capital (either local or foreign), and much of this struggle was articulated through the Kenya National Chamber of Commerce (KNCC). Through this organization the petite bourgeoisie has persistently pressured the government to open up areas of accumulation by means of *legislation* to remove noncitizen competitors. It is clear that the strong rhetorical attacks on Asians and foreign firms by the petite bourgeoisie since the mid-1960s are not merely examples of isolated racism; circumscribing nonindigenous capital is clearly in the long-term interest of the Kenyan bourgeoisie as a whole. The core elements of the Kenyan ruling class (the large-scale politicians, bureaucrats, and businessmen) do not need to indulge in degrading racial onslaughts, for they are in a position to use the state to individually appropriate particular noncitizen enterprises.

After Kenyatta's death in August 1978, with the advent of the Arap Moi regime, the government appeared to exhibit a more coherent nationalist control over the economy. These efforts seemed to be undermined, however, by the impact of economic crisis from 1979-1980 onward and by the export-oriented direction of the 1979 Development Plan. During the 1960s and 1970s in Kenya, the petite bourgeoisie acted as the ideological spearhead for the bourgeoisie in their drive to extend the area of accumulation. During the Kenyatta regime, sections of the ruling group were closely aligned with foreign firms and therefore did not need to use legislation to gain distribution rights from foreign firms. This was achieved as a matter of course by means of alliances between certain politicians and foreign firms.[27]

*Distribution of Manufactured Goods*

During the Africanization of the commercial sector, which began in the mid-1960s, Asian capital was the first to be appropriated, and government policy was not agreeable to attacks on foreign firms. From 1967 onwards, the chamber of commerce exerted continuous pressure on the Ministry of Commerce and Industry to withdraw trading licenses from Asians and to make compulsory the distribution of manufactured goods through citizen traders. For instance, in 1969, the chamber complained that noncitizen traders in River Road and Bazaar Road areas of Nairobi were being allowed to trade in specific goods, even though there were a sufficient number of African traders in the district. At the same time, the KNCC agreed with a report of the Provincial Trade Development Officer that the lack of specialization among African traders was the reason for their low success rate. It is certainly the case that, in 1969, the KNTC was appointing a large number of traders (as many as fifty) in any one commodity. Soon after, a policy was adopted of appointing only a few agents for each item, which served to regulate competition in retail trading.

Another drawback facing African traders in their takeover of noncitizen enterprises was lack of credit, a central factor in the provincial trade officer's report on local enterprises in 1970.[28] The chamber of commerce recommended to the government in 1969 that 60 percent of all money advanced for any cause through government banks should go to Africans, 20 percent to citizens, and the remaining 20 percent to anyone. The chamber also called on the government to channel all contracts for government supplies through African traders. By 1970, the KNCC was also requesting the Ministry of Commerce and Industry to take measures to Africanize the import-export trade, which proved to be a difficult task. These examples show the way in which the petite bourgeoisie favored the application of racial criteria to demarcate areas of the economy. Ironically, these tactics were similar to those employed by the state in support of settler enterprises during the colonial period.

The Kenyan government gradually acceded to the demands of the traders and took measures to appropriate Asian firms. In 1975, the minister of commerce and industry finally agreed to make compulsory the distribution of manufactured goods through citizens, by means of legislation. For six years, the chamber of commerce had pressured the government to pass such legislation, and the measure took time because of the alliance between certain prominent Kenyans and foreign firms. Some foreign firms refused to comply with the chamber's demand that the government agency, the KNTC, should appoint distributors of manufactured goods. As early as July 1969, the Africanization Committee of the chamber requested that East African Industries (a Unilever subsidiary with government shares) should "in the light of the very many African wholesalers and distributors as opposed to the practice of a few years ago when the majority of the buyers of the firm's products were Asians, be asked to consider seriously appointing African salesmen for their products."[29]

Significantly, the Kenyan chairman of East African Industries at this time was also chairman of the Kenyan Association of Manufacturers, which was itself a mouthpiece for the alliance between international capital and fractions of the indigenous bourgeoisie. The chairman of EAI consistently refused to allow the distribution of that firm's goods through the government parastatal (KNTC), and the firm continued to appoint its own distribution agents, who were often ex-employees. In July 1975, a position paper was sent by the KNCC to the Ministry of Commerce and Industry, which reprimanded the chairman of EAI for undermining the chamber's policy on the distribution of manufactured goods:

The Chamber does not hesitate to quote in the case of Kenya's economy that: never have so few enjoyed so much economic privilege at the expense of so many . . . . while Mr. Wanjui (EAI) is obliged by the nature of his job to protect his industry, he must not do so at the expense of the Africanization of distribution . . . economic expansion is enhanced by the attraction and protection of both foreign and local investors, it cannot be fully achieved by ignoring or suppressing local interests.[30]

In order to appease the tide of criticism from the petite bourgeoisie, in 1975 the government finally passed an amendment to the Trades Licencing Act making it compulsory for all manufacturers to distribute their goods through citizen agents appointed by the KNTC. This measure passed through parliament with a minimum of publicity, with the obvious intention of avoiding any kind of threat to Kenya's foreign investors.

After 1967, the appropriation of businesses from noncitizens was carried out by the provincial trade officers, who withdrew trading licenses. Between 1970 and 1977, they made a systematic effort to withdraw the trading licenses from both citizen and noncitizen Asians, and these businesses were then turned over to Africans. For instance, in 1971, 141 shops in Nairobi were issued with notices to quit; seventy-eight of these were taken over by citizens of African origin. In spite of these efforts, there were constant complaints by the chamber about "window dressing" or collusion between African owners and the former Asian proprietors, who in some cases remained in control of the enterprises.[31] In the early 1970s, therefore, large sections of the wholesale trading sector remained under the effective control of Asian businessmen. It was around this time that the most vehement racial attacks were made on Asians that were more than just rhetoric. In 1972, the chairman of the chamber of commerce (Nairobi) welcomed a delegation from the chamber in Kampala and called for the KNCC to assist Africans in Uganda with their plans for the economic takeover of the economy from Asians.[32] In the same vein, the chamber, in a review of shops taken over from Asians in 1971, reprimanded Asians for harassing Africans with "unfair" competition. At this time, the KNCC noted that the only two successful African-owned wholesale enterprises in Nairobi were both owner-managed.

The KNCC suggested several solutions to the "selfish confinement of knowledge and business tactics by most Asians," including the provision of government credit exclusively for Africans and the promotion of education in trade practices.[33] "We accept that so long as competition is healthy the consumers will gain and as such is essential, but competition posed by Asians is not only detrimental to the Africans' participation in sharing the benefits of uhuru [freedom] but it is also defeating government policy."[34] In response to such complaints, the government set up a committee to report on the progress of Africanization, chaired by the provincial trade officer for Nairobi. The resulting report reflected pressure from the petite bourgeoisie but was in essence highly nationalist and dealt with Africanization of all sectors of the economy: trade, agriculture, public services and tourism.  Its proposals were quite radical for the time, and it argued for the phasing out of all expatriates in most areas of the economy, as well as the wholesale appropriation of Asian-owned enterprises.  It recommended that immigration rules for noncitizens be tightened immediately and also that government provisions of credit and training should be greatly extended for African entrepreneurs: "The African would expect effective mechanisms to place him in business trade and displace the Asian as he has displaced the European in agricultural farms."[35]

Between 1971 and 1977, therefore, the powers of the state were used to rapidly accelerate the pace of African commerce. The Industrial and Commercial Development Corporation (ICDC) became the main funding body behind the takeover of Asian enterprises, and the provincial trade officers were themselves responsible for bringing urban trading concerns under African control.  For instance, in 1975 the Ministry of Commerce and Industry issued 463 notices to quit for noncitizen firms in Nairobi, including several major supermarket chains.  There was considerable struggle between 1975 and 1976 between those with political power and the smaller scale traders to gain the most lucrative enterprises.  By 1977, most of the commercial sector in Nairobi and other major towns had come under the control of Africans, and the supply of Asian businesses "for the picking" had diminished to a trickle.

The logic of the persistent pressure from the small traders through the chamber of commerce on the Asian merchant class and international firms has been to bring a larger proportion of the means of distribution under local control.  In other words, the petite bourgeoisie may have acted as the "ideological vanguard" for the Africanization process, although that section of the Kenyan bourgeoisie with political as well as economic power has gained most from the appropriation of Asian enterprises.

Here we have focused on the tactics used to further indigenous control over the commercial sector; elsewhere company statistics have been used to illustrate this pattern.[36]  This study shows that, by the mid-1970s, there was a concentration of local enterprises in real estate and trading amongst a few large-scale businessmen. The competitive nature and relatively low profit margins of retail trade were a further impetus to local investment in manufacturing, where capital can yield a higher rate of return in the long run.  The use of state power to appropriate the bulk of Kenya's commercial sector from noncitizens during the 1970s certainly accelerated the accumulation of merchant capital, thereby laying the foundation for a move into manufacturing.

## Indigenous Capital and Productive Enterprises

As in many early capitalist countries, the state has played a central role in supporting local investment in manufacturing industry. By the mid-1970s, the Kenyan capitalist class had accumulated a significant amount of surplus from both agricultural production and trade. Leys draws attention to "a spectacular phase of accumulation" using modern forms of plunder, such as smuggling of commodities to neighboring countries and commandeering of farms and urban real estate.[37] The increase in coffee prices after 1977 also significantly boosted the amount of revenue derived from agricultural production. By that year, most of the trading sector was in African hands, and substantial inroads had also been made into transportation and tourism. Thus, by the late 1970s, a substantial amount of surplus existed for investment in manufacturing industry. The Industrial and Commercial Development Corporation, in addition to underwriting the takeover of the commercial sector from noncitizens in the 1970s, became the primary investment agency for industry. The ICDC has a number of roles: it acts as a funding agency for African traders and industrialists, and it also enters into partnerships with foreign manufacturing firms. Up until 1971, the ICDC loans scheme had given about 80 percent of its funds to indigenous traders in order to assist their acquisition of noncitizen businesses. After that time, most of the ICDC loans dispensed were used for the purchase of businesses *and* the extension of existing enterprises. For instance, from a sample of 123 business loans dispensed between September 1974 and February 1975, approximately 95 percent were used for the purchase of equipment and stock.[38] It is interesting to note that the larger-scale businessmen with existing security always tended to receive the lion's share of loan capital. This process gave a further boost to the concentration of enterprises among a few individuals.

In 1974, the ICDC announced the formation of a confidential register of farmers and businessmen who were prepared to invest their savings in large industrial projects promoted by the corporation. The aim of such a scheme was to give the

ICDC a file on all investors who could raise more than KSh.50,000 for investment in new industrial projects. The minister for commerce and industry estimated that at least KSh.50 million would be raised from Kenyan businessmen in this way. The initial response to this request was enthusiastic and gave some indication of the potential for development of a local industrial class. The ICDC pamphlet announced that "it is hoped that those who have large funds will take this opportunity and leave the small businesses and industry to less fortunate Kenyans." A letter to the ICDC from a potential investor concurred with the aims, saying, "we are indeed proud of the efforts you are making to put some of us jointly with international investors, which has been a problem until now."[39]

The list of potential industrial investors in 1974 was drawn from the ranks of senior civil servants, large-scale traders, transporters, and big farmers. The type of investment projects in which these individuals were interested included steel fabrication, concrete mixing, printing, nail manufacture, and construction. Most of the participants in the scheme were already involved in agricultural and/or trading enterprises. A firm of local accountants expressed their interest: "I am interested in growth and hence would be ready to wait for a few years for the dividend."[40] Since most of the businessmen who were prepared to commit their savings to future industrial project were already well established in farming, trading, or professional fields, they were prepared to wait for a higher rate of return on their investments.

The state has begun to bridge the gap in terms of credit and technological inputs required for modern manufacturing. As most technologies are the monopoly of metropolitan countries, it has been necessary for the Kenyan government to enter into partnerships with foreign manufacturing firms. Once the technical and financial inputs have been secured either from multinationals or government, the returns on capital invested in industry are high.[41] The emergent local bourgeoisie has not been slow to utilize these opportunities and perceive its long-term goals as being to *internationalize* distribution, clearly the first step toward building a productive base.[42] In 1976, the managing director of a large wine and spirits business in Nairobi gave his motives for investing in a paper products factory: "Retail is easier initially but for the long term it is necessary to go into manufacturing which allows higher profit margins."[43] This firm now exports its goods to neighboring African countries as well as supplies the local market under protected conditions.[44] This is but one example of a general trend from the mid-1970s to diversify into manufacturing.

Kaplinsky and Langdon have pointed to the small size of indigenous enterprises and the unstable nature of those investments, which involved a heavy reliance on state support. We will be concerned here with the process of corporate accumulation rather than size of enterprise.

## Forms of Manufacturing Investment

By the 1970s, the predominant form of foreign investment was the partnership or joint venture between local and overseas capital. This involves a complex unity of finance and technology, in most cases under the supervision of a government agency such as the ICDC or the Development Finance Corporation of Kenya. Some of these agencies are funded by external credit, from the World Bank or the German Development Agency for instance, and they invest in large industrial projects, frequently in conjunction with multinational corporations.[45] Kenyan government ministries oversee these investments, and the terms of the partnership between local and foreign capital are laid out in the management contracts. Nationalist controls over these contracts have become more stringent during the 1970s and involve such issues as training, personnel, amount of value added, finance, proportion of local raw materials, etc. The industrial sector has increasingly come under the formal ownership of Kenyan partners, and in most cases this means the state. For instance, in the early 1970s, the government took majority ownership in oil refining, power and lighting, cement, banking, meat processing, and airlines.[46] Kaplinsky has confirmed that over 60 percent of the equity of manufacturing industry in 1977 was in the hands of Kenyans.[47] In the later 1970s, the government invested further in tourism, food processing, and transportation.

State investment in manufacturing has been accompanied by private Kenyan investment in both manufacturing and agriculture. Furthermore, the state actively encourages the participation of private Kenyan investors in industrial projects. It is important to stress that this is not unusual in the practice of capitalism in other countries.[48]

*Investment by Local Individuals, Groups,*
*and Cooperative Companies*

Since the lifting of restrictions on company formation during
the colonial period, the expansion of indigenous enterprises has
been rapid. As was noted earlier, indigenous capitalism in the
postcolonial period has been marked by the concentration of
capital into fewer units. Many of the top Kenyan directors
own from twenty to fifty different firms, and ownership has
become separated from management in these cases. The indigenous capitalist class in Kenya has often been portrayed as
a group of "petty accumulators" whose scale of investment is
insignificant next to that of foreign firms.[49] It is certainly the
case that Kenyan businessmen do not have the resources to
develop an "autonomous" industrial base due to their late start
in capitalist enterprise and the particular form of colonial experience. However, we are not concerned here with arguing
about size of enterprises but rather to illustrate the process of
capitalist relations as manifested in the corporate form.

During the 1970s, Kenyan investors consolidated their
power, either through cooperative companies or large consor-
tia. Individual firms or holding companies have moved into
new areas by two principal means: by purchasing existing
concerns or by investing in new projects. Also during the
1970s, there was a notable tendency for indigenous capitalists
to buy into foreign firms, sometimes taking a controlling interest. For instance, in 1975 Mackenzie Dalgety, one of the
largest foreign conglomerates in Kenya, was taken over by
Mawamu Holdings Ltd., whose owners included the Kenyan
chairman of Mackenzie Dalgety and the chairman of Lonrho
East Africa. This firm in 1974 had a paid-up share capital of
K£2.7 million, and it has a wide range of subsidiaries in
agriculture, trade, and manufacturing. In 1976 the local
manager of a foreign-owned paint company bought a controlling interest in the foreign subsidiary.

There is often a considerable diversity among Kenyan-
owned enterprises. For instance, one of the so-called cooperatives, which was formed in the 1970s by leading local businessmen, the Gatundu Development Company, invests in
large-scale farming and food processing.[50] Furthermore, an
examination of Kenya's top directors in 1974 illustrates the
extensive overlap of class positions within the bourgeoisie between bureaucratic, political and professional groups.[51]

In Kenya, most bureaucrats and managers of foreign firms
cultivate their own business interests while, at the same time,

holding down full-time salaried positions.  Indeed, the Ndegwa Report of 1972 sanctioned the use of official positions to further private enterprise, although it seems likely that, under the more technocratic regime of Arap Moi, the lines between public and private will become more clearly demarcated.  It is worthwhile to look at some individual cases of overlap between private and public concerns, as they tend to illustrate the pattern of accumulation that has become typical in Kenya.

Kenneth Matiba, for example (one of my top fifty directors and one of Kaplinsky's top twelve), rose to prominence through government office, having been part of the educated class during the colonial period.[52]  In the 1970s, he was both chairman of the Kenya Football Federation and chairman of Kenya Breweries.  During this time he was able to build up quite a large network of private interests, including intensive horticulture for export, hotel and catering businesses, aviation, tourism, and real estate.  The link between private business and government corporations is demonstrated by his board memberships:  in 1978, he was both director of the Kenyan Horticultural Development Authority and chairman of the Civil Aviation Board.  After 1978, Matiba was elected as one of Central Province's two members of the ruling party, KANU.  It seems to be necessary in Kenya for businessmen to legitimate their operations at the political level.

Udi Gecaga and Ngengi Muigai have been isolated by Kaplinsky as the only indigenous directors with substantial holdings in manufacturing, as well as real estate and trade. Certainly their rapid rise to preeminence in Kenya's business world before 1978 was not unconnected to their relationship with President Kenyatta.  However, these are by no means the only members of a rising group of Kenyan businessmen who are increasingly channeling their surplus from agrarian holdings into manufacturing concerns.  It is not unusual in early enterprise for individuals to move from the level of small-scale trade into production.  As Lenin noted with regard to early capitalism in Russia:

> Perhaps one of the most striking manifestations of the intimate and direct connection between consecutive forms of industry is the fact that many of the big and even the biggest factory owners were at one time the smallest industrialists and passed through all stages from popular production to capitalism.  One individual went from peasant/serf, cowherd, carter, worker/weaver, handicraft weaver, small salesman, owner of small establishment, to owner of a large factory.[53]

We will now consider one of the most significant conglomerations of indigenous capital in the 1970s, the Gema Holdings Corporation.

## Gema

This corporation has been important due to its large-scale investment and the link-up between merchant and industrial capital. The Gikuyu, Embu, and Meru organization was formed in 1971 largely as a political and economic vehicle for the most powerful section of the indigenous bourgeoisie. Given the defunct nature of the ruling party, KANU, as an organization of the ruling group, the political wing of Gema (during the Kenyatta regime) took over as a substitute. Their activities included fielding candidates for election, mobilizing funds for investment and, in general, consolidating the class power of the bourgeoisie. The national office-bearers of Gema were all prominent politicians and bureaucrats with links to both public and private sectors. Dr. J. Kiano, the former minister for commerce and industry, was the first chairman of the organization but, in 1973, national office-bearers were replaced by nonpoliticians. It was clearly becoming difficult for Gema to be identified so closely with politicians, and the new officials held prominent positions in banking and private business. In 1973, therefore, Njenga Karume, a prominent Kiambu businessman, became the national chairman of Gema with Duncan Ndegwa (governor of the Central Bank) as vice-president.[54]  Kihika Kimani, a large-scale farmer and businessman from the Rift Valley, became the organizing secretary. By 1973, the leadership of Gema was drawn predominantly from the ranks of the big bourgeoisie and included individuals with a substantial degree of economic power.

In that year, the organization began to develop its economic interests with the formation of the Gema Holdings Company, which was designed to draw on the resources of Gema members. The corporation was a public company, offering shares on the stock exchange as a way of encouraging wider participation. Forty percent of Gema Holdings' shares were to be held in trust by Barclays Bank International, which indicates a link-up with international finance capital. The directorship of Gema Holdings and several members were experienced businessmen, including Matu Wamae (executive director of the ICDC and a private capitalist), Mr. Gecau (chairman of East African Power and Lighting), Mwai Kibaki (minister of commerce and industry and vice-president after 1978)--indeed, the list reads like a *Who's Who* of Kenya and includes some of the country's most prominent politicians, bureaucrats, and private businessmen. Gema became a direct expression of the class interest of Kenya's big bourgeoisie.

Gema was also active at the political level during the Kenyatta regime. For instance, in 1976 the organization was concerned to "combat rumors" surrounding the death of J.M. Kariuki, who had been an outspoken critic of the government. There has always been a considerable overlap between Gema officials and the political process, and many of its national, branch, and executive officials between 1973 and 1978 were elected to parliament and local government bodies. After the advent of the new president, Daniel Arap Moi, in 1978, the caucus of power shifted away from Kiambu, and Gema Holding Company found itself under political pressure from the government after it was prosecuted for a minor offense against company law.[55] This reflected the changing balance of political power in Kenya, which has involved the widening out of political power from the small group that surrounded Kenyatta. The Gema organization has itself responded to such changes by widening its links with powerful individuals and groups from different sections of the bourgeoisie.

The Gema Holdings Corporation was formed in 1973 primarily to stimulate investment in property and farming, and since that time it has built up large assets. The corporation's mode of operation was exposed during the court hearing on registration offenses under the Companies Act in 1979. By 1974, Gema Holdings was functioning as an investment agency and bank for indigenous capital; it had raised K£1 million in share capital, which by 1976 had been increased to K£2.5 million, most of which went into manufacturing projects. Nevertheless, the bulk of Gema Holdings' investment has gone into land, property, and farming enterprises. By 1979 its assets were divided up as shown on the following table.

It is likely that the company's formal assets conceal the extent of its investment: according to the auditor's reports in 1979, the firm had mortgaged its assets to the Kenya Commercial Bank for twelve million Kenyan shillings, indicating a larger-scale investment program, much of it in manufacturing.[56] The link-up between productive investment and finance capital in this corporation is personified in Michuki, who is a director of Gema Holdings and Chairman of Kenya's largest government-owned bank. Likewise, D. Ndegwa, before

TABLE 5.1:  Gema Holdings

Company Owns:

(A)   2 Farms - 75,000 acres in Gilgil and Rumuruti.
      (10,000 acres distributed to smallholders.)
      With 7,000 head of livestock.

      Value of land = K.Sh. 35 million
      Value of livestock = K.Sh.7.3 million (as certified
            by professional valuers).

      Plus 1,000 acres in Narok (wheat zone).

(B)   A plot on Moi Avenue, downtown Nairobi.
      (Proposal to build a bank on this plot.)

(C)   75% share capital - Clayworks Ltd.
      Company assets professionally valued at K.Sh.
            21.3 million.


All Company Assets Gross Value = K.Sh. 70 million (roughly)
Net liabilities are on the order of K.Sh. 25 million.
Net Assets therefore = K.Sh. 45 million

Amount contributed from shares = K.Sh. 4.4 million.

Dividends:  Interim dividend of twenty percent of the ordinary issued share
capital, issued December 1980.


Source:  Registrar of Companies, Nairobi;  Company Accounts and Annual
Report up to and including the year ended December 1979, prepared by Citizens
Registrars Ltd.

he resigned as vice-chairman of Gema, connected the leadership of the organization with the Central Bank of Kenya, of which he was governor. Clearly the corporation since 1973 has taken advantage of its excellent contacts with the banking world.

The scale of investment in manufacturing enterprise is further evidence of the corporation's economic power. In 1976, it took over one of Kenya's largest brick and tile making concerns, formerly owned by an American multinational. In 1977, the corporation invested in a vehicle assembly plant in conjunction with a foreign firm. In the late 1970s, the corporation was intent on plowing its surplus from farming into manufacturing, largely by means of taking over existing firms.

It is clear that by the mid-1970s a number of locally owned firms in Kenya were setting up in manufacturing enterprise, either in collaboration or in competition with foreign firms. For instance, several of the Gema enterprises have been in partnership with foreign firms, whereas the Tiger Shoe Company and the Chui Soap factory were both set up in direct competition with powerful multinationals (the Bata Shoe Company and Unilever, respectively).[57] It was during this period, also, that financial institutions and commercial banks were extending credit through special loan schemes to African industrialists. The new African-owned enterprises were manufacturing a wide range of products that could best be described as "light industry": iron and steel products, pharmaceuticals, oil filters, leather, shoes, soap, radios, food and beverages.[58] Nevertheless, it is clear that indigenous enterprise is restricted largely to consumer goods production, much of it using a high degree of imported components.

## Relationship Between Local and Foreign Capital

It has been shown that during the postcolonial period in Kenya, the state has supported the move of indigenous capital into both distribution and production. In some instances this has been at the expense of foreign capital, but more often local firms remain reliant on foreign technology agreements to run their enterprises. Most of the larger industrial projects in Kenya are carried out under the partnership conditions explained earlier.

However, it is significant that, during the 1970s, Kenya laid down the foundations of a nationalist policy toward foreign investment. The most important bodies established in the early 1970s to control the conditions under which foreign investors could operate were the New Projects Committee and the Capital Issues Committee. The CIC was set up in 1971 by the treasury in order to vent all issues of capital stock and to prevent foreign firms from expanding into certain areas of the economy (mainly land). Since its inception, the aim of this committee has been to encourage large foreign firms to issue a proportion (at least 25 percent) of their share capital on the Nairobi stock exchange in order to promote a higher degree of local ownership. Brooke Bond, for instance, was persuaded in 1972 to issue 12 percent of its shares on the Nairobi stock exchange, most of which was taken up by the treasury itself. Through this tactic the government has acquired large holdings in the private sector.

The Capital Issues Committee also vents transfers of new stock between citizens and noncitizens, with the aim of preventing foreign firms from taking over local enterprises. For instance, the committee between 1973 and 1975 managed to block several attempts by Lonrho to take over local firms. Political intervention emanating from the late president's family ensured the success of several other takeover attempts by Lonrho.

The New Projects Committee was set up in 1973 by the Ministry of Commerce and Industry with the aim of regulating the flow of foreign capital into industry. This ministerial committee includes representatives from the Ministry of Finance and Planning, ICDC, and Development Finance Corporation, plus civil servants from relevant ministries.[59] The function of this committee is to critically evaluate proposed industrial projects against a list of criteria established by the government as being in the "national interest," such as employment created, value added, etc. The committee has in the past been subject to the same type of political pressures from above with regard to decisions on certain foreign projects.[60]

Within these regulatory bodies, considerable struggle has taken place over the controls on foreign capital. As many foreign firms and potential investors forge high-level political alliances during project negotiations, it is hard for bureaucrats to consistently impose institutional controls over foreign firms.

The Arap Moi government took power on the death of Kenyatta in 1978, with a flourish of populism. President Arap Moi attacked corruption and smuggling and released all of the detainees. As part of this campaign, the state machinery was tightened up to some extent. Nevertheless, the severe balance-of-payments crisis faced by the country from 1979 onwards has placed restraints upon a "nationalist" development policy. In *Sessional Paper No. 4 of 1980 on Economic Prospects and Policies*, a new industrialization policy was formulated that emphasized the substitution of tariffs for quantitative restrictions and an export promotion scheme.[61] The dismantling of full protection for local industry began in 1978, when Firestone Tire's monopoly over the market was terminated by the government. The government clearly does have the legal power to control licensing and investment conditions, and these latest moves to promote an export-oriented industrial strategy are partly in response to the conditions of economic crises in which the state finds itself. As Godfrey has pointed out, the new policy poses a strong threat to *both* local and foreign-owned manufacturing enterprises that are assumed not to be strong enough to survive the rigors of international competition.[62]

By the late 1970s, a large proportion of the means of production in Kenya had come under local ownership and control. This included most of the prime agricultural land and about 60 percent of manufacturing industry. The significance of this attempt to bring the productive forces under local ownership cannot be underestimated, despite the obvious qualifications with regard to industry where most inputs are imported. The control over technology still lies clearly in the hands of foreign corporations, as Langdon has pointed out. In this sense, the development of local manufacturing is closely integrated into the world economy.[63]

At one level, capitalism, whatever its nationality, has in common the extraction of surplus value from labor--a process that has been highly internationalized at this historical stage. Nationalist investment measures in Kenya, although only partially successful, do express the need of local capital to retain a higher proportion of surplus *within* the national boundary. Since independence, the indigenous capitalist class in Kenya has propelled itself into areas of accumulation previously inaccessible. It is impossible to ignore the internal social and political dynamics of a class of entrepreneurs who still base their reproduction within the social formation. At this stage, an indigenous bourgeoisie is unlikely to supplant foreign capital in any Third World country, whatever its level of development. A more likely picture is a varying degree of integration and interpenetration between the two forces, mediated by politics. To specifically condemn "peripheral" capitalism for not being balanced, self-sustaining and integrated is to confuse the quest for an understanding of the present phase of imperialism.

## Notes

1. Ann Phillips, "The Meaning of Development," Review of African Political Economy, 8, (January-April, 1977): 19.

2. For an excellent outline of European industrial history, see A. Gerschenkron, Economic Backwardness in Historical Perspective (Cambridge, Mass.: Harvard University Press, 1966).

3. E.J. Hobsbawm, Industry and Empire (London: Penguin, 1968), 50.

4. V.I. Lenin, The Development of Capitalism in Russia, Collected Works (Moscow: Progress Press, 1974), 45-47.

5. Ibid., 69.

6. For instance, in S. Amin, Class and Nation, Historically and in Crisis (London: Heinemann, 1980).

7. For a good discussion of Third World industrialization, see M. Lansberg, "Export-led Industrialisation in the Third World: Manufacturing Imperialism," U.R.P.E., vol. 11, no. 4 (1979).

8. See B. Bluestone and B. Harrison, Corporate Flight: the Causes and Consequences of Economic Dislocation (Massachusetts: Washington Progress Alliance, 1981).

9. Colin Leys, "Capital Accumulation, Class Formation and Dependency-- the Significance of the Kenyan Case," Socialist Register (1978).

10. R. Kaplinsky, "Capitalist Accumulation in the Periphery--the Kenyan Case Re-examined," Review of African Political Economy, 16 (1980).

11. M. Godfrey, "Kenya: African Capitalism or Simple Dependency?" in M. Bienefeld and M. Godfrey, eds., The Struggle for Development, National Strategies in an International Context (M. Phil. textbook, Sussex, forthcoming).

12. M.P. Cowen, "Capital and Peasant Households," mimeo (Department of Economics, University of Nairobi, July 1976).

13. Ibid.

14. For further details, see N. Swainson, The Development of Corporate Capitalism in Kenya, 1917-1977 (London: Heinemann Educational Books and University of California Press, 1980).

15. J. Heyer, "A Survey of Agricultural Development in the Small Farm Areas of Kenya since the 1920s" (I.D.S. Nairobi Working Paper no. 194, October 1974).

16. S. MacWilliam, "Commerce, Class and Ethnicity: the Case of Kenya's Luo Thrift and Trading Corporation, 1945-1972" (Conference paper for the Australasian Political Studies Association, Sydney, 1976).

17. Speech by Tom Mboya, Ministry of Commerce and Industry File in the Kenya National Archives (KNA).

18.  Colin Leys, Underdevelopment in Kenya, the Political Economic of Neo-Colonialism (London and Nairobi: Heinemann, 1975), 62.

19.  Colin Leys, 1978, op. cit., 250.

20.  Ibid., and Apollo Njonjo, The Africanisation of the White Highlands: a Study in Agrarian Class Struggles in Kenya, 1950-1974 (Ph.D. diss., Princeton University, December 1977).  Both have stressed the amount of liquid capital available for productive investment after the coffee boom.

21.  For instance, A. Gundar Frank, "The Development of Underdevelopment," Monthly Review, vol. 18, no. 4 (1966); Samir Amin, "Accumulation and Development:  a Theoretical Model," Review of African Political Economy, 1 (1974); and I. Wallerstein, "The Rise and Future Demise of the World Capitalist System:  Concepts for Comparative Analysis," Comparative Studies in Society and History, 16 (1974).

22.  Leys, 1975, op. cit., 149.

23.  M. Von Freyhold, "The Post Colonial State in its Tanzania Version," Review of African Political Economy, 8 (1977).

24.  S. Langdon, "The State and Capitalism in Kenya," in Review of African Political Economy, 8 (1977): 90-97, and S. Langdon and M. Godfrey, "Partners in Underdevelopment, The Transnationalisation Thesis in the Kenya Context," Journal of Commonwealth and Comparative Politics, no. 14, 1 (1976).

25.  N. Swainson, 1980, op. cit., ch. 6 and Conclusion.

26.  For further details on the Africanization of trade, see N. Swainson, 1980, op. cit., ch. 5.

27.  For instance, a partnership between an Asian multinational firm and Udi Gecaga, who distributed the goods.

28.  Comments on the Provincial Trade Development Officer's Report by the Kenya National Chamber of Commerce (KNCC), Africanisation Committee, 16/70.

29.  Africanisation Committee of the KNCC, July 1969.

30.  Position paper of the KNCC on the distribution of locally manufactured goods, July 1975.

31.  Minute 14/72, Wholesalers and Distribution Section of the KNCC.

32.  Minute 19/72, ibid.

33.  Ad hoc Committee on the "Implementation of Government Policy on Africanisation of Personnel," 17/10/72.

34.  Ibid.

35.  Ibid.

36.  N. Swainson, 1980, op. cit.

37.  Colin Leys, 1978, op. cit.

38.  N. Swainson, 1980, op. cit., 190.

39.  Pamphlet on industrial investment, ICDC, 1974.

40.  List of potential industrial investors, ICDC, 1974.

41.  S. Langdon, "The Multinational Corporation in the Kenya Political Economy," in R. Kaplinsky, ed., Readings on the Multinational Corporation in Kenya (London: Oxford University Press, 1978).  Langdon suggests that the rate

of return on manufacturing investment in 1974-1976 was around twenty percent.

42. Since the 1950s, there has been a significant amount of trade between Kenya and her neighbors, Tanzania and Uganda, although this was stopped after the closure of the Kenya-Tanzania border in 1977.

43. Interview with the managing director and major shareholder of a large wines and spirits firm in Nairobi, March 1976.

44. It should be pointed out that the era of full import protection ended in 1979 with the Development Plan 1979-1983; this proposes to phase out all non-tariff protection to existing industries within five years.

45. N. Swainson, op. cit., 223-227.

46. R. Kaplinsky, op. cit., and S. Langdon, "Industry and Capitalism in Kenya: Contributions to a Debate," in this volume.

47. For a list of government investments in industry for 1976, see N. Swainson, 1980, op. cit., 246-249. Also in 1977, the government took over the airline business with the formation of Kenya Airways Ltd., while hiring off charter and tourist lines to private firms.

48. Note, for instance, the current practice of large industrial firms in the United States (such as Ingersoll Rand in Greenfield, Mass.) threatening to move their operations to cheap labor zones if local governments do not heavily subsidize the construction of a new plant.

49. In R. Kaplinsky, op. cit.

50. Weekly Review, Nairobi, 5 January 1979.

51. N. Swainson, 1980, op. cit., 200-208.

52. See Weekly Review, Nairobi, 24 November 1978, on Matiba.

53. V.I. Lenin, op. cit., 541-542.

54. For a case study on Njenga Karume, see N. Swainson, 1980, op. cit., 204-206.

55. Much of this information on GEMA came from Weekly Review, 2 February 1979.

56. The details of this loan are also attributed to the above article.

57. One of the major shareholders in this shoe firm was the national chairman of GEMA, Mr. Njenga Karume.

58. N. Swainson, 1980, op. cit., 225.

59. For details on the functioning of this committee, refer to ILO Report on Employment, Incomes and Equality in Kenya (Geneva, 1972).

60. An example of this being the proposed vehicle assembly plants in 1976.

61. M. Godfrey, 1981, op. cit., 19.

62. Ibid.

63. Langdon, 1980, op. cit.

# Part 3
# The Agrarian Origins of African Capitalist Classes

If nothing else, the contemporary crisis of African agriculture provides a test of the Marxist assumption that crises generate solutions which deepen the interdependence and technical components of capitalist production. In a continent once self-sufficient in food and a major exporter of agricultural staples, per capita food production is expected to decline, while population is predicted to soar throughout the 1980s. In the Kenyan case, white settler farming and differentiation among the peasantry were noted as the two sources of Kenya's agrarian capitalist class. In the cases of Nigeria and the Ivory Coast, differentiation of the peasantry is complemented by either direct state intervention in the form of capital-intensive, state-managed irrigation schemes, or the entry of urban merchants and civil servants (e.g., retired army officers) into capitalist agriculture--usually with state subsidization.

The climatic variation, land size, and uneven development of capitalism in Nigeria allow multiple forms of capitalist agriculture to exist. Despite the enormous sums of capital expended on agriculture and irrigation, it is noteworthy that Nigerian peasant households still account for the overwhelming majority of output. Yet the trend is clearly toward capitalist agriculture. Currently, the crisis in urban-centered forms of accumulation and the difficulty of importing foodstuffs, due to declines in foreign exchange, have encouraged urban entrepreneurs to take up capitalist agriculture with state support, especially in sparsely settled areas.

Oculi's paper offers a scathing critique of the "green revolution" as it was institutionalized by the now-discredited Shagari administration. Rooted in the dependency perspective and a populist sympathy for the victims of state intervention in the countryside, Oculi marshals available evidence to expose the waste, exploitation, and distortion of the agrarian sector associated with the green revolution. Consequently, the green revolution undermined peasant agriculture, enriched international firms and advisors for the World Bank, and fed the overseas bank accounts of the Nigerian political elite--whose dependent alliance with the center states was further entrenched.

For the case of the Ivory Coast, Anyang' Nyong'o analyzes coffee production from the postwar period to the mid-1970s, illustrating how the indigenous planter bourgeoisie secured labor from the north for its farms and thus displaced the French *colons* from agrarian production. Throughout his detailed empirical account of the dynamics of the rural economy during the postwar period, Anyang' Nyong'o pays close attention to the role of the Ivorian state in structuring commodity production for the world market through credit schemes, labor recruitment, and technical services. Above all else, the chapter illustrates how the planter bourgeoisie instituted itself as the "ruling class" through careful use of state institutions and the manipulation of foreign labor. In his final section, the problem of differentiation of the peasantry is discussed in light of the problems associated with declining fertility and yields that follow universally from extensive cultivation of export crops.

*Paul M. Lubeck*

## Okello Oculi

# 6 Green Capitalism in Nigeria

The incorporation of Nigerian agriculture into the world capitalist system has gone through three phases. The first phase, from 1900 to 1957, was the colonialization of peasant production. During this phase, the state intervened to transform peasant production so that labor would be used either for the production of export crops or for the construction of infrastructures, such as railways and roads, and work in the mines of Jos and Enugu. State colonial policy resisted efforts to introduce plantation agriculture on a large scale. Instead, it emphasized mobilizing production by peasants, who also subsidized export production and export prices by producing their own food and by responding to new markets, such as the mineworkers and urban laborers. The emphasis on small-scale peasant production, which was only slightly improved by the introduction of the plough and new farming techniques, such as ridging and new seeds from government research stations, inhibited the emergence of a large-scale farmer class of indigenous plantation owners. The colonial state did not protect either the peasant industrial sector against competition from imported goods or the peasantry against low prices paid by colonial companies; nor did the state prevent the expropriation of surplus by marketing boards after the Second World War. All these factors combined to impoverish the peasantry in the northern region. According to Tiffen:

As Gombe farmers produced about ten percent of Nigerian cotton production, about ten percent of the total Marketing Board surplus (1950-1966) on its cotton account was due to them. Let us assume that if they had received this sum amounting to about £400,000, they would have invested only ten percent, and consumed the rest. This would have meant an additional investment of £40,000 over and above the

167

£600,000 calculated to have been actually invested by Gombe farmers, 1947-1967.[1]

Despite poverty and the exactions of the colonial state and foreign firms, however, the peasantry continued to produce food for the urban areas during this period.

During the second phase of Nigerian agricultural development, from 1957 to 1966, the foreign trading companies and the state continued to exploit the peasantry. What was new was the entry of the African political-administrative class, which took responsibility for marketing boards at the regional level in this period. Excluded from opportunities to accumulate capital in shipping, insurance and banking, and the industrial sector, and without a *latifundia* base in agriculture, the political-administrative class and its allies in the private sector turned to the state as a medium of expropriation and accumulation. Because the main source of accumulation in the state sector was export crop sales, this class wanted to increase the production of cocoa, oil palm, groundnuts, cotton, and rubber for export. Herein lay the first moment of contact between the material interests of the political-administrative class and Nigerian agriculture. Some members of this class alliance, most notably those from the traditional ruling class in western Nigeria, had already made money from agriculture as produce-buying agents or as large-scale farmers.[2] In their desire to use agriculture as a means of generating surplus for the state, the political-administrative class was now in harmony with the policies of the colonial state and the metropolitan capitalists, who were dependent on these export crops.

In order to increase the production of export crops, an emphasis was put on government plantations and settlement schemes, especially in the western and eastern regions, in the period from 1950 to 1970. The schemes were capital-intensive, costing as much as £10,000 per settler in the western region during 1959 to 1964, and they involved only an estimated 7,187 settlers. These policies persisted despite constant scheme failures, low returns from plantations and farm settlements, and evidence that, given good prices and appropriate financial support, peasant producers would achieve better results. During 1967-1968, for example, plantations and farm settlements contributed only one percent of the cocoa output from western Nigeria.[3] Only in the northern region was considerable emphasis put on funding agricultural extension services to reach peasants; yet, at the same time, colonial authorities there studied and experimented with irrigation schemes, notably the

Chad Basin, the Sokoto-Rima Basin, and the Hadeija Basin schemes.

Both the northern and southern political-administrative classes ignored the peasantry's need for capital to increase production and income. Instead, both elites continued the colonial policy of drawing surpluses from the peasantry, thus undermining peasant productivity. Furthermore, just as the colonial elites had exported marketing board surpluses to rebuild the war-torn British economy, the African political-administrative class expropriated the peasant surpluses for purposes of personal accumulation, political patronage, and competition for control of the national state apparatus. The agricultural sector thereby became subordinated to the needs of the political-administrative class and its allies, and the state's resources served their personal and class needs:

> Award of contract has come to be regarded generally in this country . . . as a very lucrative transaction. So eager is everyone in the hierarchy of any organisation to engage in the transaction that no matter how perfect and corrupt-proof the procedures laid down may appear on paper, some subtle devices are thought out to defeat their purposes . . . contracts provide the most popular avenue for acquiring wealth by corrupt and fraudulent means.[4]

The effect of these policies and practices on the peasantry during this phase (1957-1966) was to undermine the viability of the rural economy. Rural-to-urban migration increased, thus increasing the demand for urban foodstuffs. At the same time, the agrarian sector's ability to produce food was reduced by the loss of surplus labor and the absence of more productive technologies.

The pattern of industrialization that took place during this period was aimed at satisfying the consumption needs of the political-administrative class and the lower bureaucracy. It was heavily biased toward labor-intensive luxury goods such as textiles, processed foods, alcohol, and tobacco. After the 1960s, these commodities were replaced by more sophisticated and expensive consumer goods, such as motor vehicles, television sets, furniture, refrigerators, radios, etc., which were more capital-intensive industries. Low incomes prevented the peasantry from consuming such goods. In 1973, the food, beverage, and tobacco industries contributed 42 percent of the value added of the Nigerian manufacturing sector, as compared to a mere 7 percent in the machinery and metal products manufacturing industries.[5] This capital-intensive mode of industrialization, directed by multinational corporations (MNCs), was aimed at preempting competition from foreign manufacturers; because the MNCs exported profits, a source of investment capital was denied to the agricultural sector. As the African political-administrative class intensified its expropriation of public capital income, it also diverted state funds away from services and capital investment for the peasantry.

The phenomenon of elite expropriation of the state's resources has been widely discussed by Nigerians and others. It is generally viewed as a manifestation of a peculiar cultural trait in Nigerians, characterized by alleged "moral decadence," "greed," or "lack of discipline." Such an interpretation neglects the problem created by the survival of feudal classes in Nigeria, which controlled local-level government under colonialism, benefitted from colonial education, and prospered from colonial export crop farming opportunities. Since colonialism lasted only half a century in Nigeria, the survival of these classes was not seriously threatened: with the state as its only source of income and resource extraction, the political-administrative class that emerged from the precapitalist political elite, especially in the Muslim north, used state power for *personal* accumulation, rather than public services.[6] Tiffen comments on this problem:

> The liabilities of Nigeria are in a sense the reverse of its assets. The ability of its farmers and traders to seize opportunities for gain is equally present in civil servants, politicians and policemen, and as a result, it is almost impossible to prevent corruption in enforcing government regulations, in allocating licenses or loans, or in providing 'free' government services. In these circumstances, a development policy based on detailed government control over the direction of economic activity is almost certain to result in the gross waste of resources and the diversion of public funds into private pockets.[7]

The expropriation of public resources by members of the political-administrative class is unlike the process of primitive accumulation that occurred in metropolitan states, for, in the latter case, the bureaucracy exercised some modicum of discipline over primitive accumulation, and the resources, once taken, were invested in productive economic activity. Tables 6.1 and 6.2 indicate the pervasiveness of the phenomenon of elite expropriation at the local level, from 1972 to 1973.

In the Western State, for example, the value of public funds lost by civil servants at the state level went from N11,143 in 1972 to N67,598 in 1973. State officials had, by that time, advanced up to 57 million naira for the purchase of personal vehicles by other eligible officials. The auditor gen-

TABLE 6.1:  North-Central State:  Abuses in Contract Awards, 1972-1973

| Type of Query | Ministry | No. | Amount (naira) |
|---|---|---|---|
| | Works & Housing | 12 | 37,834.23 |
| Contracts Awarded without Prior Approval | Agriculture | 1 | 59,907.30 |
| | Secretary to the Military Government | 1 | 1,656.00 |
| | North-Central Water Board | 1 | 40,000.00 |
| | Total | 15 | 139,397.53 |
| Purchase in Excess of Contract Rates | Water Board | 1 | 148.00 |
| | Health | 4 | 581.00 |
| | Total | 5 | 729.00 |
| Split of Contract | Works & Housing | 5 | 82,603.82 |
| | Agriculture | 1 | 12,317.24 |
| | Total | 6 | 94,921.06 |

Source:  Report of the Auditor-General on the Accounts of the Government of North-Central State of Nigeria for the Year Ended 31 March, 1973 (Government Printer, Kaduna).

TABLE 6.2: Selected (out of 200) Cases of Misrepresentation, Western State, 1972-1973

| Ministry | | Case | Amount (naira) |
|---|---|---|---|
| Home Affairs & Information | 1. | Theft of government funds | 28,471.08 |
| Lands & Housing | 2. | Fraudulent land claim (Ibadan) | 4,456.80 |
| | 3. | Fraudulent compensation claim (Ibadan) | 2,154.33 |
| | 4. | Compensation to fake claimant (Ibadan) | 6,158.57 |
| | 5. | Loss of stationery | 2,056.77 |
| Works & Transport | 6. | Loss of petrol, superintendant engineer's office (Ibadan) | 8,029.40 |
| | 7. | Loss of stores in farm settlement | 5,522.75 |
| | 8. | Loss of sundry building material | 2,634.32 |
| High Court of Justice | 9. | Misappropriation of court revenue and deposits (Ibadan) | 27,534.88 |
| Agricultural and Natural | 10. | Loss of fuel at principal agricultural engineer's office | 16,061.08 |
| | 11. | Misappropriation of deposits | 15,011.77 |

Source: Report of the Auditor-General on the Accounts of the Government of the Western State of Nigeria for the Year Ended 31 March, 1974, 22-28.

eral feared that "a large number of advances which had remained dormant for many years may have to be written off as
no worthwhile recovery actions" were being taken, possibly
amounting to as much as 20 percent of the total advanced.[8]
Note that this situation does not coincide with Alavi's analysis
of the functions of the postcolonial state:

> The apparatus of the State, furthermore assumes also a new and rela-
> tively autonomous economic role, which is not paralleled in the classical
> bourgeois State.   The State in the post-colonial society directly
> appropriates a very large part of the economic surplus and deploys it in
> bureaucratically directed economic activity in the name of promoting
> economic development.[9]

My contention is that the agrarian crisis in Nigeria is a
direct result of state appropriation of peasant-produced surplus
which, unlike in Alavi's description of the postcolonial state,
was consumed by the political-administrative class and its allies.   In part, because of the continuing role of backward,
semifeudal classes within the political-administrative class, little viable economic development occurred, least of all in
agriculture, as a result of state intervention.   For example, the
corruption and incompetence of the political-administrative
class was the principal cause of the peasant rebellion that occurred in the Western Region in 1968.[10]

The third phase of Nigerian agricultural development,
corresponding to the period of civil war and the onset of the
petroleum economy, was marked by a food shortage.   Arthur
Lewis had already pointed out in 1967 that government policy
discriminated against farmers, noting that "between 1950-1952
and 1961-1963 the overall index for Southern Nigeria prices
paid to farmers fell from 100 to 73, while that for wages paid
by the Federal Government to unskilled labor increased from
100 to 297."[11]   Table 6.3, below, gives some indication of the
level of generalized food shortage (keeping in mind the
"optimism" of official estimates).   The most visible economic
manifestation of the food shortage was the massive entry of
food importers into Nigeria and the outflow of foreign exchange for food imports (table 6.4).

The oil boom, which dramatically increased government
revenues from N108 million in 1962-1963 to over N13 billion
in 1979-1980, shifted the means of elite expropriation of the
state significantly from agricultural export sales and investment to oil revenue.   The general neglect of and bias against
peasant producers was thus deepened, since fluctuations in
their levels of earnings and crop production no longer had a

TABLE 6.3: Projection of National Accelerated Food Production Program (NAFPP) Crops in 1982, as Compared to 1977 Practices if NAFPP Is Implemented

| Crops | 1977 level (million tons) | NAFPP 1982 target (million tons) | NAFPP national gap estimates (thousand tons) |
|---|---|---|---|
| Maize | 1.117 | 1.463 | -34 |
| Millet | 1.974 | 2.906 | -239 |
| Sorghum | 2.760 | 4.379 | -678 |
| Rice | 1.164 | 1.358 | +653 |
| Wheat | 0.038 | 0.060 | -190 |
| Cassava | 10.307 | 13.316 | +471 |

Source: Proceedings of 2nd NAFPP Workshop on Sorghum, Millet and Wheat, April 17-19, 1978, Zaria, 172.

TABLE 6.4: Imports of Grains to Nigeria, 1974-1977 (Value in naira)

| Commodity | 1974 | 1975 | 1976 | 1977 (Jan-Aug) |
|---|---|---|---|---|
| Wheat | 50,744,534 | 54,956,770 | 97,838,367 | 68,510,861 |
| Rice | 1,497,534 | 2,376,879 | 20,136,490 | 94,054,463 |
| Maize | 608,289 | 429,999 | 1,422,338 | 3,490,112 |
| TOTALS | 52,850,357 | 57,763,648 | 119,397,195 | 166,055,436 |

Source: Federal Office of Statistics, Lagos, in G.O.I. Abalu and B. D'Silva, "Socioeconomic Aspects of Semi-Arid Tropical Regions of Nigeria," Workshop on Socioeconomic Constraints to Development of Semi-Arid Tropical Agriculture, ICRISAT (19-23 February, 1979), 8.

direct impact on the material interests and surpluses for which
the elite had to compete. Consequently, the issues of adequate
transfer of capital to the peasantry and high prices paid for
crops were virtually swept out of the policy arena. It is in-
structive to note that it was only in November 1980, that
Phillip C. Asiodu, a key figure in policy-making under the
Gowon oil regime, proposed a change in Nigerian agricultural
policy:

> A more extensive programme of profitable producer prices for all major
> foodstuffs should be introduced. At the same time we should set
> effective country-wide government-financed buying organisations to
> buy from the farmers at harvest time all their products they are willing
> to sell . . . . Such producer prices should be fixed taking into account
> the prices of fertilizers and other essential inputs which the farmer
> would need to buy from effective and efficient private commercial
> distributors of such inputs including tractor and other equipment
> services [emphasis added].[12]

Food imports, funded by petroleum revenue, cushioned the
urbanized political-administrative class and the urban workers
politically and materially against the pains of severe food
shortages, while the massive food subsidization process, on the
whole, neglected the needs of the peasantry and the urban
unemployed. Such policies stimulated the expansion of a class
fraction of urban food distributors who were structurally
linked to foreign food imports. This is a class fraction that is
understandably not excited about new policies that would
promote domestic food sufficiency, since its existence was
brought about by the domestic food crisis. In a recent scandal
over rice shortages, involving federal legislators including the
senate leader, it was revealed that as many as thirty-seven
companies had been awarded contracts by the Shagari government to import 100,000 metric tons of rice.[13] It has been suggested that these opportunities for accumulation are given only
to supporters of the ruling party at the federal level (NPN)
and its allies (NPP), "as a way of repaying campaign expenses
to party supporters."[14] A comment from a paper published by
a leading NPN supporter suggested as much:

> The UPN Press is shouting its head off over the N75 million contracts
> awarded by the Federal Government to prosecute the federal housing
> scheme. We suspect that all the noise arose from the fact that Papa
> (Chief Awolowo) was not in the position to award those contracts.[15]

Only a section of the political-administrative class benefitted from the food import trade however, even under mili-

tary rule, and they did not make policy.  More significant voices came from sections of the military, where some officers, in anticipation of a retreat from politics, wanted to secure a large agrarian estate on the Latin American model. Both the last military head of state and his deputy acquired considerably large tracts of land and indicated their desire to leave the army for farming.  In this inclination they found sympathy from international agencies such as the World Bank, which increasingly saw Nigerian agriculture as an important new market for various types of industrial imports, including fertilizers, irrigation pipes and pumps, new hybrid seeds, tractors and earthmovers, technical consultants, etc.

In a recent policy dispute between the Kaduna State governor and the federal minister of agriculture over World Bank participation in the Integrated Rural Development Program, the governor voiced his opposition to several World Bank demands.  Among many, the most important concern was the following list of conditions of remuneration for World Bank consultants and managers:

1.  The salary of each World Bank official will be about 40,000 naira per annum, tax free and paid in foreign currency in foreign banks
2.  They shall each receive, in addition, 78 percent of the gross salary as cost of living allowance
3.  N733 per annum per dependent as dependent allowance
4.  25 percent of the gross salary as "post allowance"
5.  75 percent  of their children's school fees to be paid abroad in foreign currency
6.  Free air-conditioned and chauffeur driven vehicle;
7.  Free air-conditioned and "furnished-to-taste" housing
8.  Free electricity and water supply
9.  Free trip return air ticket to anywhere in the world for annual vacation
10. Forty working days leave per annum

As the governor's statement noted, the value of this commodity ("technical experts") "would cost about N12 million per annum."[16]  The entire project would cost N100 million.

The orientation of subsequent new policy was similar in some aspects to earlier policy phases in Nigerian agriculture, particularly in its revival of irrigation projects that had been articulated during the colonial period.  As large-scale projects, the irrigation systems ignore the general mass of peasant producers and emphasize capital-intensive production units.  Wallace reported that in the Kano irrigation scheme at Kadawa, some peasant farmers were forced off their land by the project's land needs, while others were displaced by absentee businessmen and civil servant farmers based fifty kilometers away in urban Kano.[17] Furthermore, the irrigation schemes are oriented to supply urban consumers rather than the needs of peasant consumption. The cost of these schemes is enormous, especially if compared to the funding of peasant production projects:  the Bakalori scheme, for example, has an estimated cost of over 300 million naira. The costs of the irrigation projects per hectare are also high:  N2,000 in Bakalori, N1,750 in Chad 1, and N1,200 in Chad 2.[18]  The average peasant does not earn even ten percent of these overhead costs in a year.

How does one explain the government's implementation of these high-cost schemes?  First, they offer opportunities for accumulation to the political-administrative class and its allies. Second, bureaucrats benefit from "kickbacks" received when the contracts are awarded, as noted by a commission of inquiry during the 1960s:

> We require a machinery which will ensure that government and public corporations' contracts will no longer be the chief source from which political parties derive their revenues . . . .[19]

In Bakalori, for example, the contract with Impressit, giving the company an award to both design and construct the project, was signed in haste by a local official on the Sokoto-Rima Development Board.  Such a contract, worth over 100 million naira, should have been signed only at the ministry headquarters in Lagos.  It is difficult to quantify the general level of corruption, but it is clear that agricultural development, as such, was an effective means of expropriation of the state by the political-administrative class, the members of which did not necessarily participate in production.  Certainly the largest share of government investment in agriculture in the 1974-1980 plan--535 million naira--went to irrigation schemes, followed by N150 million to the Nigerian Agricultural Bank and N132 million to large-scale food farms.[20]

Irrigation has also been an avenue by which direct linkages have developed between the international capitalist system and Nigerian agriculture.  As mentioned above, equipment and infrastructures needed for irrigation schemes--earthmovers, bridges and dams, erecting pumps, building irrigation channels, establishing spray pumps, setting up electrical installations at dam sites, etc.--have had no backward linkages with Nigeria's peasant sector and little with the industrial sector.

As in the colonial and early postcolonial phases, these projects provide a lucrative way for MNCs to profit by trading with the Nigerian agricultural sector, despite a considerable decline in export crop production. Little effort has been made to enhance the use of traditional river basin irrigation (*fadama*). In fact, in both Bakalori and Hadeija irrigation schemes, thousands of acres of land traditionally farmed by means of *fadama* have been drowned, and the *fadama* farmers have had to abandon an established cycle of dry season farming. Without alternative sources of land, food production has suffered from this intervention.[21]

The main effect of import substitution as a phase of Nigerian agricultural policy, however, has been the transition from a state that merely extracted surplus from the peasantry to one that intervened in land acquisition and the establishment of farms and poultry and dairy ranches. In the northern states, civil servants and state and federal political functionaries exploited the power of traditional local rulers to acquire land. Traditional rulers themselves have gone directly into farming. The emir of Daura, for example, won a local "Farmer of the Year" award in 1978, and another emir established an N11 million poultry project.

In the revised Third Year Plan, the government allocated N150 million to the Nigerian Agricultural Bank for loans; N132 million for the establishment of state farms in each of the nineteen states, with the understanding that such farms would eventually be handed over to private individuals; and N100 million for the purchase and distribution of fertilizers to farmers. As we have seen, it is reasonable to assume that the political elite will be the main beneficiaries of the 4.4 billion naira that the federal government plans to spend on food production during 1980-1985.

The development of a political-administrative class with a landed interest is linked to the invitation extended to MNCs to expropriate land and participate in direct production. The central bank has been instructed to oversee the investment in agriculture by commercial banks, and foreign companies were promised as much as sixty percent ownership in agricultural ventures. On his first visit to the United States, in 1980, the Nigerian president invited U.S. companies to enter agricultural production in Nigeria; there already exists a Nigerian-U.S. commission charged with facilitating this process. Asiodu summarizes the policy:

> The new attitude we need if we are to increase the impact of oil revenues in this regard is to boldly and freely use imported foreign exper-

tise, and foreign-controlled enterprises as well to achieve these things. Foreigners cannot uproot and take away the farms they develop nor can we fail to benefit from the production of abundant food in Nigeria even by foreign-owned firms. And we must have confidence in the ability of our people to emulate good practices and to compete effectively.[22]

All of the above indicates that state policy is directed toward an alliance with international capital to develop Nigerian agriculture in a capital-intensive, urban-biased, and dependent capitalist direction. Never was there a serious attempt to mobilize the individual and collective energies of the Nigerian peasantry toward the goal of agricultural modernization.

Table 6.5 below details the production and ownership criteria envisaged under the joint-venture formula. It should be noted that more emphasis is placed upon the industrial-processing sector of agriculture than on food production.

Except for poultry farming, where the political elite shows confidence in handling production on its own, foreign companies own a sixty percent share of most large-scale farming operations, i.e., plantation agriculture for tree crops, grains, and other cash crops (including sugar). A closer look at poultry farming reveals that it consists mainly of *imported* birds for meat and laying eggs, thus avoiding the difficult enterprise of raising one's own breeding stock from local chickens, guinea fowl, ducks, and bush hens. The imported birds are fed mostly on imported feed, or feed milled from maize and mixed with imported concentrates containing fish, bone, groundnut cake, cotton seed, medical components, and vitamins. The products, notably meat and eggs, are in great demand in urban markets. The automated equipment for breeding and collecting eggs from layers is imported and relatively simple to operate. Disease is the only major risk in poultry production: the Kuru livestock farm in Plateau State, for example, suffered a loss of more than 90 percent of its stock (from 9,000 birds to 700) in 1980, due to an epidemic. But insurance is available to cover such losses, making poultry farming almost risk-free and bringing returns in a matter of weeks. Little managerial skill or capital is required, and poultry farming is thus an ideal investment for the political-administrative class.

In view of the above, the question arises of whether the role of MNCs will expand to undertake plantation farming and increase Nigerian dependency on secondary production needs such as machinery and fertilizers. These corporations will restructure Nigerian agriculture when they make decisions such

TABLE 6.5: Food Sectors in the Indigenization Schedule

Schedule 1
Enterprises exclusively
reserved for Nigerians

1. Bread and cake making
2. Poultry farming
3. Rice milling

Schedule 2
Enterprises in which Nigerians
must have at least
60 percent equity interest

1. Fish and shrimp trawling and
   processing
2. Fertilizer production
3. Grain mill products
4. Manufacture of biscuits
5. Manufacture of cocoa, chocolate, and
   sugar confectionary
6. Manufacture of dairy products,
   butter, cheese, milk and milk
   products
7. Manufacture of yeast, starch,
   baking powder, coffee toasting,
   tea leaves to black tea
8. Oil milling and cotton ginning
9. Plantation sugar and processing
10. Petro-chemical feedstock industries
11. Slaughtering, storage associated with
    industrial processing, and
    distribution of meat

Schedule 3
Enterprises in which Nigerians
must have at least
40 percent equity interest

1. Manufacture of agricultural
   machinery and equipment
2. Manufacture of food machinery
3. Plantation agriculture for tree
   crops, grains, and other cash crops

Source: Federal Republic of Nigeria, Joint-ventures Enterprises.

as what types of seed to use, which machines to use for weeding, harvesting, threshing, and milling, and where imports will come from. For example, a Nigerian branch of an MNC would be likely to import seeds from one sister subsidiary, import pesticides and insecticides from another, and use seeds that can only be weeded, harvested, threshed, and milled (in the case of grain) by machines imported from a third subsidiary of the same parent company.[23]

Here conflicts may arise when new crop strains are introduced that meet the needs of the imported machinery but fail to supply peasant farmers' other needs, such as non-grain fodder resources. Evidence of this conflict occurring on a large scale already exists on Bokkos farm in Plateau State. The farm was started in 1974 as a joint venture between Benue-Plateau State and a German firm, Rau Imex, Ltd. The latter provided the machinery, established the farm itself and trained Nigerian staff to manage it. The farm grows mainly maize hybrid X 396B, and the reason for this is clearly stated in an official pamphlet:

> One would tend to wonder why some grains like the tall G/corn and millet are not grown. This is actually because the farm is fully mechanized and this has contributed to crop restriction so as to suit the kinds of machinery available.[24]

Such backward linkages among MNCs distort the use and production of food. For example, the maize hybrid grown is fed to livestock on the farm, and the seeds are sold to local farmers who have "taken to large-scale growing of maize" because it has "a ready market with the presence of poultry farms around."[25] The long-term effect of this scenario is that local farmers turn to maize production as a cash crop because it can be easily sold to poultry farmers, who produce eggs and meat for the richer urban markets. In the meantime, local farmers are destroying their fodder and food base by not growing traditional food crops, mainly millet and sorghum (guinea corn). Additional conflicts arise in the area of dependency on imported strains, loss of traditional, resistant varieties, and the monopolization of genetic materials by the MNCs.

Joint-venture agricultural production is seen as a way of making foreign companies increase their "industrial contribution to the national economy."[26] This is obviously true in one sense. On the Kuru livestock farm, for example, a Danish firm, ATALS Co., supplies equipment for the piggery, while a British firm, Pig Improvements Co., supplies the pigs. There is a feedmill on the farm that produces five tons of feed per hour. On the Bokkos farm, there are silos for storing up to 15,000 tons of grain, combine harvesters, and other machinery and vehicles. The farm hires planes from Ciba-Geigy West African Chemical Co. to spray for pests. Agriculture is thus capital-intensive and import-intensive. There is no linkage between this technology and the Nigerian peasant or the local industrial sector. Nigerian agriculture is therefore becoming increasingly dependent upon foreign firms. Furthermore, the cost of such technology is high, and should production fail to meet the food requirements of the constantly expanding urban population, Nigeria will be strapped with a large foreign debt. Compounding this problem is the political-administrative class and their allies, who expropriate money from agricultural banks, from the food-import trade, from irrigation schemes, and elsewhere, and transfer the money away from farming and indigenous industrial innovation into personal consumption (i.e. construction of houses for rent or personal use, or purchase of shares in manufacturing industries).

Since the onset of colonialism, Nigerian agricultural politics have exploited the peasantry, undermined the autonomy of a successful system and transferred agrarian wealth from the direct producers to the urban-based administrative class and their allies in the private sector. Even more alarming than the past record, however, is the solution proposed by the current regime to correct the problems created by earlier policies. As I have argued here, the opening up of the agrarian sector to multinational corporations and agencies such as the World Bank threatens to marginalize peasant production and render agrarian production dependent on foreign inputs, technologies, and genetic materials. The foreign exchange costs alone threaten to generate an agrarian crisis. With the Nigerian political-administrative class at the helm, the only visible constraint on this process is to be found in the populist policies of several state governments and in the resistance of the peasantry, as demonstrated by the recent Bakalori protests.

## Notes

1.   Mary Tiffen, The Enterprising Peasant:   Economic Development in Gombe Emirate Northeastern State, Nigeria, 1900-1968, Overseas Research Publication No. 21, Ministry of Overseas Development (London, 1976), 94.

2.   Gavin Williams, Nigeria:   Economy and Society (Oxford:   Oxford University Press, 1976).

3. S.A. Agboola, An Agricultural Atlas of Nigeria (Oxford: Oxford University Press, 1979), 192.

4. Report of the Working Party on Statutory Corporations and State-owned Corporations, 1968, Nigeria, Federation, 22.

5. B.U. Ekuerhare, "The Impact and Lessons of Nigeria's Industrial Policy under the Military Government 1966-1979" (Paper presented at Department of Economics seminar, Ahmadu Bello University, 23 January 1980), 5.

6. Yakubu Mohammed writes: "At the State level, at least, what makes the legislators envy the Governors' men is the power of patronage which the latter enjoy, but which the former don't seem to, like contract awards . . . . We still regard politics in this country as an avenue for money-making . . . ." New Nigerian (1 November 1980).

7. M. Tiffen, op. cit., 170.

8. Report of the Auditor-General on the Accounts of the Government of the Western State of Nigeria for the Year Ended 31 March, 1974, no. 2 (1976): 2-7.

9. Hamza Alavi, quoted in John Saul, The State and Revolution in Eastern Africa (London: Heinemann, 1979), 169. Peemans also noted this phenomenon taking place in Zaire in the 1960s. He wrote: "The use of the State power is likewise the means by which individual members of the emerging class can insert themselves into the structures of capital ownership, not only as administrators of State and 'mixed economy' enterprises, but also through savings on high salaries, various earnings and sideline incomes channelled by the exercise of public authority. Savings can be invested in trade, transport or real estate, or converted into land." J.P. Peemans, "The Social and Economic Development of Zaire since Independence: An Historical Outline," African Affairs 295 (April 1975): 163. To the extent that the ruling class in an African country is dominated by remnants of a feudal past, the level of expropriation of the state for personal accumulation and the disregard for the role of the state in providing public services and developing the economy deepen accordingly.

10. G. Williams, ed., op. cit., 136-153.

11. A. Lewis, Reflections on Nigeria's Economic Growth (Paris, 1967). A Government brochure now reads: "FOOD IMPORT BILLS ROSE TO OVER $3.7 BILLION--An Invitation to Invest in Plantation Agriculture/Animal Husbandry and Food Processing."

12. Phillip C. Asiodu, "The Impact of Petroleum on Nigerian Economy," New Nigerian, 21 November 1980.

13. The Nigeria Standard, 31 October 1980.

14. Tunji Braithwaite, in The Nigeria Standard, 1 November 1980.

15. National Concord, 20 November 1980. The level of accumulation that this class makes from their control of the imported food trade can be gleaned from recent cost of living reports. In Lagos, the price of imported rice went up from N35 per kilogram bag in June 1980 to N60 in August 1980. The price of imported brown beans went up to almost double its former price of N60, and the price of stockfish also went up by 50 percent in the same period. The Nigeria

Standard, 8 August 1980.

16. New Nigerian, 20 November 1980.

17. Tina Wallace reports that 113 out of 307 farmers at Chiromawa had lost some of their land, and of these, sixty-nine who tried to make up their losses by buying new land could not do so due to inflation in land prices. Tina Wallace, "Planning for Agricultural Development: A Consideration of Some of the Theoretical and Practical Issues Involved" (Revised version of a paper presented at the 9th World Congress of Sociology, Uppsala, Sweden, August 1978).

18. Brian C. D'Silva, Yahaya A. Abdullahi, and M.R. Raza, "Policies Affecting Rural Development in Nigeria" (Paper prepared for presentation at the 5th World Congress of Rural Sociology, Mexico City, 7-12 August, 1980), 10.

19. Sayre P. Schatz, Nigerian Capitalism (Berkeley: University of California Press, 1977), 190.

20. Asiodu writes: "By far, the bulk of the greatly increased resources from oil has been publicly saved and has financed a tremendous programme of infrastructural expansion and improvement. The figures of the plans--308 million naira in 1955-1962; 2.2 billion naira in 1962-1968; 3.2 billion naira in 1970-1974 and 30.0 billion naira in 1975-1980; or the 108 million Sovereignty Budget in 1961-1962 compared with 11.8 billion naira in nine months of 1980--underscore the vastly altered circumstances." New Nigerian, 22 November 1980.

21. A census of MNCs or their subsidiaries involved with irrigation in Nigeria, by category of line of specialization, is being put together. Of fadama land that is lost, Tina Wallace writes: "The Bakalori dam has affected 20,000 hectares of fadama land, all of which was highly productive in the wet season . . . . Yet the scheme will only create 24-26,000 hectares of irrigated land." Tina Wallace, "Agricultural Projects and Land" (February 1980): 8.

22. New Nigerian, 21 November 1980.

23. See Michael Hodges, Multinational Corporations and National Government: A Case Study of the United Kingdom's Experience, 1964-1970 (Lexington Books, 1974), 5.

24. Plateau State, Agricultural Ventures: Bokkos Farm Project, Kuru Livestock Farm, 2.

25. Ibid., 10.

26. Federal Republic of Nigeria, Joint-ventures Enterprises, 1.

*Peter Anyang' Nyong'o*

# 7 The Development of Agrarian Capitalist Classes in the Ivory Coast, 1945-1975

There are some important lessons to be learned from the attempts to promote commodity production in Africa during colonial times. In the cases of Kenya and the Ivory Coast, for example, participation by Africans in commodity production, either as capitalists or as various types of exploited labor, differed both in the ways production was organized and in the periods during which the different forms of surplus extraction were introduced. In short, the colonial systems of agriculture were different in each case not simply in terms of commodities produced for export, but also in the ways in which surplus was extracted and in the role of the state in changing the character of the precapitalist societies. This meant that the emergence of African capitalist and other classes of property was likely to follow different paths in each country, resulting, no doubt, in the different forms of class alliances and class struggles that gave the postcolonial states in the two countries their distinct characteristics.

Many scholars have talked about the "middle classes" leading the nationalist struggle for independence in various African countries. There is a simplistic notion that these middle classes all had the same bourgeois aspirations, and that they would generally be the domestic cushion on which neocolonial regimes would thrive. Although their political slogans and ideologies have at times differed, this simplistic notion also reduces the differences to "mere appearances."

The argument of this chapter, however, will be based on the premise that, given the specific political economy of each colony, the emergence of ruling classes in postcolonial Africa must be traced to their evolution in colonial times. Indeed, it is the class dynamics within these colonies that explain how

185

certain sections or fractions of the middle classes managed to put together power blocs  capable of exerting power in the postcolonial state.  In the case of the Ivory Coast, it was the small African capitalist class, emergent in the prewar era but consciously nurtured by the colonial state in the postwar era, which, having developed strong alliances with the rural small masters, became the center of this ruling bloc.

For the purposes of this chapter, we shall concentrate on the Ivory Coast, but without hesitating to draw comparative lessons.

The essential elements of the colonial system in the Ivory Coast were:  (a) African labor, exploited by the *colons* (the small community of French settlers), the trading houses, the colonial administration (especially in forced labor on public works), and a minority of the African "small masters";[1] (b) the *colons* and traders, though belonging to different sectors of the economy (the former predominantly rural and agricultural with much smaller capital and the latter urban and international with more capital in small-scale manufacture and commerce); and (c) the colonial state, interested not only in the fiscal health of the colony as a way of reducing the costs of administration (otherwise paid for by the metropolitan state) but also in the economic development of the colony, given the predominant interests of the trading houses and the vital interest of the French economy.

Like other European colonial empires during the Second World War, French colonialism suffered a serious crisis.  When the war was over, the crisis had so shaken the French Empire that the requirements of capital accumulation on a world scale compelled France to dismantle her colonial empire and reorganize the economic basis of the Overseas Territories in Africa. The new program, initiated from above but realizing its objectives by articulating with the existing colonial modes of production, created, in that process, new class relations.[2]

One factor in this creation was the existence of a political atmosphere in which the African "small masters" could express their economic interest in political terms, thus coming into direct conflict with the *colons* but finding allies, within the nationalist movement, in the very share-croppers and piece-jobbers they would exploit.  A second factor was the infusion of global political and economic relations (read imperialism) into the local scene, creating parameters for certain local political and economic battles, hence asserting imperialist hegemony on whichever class emerged the victor.  This, perhaps, is the tragedy of dependence.

This chapter is divided into two sections: the first section will discuss the collapse of the colonial system in the Ivory Coast and the emergence of the conditions for the development of African capital in agriculture between 1945 and 1960; the second section will cover the dynamics of state-sponsored capitalism in agriculture, class formation and class struggles from 1960 to 1975.

## The Collapse of the Colonial System and the Emergence of Conditions for the Development of African Capital in Agriculture

### Labor and Land Ownership Practices in the Colonial Ivory Coast

Forced labor for private enterprise (i.e., plantations of the *colons*) and public works (e.g., construction of roads) was overextended in French West Africa during the Second World War.[3] Not only did the war require that francophone Africans be drafted into the French army, it also necessitated reorganizing economic activities and social and administrative services to meet France's war needs. This entailed the reallocation of available manpower, leading to the prosperity of certain sectors of the economy at the expense of others.[4] Import-substituting industries were the first to mushroom under this "war economy."

Within the Ivory Coast, forced labor for private export production benefited mainly the French settlers.[5] In 1939, when the war broke out, there were barely 250 European *colons*, most of whom were found in the Gagnoa-Daloa region, mainly as coffee farmers. But *colons* also dominated the banana and timber industries, both of which were important in the export earnings of the Ivory Coast territory of the French West African Federation at this time.

The ways in which the *colons* obtained forced labor have been documented sufficiently by Frechou (1956) and Berg (1960).[6] Suffice it to say that the *colons'* close alliance with the traders and administrators meant that the whole colonial state machinery would be geared toward serving their common interests. During the war, opportunities for exporting certain kinds of commodities to France were limited, first because military material took priority in sea transport and second because, when France was occupied by Germany, the "home market" to which most of these commodities traditionally went was temporarily lost.[7] In certain cases, trade was directed toward the United States, creating new problems for France after the war. But since the traders had been used to supplying a few overpriced imported goods to the local market and exporting a few very cheap commodities, the war economy in the Ivory Coast actually promoted their interests.[8] In the case of coffee, Algeria was found as a new market with a big enough population to sustain Ivorian exports.[9] Moreover, because of the rationing of imported goods, the traders were even more assured of their sales and profits and could plan even better. The *colons*, on the other hand, provided a ready market for the high-priced consumer goods with the easy money they earned through the collaboration of the colonial state. In 1944, a state decree declared a premium of 1,000 francs per hectare for all planters who had twenty-five or more hectares of each crop under cultivation. In addition, for every kilogram of coffee harvested, a remuneration of six francs was given to the planter, qualified under the first clause.[10] All this meant that a *colon* was assured of at least some freely earned income which, given the limited quantity of consumer items available and a mentality of being besieged by a war, he could spend thriftlessly, much to the delight of the traders.

Only about fifty Africans benefited from this special decree, however. Others had to abandon their gardens and resort to shifting cultivation to crops they could sell more readily within the local environment. This frequently meant a move of several kilometers away from the coffee plantations to establish new sites for cultivating such crops, because few people wanted to interplant coffee with food crops at this time; that would have meant maintaining the coffee plants while also maintaining the useful food crops. The latter could be sold, while the former was almost always wasted. Moreover, since the market for the imported consumer goods was particularly bad for the Africans, emphasis was laid on self-sufficiency and essentials. Retail traders in the rural areas were given vouchers to buy only essential goods, such as rice, salt and cooking oil. Other goods--bread, petrol, fabrics, and sugar--were reserved for the Europeans. The black market flourished at all levels. When some retailers presented their valid vouchers to the French wholesalers (*commerçants grossistes de l'économie de traite*), they were often refused the purchase of the goods they wanted or were forced to buy worthless goods at exorbitant prices in addition in order to get the actual commodities marketable in the villages.[11] When such goods finally reached the village market, it was the peasant cultivator who had to pay for the losses of the retail trader.

The overall effect of this on the African peasants was to cause their momentary withdrawal from cash crop production. Shortages of consumer goods, very high prices, and inability to sell the cash crops meant that the little money the peasants had was almost valueless in practice. Concentration on subsistence agriculture was only rational action.

*Land ownership.* In the practice of share-cropping, it was recognized that those who welcomed immigrants reserved the right to receive a share of the harvest for a certain period of time. After this period was over, the immigrant himself became the rightful possessor--not actual owner--of the piece of land he had "mixed his labor with." Even in situations where settlement had resulted from conquest of the native occupants of the land by the immigrants, the former reserved ownership rights to this land; the latter merely enjoyed usufructuary rights. The Abron of the eastern Ivory Coast, for example, conquered the Koulango who were the original inhabitants of the area around Bondoukou. The Abron had no right over the forest in the area. In the beginning of the century, when an Abron wanted to harvest rubber or plant cocoa, he had to get the permission of the N'Goulango who was the descendant of the first occupant, and he had to pay a royalty, which consisted of half of one-third of the crop harvested. Similarly, if the land belonged to the Abron (as was the case in areas which were uninhabited when the Abron arrived and to which the Koulango did not lay claim), then a stranger who wanted to harvest rubber had to give one-third of his harvest to the Abron chief.[12] This is exactly what happened in the rest of Agni society in the Indénié and Sanwi kingdoms.[13] This was the framework within which primitive accumulation took place among the indigenes.

These mechanisms by which immigrants could become independent planters were, therefore, the same mechanisms that deprived the original landowners of their sources of surplus product, i.e., migrant labor. It would seem that the indigenous planter would eventually move to change this structure, to ensure stable extraction of surplus from those already installed as immigrants.[14] Two conditions, however, militated against this change. The first was the disequilibrium created in Baoule society (the source of the majority of migrant laborers) by the forced labor system of the colonial administration to

provide labor power for public works and the *colons'* plantations.  In the Agni country, due to the absence of *colons*
(except in the banana plantations of the Agboville-Abidjan
axis)[15] and the fear of "voting with their feet" as they had
done before, there was comparatively much less recruitment of
peasants into the labor services of either *colons* or the administration.  Secondly, being sparsely populated, the Agni of
Sanwi and Indénié welcomed immigrants as allies and people
who, once absorbed into the society as equals, would thereby
be integrated and help defend the realm.  Land, the Agni were
aware, was abundant, and it was a common practice for a
Baoule or even a Dioula immigrant to set himself up directly
as a planter if an Agni noble would concede to him some virgin forest over which to establish usufructuary rights.[16]  Such
immigrants were welcome both for the rents they paid and for
the manpower they added to the community as a whole.[17]

Legally, the colonial administration had made unused land
a property of the state.  A decree of 23 October 1904 made
the French state the owner of "vacant and ownerless lands;"
this included all virgin forests not effectively used for cultivation by the Africans.[18]  For Africans to have a legal right to
any lands--even those they used--they had to register the
lands and establish their ownership under common law.  The
law of 8 October 1925 declared the issuing of title deeds--not
necessarily with registration--to be the means of establishing
ownership rights.  Such rights were diametrically opposed to
customary land rights in the tributary or communal societies of
precapitalist Ivory Coast, but the Europeans successfuly used
them to get land concessions in the forest region.  In November 1935, a new decree was passed annulling all previous ones
and recognizing--in theory at least--customary land rights.  In
practice, this decree gave the administration a free hand by
providing a basis in law for the rejection of claims on land
already earmarked as concessions to Europeans or to be preserved as public domains in the manner of Crown lands in
British colonies.  It redefined "vacant and ownerless lands"
preventing, in many cases, the claim to customary ownership.

Article 1 of the new decree grouped in the "vacant and
ownerless lands" category all "lands not subject to a regular
and legal title deed of ownership or use and remaining untitled
or unoccupied for more than ten years."  Thus land that was
neither cultivated nor in common use (for example, pastures,
forests, and hunting districts) could legally and without process
of law be confiscated and allotted by the state to other persons.  The same applied to lands lying fallow for a longer pe-

riod (fallow periods of ten years or more were frequent and even normal in many of the areas under cultivation). It was not until after forced labor was abolished and the Africans had access to "free labor" that the restrictions these laws imposed on the manner in which the Africans could expand their plantations became entirely clear. Only then did land and its mode of acquisition become a political issue, an object of real class struggle.[19]

*Labor.* The war policies did heighten the issue of labor, however, and coagulated class struggles around it. On the one hand were ordinary peasants, fed up with forced labor and its attendant economic and social consequences; on the other were the emerging African cash crop farmers requiring more than family labor to keep their units of production profitable. These men, be they Bete, Baoule, Gouro, Agni, Attie, Abron, or Dioula, needed to bleed surplus labor out of the native or foreign migrant labor to stay in the business of being "planteurs."

Originally, the Ivory Coast posed a classic obstacle to the establishment of plantation agriculture:

> Where land is very cheap and all men are free, where every one who so pleases can easily obtain a piece of land for himself, not only is labor very dear, as respects the laborer's share of the produce, but the difficulty is to obtain combined labor at any price.[20]

The solution was forced labor of various kinds. But as the Africans became agricultural entrepreneurs, there emerged, first, the formation of self-employed workers (petty commodity producers) and, second, the hiring of a share-cropping strata in the forest belt. The possibilities for forced laborers to reinsert themselves into precapitalist forms of life by sharecropping made it imperative that *colon* capitalist agriculture appropriate land from the Africans or risk losing their labor. During the war, this was done in the *cercles* of the southern Ivory Coast. A commission of inquiry of the French National Assembly, set up under the auspices of the Communist group, reported that, by 1947, concessions of land to Europeans and classified forests in the south deprived Africans of almost three-quarters of their land.[21] The commission recommended that, in addition to abolishing forced labor, the people released from forced labor had to be given access to land and the technical know-how to use it rationally. The territorial assemblies, which represented the native residents, had the authority to grant concessions and decide what land would be used for public purposes (e.g., classified forests).

The right to determine one's own destiny in the postwar era, to use one's own resources for self-improvement, and to belong to a community of nations where bourgeois democratic rights provided the ideological framework for organizing social relations,[22] was imposed upon Ivorian society from above, just as it was forced upon France by the totality of the conjunctural social forces.[23]   But this does not mean that local class struggles played no role in shaping the form of political domination in the postcolonial society.   These struggles, and the local historical conditions under which they occurred, differentiate the specific postcolonial regimes that emerged in Africa after the Second World War.

## Emergence of State-supported Capitalism in the Peasant Economy

After the war, in spite of the tremendous disadvantages during the war, African coffee/cocoa production was quick to recapture prewar levels and even surpass them, and it was clear then that export agriculture was effectively in the hands of the Africans.[24]   Only the unfair practices of the colonial administration and the *colons* retarded their contribution to the metropolitan economy.   A 1948 annual report of the Department of Agriculture, which reviewed past policies and recommended new ones, stated the issue as follows:

> Coffee has remained a gathering crop (produit de cueillette) in Abengourou, Grand Lahou and Sassandra, but even more so in Abidjan, Aboisso, Agboville and Grand Bassam.   Planters lose about fifty percent of their production, due no doubt to the lack of labor but also to the lack of equipment and poor economic policies pursued by both the state and the trading houses up to now.
>
> Coffee production requires technical training, which should be provided by the state.   So far, Native Provident Societies, lacking qualified personnel, have done an insufficient job.   But even if the Africans were trained, they would require some capital to buy equipment and employ labor.   All this has not been forthcoming.
>
> If we are to expect anything from our 'emancipated subjects,' we must be prepared to pay for the anarchical methods and policies that we adopted towards the African growers in the period of 1933-1938, methods simply aggravated by the war, not caused by it.   Having had no concrete guidelines as to how coffee could be planted, having allowed both the administration and the colons to disrupt the labor

processes in the peasant households, we must, by criticizing what happened during that epoch, now create something that can promote the rational use of the resources of this country by her own people.[25]

The report then made the following recommendations: (a) of plantations neglected during the war, those which were completely tired (having produced coffee/cocoa for more than twelve years without use of fertilizers) were to be abandoned; (b) African planters should be grouped in blocks of ten hectares, each planter with his own parcel within the block, using good quality land, properly cleared and planted with selected seedlings from state nurseries certified by the French Institute of Coffee and Cocoa, and using machinery to maintain the plantation; and (c) given the preceding recommendations, the state itself should undertake responsibility of the technical formation of African planters and the advancement of capital to them.

State capital could be used then to accumulate more capital, both by those who advanced finance capital to the coffee growers (the state and other, private financial institutions) and by some of the capital recipients, who used it to hire the free labor. The solidification of the economic base of "small masters," the emergence of rural capitalists among them, and the development of their dominance in rural Ivory Coast constituted both a political project of the postcolonial state to create "support classes" among the cash crop growers and a logical outcome of class struggles in the Ivory Coast from 1894 to 1950.

Support for the formation of petty commodity producers--rich peasants, small masters, middle peasants, in short, a social layer using modern technical methods of production and borrowing money from the state to do so--had been proposed and attempted in various programs well before the Second World War. The difference between the prewar efforts and those of the postwar period was that the former lacked the full backing of monopoly capital. In the former period, the Ivory Coast was the backyard of Senegal,[26] a forest reserve in which a few *colons* made their first attempts at commercial agriculture.[27] Trading houses manipulated the import-export business, realizing tremendous profits;[28] the fiscal basis of the colonial state was based on direct and indirect taxation;[29] and the African ruralites, still conserving their natural economies, only produced surplus for the colonial economy upon compulsion, or, in cases where surplus labor was offered voluntarily, it was dovetailed to fit in with the production cycles of the subsistence economies.[30] In the postwar period, the efforts of the colonial state to create farmers out of the cultivators were updated by the infusion of capital and technology into rural agriculture. The Ivory Coast is no longer the backwater of Senegal;[31] it is rapidly becoming the center of the West African periphery.[32] In fact, Sarraut's age-old *mise-en-valeur* thesis is updated and executed, with the exception that *spécialisation à l'ivoirienne* is done on more than one front in the sphere of agricultural commodities:  it is a multi-cash-crop specialization with the surplus from coffee/cocoa production as its local base.[33] The state itself becomes a partner with private enterprise in economic development.    To the rural coffee farmers, depending on their class positions, the state can be a landlord, a shareholder, or simply a trader mediating between the coffee producers and the impersonal international world market.

Let us now trace the genesis and evolution of these various modalities of state intervention in cash crop production and see how, by 1975, the percentage share of coffee in total export earnings had been reduced significantly relative to other sectors of the economy.   What implications does this have on the surplus extracted from the coffee economy?   Which class has hegemony in the Ivorian society:   small masters in the countryside,   the   national   bourgeoisie,   or   the   international bourgeoisie?[34]   Or, in this context, do we only have capitalist classes, classes of property, and not a national bourgeoisie?

*Modalities of State Intervention:*
*Modernizing Techniques of Production*

*The colonial heritage.*   There is ample evidence in the national archives of the Ivory Coast that French administrators often took time to learn about African tools and techniques of work   and   to   write   monographs   that   proved   useful   to metropolitan industries interested in making tools adaptable to the African modes of production.[35]   Whenever expositions and shows were held in France, African tools were put on display, partly to attract the attention of toolmakers who could then produce simple tools to replace those made by the local blacksmiths and ironmongers in Africa.   Thus the need to plant cocoa/coffee for the exchange economy soon led to the need to buy industrially produced hoes, slashes, axes, and chopping knives; this, in turn, led to the demise of the Ivorian iron works of such places as Dume.   The need to export groundnuts led to the requirement that part of the harvest be set aside as next year's seedlings. These new methods of production and new techniques in the labor process required training and technical formation, argued the colonial administrators. To that end, in 1909 the colonial regime founded Indigenous Provident Societies (Sociétés indigènes de prévoyance--SIP) in French West Africa, beginning with operations in Senegal.[36]

It was argued that the natives of West Africa could not produce enough in export agriculture because they used archaic methods, employed unsophisticated tools, lacked capital, and were almost wholly at the mercy of nature.[37] The SIPs were founded, therefore, to train, provide credit to, and equip native labor to produce for the metropolitan market. But in the Senegalese Sine Saloum valley where they originated, the so-called cooperatives, formed to coordinate seed provision to the peasants, ended up as mechanisms for primitive accumulation by the colonial administrative officers and the African presidents of the SIPs.

In the Ivory Coast, SIPs did not begin to do real work until after 1931. But, whereas their principal aim was to organize the Ivorian cash crop growers in the production, transportation, and sale of their commodities, the administrators used them as a method of personal accumulation, just as had happened in Senegal.[38] Members would contribute annual dues for the purchase of farming equipment, but the funds would end up in the *cercle* commander's pockets or in those of local notables on the board of management. Belonging to the societies paid off, however, in that the administration recognized members as an elite group, men who could avail themselves of the use of more advanced productive forces and thus be an example to their primitive brothers and sisters.[39] There was always the publicly professed belief that *sociétaires* would get privileged treatment from the administration, even if the latter was slow to translate its promises into deeds.

The African coffee/cocoa growers' lack of enthusiasm for the SIPs was not because they opposed cooperative work or because they did not want to use modern methods; their withdrawal from the SIPs was due to the way the SIPs operated--very often for the personal enrichment of those who had political sway over the colonial state apparatus.[40] If the SIPs had had their own resources, instead of having to rely on the meager dues (*cotisations*) of the peasants they informed, they would have had greater success. Coffee production, argued an official of the Agricultural Service in 1948, would not have been a mere "produit de cueillette"[41] as it had been throughout most of the colonial period.

*The era of transition.* With the end of the Second World War and the commitment of France to consolidate the economic foundation of the cash crop growers, it would have been a contradiction to rely on the infamous SIPs as the state organism for the technical formation and animation of the peasantry. Thus the Investment Funds for the Economic and Social Development of Overseas Territories (Fonds d'investissement pour le développement économique et social-- FIDES) were established in 1946 as part of the program to modernize and equip the French colonies.[42] Some of the most important recipients of this fund were the research institutes, government training centers, and extension services, all of which were meant to do the work that the SIPs had failed to do. But these agencies, although they were equipped and ready to work, could not accomplish much without a well developed social and physical infrastructure.[43] Thus the first FIDES budget was heavily weighted on infrastructural development, this accounting for roughly 40 percent of the budget between 1946 and 1958.[44] Agriculture was next on the list, receiving about 20 to 25 percent of the total budget, and industry and utilities came third.[45]

Agricultural development was considered so important that, in 1949, a special Fonds d'équipement rural de développement économique et social (FERDES) was created by the French state to undertake rural development projects in French West Africa, especially through the modernization of productive forces: land redevelopment, creation of collective granaries, construction of market places, provision of seedlings, etc. (Table 7.1, below, shows the distribution of FERDES funds on various rural development projects as of 1958.) FERDES, unlike FIDES, was financed solely from funds raised within French West Africa: the federal budget, resources from the SIPs, municipal funds, and material contributions (e.g., seeds) from the peasant producers themselves.[46] From 1935, the coffee/cocoa funds raised by the Caisse in the Ivory Coast were a major contributor to FERDES.

Here again, however, we find the pattern of uneven development favoring the south and following the structure of development laid down by the colonial economy. Taking the example of road development, a total of 9,650 million francs *cfa* were spent between 1949 and 1958 from the combined resources of FIDES, FERDES, local/general territorial budgets,

TABLE 7.1:  FERDES Funds Spent According to the Nature of the Rural
Development Projects as of 1958 (in million francs cfa)


SOCIAL PROGRAMS

|  | Rural Schools | Sanitation | Paths, wells | Water development |
|---|---|---|---|---|
| $ of project | 178.0 | 78.0 | 14.6 | 66.0 |
| Amount | 465.0 | 121.6 | 370.5 | 203.3 |

ECONOMIC PROGRAMS

|  | Markets | Storage, etc. | Land Redevelopment |
|---|---|---|---|
| $ of project | 66.0 | 19.0 | 62.0 |
| Amount | 63.3 | 27.4 | 115.7 |

TOTALS

|  |  |
|---|---|
| $ of project | 615.0 |
| Amount | 1,367.0 |


Source: Inventaire économique, 241.


cocoa and coffee funds, and a special Road Development Fund
(*Fonds routier*).  Of this amount, 1,145 million francs *cfa*, or
11.87 percent, came from cocoa and coffee funds.  While this
might not appear significant at first, it must be remembered
that the local budget, contributing nearly 2,615 million francs
*cfa*, or 27.1 percent, to the road development project, raised
33.79 percent of its revenues (1948 figures) from direct and
kindred taxes from the people whose principal source of income was cash crop production.[47]  If cocoa and coffee production financed the dominant portion of the road development project, then one might conclude that it is not unfair
that most of the roads constructed were within the forest
zone--the coffee/cocoa region.  This cannot be measured in
terms of the lengths of roads built per *cercle*, since the figures
are given in global terms, but rather in terms of the number
of motor vehicles in use per *cercle*, which increases in proportion to the availability of good roads.[48]  The relationship between road development and coffee production is also evidenced by the fact that those who had surplus from coffee
production could invest in taxis and trucks.[49]  (The two phenomena reinforced each other:  as road transport was improved

and more people took the opportunity to try their luck at transport, the cost of transport was itself reduced.)[50]

*The neocolonial society and the technical formation of the direct producers.* A worker who works efficiently, argues Braverman, pays back to the employer much more than the employer "invests in him" in terms of education and technical formation.[51] The acceleration of work--whether by the use of machines, improvement of communication, or better trained manpower--leads to one goal: increase in the relative surplus value in capitalist society.[52] When the capitalist mode of production articulates with the precapitalist modes, suplus can be transferred from the latter to the former in two ways: by lengthening the working day of subsistence peasants in their efforts to produce commodities (absolute surplus value), or by the aforementioned acceleration of work (creating relative surplus value). What distinguishes the precapitalist from capitalist epochs, in which these forms of surplus value are realized, is that, in order to produce relative surplus value, economic life must be organized more and more on a voluntary basis, whereas for the extraction of absolute surplus value compulsory labor will often suffice. The latter is typical of the pillage economy and the economy of colonialism; the former is the *raison d'être* of neocolonialism.

We noted earlier that the failure of the SIPs was not only that members' dues were misappropriated but that the societies had failed, due to lack of capital and manpower, in the technical formation of the cash crop grower. Although accurate knowledge of the productivity of the peasant gardens was hard to come by, due to negligible land registration and the fraudulent weights used by the traders, some global calculations can be based at the *cercle* level to demonstrate that there were low yields in the subsavanna marginal zones (especially the Dimbokro-Bondoukou-Séguéla "V") and in the areas where coffee, as a *produit de cueillette*, had been grown for the longest time (see table 7.2). Figures for 1948 reveal that productivity was below average (253.6 kilograms/hectare) in the following circles: Abidjan, Agboville, Grand Lahou, Daloa, Dimbokro, Tabou and Séguéla. Even after the call by the Department of Agriculture to correct the archaic techniques being used, productivity seems to have decreased systematically (except in Dimbokro and Aboisso) during the years 1948-1958; the 1958 average yields per hectare were 17.4 units below those of 1948.

The Department of Agriculture's *Annual Reports*, 1948-1958, consistently blame the growers' lack of proper tech-

TABLE 7.2: Productivity in Cercles: 1948 and 1958 (in kilograms/hectare)

| Cercle | 1948 | 1958 |
|--------|------|------|
| Abidjan | 222.8 | 179.7 |
| Aboisso | 254.6 | 194.7 |
| Agboville | 215.3 | 138.2 |
| Sassandra | 265.3 | 173.6 |
| Grand Lahou | 250.0 | 200.0 |
| Gagnoa | 316.9 | 226.1 |
| Daloa | 217.1 | 175.8 |
| Abengourou | 466.7 | 248.9 |
| Bondoukou | 342.9 | 228.1 |
| Dimbokro | 204.9 | 339.7 |
| Man | 323.2 | 272.5 |
| Tabou | 200.0 | 250.0 |
| Bouake | 290.7 | 248.1 |
| Kitiola |  | 40.0 |
| Séguéla | 200.0 | 97.62 |

Source: Inventaire économique, 72-73.

niques for the low yields. Even where phytosanitary products were provided by the Provident Societies, the insecticides were applied too late to affect the damage already done by insect pests. A special service was needed for animation, a service both well-equipped and properly integrated into the state machinery of planning and research.[53] To achieve these goals, the Société d'assistance technique pour la modernisation agricole de Côte d'Ivoire (SATMACI) was founded under the auspices of the French government in 1958.[54] Its objectives were defined as follows: (1) to participate in the agricultural education and training of farmers; (2) to ensure the delivery of technical services and equipment to them so as to improve productivity; and (3) to participate in all studies and surveys aimed at establishing programs of development.

In the beginning, SATMACI had under its jurisdiction all the cash crops in the Ivory Coast: palm oil, bananas, rice, coconut, fruits, vegetables, coffee, and cocoa. As production increased and some of these crops expanded beyond the capabilities of SATMACI, special public corporations were created

to take charge of them and, after 1970, SATMACI was left
with only coffee and cocoa.[55]  While SATMACI had all the
other crops to deal with, less energy and resources were devoted to the animation and technical formation of co-
coa/coffee growers.

The program that SATMACI devised for improving productivity was that of monopolizing the growth of seedlings and
supplying them to farmers (still using extensive methods) who
wanted to start new gardens or replant old ones.  Because of
the larger amount of capital required, the intensive methods
were applied only to a small number of peasants who volun-
teered to regroup their gardens and cultivate in blocks closely
supervised by SATMACI.  In such cases, virgin lands were
cleared, and each member of the group owned at least a
hectare within the block.

But SATMACI, too, needed the technical formation of its
agents.  This, in the improvement of coffee and cocoa growing, was provided by the Institut français du café et du cacao
(IFCC).  The activities of the IFCC as a publicly financed research institute can be understood within the framework of the
state's role in regenerating the colonial economy after the Second World War.  While French businessmen had to look for
new areas of capital investment in Africa after the Indo-Chi-
nese debacle, private capital was not prepared to finance the
necessary unproductive preinvestment research.  The state, unlike private companies, could finance this research to the
eventual benefit of private capital and pass the costs on to the
taxpayers.

*Modalities of State Intervention:*
*Capital, Credit and Market Prices*

*Credit institutions: the colonial era.*   In colonial French
West Africa, finance capital had been the preserve of trading
houses with strong connections to the banks, particularly the
Banque de l'Afrique Occidentale (BAO).  BAO, although subjected to increased government control when it became the
sole bank of issue for French West Africa in 1901, continued
to be dominated by private interests in capital, management,
and policies.[56]  It became the principal deposit bank and, from
1904 on, enjoyed the right refused to the Banque de France to
participate in the constitution of companies, on the condition
that the total sum of its participation did not exceed one
quarter of its reserves.[57]  Unlike the Banque de France--which

was essentially a "bank of banks"--BAO was a bank of issue, a commercial bank, and a deposit and broking bank.[58]

Closely attached to the BAO was Crédit foncier de l'Ouest Africain (CFOA), the most important land bank in French tropical Africa, with over half its capital invested by real estate companies.[59]  For French West Africa, these were the major sources of finance capital and credit during most of the colonial period, and, like their parent trading companies, they chose their clients carefully and invested as little as would ensure maximum profits with the fewest risks.[60]  Trade and real estate accounted for 48.5 percent of the French private capital invested in Africa by 1940; banks and industries, 17.1 percent; mines and transport, 3.6 percent; plantations and stock raising, 30.8 percent; and forests, 12.5 percent.[61]  Public investments were merely identified as colonial loans, and the colonial administrators themselves were constrained to use those monies in manners that would ensure their eventual repayment.[62]

African cash crop producers did not receive credit from the state or private banks.[63]  The qualifying conditions for any loan immediately eliminated the peasant producer.  Therefore, credit institutions, such as the Caisses locales du crédit agricole, served primarily the needs of the European *colons* and traders.[64]

On 29 January 1929, the French government gave the BAO rights to furnish certain resources to the treasury, destined to help in the development of agriculture in areas where problems of capital arose.  Bringing in the bank at this particular time was important because the economic crisis of the worldwide depression made it very difficult even for the European traders and *colons* to raise the basic capital for the *caisses locales*.  But the BAO was the center of the financial power of the French import-export houses, and although nominally brought under the state's control in 1929, it remained essentially under the control of the "empire of high finance."[65]

The colonial administration reacted to financial problems of agrarian production by creating cooperatives and agricultural associations for Africans.  For then-Governor Reste, the major objective of these cooperatives was to pursue the goals that the European cooperatives were pursuing for their members.  The administration created two cooperatives for the Africans:  the Association agricole indigène de l'Indénié (AAII) based in Abengourou, and the Association agricole indigène de la Basse Côte d'Ivoire (AAIBCI) at Grand Bassam.[66]  The African cooperatives did not succeed, however.  First, having been instituted from above, they lacked the support of their supposedly native members. Second, when they did achieve some measure of success, their leaders imitated the behavior of the SIPs' leaders by misappropriating the funds.[67] The 1936 annual report of the Caisse national du crédit agricole showed the cooperatives in debt to the Crédit mutuel.[68] Nothing was done to improve the situation until after the Second World War.

*Credit and capital in a period of transition.* After the First World War and the Depression, the metropolitan state had attempted to stabilize the prices for agricultural commodities and to help reconstruct the French economy by establishing imperial preferential treatment for West African rubber and coffee (1931), bananas (1932), and vegetable products (1933-1934), with the support of the *caisses de compensation.* These compensation funds were built up by levying a surcharge on foreign imports of these products at French ports of entry and were then paid out to support producer prices in the colonies at times when they fell below a certain minimum level. Ivorian coffee growing increased as a result of this policy. During the Second World War, however, such preferential treatment and supported prices were discontinued. The United States increased its trade with French African colonies, thereby threatening to destroy the monopoly established by French trading houses during the colonial period and putting France in a difficult position with regard to its monetary policy in the overseas colonies.[69] The compensation system would obviously have encouraged colonial exports to France. At the same time, if the Overseas Territories discontinued their imports from France because of the higher prices, they would then spend their "francs" buying foreign goods and thus transfer their increased earnings to dollar or pound zones. Moreover, France needed its colonial possessions to export to the dollar zone, in particular to gain the foreign exchange for settling its debts.[70] Under these circumstances, empire trade conducted on a selective tariff basis--imposing quotas on goods imported into the colonies from outside the empire, with exchange controls employed to conserve stocks of gold and dollars--became the basic framework of monetary and commercial policies toward the colonies in postwar times.

The maintenance of privileged access to colonial markets was therefore translated into economic and, above all, monetary regulations, in particular as regarded the convertibility of colonial currencies into French francs and the fixed parity of these currencies.[71] Under the pretext of protecting colonies, which were becoming increasingly dependent on imports from the other monetary zones, the *cfa* (*colonies françaises d'Afrique*) franc was created under the currency board of the Caisse centrale de la France d'Outre-Mer in 1945.[72] In this way, French West Africa acquired a separate currency from the metropolitan franc, the principal difference being that the *cfa* franc did not follow the several devaluations of the metropolitan franc after the war and therefore had a higher value. Thus, the colonial commodity producers would not necessarily seek to sell in either the sterling or dollar zones simply because those currencies were stronger.[73]

While certain colonial export products, such as coffee, could be sold on the world market after metropolitan needs had been satisfied, other crops, notably groundnuts and cotton, were reserved for French buyers. Even here, however, a marketing arrangement was created which, while aiming to stabilize commodity prices for the direct producers, eventually gave the postcolonial state an opportunity to accumulate capital derived from the coffee/cocoa trade while simulataneously ensuring superprofits to the trading companies. On the surface, it was argued that the support funds were actually aimed at ensuring stable incomes to the producers, thus giving them an opportunity to save what they earned.[74] In reality, however, the funds functioned as insurance for the trading companies, who were now not only assured the market but would also receive "soutien" from the Caisse in periods when they had to buy from the producers at prices higher than the world market prices.[75]

*Price mechanisms and surplus: the coffee case.* The single most important institution to emerge during the period of transition, to consolidate the hegemony of the trading houses in the coffee economy, and to give the postcolonial state influence over the direction of coffee surpluses was the Caisse de stabilisation et de soutien des prix des produits agricoles (1962), referred to hereafter as the "Caisse" (originally the Caisse de stabilisation des prix du café--1955--et du cacao--1956).[76] The Caisse functioned within the context of extraction of surplus from coffee producers while increasing and stablilizing their income. In postcolonial times, the Caisse is one of those state apparatuses for the formation of classes and consolidation of the position of the dominant classes, notably the capitalists and technocrats, which have had significant influence over the use of state power.

In spite of the French efforts to encourage coffee imports from the Overseas Territories, metropolitan coffee drinkers preferred the more "aromatic" flavor of Brazilian coffee. And because of the Inter-American Agreement, which established the principle of quotas, it was possible for Brazil and other Latin American countries to sell in nonquota markets at prices that could easily undercut the French import-export houses. After the Second World War, the metropolitan state, not willing to pay for any support prices, decided to levy an export tax on coffee and cocoa to be used in the support funds when prices fell below world market levels.[77]    In French West Africa, this move was resisted by both the traders and the planters.[78]    The reasons can be found in the "budget politics" of the French West Africa federation at that time.[79]

The demands by Ivorian coffee growers for "price protection" against other, notably Brazilian, producers made it easier for the metropolitan state to introduce the idea of the Caisse de stabilisation des prix du café in 1955.[80]    The Caisse was to guarantee to the Ivorian producer a minimum revenue, while acting as a mechanism of compensation to reduce the effects of fluctuating world prices on the local market, and to reduce the difference between the world and local prices so as to improve the quality of Ivorian coffee by thus encouraging the producers.[81]    Since this was the same year that prices dropped below previous levels, the planters were enthusiastic in their support for the scheme. Previous sudden falls in world prices without the remedy of stabilization schemes had led to a sudden loss of income for the cocoa growers.[82]    Surplus during periods of plenty would, in fact, "support" the producers' revenues during periods of low world prices.[83]

Given France's low consumption of the robusta from its African colonies, only a liberalized protectionist policy within the rubric of stabilization schemes would ensure access to other monetary zones.[84]    Even after the Treaty of Rome, the Ivory Coast has needed access to other markets to dispose of all its coffee.[85]    But, with the stabilization of prices, coffee growing expanded both in area[86] and in terms of the actual number of producers.[87]    Their geographical distribution was more or less even in the forest zone, and it is in this zone that support groups for the independent ruling class emerged.

*Modalities of State Intervention: Mobility and Legitimation*

Increased production of coffee by the Ivorian peasantry, encouraged by the availability of labor from the north and rising world prices in the 1950s, led to an increase in the wealth of the peasant households in the forest zone. There was a general upward mobility in the southern rural economy, which contrasted sharply with the relative stagnation of the north. While the southern revenues from cash crops grew from 9.4 billion francs *cfa* in 1950 (at 1965 values) to 33.1 billion in 1965, northern revenues only increased from 750 million francs *cfa* to 2.1 billion.[88] The rate of growth in the two regions was more or less the same, but absolute wealth differed radically. This is demonstrated much more clearly when we look at per capita income in the two regions.[89]

Since the north served as a labor reservoir for the south, it helped create the surplus value with which the small masters of the south became upwardly mobile. In other words, the north was underdeveloped by the very process in which northern human resources, through the active participation of the state in such bodies as SIAMO (Syndicat interprofessionel d'acheminement de la main-d'oeuvre), developed the south.

But the south itself was not evenly developed. The eastern region, for example, had established a historical lead in the evolution of small masters, which was consolidated by the economic boom of the 1950s. Between 1950 and 1960, rural incomes from coffee and cocoa more than doubled in the southern zone. These incomes contributed the major share of income from cash crops in the peasant households within the zone. In the eastern region, coffee/cocoa incomes per capita rose from 140,000 francs *cfa* in 1950 to 169,000 in 1965 (at 1965 values). In global figures, however, the increase from 4.3 to 12.2 billion francs *cfa* meant that per capita revenues in the central region approximately tripled. This means that annual per capita revenues in the central region were just one-third of those in the eastern region. In other words, the east continued to gain both in labor and in income, showing that the pattern of economic growth inherited from the colonial era was not changed but consolidated.

At the level of the individual peasant households, the general upward mobility--with varying amplitudes within the forest zone--was not always maintained throughout the decade of the 1950s. Whenever coffee or cocoa prices fell, individual households surviving on less than two hectares of productive coffee/cocoa land were likely to be reduced to subsistence.

This vacillation in wealth, cyclical by the very way in which good and poor harvests naturally follow each other in the coffee culture, did not usually reduce these poor peasants to utter poverty except in the marginal zones of the central region, and even here the phenomenon of utter impoverishment was not felt until the late 1960s and early 1970s. There are various ways, however, in which the peasants struggled against this tendency to become impoverished; one was migration to new lands.

Among the medium and rich peasants, the general tendency was to seize opportunities to accumulate capital, especially by organizing and dominating the labor market via SIAMO, thereby becoming notable Ivorian planters. And the mark of a successful planter was not to be seen just in rural wealth, but in social wealth as well: ownership of means of transport, real estate, shares in parastatals, etc. The general interests of these upwardly mobile small masters converged in the ruling party to influence the state apparatus in making this mobility possible, albeit without unnecessarily ensuring that each small master achieved the same level of fortune as his cohorts. Thus, political decolonization was on the international agenda at a time when upwardly mobile peasants in the Ivory Coast were also anxiously seeking political power to back their economic programs. If the Africanized old economy had the promise of working to the economic advantage of the small masters, there was no political program more suitable to their interests than that which would consolidate this old economy.

The struggles of indigenous peoples versus nonindigenous peoples, of northerners versus southerners, and of small planters versus big planters were all fought around the issue of labor and terms of labor contracts during the '60s. With the state now stepping in with loan capital and making it possible for certain planters to run their operations as commercial enterprises, a polarization of wealth soon occurred among the coffee/cocoa growers whereby real capitalists emerged among the small masters. But as long as fractions of classes among the small masters had hopes of rising above their class, this social category remained, as its name suggests, a category: a differentiated social mass with its hopes pinned above its present achievement. Characteristic of all capialist societies, such a mass has a tendency toward conservative politics.[90]

Where this mass actually became the majority, and enjoyed full rights of citizenship while those from whom they did or could extract surplus labor were considered noncitizens, it can be seen how dependent the former group became on the state as a mediator in recruiting this labor from outside and in denying it full political power within. This role of mediation was also the source of legitimacy of the state as far as those planters were concerned. In the second part of this chapter, we discuss how the ruling class, with its capital accumulated essentially from agriculture, has sought to cement this alliance and to reproduce it over time through the use of state apparatuses and the share and distribution of surplus.

## State-sponsored Capitalism, Class Formation, and Class Struggles in Ivory Coast, 1960-1975

### The SAA

Out of the ashes of the Second World War, in response to the discriminatory practices of the colonial administration in favor of the *colons* and their refusal to buy from the African planters--thus denying them the source of capital accumulation and leading to the ruin of their fields--the African planters united in a trade union called the Syndicat agricole africain (SAA). The main objective of the SAA was:

> to take into its own hands the defence of the native interests by lead-
> ing, from 1944 onwards, an open struggle against the colons whose
> interests were diametrically opposed to those of the Africans.[91]

SAA membership was officially restricted to those with at least two hectares (approximately five acres) of land, but in practice it was open to smaller farmers willing to pay the annual dues of 300 francs. By the end of 1944, membership had grown to 8,548 with nearly half the members concentrated in the two Baoule-dominant circles of Bouaké and Dimbokro. Most of the other members were scattered throughout the forest zone, with the exception of the southeast region. This area, which produced 53 percent of the coffee and cocoa grown in the Ivory Coast, accounted for only 10 percent of SAA membership.[92] How was it that the most developed region in the Ivory Coast was, at the same time, the least interested in union politics?

*Structural contradictions for the SAA.* There were, first of all, regional contradictions created out of the unequal development of capitalism in Ivorian agriculture. The development of cash crop production in French West Africa had been carried out in terms of regional specialization. Within the Ivory

Coast, little was done to encourage the cereal economies of the north--to develop them for exchange--and the result was the use of this part of the country as a labor reservoir for the south.

Within the forest zone itself, there was equally uneven development. Houphouët-Boigny's contention was that forced labor was necessary within the forest region partly because there were risks in transporting labor from the north.[93] If we accept this argument, then the Baoule, living in the center of the wood-cutting industry with the main railroad and interterritorial highway bisecting their country and connecting their two principal towns, would be the people most vulnerable to the regime of forced labor. Baoule country also had one of the highest concentrations of *colons* in the colony (following after the Krou *cercles* of Daloa and Gagnoa); thus the Baoule were accessible for forced labor in the *colons'* cocoa/coffee plantations. In addition, the Baoule have always been the single largest ethnic group in the Ivory Coast (about 20 percent); everything else held constant, they would probably have provided the highest number of forced laborers compared to other ethnic groups.[94]

The uneven development between regions affected the Baoule-Agni relationship in colonial and postcolonial Ivory Coast. The Agni emerged as the least affected by forced labor. Having had access to cash crops earlier than others, and with a political formula that gave some autonomy to their precolonial political institutions, the Agni had more successful small masters than other regions. Thus, ethnicity became politicized and regionality a subject for class struggle.

Forced to emigrate out of their own region for the reasons given above, the Baoule found Agni country a hospitable place to settle. Speaking almost the same language and with similar cultural practices, the Agni--with a low density of population and enough land for all--were ready to welcome the Baoule, first as surplus labor and then as *chefs d'exploitation*.[95] Apart from the banana colonies of Agboville, Nieky, Sikensi Tiassale (in neighboring regions of the Lagoon tribes), and Aboisso and Anyama (inside Agni country), the Agni did not experience much European settlement. The banana colonies did not even produce in any major way until the mid-1950s, this in spite of much politicking by the banana groups in the 1930s.[96]

Moreover, after their emigration into the Gold Coast in 1916-1918, a more or less implicit permanent rapprochement was maintained between the Agni and the colonial authorities until the debacle of the Second World War when, once more,

Prince Kouame Adingra of Bondoukou (Indénié Agni) migrated with his people into the Gold Coast, declaring Agni solidarity with Free France.[97] It was the Baoule of Bouaké, the Voltaic people of the northern savanna, and the Adioukrou of Dabou who were left behind to fight the rubber war and provide cotton, rubber, oils, and fats to the Services du travail obligatoires.[98] By the end of the Second World War, the southeast had the highest number of immigrants from other regions of the Ivory Coast.

A SEDES study in 1967 noted that 2,400 Ivorians from outside the southeast region were permanently settled there by 1939. These immigrants, particularly in Agboville and Aboisso, were mainly Baoule.[99] Some had immigrated as early as 1915.

The distribution of the Baoule emigrating from their own homelands to settle in other parts of the forest region amenable to cash crop production was given by Etienne and Etienne as follows:    30 percent within the periphery of Baouleland (the "no man's land"); 29.6 percent in Agni country; 31.6 percent within the forest region between the Bandama and the Sassandra; and 8.8 percent in the southern regions of Grand Lahou, Agboville, and Grand Bassam, where, in any case, cash crop production tended to be organized more and more on the plantation scale (rubber in upper Dabour, bananas in Agboville, coconut on the Abidjan-Grand Bassam, route and palm oil in pockets along the coastline).[100]

During the SAA mobilization period, most Agni planters looked upon themselves as potential employers of labor from any part of the Ivory Coast. A threat was therefore posed to their social mobility by SAA politics that tried to emancipate Ivorian labor and turn to the Upper Volta for hired labor to replace the Ivorian laborers, "now become small masters," emanating from all parts of the country.[101] Because the Agni small masters were upwardly mobile well before the advent of the SAA, it stands to reason that they had less to gain from SAA politics, when compared to the Baoule, for example.[102]

*The SAA political program.*[103] The political program of the SAA was implicit in the resolutions of its first congress in Abidjan in September, 1944. These resolutions were to secure premiums for African producers, to organize cooperative sales in order to eliminate middlemen, to obtain a quota of imported cloth and agricultural implements, and to secure a more equitable allocation of manpower for its members.[104] Thus, when SAA president Houphouët-Boigny ran for the Constituent Assembly, one of the main reasons for his winning was that

he promised the electorate freedom from forced labor, more consumer
goods, the opening of new schools and dispensaries, and the suppression
of taxes.[105]

The Parti démocratique de la Côte d'Ivoire (PDCI)--the
Ivorian branch of the French West Africa Rassemblement
Démocratique Africain (RDA)--was built out of the organizational strength of the SAA as a trade union. After four to six
years of political resistance--which became violent between
1948 and 1950, when PDCI leaders tried to curb the militancy
of their followers--the local *colons* and traders realized that
the PDCI meant to harm them economically. They decided it
was necessary to collaborate with the PDCI rather than es-
trange it through the Estates General of French Colonisation
(Etats généraux de colonisation française).[106]     Houphouët-
Boigny himself made it very clear that the PDCI was a party
whose primary concern was to win economic advantages for its
members and not to flirt with political ideologies. His famous
statement before the Damas commissioners, asserting that it
was incomprehensible to think that he, a Baoule chief with
several wage-workers and a big plantation, would be a Communist, clarified his own class interests.[107]

The PDCI leadership was willing to make coalitions and
alliances even at the expense of some of its militant supporters. In this way, PDCI nationalists consolidated themselves in
political power with the trade unionist programs of the SAA,
and it was no wonder that, as the party assumed state power,
the trade union outlived its usefulness and found its resting
place in the party archives.

The battle to ensure French imports of Ivorian coffee and
to grant it protected prices and the fight to keep Ivory Coast
out of the French West Africa federation because of its fiscal
advantages were both examples of economic demands for
which the Ivory Coast leaders depended heavily on cooperation
from the metropole.[108]     These were issues that did not question the foundations of the Ivorian economy; to the contrary,
they took the foundations as a given and worked for the economy, as it was, to be organized to the advantage of the most
dominant classes in the nation.

## SIAMO

Once forced labor was abolished and the Baoule and others
"emancipated" to be small masters in their own right, there was
a "labor rush." The people abandoning forced labor in the

European plantations moved either into new frontiers (mainly towards the west) or to the "no man's lands" within their own regions, to begin their lives as *chefs d'exploitation*. Given the labor required to establish a fresh plantation, most potential planters needed surplus labor to cooperate and enter into sharecropping arrangements for at least the period of the first harvest. The only place this surplus labor could be found was in the non-cocoa/coffee-growing region of the north: the savanna country of the Mossi and other Voltaics.

But the Mossi had established a system of migrating to the Gold Coast and had avoided the low wages and forced labor conditions in the Ivory Coast. They too had a *petit frère* practice for recruiting labor, and a sudden change in market conditions would not necessariy alter this pattern immediately. Moreover, given that, as target-workers, they had already established their seasons of migration in accordance with their work schedules, it was difficult to change this unless more than economic forces influenced their initial behaviors.

It was therefore necessary that a system be found by which the Mossi laborer would be made aware of market conditions in the Ivory Coast and be led to make the choice to migrate there instead of to the traditional market of the Gold Coast. Under the auspices of the SAA leaders, the Syndicat interprofessionel d'acheminement de la main-d'oeuvre (SIAMO) was founded in 1951, organized in conjunction with the Labor Department (Office de la main-d'oeuvre), to recruit labor in Upper Volta (now Burkina Faso) and the northern savanna region of the Ivory Coast for work in the forest region. Just as the state had previously stepped in to help recruit forced labor for the *colons*, so it stepped in now to recruit free laborers for the colonized. In other words, economically the colonized were already in the process of being decolonized: colonial political relations had fast become antiquated with the rapid success of this economic development.

Before the creation of SIAMO, it was very difficult for the African coffee and cocoa farmers to get labor from Upper Volta. The *colons*, however, had a system by which the Moro Naba, paramount chief (or king) of the Mossi,[109] and Gbon Coulibaly, the chief of the Senoufo, supplied 30,000 and 6,500 forced laborers respectively to the southern European plantations.[110] Although this human traffic was abolished by the general abolition of forced labor in 1946, Coulibaly and the Moro Naba continued to want the surplus they obtained by trafficking their young men to the south. Approached by

Houphouët-Boigny and the SAA men for a deal, Coulibaly, then about 100 years old, said:

> We would like, with Houphouët, to try an experiment, because it is very painful for us to recruit by force, each year, 6,500 of our young men-- some of whom never come back--to work in European plantations. Those who come back are lean and exhausted.[111]

The next day Houphouët-Boigny recruited 4,500 voluntary workers. He then went to Upper Volta where, with the Moro Naba's consent, he got 3,500 volunteers. The terms of work Houphouët-Boigny offered were attractive. The worker could opt for either sharecropping or monthly salaries. There were to be two types of sharecropping: *abu-sam* (or sharing in thirds) and *abu-dyan* (sharing in halves). Cocoa work was regulated by the former method and coffee work by the latter. In addition, each worker would get accommodation and food from his landlord; in the case of the salaried wage laborer, twenty francs per day was the agreed-upon rate, instead of the 3.5 francs paid by the European *chantiers* and *colons*. The SAA labor market won the day,[112] and the result was the ruination of the *colon* plantations, which not only lost labor already hired out but also could not resort to fresh supplies from the northern labor reservoirs.[113] The foundation was now laid for the economic triumph of an African rural bourgeoisie.

Dwelling on this theme, Houphouët-Boigny said to the Damas commissioners:

> A lot has been said about an African elite, and most among you have been led to believe that this elite comes from an old African bourgeoisie, that they are bourgeois by birth . . . Error, error, error; gross error! Of any ten people who are members of this young elite, you would rest assured that in the Ivory Coast, only two would be descended from old bourgeois families.[114]

In other words, some small masters, "descended from coffee and cocoa," had also climbed to the top. And now the state, through SIAMO, was to consolidate its roots on that plateau of men who had arrived there without necessarily working for what they had.

The first year of SIAMO operation was a great success. Just over 50,000 workers were recruited at a total cost of 30.63 million francs *cfa*: 20,000 for African planters and 30,000 for the European farmers and woodcutters.[115] During the following years, as European plantations diminished because they could not afford to compete with the Africans since the abolition of forced labor, SIAMO's services focused increasingly on the demand for labor by the African planters. But, at the same time, it was becoming more and more expensive to recruit. While it had cost 30.63 million francs *cfa* in 1951 to recruit 50,000 workers, in 1958 it cost 54 million francs *cfa* to recruit 20,740 workers.[116] It was clear that the Mossi were taking advantage of the "relatives clause" in the work contract (which paid the transportation expenses of the recruit's family to the new work site). Records kept by SIAMO were also not very accurate in distinguishing between those recruited by their particular employers, hence needing reimbursement, and those recruited by SIAMO. Thus reimbursement became a mechanism for primitive accumulation by officials and transporters. In any case, as the Voltaics became more aware of the market conditions in the Ivory Coast, SIAMO became an increasingly irrelevant institution.

*The Availability of Labor and Regional Social Structures*

The availability of labor for most of the small masters in the coffee/cocoa economy during the 1950s and 1960s altered the social structure of the regions. The southeast region quickly lost its dominance of coffee/cocoa production. There were approximately 40,000 cocoa and coffee farmers in the Ivory Coast in 1944, 120,000 in 1956, 200,000 in 1959 and 550,000 in 1974.[117] While the southeast region produced 53 percent of these cash crops in 1942, compared to the center's 22 percent and the west's 25 percent, in 1957 production was more evenly distributed at 34, 31 and 35 percent, respectively.[118] (See table 7.3, below.)

It is to be noted that coffee revenues did not even out during these years, however, due to the different productivities of the regions. Rather, coffee/cocoa revenues remained more or less constant in the eastern region--the oldest coffee/cocoa-growing region--due to the age of the trees and the small expansion of gardens following the scarcity of labor. The tremendous increase in the west is accounted for by the fact that this was a "new frontier," while in both the center and the center-west the expansion of already existing fields by "emancipated" laborers and immigrant labor explained the great growth in cash crop income.

Thus, since 1960, coffee production continued to increase more or less in the same pattern in the four regions. (See table 7.4, below.)

TABLE 7.3:  Regional Distribution of Coffee and Cocoa Revenues, 1950-1965

| Region[a] | Revenue per head | | Percent increase |
|---|---|---|---|
| | 1950 | 1965 | |
| East | 14.0 | 16.9 | 20.7 |
| Center | 3.0 | 11.0 | 266.7 |
| Center-west | 4.2 | 10.7 | 154.8 |
| West | 1.2 | 7.2 | 500.0 |

[a] The eastern region here includes the former Circles (now Departments) of Abidjan, Agboville, Aboisso, Abengourou and Bondoukou; center comprises Dimbokro and Bouaké; center-west, Daloa, Gagnoa, Bouaflé and Divo; and west, Guiglo, Man Biankouma, Danané and Sassandra (formerly Sassandra, Soubre, Tabou and Guiglo).

Source:  Samir Amin, Le développement du capitalism en Côte d'Ivoire (Paris: Editions Minuit, 1967), 290-291.

TABLE 7.4:  Coffee Production by Region, 1960-1970

| Region | Production in tons (000) | | Percent Increase |
|---|---|---|---|
| | 1960 | 1970 | 1960 to 1970 |
| East | 56.0 | 77.1 | 37 |
| Center | 59.0 | 56.0 | -5 |
| Center-west | 47.0 | 71.0 | 51 |
| West | 25.5 | 40.2 | 58 |

Source:  Ivory Coast, Ministry of Agriculture, Statistique agricole (1973): 65.

The decrease in coffee production in the central region, particularly in north Dimbokro and east Bouaké, is due to the increasing marginality of these areas. Coffee incomes have decreased there because of exhausted soil conditions resulting from the extensive methods of cultivating coffee used since the 1950 coffee boom. The Baoule coffee growers have reacted to this decrease in three ways: by turning to other cash crops, i.e., diversifying their cash crop dependence; by migrating out of the marginal coffee zone into the emergent coffee zone of the western region; and by intensifying other forms of petty commodity production (e.g., village artisanry) as alternative sources of money incomes. These forms of class struggle are replicated in the west and center-west regions, but their magnitude and intensity vary according to the class locations of planters affected and whether or not decreasing returns are also due to the factor of labor availability.

The first type of reaction, diversification of crops, is induced mainly by the state, which has encouraged rice-growing in the central region, vegetables in the Ferkessedougou area, palm oil along the coast, and pineapples in the Ono-Bonoua region. Except for rice, all these are grown by peasants as part of *outgrower projects*, attached to industrial plantations run on a private or semiprivate basis. Migration from marginal regions to new coffee lands of the west (the second reaction to decreased coffee incomes in the center) implies the export of class contradictions from areas abandoned by the emigrants to the new lands in which they settle. The Ivorian state has taken action, however, to restructure relations of production by becoming the proprietor of coffee plantations (the CEDA program) and by limiting its outgrowers to people not previously engaged as coffee/cocoa *chefs d'exploitation*. Regarding the third type of reaction, there is almost no available data correlating wealth of peasant households and nonagricultural or artisanal activities. The 1974 *National Agricultural Census* and the Ministry of Planning analysis of nonagriculutural activities based on the data of the census both give mainly global figures, breaking them down by administrative units and types of activities.[119]


*The State and the Formation of Classes in Agriculture*

The 1974 *National Agricultural Census*[120] of the southern region (forest zone) revealed that there were approximately 443,400 units of production (small holdings, farms, and medium-size plantations) in the forest zone, each accounting for 7.4 residents, with a total population of 3.3 million people --56.9 percent of the total Ivorian population.[121] Within this agricultural population, only 15.6 percent grew neither coffee nor cocoa; 78.6 were predominantly coffee growers.  Only 1.4 percent of the units of production had solely palm oil (mainly in the departments of Abidjan and Sassandra along the coast); 1.8 percent had only coconut (in the same departments); and less than 1 percent had bananas, cotton, pineapples, groundnuts, and vegetables as the only crops produced.[122]  In other words, coffee and cocoa production is still dominant, and diversification programs have only affected a minority in the forest zone.

In general, therefore, larger plantations hire more wage labor--permanent or seasonal--than smaller ones (see table 7.5, below).  Medium-size plantations rely more on seasonal sharecroppers and task-jobbers, while small household farms depend predominantly upon family labor.  Where farm size varies according to region, wage labor will vary likewise. Thus, as the central region becomes less productive because of its marginality as a coffee-producing area, household farmers migrate to the west to find new plantations and, because of their limited capital, set up household farms similar to those they could not maintain in the region they just left.[123]

TABLE 7.5: Labor and Capital by Farm Size in the Forest Zone

| Size (in hectares) | Number of farms | Percent hiring permanent labor | Percent hiring temporary labor | Percent belonging to SATMACI[a] |
|---|---|---|---|---|
| 0.5-1.99 | 266,108 | 6.99 | 52.43 | 4.93 |
| 5.0-19.99 | 167,745 | 28.03 | 67.69 | 11.97 |
| 20.0-99.99 | 9,442 | 66.96 | 81.92 | 20.75 |
| Over 100[b] | 100,150 | 00.00 | 100.00 | 100.00 |

[a] SATMACI, as we shall see later, provides means of production to farmers by credit arrangements that necessitate capital investment.

[b] Plantations over 100 hectares were not included in the census; they had a separate census that was not published by 1975. These figures are based on Ministry of Agriculture estimates.

Source: National Agricultural Census (1974).

Because of the continued use of the extensive method, neither use of more labor nor size of farm relates to productivity. Those who receive capital and technical assistance from SATMACI, however, are beginning to have higher yields.[124] It has been increasingly necessary to improve productivity and control total production because of the constraints put on producer countries in the Third World by the limited demands of the world market.

*The International Coffee Agreements.*[125]    Central to the International Coffee Agreement of 1962 (ICA-I) was the establishment of a system of quota allocation based on production capacity and share of market--with a view to maintaining a long-term equilibrium between production and consumption. This would ensure remunerative prices for producers.    The parties to the agreement recognized the necessity of ensuring that the general level of coffee prices did not fall below the 1962 level.[126]

The effect of this agreement on producer countries was that they had to tailor their coffee production within the limits of exportable production.    A diversification fund, set up by the same agreement, was aimed at redirecting productive activity to cash crops other than coffee.    From the point of view of direct producers and *chefs d'exploitation* in the Ivory Coast, however, this meant diversification of dependency at two levels:    first, at the level of dependence on the state as the only institution that could redirect capital investments into new areas of cash crop production, since to sell to the international market, it is necessary to pass through parastatal marketing institutions such as the Caisse; and second, dependence on international social forces that regulated which commodities were in demand on the international market.[127]

*State Response to the Requirements*
*of the World Coffee Economy*

The Ivorian state had actually responded to the demands of the world market by encouraging and/or starting diversification programs in pineapples, palm oil, rubber, cotton, and bananas. Thus, while coffee/cocoa had accounted for about 68 percent of the commodity exports of the Ivory Coast in 1963, by 1973 their share had fallen to 38.2 percent, although in absolute terms coffee/cocoa exports earned 37,025 million francs *cfa* more than the 1963 figure.    Wood accounted for 22 percent of export earnings in 1963 and 30 percent in 1973; tropical fruit (mainly bananas and pineapples) and vegetables provided 7.6 and 3.1 percent in the two years; vegetable oils, exported in semifinished form, were also becoming more important in Ivorian foreign trade.[128]

Two important state projects provided the mechanisms for this diversification scheme: (a) intensification of petty commodity production to conserve on labor and destructive use of land; and (b) expansion of state participation in cash crop production by increasing capital investment in plantation agriculture in an alliance with foreign private and public capital.

Within the coffee economy, intensification of production was undertaken by SATMACI, using the block system and technical animation and formation of individual planters who offered to be SATMACI adherents. Such a person would be committed to using intensive methods of coffee production according to SATMACI guidelines, which required the use of selected seedlings, fertilizers, insecticide treatment, mulching, pruning, and systematic and regular weeding of fields.[129] This entailed working according to a strict agricultural calendar dovetailed with the annual cycles of the traditional coffee culture. SATMACI worked out which food crops could most suitably be interplanted with coffee, to ensure regular food supply to households cultivating coffee or cocoa. In general, it was those able to afford more temporary or permanent hired labor who could have the surplus labor necessary to produce according to the SATMACI calendar. Poor peasants, those with less than five hectares of cocoa and relying mainly on family labor, could adhere to SATMACI only to become a true proletarian working at home.

Coffee producers, as petty commodity production is intensified, become more subjected to capital in different ways. In addition to relying increasingly on the state for capital investment and technological formation, they become more and more divorced from other petty commodity forms of exchange as the state and monopoly capital invade most relations of exchange in the rural areas: buying and selling agricultural produce, for example, or drying and deshelling coffee, transporting coffee to export centers, lending money, building homes, etc.[130]

*The SERIC formula.* One aspect of the elimination of petty commodity trade in the rural coffee economy was the establishment of SERIC (Société d'études et de réalisations pour l'industrie caféière et cacaoyère) in 1970. With 55 percent state and 45 percent private capital (including capital from the local import-export houses of the Société Nouvelle, Compagnie Ivoire Café, Jean Abile Gal, Daniel Angel et Fils, Compagnie Ivoirienne de Promotion pour Exportation et Importation, Eburnea), SERIC was meant to take over the buying and deshelling of coffee in the countryside, its conditioning, and its embarkment to the port of export, Abidjan.[131] A factory capable of treating 10 to 12 percent of the national coffee product (67,000 tons) while in dry berries would decorticate, select, store, and condition them, thereafter to be delivered to the import-export houses, who would receive quantities according to a formula worked out annually by the Caisse.

The effect of the SERIC program was that petty traders in circulation and decortication would be eliminated from the process of production, as would traders and transporters. Among the 8,317 decortiquers in the forest zone, only 1,081 were owned by artisans whose only means of livelihood was the decortication trade.[132] The first SERIC factory in Toumbokro[133] displaced a maximum of sixty-five decortiquers within the department of Dimbokro alone,[134] but it was held that the machines were sold to other regions where SERIC had not extended its activities.

SERIC's aim is to eliminate both the village buyer and the trader as elements in the process of commercialization and to encourage buying products by SERIC from *groupements à vocation cooperative* (GVCs). Transporters would then remain as intermediaries, but their remuneration would come neither from the exporters nor the GVCs: it would be paid by SERIC directly from its receiving points at the factories. Moreover, most transport trucks would, eventually, belong to the GVCs. This would not only simplify the process, it would also reduce the many temptations for buyers to cheat producers on weights in order to earn higher commissions from their traders.

The SERIC program would, secondly, reduce the tendency of buyers to do business with planters. Quite frequently, in the past, the buyer consented to buy rice, mattresses, paraffin, etc., from Aboisso and to deliver them to planters in Mafere or Kohourou, on the condition that the money was deducted from the price the buyer paid the producer for his coffee or cocoa. It was always likely that the buyer would cheat the planter and deduct more than the goods were worth. More serious was the borrowing of money by planters from the trader or the buyer, money they were forced to pay back in coffee or cocoa. Often the small planter ended up getting nothing from his harvest because the buyer had charged enormous interest on the money loaned. Since the buyer/trader monopolized the market, the planter had no alternative but to go further into debt for the coming year. The immediate struggle of such a planter was not so much against the general low prices of cocoa/coffee as dictated by the world market, but rather against the village buyer or local trader with whom he traded.[135]

Finally, this system did not allow the planter to value quality production. The village buyer, as well as the trader, is interested above all in quantity rather than quality. Buying from so many planters at once, he does not have the time to test and examine each delivery. Hence planters make no effort to innovate and improve their methods of production in order to harvest better quality coffee. The new SERIC program would have facilities to grade coffee once it arrives at the factory, giving each GVC delivery its grade per sack and thus allowing a GVC to know which one of their members delivered what grade of coffee. Although the plan to pay planters according to grade and quality was unlikely to be executed, it was nonetheless a potential threat to the GVCs and motivated them to insist their members improve the quality of their produce.

We have seen how local traders and owners of decortiquers are eliminated from the commercial network. In the meantime, the state, through SERIC, prepares to appropriate the surplus formerly appropriated by the decortiquers, albeit "for better services" to the planter. In a similar way, the surplus on which local traders and buyers--mediating between the producer and the import-export houses--used to survive will either go to the state, to the state-appointed transporters or to the GVCs.

Where the state has encouraged these village cooperative societies[136] to coordinate the selling of coffee, more and more village small traders have been put out of the coffee and cocoa business. The big transporters, clients of the Caisse, stay in business. If the cooperatives completely took over the transportation of coffee from the planter to the SERIC factory using their own vehicles, the big transporters would simply intervene between the SERIC factory and the port of embarkation. While this would be an efficient arrangement for the big transporters--most of whom are owned by the import-export houses and wood-processing companies--it also makes it likely that the state, with or without some elements of national capital, would move into the transportation business.[137] In recent years, the traditional local French trading houses have there-fore reacted cautiously to such state-sponsored ventures.

On 30 December 1975, a meeting was held in Abidjan by the coffee exporters. At this meeting, the exporters decided to recommend to the government that the SERIC program be radically altered, that it would be both politically rewarding and economically rational if twenty to thirty decortiquers, each processing about 20,000 tons of coffee, were built in different regions of the Ivory Coast, instead of the five previously en-visaged by the SERIC plan. The Toumbokro experiment, the exporters argued, had been too expensive to run: the roof of the storage building had collapsed at the height of the harvest, holding up work for thirty days, while chains of trucks stood in wait with coffee in them. With smaller factories, such dis-asters would be avoided or at least their scale reduced. It was not quite clear whether the Toumbokro failure should be blamed on the Jean Abile Gal managers or on the very way in which the factory was conceived: one contention was that the factory had been poorly designed and could not work. But, argued the exporters, whatever juridical formula was retained, even if there were to be an increase of SERIC capital in cre-ating new factories that conformed to the interests of the ex-porters, the management of those decortiquers should be in the hands of the profession, that is, the import-export houses. The profession should therefore be prepared to demonstrate its dynamics by running these factories at a profit.[138]

Here, then, a professional class is found which, without taking part in production, captures the management of pro-duction as a whole and economically subjugates the producers to its rule. These professionals make themselves the indis-pensable intermediary between the two producers, exploiting them both. On the pretext of saving the producers the trouble and risk of exchange, finding distant markets for their prod-ucts and thus becoming the most useful class in society, a class of parasites arises, genuine social sycophants who, as a reward for very significant real services, skim the cream off produc-tion at home and abroad, rapidly amass enormous wealth and the corresponding social influence and, for this reason, are destined to reap ever new honors and gain increasing control over production.[139]

*BNDA loans.* The National Bank for Agricultural Devel-opment (BNDA) is a postindependence successor to the Na-tional Caisse for Agricultural Loans (CNCA) which, though founded by the new Ivorian regime in 1959 to finance agricultural development for small farmers, had limited capital to draw from. The CNCA was financed mainly by public funds, ten percent of the yearly profits realized by the Caisse from 1966 on; before then, it had functioned on small annual loans from the Special Budget for Equipment and Investment. Because it was a public body whose operations were politically inspired, CNCA loans were not properly repaid. After its first two to three years in operation, the CNCA cut back drastically on loans to small farmers. In its 1966-1967 Annual Report, the director wrote:

> Our contribution of loans to village planters, who are the majority of our clients, remains the smallest because of the absence of guarantees. The only way that this situation can be remedied is to find some extension service--or similar such organization--which can administer loan repayment on behalf of the peasants.[140]

The BNDA was therefore formulated as a parastatal institution to handle agricultural credits on a commercial basis and to "take politics out of the financing of agricultural development."[141] It was established that, for channeling loans to small-scale farmers (those with less than ten hectares), appropriate public extension services would be used to handle the distribution and repayment of the loans. For the coffee/cocoa program, the services of SATMACI were readily available to the BNDA. Given the fact that SATMACI was committed to intensifying coffee/cocoa production, an offer of channeling capital investment to its predetermined programs was a welcome opportunity.

SATMACI handled only emergency loans for the BNDA. These have a duration of seven to eight months. Given out every year at the commencement of the harvesting season, they are intended to help the farmers solve emergency problems caused by the rush to get crops in on time for the traders. But as the beginning of the harvest season coincides with the opening of the school year, most farmers use this money for paying school-related expenses, in other words, investing outside of agriculture.[142]

Just before the harvest season begins, usually around July, a group of ten to thirty villagers appeals to the nearest BNDA office for the loans, making their demands on the basis of the harvest each member expects at the end of the year. From the records held at the local SATMACI office, BNDA can cross-check their figures before granting the loan. While the loans are paid directly to the individual members of the group, the group as a whole is responsible for the repayment by each member.

On the average, emergency funds amount to 15,000 francs *cfa* per recipient. Given that the average productive farm size is 0.536 hectares[143] and that the average yield per hectare is 407 kilograms, this figure represents 22 percent of the village farmer's annual income from coffee calculated at 170 francs *cfa* per kilogram (1975 prices) of green coffee.[144]

The BNDA managed to reach 24 percent of the Ivorian households through the emergency funds in 1975, with regions having higher concentrations of cash crops receiving the greatest number of loans. Thus, in the *sous-préfecture* of Aboisso, the leading coffee-growing village, Kohourou, surpassed all the other villages in the number and total amount of emergency loans received.[145] Djatokro and Bafia, marginal coffee-growing villages, were at the bottom of the scale. The cereal-growing north is almost totally untouched by BNDA loans.

*The Caisse.* The Caisse functions as a mechanism for determining how part of the surplus value realized in coffee/cocoa production will be appropriated. It appropriates part of the surplus value for itself and, through the state's Special Budget for Investment and Credit (BSIE), channels some of it to finance development projects. As table 7.6 shows, the Caisse increases its contributions to the BSIE treasury as diversification programs are undertaken. In other words, coffee/cocoa surpluses finance a good part of the cotton, rice, palm oil, sugarcane, paper-making, and other projects.

The Ivory Coast budget depends regularly, and to a considerable degree, on withdrawals from the Caisse funds to finance various activities and projects. During the course of its

TABLE 7.6:  Contribution of the Caisse to the BSIE Treasury

| Year | Percent Contribution |
|------|---------------------|
| 1973 | 1.09 |
| 1974 | 5.62 |
| 1975 | 23.20 |

Source:  Marchés tropicaux 1563, 42.

nine-year history (up to 1975), the Caisse contributed 29.3 billion francs *cfa* to the BSIE and allocated 13.9 billion francs *cfa* in direct subsidies (in addition to the 2.5 billion francs *cfa* in contributions to international organizations) from a total revenue of 52,963.5 billion francs *cfa*. An explanation of how the Caisse gets its capital follows.

At the beginning of every harvest season, a minimum price for coffee bought from the planters is set by the Caisse after consultation with exporters. During these consultations, the amount to be exported by each commercial house, as well as the *differentiel* (all expenses and remunerations to all agents who intervene in the export of coffee between the planter and the port of embarkation determined in the freight-on-board price), is set. From this, the Caisse obtains the CAF, the cost, insurance, and freight price that is guaranteed to the exporter, whatever the selling price at the market of destination turns out to be. If the exporter sells at a price superior to the CAF guaranteed price, he gives back to the Caisse the difference (this is called *reversement*); if the exporter sells at an inferior price, it is the Caisse that will reimburse the difference (*soutien*).

Once they are assigned their export quotas, most exporters borrow money from commercial banks to make advances to their traders, who buy the coffee from the collection centers in the rural districts. Traditionally, most of these traders were Lebanese, Syrians, and Dioula, but native Ivorians are also beginning to form an important fraction of the transporters; their future in the coffee trade is threatened, however, if the GVCs take over the trade completely.[146]  The advances made to traders are basically a question of confidence between the trader and the exporter, as legal contracts are only entered into in a minority of the transactions.

The value that the exporter adds to the coffee is mainly in terms of conditioning, storage, and delivery to the harbor of export, where maritime commerce takes over. At the port, the final grading of the coffee is done, although most exporters have already done their own grading in the factories and only wait for the control service to confirm their findings. The coffee can then be exported to two types of markets: the traditional markets (Western Europe and North America in particular) and the new markets (the Annex or "Schedule B" countries--the Soviet bloc, Japan, and most Third World countries).

Since 1959, the Caisse has consistently cultivated its U.S. market, where Ivorian robusta is useful in making soluble coffee. By 1973, the United States had become the Ivory Coast's leading market, receiving 33 percent of the total coffee exported; France followed with 28.5 percent, and then Japan with 8.6 percent.[147] Because the Caisse sells directly to the U.S., the scale of operations of the traditional import-export houses has been curtailed, making the SERIC program even more of a threat to them should it become increasingly dominated by the state.[148]

*CEDA and arabusta.* Until very recently, the Ivorian state had not participated directly in improving coffee production, as it had in the palm oil industry in conjunction with Palmivoire-Palmindustrie.[149] But during the last ten years, there has been constant research to find ways and means of improving coffee productivity; this is in response to the tremendous reduction of village plantations' yields, due to the archaic production methods used, the exhaustion of the soil, and the frequent occurrence of crop diseases. The results of IFCC laboratory experiments and experimental fields show that productivity could be increased by increasing the use of fertilizers, by improving irrigation, and by using insecticides to control the spread of disease.

In 1974, the government created a parastatal body to promote the growth of arabusta, a disease- and drought-resistant variety of coffee cross-bred from *cafea arabica* and *cafea robusta*. This body, called the Centre d'étude de développement de l'arabusta (CEDA), is based in Soubre and run under the auspices of the IFCC and SATMACI. Its first project was an experimental 500 hectares of arabusta, and the goal of this operation was twofold: (a) to create an example of the growth of arabusta in a zone where the ambiance is good in terms of labor, soil conditions, and climate, with the labor to be used coming mainly from foreign immigrants and local outgrowers with no previous experience in the coffee culture; and (b) to organize the arabusta program on sound economical and commercial plans such that, should its estate system prove successful and profitable, it would replace the village extensive system.[150] Properly taken care of, arabusta should yield up to 2,400 kilograms per hectare as compared to the 407 yielded by the average village plantation.

SATMACI officials justify the CEDA program on the grounds that, given the limits on exportable coffee, the decreasing availability of labor for the planters, the unproductivity of the extensive method, and the "unwillingness" of the peasants to adapt to intensive methods; it would be much easier for the state--having access to enough capital--to eventually take over coffee production so that the peasants can concentrate on producing food. Or, in regions where other cash crops are being encouraged, former coffee/cocoa growers may be released to join diversification programs.

*The Sodepalm experience.* Part of the state policy to diversify Ivorian export production was the extension of palm oil and coconut production. Thus, in 1963, the government created a public corporation called Société pour le développement et exploitation du palmier à huile (Sodepalm).[151] The aim of Sodepalm was to increase production of palm oil and coconuts, using domestic labor and foreign capital brought together by the state. Sodepalm, a body fully owned by the state, runs the plantations and gives technical assistance to the outgrower smallholdings surrounding each estate within a radius of twenty kilometers. Until mid-1969, Sodepalm owned and operated all oil palm estates, palm oil mills, and coconut estates established under the government's oil palm and coconut programs and was responsible for oil palm and coconut outgrower schemes.

In 1969, however, two new companies were formed: Palmindustrie, to take over ownership of the Sodepalm oil mills and to construct new milling facilities, and Palmivoire, to construct the Palmindustrie mills and the Sodepalm oil palm estates. The 1969 changes were made to permit the introduction of private investment in the country's palm oil development program--at a time when vegetable oils were again becoming lucrative on the world market--through the sale of shares in Palmindustrie and Palmivoire to foreign companies and banks and to Ivorian companies and individuals. Management by Palmivoire would ensure that the industry was run strictly on a profit-making basis.[152]

Upon the establishment of the two newer corporations, Sodepalm, Palmindustrie and Palmivoire entered into a contract of association and participation on 31 October 1969 for the development and operation of the industrial palm oil estates and mills. Palmivoire collects, processes and sells the outgrowers' production; Palmindustrie acts as the marketing company for the participation. The technical formation and supervision of the work of the outgrowers remains the responsibility of Sodepalm--the wholly state-owned of the three partners.

The eight Sodepalm estates were founded in thinly populated areas or in virtual virgin forests previously left wild and unused as *classed forests*. The state demands that labor for these estates be recruited specifically from among the Voltaic immigrant workers, who may no longer be able to establish themselves in the forest zone as coffee/cocoa growers due to reduction in coffee growing there. Voltaics were, in addition, regarded as more adaptable workers and, given the opportunity to be outgrowers, would not, as foreigners to the lower Ivory Coast, be tempted to engage in other agricultural activities diverting their attention from palm oil. Since palm oil harvests come almost every month, and since the Sodepalm-Palmivoire-Palmindustrie arrangement ensures regular collection of the harvested product, Voltaics coming out of the share-cropping coffee arrangements find setting themselves up as Sodepalm outgrowers a welcome opportunity for becoming *chefs d'exploitation* in their own right.

With employment opportunities presumably opening up in the industrial sectors, most young native Ivorians tend to move to the urban areas with the hope of finding semiskilled positions instead of the *travail voltaïque* that agriculture offers. In the Aboisso estates of Ehania, Toumangue, and Adiake, not only is labor overwhelmingly Voltaic but 70 percent of the outgrowers also are either Voltaic or other foreigners.[153] The result is that, with the intrusion of the palm oil industry and the attraction of immigrant labor to it, the source of labor for coffee/cocoa small masters has been further reduced. Some of these may return to being ordinary peasants, growing one or two hectares of coffee intermixed with food crops. But even this a family can do only for a short while, for coffee must be increasingly intermixed only with those crops that SATMACI recommends, or else the peasant's poor yields may eventually force him out of the coffee business.

*Sodepalm's implications for CEDA.* Because CEDA is set in the "new frontier" of the western region, it will have to rely on immigrant labor for its outgrowers and farmworkers, or those already settled in the region will be converted into the workers and outgrowers as the program gradually eliminates the production of coffee on a household basis. But there is also the possibility of existing outside the cash economies of coffee and palm oil. The Baoule migrating from their homelands in Daoukro, Bouaké, or Dimbokro, where cotton as a cash crop has not been very appealing to them, are more familiar with such "possibilities."[154] The predicament of the peasant already involved in the cash economy as a petty commodity producer is that of immense weakness against the power of capital, be it from the state or from private business. Native Ivorians in the rural economy still try to resist complete proletarianization. It is not that peasants are "unwilling" to adopt appropriate methods of production in order to survive under the new requirements of capital accumulation, but that, given these new requirements, they can only adapt as wage-workers, small masters, or outgrowers. To say that they can adapt is, in actual fact, a euphemism; they can *struggle*, and they do struggle, to better their livelihood given the social structure into which they are born and the social power that they can wield in society with those sharing their class situation. By weaving a class alliance with propertied classes and fractions of classes at various levels of society, we have seen how the bourgeoisie, in the sphere of agriculture, maintains its hegemony in the Ivory Coast.


## Conclusion

Studies of rural development in Africa are best understood in terms of articulation of modes of production. A theory of rural development is therefore a theory of modes of production in agriculture and changes that occur in them, once they are in contact with other modes. A study of the mechanisms of this contact, often involving the transition from precapitalist modes of production to the capitalist mode during periods of primitive accumulation, becomes a study of class formations and class struggles as well. From this perspective, social inquiry into problems of rural development cannot be a preserve of any single discipline as they are organized and reproduced in the social sciences today. Rural development studies must be an interdisciplinary concern with a single epistemological foundation. In the language of Marxist political economy, we can summarize this argument by saying that "historical materialism knows no disciplines."

What this work has attempted to do is organize already available data on commodity production in the Ivory Coast, particularly coffee, in a way that provides an analysis and interpretation that may lead us to understand the history of the Ivory Coast as that of capitalist development, set in motion within a specific environment--the world capitalist system-- and giving rise to classes and class struggles specific to that social formation. The struggles of these classes will determine the future of the Ivory Coast. But we cannot predict with any degree of accuracy how these classes will struggle and what will be the outcome. What we can predict, however, are the alternatives open to them; in fact, we do not need to predict these--we know them. The alternatives are not determined by the subjective desires of this or that individual within this or that class, but by the structural prerequisites of the modes of production.

Certain classes are indeed structurally "at the crossroads" and can, by subjectively committing "class suicide," struggle for the socialist revolution. This is the position in which various fractions of the petite bourgeoisie in town and country can be found. Caught up in a process of social mobility whose future is uncertain but past known and not fully rewarding, these elements can fall on the side of the revolutionary forces should the latter command social power in society. Political education and ideological training becomes an important task in creating revolutionaries out of these fractions of classes. But only by understanding the objective conditions under which this revolution is to be made can the petit bourgeois intellectual, undressed of his class interests, become a true social praxician. Any romanticism of the structure of society, and hence of the classes that comprise it, can only lead to utopianism or petit bourgeois populism.

This work has attempted to expose what the social structure of the Ivory Coast looks like, how it has evolved from colonial times, and what kind of political consciousness a social praxician may expect from the rural classes--the so-called masses--if he could propose a socialist program to them. Our original hypothesis was that, given the dominance of the small masters in the rural economy, the tendency within rural politics would be to defend the regime of private property and the conditions that make upward mobility possible under this regime. Insofar as this mobility is still possible for the small masters, their hopes and faith in this regime cannot be crumbled by mere moral criticism of it. What need to be demonstrated, even to the small masters, are the contradictions that this assumed mobility eventually leads to. For people cannot change the conditions under which they live simply by the whims of one individual; nor can they struggle to change existing relations of production simply because those relations do not always work in their favor. People must be convinced that an alternative social system is possible, that their gains today, given the social system under which they live, will be their losses of tomorrow, and that the only social system in which they can safeguard these gains--which become the losses of the social classes in contradictory locations to them under the present social system--is the one whose advent is achieved by revolutionizing the present society, in our case through a socialist revolution.

It is not the task of this chapter to discuss what this revolution entails. We end by pointing out that, in the case of the Ivory Coast, it remains for Ivorians themselves to spell it out for their society. Our only contribution was to lay bare the raw material that an Ivorian social praxician would have to use in that process of revolution: the Ivorian masses as they are in the countryside.

## NOTES

1. The category of "small master" is used here as Marx uses it in volume one of Capital. For the capitalist to appropriate surplus beyond the necessities of his own subsistence, he must set at the disposal of the laborers means of production with which this extra surplus value can be produced. To effect this transformation, a certain minimum of money or exchange value must be presupposed in the hands of the individual potential capitalist. But where this is lacking, the potential capitalist can, like his laborer, take to work himself and participate directly in the process of production. He is then a hybrid between capitalist and laborer, a small master. Capital, vol. 1 (New York: International Publishers, 1973), 308.

2. The effect of capitalist penetration is to bring previously independent modes of production into contact with each other, as it simultaneously articulates with them and extracts surplus values from them. Relations of production thereby created are functions of a double articulation: (1) articulation among these precapitalist modes of production as it is subsumed by (2) their articulation with the capitalist mode of production. See, for example, Marx, op. cit., 351-354.

3. See, for example, Suret-Canale, Afrique noire occidentale et centrale: de la colonisation aux indépendances (Paris: Editions Sociales, 1961), 9-28; R.S. Morgenthau, Political Parties in French-speaking West Africa (Oxford: Clarendon Press, 1964), 1-10.

4. A.G. Hopkins, An Economic History of West Africa (New York: Columbia University Press, 1973), 263.

5. Morgenthau, op. cit., 170; H. Frechou, "Les plantations européenes en Côte d'Ivoire" (Ph.D. diss., University of Bordeaux, 1956), 186; F.J. Amon d'Aby, La Côte d'Ivoire dans la cité africaine (Paris: Larose, 1951), 111.

6. Frechou, op. cit.; Morgenthau, op. cit., 166-176; E.J. Berg, "Recruitment of Labour Force in Sub-Saharan Africa" (Ph.D. diss., Harvard University, 1960), 167 ff.

7. It should be remembered that the June 1940 armistice signed between France and Germany, whereby southern France remained in French hands under the so-called Vichy regime of Marshal Petain, also stipulated that France's colonies were to be neutralized. This meant the disbanding of the majority of France's black army, from 180,000 to 25,000.

8. C. Coquery-Vidrovitch, "L'impact des interêts coloniaux: SCOA et CFAO dans l'Ouest Africain, 1910-1965," Journal of African History 16 (1965).

9. Before the fall of France, French West Africa supplied the metropole with foodstuffs. In rice-growing areas, villagers were required to supply the administration with certain amounts regularly, even if this disrupted the organization of labor for providing for their basic needs. After the fall of France brought imports and exports to a virtual standstill, production of groundnuts, cocoa, and timber in Senegal and Ivory Coast fell drastically (see d'Aby, op. cit., 496-497; and Morgenthau, op. cit., 168). With the changeover from Vichy to the Allies in November 1942, French West Africa was once again in the war effort. Emphasis was put on groundnuts, palm oil, and rubber. To increase production, the administration requisitioned fixed amounts of produce from each village and rarely cared whether the required product could or could not be grown in a particular locality. Quite often, peasants had to travel long distances to buy the commodity elsewhere, depleting their limited monetary resources, as well as disrupting their work on subsistence crops. See J.J. Lauer, "Economic Innovations Among the Dou of Western Ivory Coast, 1900-1960" (Ph.D. diss., University of Wisconsin, Madison, 1973).

10. Houphouët-Boigny gave the example of a M. Pon's 800-hectare plantation near Bingerville--a plantation whose coffee was not, in any case, of good quality--with a claimed yield of twelve tons, for which M. Pon received 72,000 francs for the coffee harvested and 800,000 for the area cultivated. See Damas Report, "FHB Testimony."

11. This is the testimony received from Dioula villagers in Aboisso who decided to give up trading as a way of life and invest their energies in coffee growing in 1942, with the idea that, after the war, they would stand a better chance of a sustained income since, in spite of the war, coffee prices continued to rise in Abidjan.

12. Tauxier, Le Noir de Bondoukou (Paris: Payot, 1921), 306 ff.

13. The mechanism by which immigrants could soon become independent meant that the "first occupants" were constantly losing the sources of their surplus product. But economies of the savanna compelled operation in a money system, and savanna types were equally compelled to look for money wages in the forest zone from time to time.

14. Beginning in 1930, the use of automobiles and trucks replaced the use of porters. Authorities in the Ivory Coast estimated that one large truck, with a chauffeur and his assistant, replaced no less than 2,000 porters during the cocoa season. The Ivory Coast's pool of 2,000 trucks in 1935 was thus able to handle the cash crop output without heavy demand for the labor of porters. The colons applied pressure for the released labor to be sent to their plantations. The

Baoule, in turn, moved out of their localities to seek more favorable arrangements for earning money in the Agni country. See E.J. Berg, op. cit., 145-150.

15. But, because these connected to the northern savanna region by railway and production did not begin seriously until after the war, they relied mainly on Voltaic labor from the north (see Jean Tricart, "Les exchanges entre la zone forestière de Côte d'Ivoire et les savanes soudaniennes," Cahiers d'Outre-Mer 35, July-September 1956, 209-238), some of whom were brought to Abidjan by plane. The wages offered could not attract local people, who had better sources of money income--their own cash crop gardens. Bananas, unlike coffee, are a crop that cannot lend itself so easily to forced or semiforced labor unless under very strict supervision; see G.L. Beckford et al., Agribusiness Structures and Adjustments (Boston: Harvard University GSBA, 1966). But, as Frechou noted, management was both lacking and expensive for the colons. Their plantations rarely exceeded 200 hectares in size: see C.R. Hiernaux, "Les aspects géographiques de la production bananière de la Côte d'Ivoire," Cahiers d'Outre-Mer 1 (January-March 1948); they could not function at high costs of management and labor risks. Thus the Voltaics, though transported under conditions of compulsion, knew that they would be free at the end of their contracts and would take home their pay. Although even banana planters defaulted on this, the colonial administration encouraged the supply of this seasonal labor from afar because they could not escape as easily as either the Baoule or the Agni. In postcolonial times, almost any Malian, Guinean, or Voltaic may still be preferred over a local Ivorian as agricultural labor for this very reason. The demeaning of agricultural labor as "travail voltaïque" by the Agni, therefore, has deep historical roots, which connect the neocolonial economy to its colonial heritage.

16. The Dioula and the Hausa were the two leading groups of professional long-distance traders in precolonial West Africa. The former were of Mande origin, and were especially important in the Ivory Coast where they handled the north-south trade in livestock, fish, and cloth, buying kola nuts and slaves from the forest zone (Hopkins, op. cit., 61). In colonial times, the Dioula migrants settled in the forest zone as farmers in the 1910s. Some Dioula financed their agricultural ventures with funds they had accumulated in precolonial trading activities, but these were a minority. The majority, like the Baoule immigrants, started off as sharecroppers or were given "no man's lands" freely. The village of Kohourou in Aboisso, today boasting the best coffee gardens in all of the Aboisso prefecture and a population of over 4,000, was founded by one immigrant sharecropper turned planter in a virgin forest given him freely by an Agni hunter in 1940 (from field interviews, December 1975).

17. Hopkins, op. cit., 213.

18. See M. Dupire, "Planteurs autochtones et étrangers en Basse Côte d'Ivoire Orientale," Etudes éburnéennes 8 (1960), 7-237; and A.J.F. Kobben, "Le planteur noir," Etudes éburnéennes 5 (1956), 7-185.

19. In November 1948, J.B. Mockey demanded in the Ivory Coast Territo-

rial Assembly that the granting of freehold land to outsiders--under the decree of 1935--be abolished and replaced by long-term leases, with all land registered in the name of the Ivory Coast rather than France. A. Zolberg, One-party Government in the Ivory Coast (Princeton: Princeton University Press, 1969), 123-124. It is interesting to note that Mockey did not raise the questions relating to how access to land should be regulated among the Africans themselves. In the Ivory Coast, unlike in Kenya for example, it was enough to assert the Africans' traditional rights to their land to be labeled a "revolutionary."

20. K. Marx, op. cit., 766.

21. France, Journal officiel, Documents parlementaires Assemblée Nationale, Session de 1951, Séance du 15 février, 1959, 225 ff.

22. See, for example, "The Roosevelt-Churchill Eight Points and Africa's Future," The Atlantic Charter, 30-64; and F.A. Huxley's "Colonies in a Changing World," The Political Quarterly 13 (October-December 1942), 384-399.

23. One of the most important developments of the war was the hegemony the United States managed to establish in the world as a result of the weakening of Europe and Japan. The Soviet Union, having fought alongside the Allies and having sacrificed a great deal of resources to defeat the Nazis, won for itself hegemony in the Communist bloc. The two powers had a common interest in abolishing colonial relations but for different reasons. The United States had, through the Marshall Plan, invested a lot of capital in Europe; it could not sit back and see Europe use this capital, while denying U.S. access to the raw materials of France's and Britain's overseas empires.

24. Ministère du Plan, Inventaire économique et social de la Côte d'Ivoire, 1947-58 (Abidjan: Imprimerie du Gouvernement, 1960, 72-73.

25. Ivory Coast, Service de l'agriculture, Annual Report 1948, "Deuxième partie économique."

26. S. Amin, Neo-colonialism in West Africa (New York: Monthly Review Press, 1973), xi.

27. Frechou, op. cit.

28. C. Coquery-Vidrovitch, op. cit. "The import-export houses were typical merchant capitalists whose capital always remained within one sphere of circulation, was never applied either to agriculture or to industrial production in any innovative fashion."

29. C. Newbury, "The Government General and Political Change in FWA," St. Anthony's Papers 10 (London: Chatto and Windus, 1961).

30. E.P. Skinner, The Mossi of the Upper Volta (Stanford: Stanford University Press, 1964).

31. S. Amin, op. cit., vx.

32. In 1972, the Ivorian Chamber of Commerce published a report on the balance of payments of some francophone African countries in which it was revealed that the Ivory Coast's exports amounted to 140 billion francs cfa and its imports to 114 billion--a positive balance of 26 billion; Cameroon followed with 56 billion in exports and 76 billion in imports--a negative balance of 17 billion

(Côte d'Ivoire en chiffre, Abidjan: Imprimerie de Gouvernement, 1976, p. 36).

33.   Coffee and cocoa contributed the following amounts to the export earnings of the Ivory Coast in the postwar period:

TABLE 7.7

| Year | Earnings from coffee/cocoa | Total export earnings | Percent value of coffee in total exports |
|------|------|------|------|
| 1950 | 7.9 | 14.4 | 38.0 |
| 1960 | 13.9 | 33.7 | 41.3 |
| 1965 | 28.4 | 68.4 | 35.3 |
| 1970 | 60.9 | 130.2 | 46.8 |
| 1973 | 72.8 | 190.9 | 38.1 |

Source:  S. Amin, Le développement du capitalisme en Côte d'Ivoire (Paris: Editions du Minuit, 1967); B. Dusabeyezu, "La place du café dans l'économie africaine" (Ph.D. diss., University of Fribourg, 1971), 6; La Côte d'Ivoire en chiffre, op. cit., 39, 85 and 87.

34.   In 1958, the share of coffee in export earnings was 59.6 percent; in 1960 it was 41.3 percent; 1966, 39.5; and by 1973 it had dropped to 23.7 percent.  The importance of coffee earnings can be seen in the accounts of the Special Budget for Equipment and Investment (BSIE).  In 1975, the total revenue for this budget was 54.041 million francs cfa at current prices.  Of this, 17.782 was received from the BSIE treasury, i.e., capital contribution from the Caisse, whose revenues come mainly from the coffee/cocoa trade.  In other words, through the Caisse and the BSIE, coffee/cocoa surpluses have actually financed the development of other sectors of production in the Ivory Coast.  This phenomenon is not apparent to the direct producers in their daily lives, but it is much clearer to the Voltaics, who, knowing that the only thing they can take back with them to Upper Volta is their wages, frequently express the opinion that they have done more to the Ivory Coast than they get out of her (from personal communications).  But this basic reality of Ivorian development need not translate itself immediately into political practice by those exploited in the process.  It is, indeed, the aim of the hegemonic state to ensure that the state does this without any resistance from those exploited, i.e., by keeping politics out of questions of development.

35.   Tauxier, as the administrator of the colonies in West Africa, wrote several monographs on the people of the Ivory Coast which have remained "classics."  These could serve as good sources of information for any metropolitan industrialist who wanted to know certain facts about techniques of production in these precapitalist societies.  See, especially, Le Noir de Soudan--Pays Mossi et Gourounsi (Paris:  Editions Ernest Laroux, 1917); Le Noir de Bondoukou, op. cit.; Nègres Gouro et Gagou (Paris:  Librairie Orientaliste, 1926).

36.   M. Delafosse, "Les Sociétés indigènes de prévoyance en Afrique de

l'ouest française," Revue indigène (July-October 1919), 139-153.

37.  Ministère de la France d'Outre-Mer, L'Equipement des territoires français d'outre-mer, 1947-50, 22.  Suret-Canale points out that the original motivation of the SIPs was the failure of the Senegalese peasant to conserve enough seeds for the following year's crop and to protect himself against lean years, once he started producing for the capitalist market.  These problems arose not so much from the peasants' improvidence, as the French thought, as from an economic system where, through taxation and coercion, he was forced to produce cash crops to the detriment of his subsistence crops, where his able-bodied workers were taken away for the army or compulsory labor, and where he was paid prices lower than the real economic value of his produce.  See Suret-Canale, French Colonialism; Crowder, West Africa Under Colonial Rule, 316-333; and d'Aby, op. cit., 116-118.

38.  Crowder, West Africa Under Colonial Rule, op. cit., 235-244.

39.  Compare, for example, the phenomenon of "better farmer" in Kenya.  Following the introduction of the Swinnerton Plan (a project to intensify petty commodity production among the peasant population) in 1954, the Department of Agriculture instituted a program for the "encadrement" and "animation" of a few "better farmers" in select regions whose farms would be examples to their neighbors.  These farmers used select seeds for their maize fields, planted in straight lines, used fertilizers, and received periodic visits from agricultural and veterinary scouts.  The instructions from these civil servants were so limiting and their schedules so demanding that some better farmers backed off and returned to subsistence agriculture.  As the Chronique coloniale put it in the West African case:

> When the whole problem at present consists in developing colonial consumption in France and French exports to the colonies, to attempt to solve it without the collaboration and the interest, without the nationalisation of the labour of these sixty million human beings and all that this has that is moral and fertile, would be folly.  (Chronique coloniale, 30 June 1931, 246.)

40.  It should not be forgotten that in certain cases the actions of the SIPs benefited some African coffee/cocoa growers.  In the sous-préfectures of Dimbokro, Abengourou, and Aboisso, there was strong adherence to SIPs mainly because it was through the SIPs that the planters received insecticides and insecticide pumps with which to fight the scolyte.  It was also through the SIPs that they received good robusta seedlings.  Soon after the Second World War, there was resurgence of the SIPs for the same reason, especially with the task of the regeneration of the coffee gardens to be faced.  (From interviews in Aboisso, Daoukro, and Ayame.)

41.  Ivory Coast Service d'Agriculture, Rapport annuel 1948.  The 1931 "Plan Maginot" sought to advance credit to African cash crop growers in the Overseas Territories, but its interest rates were prohibitive.  As can be seen in the study of the credit system, only the colons benefited from the "fall-offs" from

the Maginot Plan.

42. FIDES cannot be treated in isolation from the general political program that France envisaged for her colonial subjects after the war. The laws of April and May 1946 (abolishing forced labor and bestowing citizenship upon former subjects, respectively) were meant to liberalize France's relations with her colonies, which had sacrificed so much for the liberation of France herself. The difficulties in the colonies, argued France's Minister for the Overseas Territories, Marius Moutet, on 23 June 1946 at the Bordeaux Exposition, cannot simply be solved by abolishing forced labor, but had to be seen in terms of the underdeveloped nature of the techniques of production (equipment) and the necessity to modernize them. See Marchés coloniaux 34, July 1946, 663.

43. By social infrastructure we mean essentially all those institutions and social services that make possible social communication among human beings (e.g., hospitals, schools, sanitation services, mass media). By physical infrastructure we mean roads, railroads, post and telecommunications, air and water transport, electricity, i.e., all those institutions and material means that make possible the physical communication of human beings in the process of production and in the circulation and exchange of commodities.

44. Between 1949 and 1958, of the 9,650 million francs cfa ($55.09 million) invested in road development in the Ivory Coast, 5,430 million ($31 million) came from FIDES. Over the same years, the federal and local budgets provided only 460 million francs ($2.6 million) while two other sources of revenue--the Road Fund and the Coffee and Cocoa Funds--added 2,615 and 1,145 million francs cfa ($14.9 and 6.5 million) respectively. (Ministère du plan, Inventaire économique, op. cit., 119.)

45. A.G. Hopkins, op. cit., 282; Inventaire économique, op. cit., 223-239. The greater part of public investment in the physical infrastructure was spent on road improvements. The only railway construction was Abidjan-Niger railways from Bobo-Dioulasso to Ouagadougou (capital of Upper Volta), in 1955. This was very useful in the movement of the Mossi migrant labor to the Ivorian forest belt in the 1950s and early 1960s. The opening of new roads enables the use of trucks in the transportation of coffee and cocoa, hence leading to the rapid development of the forest belt, which can be measured both in terms of quantities of commodities produced and in terms of the number of people involved in commodity production.

46. Amin, Le Développment, op. cit., 200.

47. Inventaire économique, op. cit., 250 ff.

48. On the evolution of roads in the Ivory Coast, 1947-1958, see table 7.8:

TABLE 7.8

|  | Length in kilometers | | |
| Category of road | 1947 | 1956 | 1958 |
| All-weather roads: | | | |
| tarmac and beaten-earth | 3,670 | 8,720 | 10,570 |
| Seasonal: rural paths | 7,230 | 8,020 | 14,618 |
| Total: | 10,900 | 16,740 | 25,188 |

Source: Inventaire économique, op. cit., 118.

49. Inventaire économique, op. cit., 121.

50. Marches coloniaux 2 (1947), 761; vol. 3 (1948), 468; vol. 4 (1949), 413. Also Inventaire économique 1958, 123. The actual cost of the transportation is taken as an arithmetric average obtained through surveys.

51. Harry Braverman, Labour and Monopoly Capital: The Degradation of World in the Twentieth Century (New York: Monthly Review Press, 1974), 44-58.

52. Marx, op. cit., 312-321.

53. The reorganization of the Department of Agriculture accompanied this new perspective of planning, research, and technical formation. The cercles were rearranged into nine sectors (instead of the previous six), each sector coinciding with a particular agricultural activity and its level of development. The Abidjan sector (Abidjan, Aboisso, Agboville, and Grand Bassam)--the most heterogenous of them all--remained unchanged; the second sector of Daloa (Daloa, Gagnoa, Sassandra, and Grand Lahou) was divided in two--the new, dynamic, and almost predominantly coffee-growing cercles of Daloa and Gagnoa became sector 5, while Grand Lahou and Sassandra were grouped under sector 2; the previous third sector of Dimbokro (Dimbokro, Abengourou, and Bondoukou, of which Dimbokro was rapidly becoming the coffee post of the Ivory Coast) was also divided in two--Dimbokro became the sector 4 by itself, while Abengourou and Bondoukou were left in sector 3, henceforth known as Abengourou sector; Bouaké sector 4 remained as it was (coffee, cocoa, cotton, rice, and corn) but was renamed sector 7; Man, itself, was sector 6; Ferkessedougou (Korhogo and Odienné) sector 8; and Tabou sector 9. See Ivory Coast Service de l'Agriculture, Rapport annuel 1955, op. cit., 60-63.

54. Parastatal bodies such as SATMACI were products of the FIDES/FERDES projects originating from 1946. It was then that the French Overseas Ministry, acting on behalf of French capital--in view of the preparation of the ten-year development plans of which FIDES was an integral part--decided to create state corporations which would function in socioeconomic projects with the drive and method of private enterprises. These corporations would,

nonetheless, enjoy the juridical protection of the post-colonial state, and some of their unproductive undertakings (e.g., administration) would be underwritten by the state. Crédit de Côte d'Ivoire (CCI), founded in 1955, was among the first of these parastatals. SATMACI followed in 1958, eventually to give birth to Sode-palm, Soderiz, Sodheavea, etc. We should, at this point, recall our earlier theo-retical statement that the postcolonial state is both a cohesive mechanism for the Ivorian social formation dominated by a power bloc of local "support classes" and a formal legal institution through which the general purpose of capital accumu-lation on a world scale is realized. Almost all of the most important Ivorian state corporations were founded with French public capital investment in part or in whole. For example, the French state owns 13.9 percent of the capital of Energie électrique de Côte d'Ivoire (EECI), 10.3 percent of Société ivoirienne de con-struction et de gestion immobilière (SICOGI), 54 percent of the SATMACI cap-ital. The Caisse centrale de cooperation économique, a French public corpora-tion, owns 7.9 percent of BIDI, and 16.7 percent of the CCI. Electricité de France has a share capital of 9.3 percent in the EECI, while the Société centrale pour l'équipement du territoire (SCET) has significant shares in several state corporations, particularly SICOGI. Finally, most capital in Ivorian banks and credit institutions is owned by French nationalized banks such as Crédit lyon-nais, which has the majority capital in Société ivoirienne de banque (SIB); So-ciété générale de banque en Côte d'Ivoire (SGBCI) is partly owned by Société générale of France; and the Banque nationale de Paris (BNP) has significant shares in BICICI (Banque internationale pour le commerce et l'industrie en Côte d'Ivoire). See J.D. de la Rochere, "L'état et le développement économique de la Côte d'Ivoire," Série Afrique Noire 6 (1976), 46-48, published by Institut d'études politiques de Bordeaux, Centre d'études d'Afrique Noire.

55. The interest that foreign public and private capital took in the devel-opment of palm oil required that the industry be run on a much different basis than either coffee or cocoa. Rice, too, poses different problems, as the marketing of rice becomes a question of having internal marketing policy rather than a pol-icy specifically oriented toward the international market.

56. In 1923, its board of administration, presided over by Paul Boyer of the Comptoir d'escompte, which no doubt represented the interests of French high finance, showed a majority of Bordeaux interests (Maurel, Gradia) and their as-sociated companies (Dalmas). See Suret-Canale, French Colonialism, op. cit., 168.

57. M. Capet, Traite d'économie tropicale (Paris: Pichon et Burand-Auzias, 1958), 174.

58. Suret-Canale, French Colonialism, op. cit., 168.

59. Ibid., 169.

60. J.B. Frankel showed in 1938 the smallness of private investments in the French African territories compared to the British ones. Global investments for most of the pre-Second World War period shows the preponderance of public in-vestments raised mainly from the local territorial or federal budgets. These bud-gets, which included loans, repayable with interest by the colonial treasuries, by

investing in public utilities and infrastructures helped mainly in adding to the surplus transferred to the metropolitan economy.  Thus, for example, while total foreign capital invested in British West Africa for those sixty-six years came to £116,730,000, that for French West Africa was only £30,426,000; for the Portuguese colonies of Angola and Mozambique, £66,732,000, that is, twice that of French West Africa.  See S.H. Frankel, Capital Investment in Africa: Its Course and Effects (New York: Oxford University Press, 1938), 158-159.

61.  Suret-Canale, French Colonialism, op. cit., 162.

62.  Ibid., 163.  See also M. Piquemal, "Exportation des capitaux aux colonies," Economie et Politique (August-September 1957).

63.  Lack of proper credit institutions gave way to usury in the countryside, a practice of primitive accumulation used mainly by merchants.  A Dioula or Libano-Syrian trader would buy coffee or cocoa from villagers and, in return, sell them imported consumer goods.  In the event of the villager not having enough money to buy, goods would be advanced to him on credit, tying up the delivery of the next coffee/cocoa crop to be given with interest to the trader.

64.  A 1940 study by the Colonial Ministry revealed that negligible private investments went into African agriculture.

65.  See G. Leduc, Les Institutions monetaires africaines: pays francophones (Paris: Editions A. Pedone, 1965), 10-39.

66.  This is the same body d'Aby refers to as the Cooperative des planteurs de la Basse Côte d'Ivoire, founded by Georges-Emmanuel Vilasco (a Grand Bassam trader and delegate to the administrative council of the colony) in 1933, which failed because it lacked the support of the two big cocoa-growing regions. See Amon d'Aby, op. cit., 110-111.

67.  See the 1936 report of the Caisse national de crédit agricole, Abidjan, BNDA Library.

68.  Ibid.

69.  Hopkins, op. cit., 284.

70.  Ibid.

71.  See B. Campbell, "The Social, Political and Economic Consequences of French Private Investment in the Ivory Coast, 1960-70" (Ph.D. diss., University of Sussex, 1973), 132; and de la Rochere, op. cit., 96-109.

72.  In 1947, fifty-four out of 178 commercial and private automobiles imported into the Ivory Coast (that is, 30 percent) came from outside the franc zone; that same year 212 out of 686 (31 percent) trucks and pick-ups were imported from "foreign" sources.  Ten years later, only 131 out of 2,301 private and commercial vehicles (about six percent) were foreign in origin, while 228 trucks and pick-ups out of 1,709 (less than 13 percent) came from outside the franc zone.  See Inventaire économique, op. cit., 112.

73.  Hopkins, op. cit., 285; Suret-Canale, Afrique Noire, op. cit., 84-86, 147-149.  The initial value of the franc cfa was set at 1.70 metropolitan francs; in October 1948 this was increased to two francs.  As a result of the introduction of the new French franc, the exchange value of the metropolitan currency, as of 1959, was equal to 0.02 francs cfa.

74. Ibid., 134; Câmpbell, op. cit., 136.

75. Caisses de soutien, guaranteeing minimum prices for most of the export crops, were established between 1946 and 1949.

76. Y.-C. Ramboz, "La politique caféière de Côte d'Ivoire et la reforme de la Caisse de Stabilisation des prix du café et du cacao," Revue juridique et politique 2 (April-June 1965), 194-218. See also A. Zolberg, op. cit., 163-170, for the political struggles behind the formation of the Caisse.

77. Y.-C. Ramboz, op. cit. This became an important issue soon after the Second World War because of the behavior of the world prices and the consequent reaction of planters and merchants. From 1946 to 1948, the Federation's coffee exporters received more than the world price in the sales they made on the French market, and the profits of the metropolitan coffee-purchasing organizations amounted to nearly three billion francs. A drop in the market beginning in 1948 involved both in losses, but late in 1949, the price paid for coffee in the Federation rose suddenly from .70 to 1.30 metropolitan francs per kilogram. Planters at this time claimed that they were not profiting as much as traders from the boom, and they also resented an increase in the export duty on coffee, which had been raised from 6 percent to 10 percent ad valorem. V. Thompson and R. Adloff, French West Africa (Stanford: Stanford University Press, 1958), 476.

78. Zolberg, op. cit., 158-168.

79. Ramboz, op. cit., 204.

80. Ibid., 206-208.

81. Ibid., 205, 208.

82. We are here referring to the 1949 33 percent drop in the world price of cocoa and the refusal of the French chocolate manufacturers to accept 8,500 tons of cocoa that they had already contracted to buy, with the GNAFCO, the national cocoa-buying organization, stopping purchase of Ivorian cocoa. When buying resumed a few months later, GNAFCO offered even lower prices than those previously guaranteed. Although GNAFCO's purchasing monopoly was later rescinded and the 600 million francs cfa that had accumulated in the supporting fund distributed among Ivorian producers, the fear of peasants withdrawing from cocoa-growing--as the Ghanaian cocoa farmers had done under similar circumstances in 1933--haunted the metropolitan government. See Thompson and Adloff, op. cit., 472-473.

83. By paying more for franc-zone coffee, the French consumer also paid for this "support scheme." It is problematic to determine exactly how this surplus was distributed: two obvious recipients must be the import-export houses themselves and the state. Why? Because in the commercialization process, it is they who survive solely on the surplus realized.

84. M. Lachiver, "Le marché du café dans l'Europe des six," Cahiers d'Outre-Mer 60 (October-December 1962), 281-406.

85. Ibid., 390 (percentages calculated from table 7.7).

86. Calculated from Inventaire économique, op. cit., 72-73.

87. Zolberg, op. cit., 25.

88. Amin, Le développement, op. cit., 82.

89. Ibid.

90. In the course of social change, the character of the various political trends reveals the inherently contradictory class structure of this mass, its petit-bourgeois character, the antagonism between the proprietor and the proletarian trends within. The vacillation of the impoverished small master between the counterrevolutionary bourgeoisie and the revolutionary proletariat is as inevitable as the phenomenon, existent in every capitalist society, that an insignificant minority of small producers wax rich, turn into bourgeoisie, while the overwhelming majority are either utterly ruined and become wage-workers or paupers, or eternally eke out an almost proletarian existence. See V.I. Lenin, The Development of Capitalism in Russia (Moscow: Progress Publishers, 1972), 31-32.

91. Damas Report, "FHB Testimony"; d'Aby, op. cit., 110-112.

92. Zolberg, op. cit., 67.

93. See, for example, Berg, op. cit., 145 ff.

94. In a total estimated population of four million in 1965, 765,000 were Baoule. (Ivory Coast, Côte d'Ivoire population, 1965, Abidjan: Imprimerie du gouvernement, 25.)

95. The cercle of Bondoukou in the Indénié had the lowest population density next to the remote western circle of Tabou. It had 3.7 people per square kilometer, while Bouaké, in Baouleland, had 19.5, the highest in the country. If the 2.3 percent population growth was even throughout the colony, then we can safely assume that this distribution applied to the precensus years as well. See Inventaire économique, op. cit., 35.

96. See part 1 of this paper, the section on credit institutions.

97. Thompson and Adloff, op. cit., 122.

98. Agriculture Service, Department of Forced Labor.

99. P. Etienne and M. Etienne, "L'émigration Baoule actuelle," Cahiers d'Outre-Mer 82 (April-May 1968), 162.

100. Immigrant population into the southeast region in postwar times still showed the Baoule to be in the majority, i.e., 30.6 percent, followed by the Mossi's 23.7 percent, and the Malians' 20.5 percent. See the SEDES Study, 1967, 1, 119.

101. The Baoule-Agni type of conflict was repeated in other areas. In Daloa and Gagnoa, it was the Dioula and Baoule versus the originaires (i.e., natives of the area): the former had enjoyed similar economic opportunities in a foreign region whose natives were underprivileged. See B. Lewis, "Ethnicity, Occupational Specialisation and Interest Groups: The Transporters' Association of the Ivory Coast" (Ph.D. diss., Northwestern University, 1971).

102. For the discussion of a similar problematic, see M. Mamdani, Politics and Class Formation in Uganda (New York: Monthly Review Press, 1976); L. Cliffe, "Rural Class Formation in East Africa," Journal of Peasant Studies 4 (January 1977): 193-224; C. Leys, Underdevelopment in Kenya: The Political Economy of Neocolonialism (Berkeley and Los Angeles: University of California

Press, 1974).

103. It was not possible to look through SAA files and documents in Abidjan, while staying there in 1975-76, due to the reorganization of the National Archives and the delay in the opening of the Houphouët-Boigny Foundation where these documents are to be deposited for posterity. Most of this information, therefore, is from secondary sources.

104. Zolberg, op. cit., 67.

105. Adloff and Thompson, op. cit., 124.

106. The Estates General was a grouping of conservative interest groups formed in France, in 1946, to put pressure on the public and the Constitutent Assembly not to grant liberal concessions to the colonies or the Overseas Territories nor to increase public investments there in the interest of the natives. It proved a flexing of muscles which, once assured of neocolonial political arrangements, quickly reconsolidated their economic power with the African nationalists in political power.

107. Damas Report, op. cit., "The FHB Testimony," 137.

108. Zolberg, op. cit., 159-170.

109. Mossi society was dominated by the tributary mode of production. See Thompson and Adloff, op. cit., 171-178); E. Skinner, op. cit.

110. Although the two chiefs were under obligation to do so, they did receive gratutities for the men they delivered.

111. Damas Report, op. cit., "FHB Testimony."

112. Ibid.

113. The basis of the 1948-1951 civil strife in the Ivory Coast can actually be traced to the labor crisis for the colons. The utter contempt in which they held the SAA, and their anger at being unable to recruit SAA men as laborers--to regard them as employers in their own right--brought racist violence by the white colons against the Africans. (See Damas Report, op. cit., "FHB Testimony.")

114. Ibid.

115. Berg, op. cit., 169; Inventaire économique, op. cit., 194.

116. Inventaire économique, op. cit., 194.

117. 1944-1959 figures from Zolberg, op. cit., 25; 1975 figure from Ivory Coast, National Agricultural Census, 1974.

118. Zolberg, op. cit., 25.

119. See Ivory Coast, Ministry of Planning, Direction des études de développement, Les activités non agricoles dans la zone sud (January, 1975).

120. This census will always be referred to as the Agricultural Census.

121. Official figures put the Ivorian population at 5,796,000 in 1973. (See Côte d'Ivoire en chiffre, op. cit., 12.)

122. The average coffee farm is 3.24 hectares; that of cocoa is 3.48; palm oil 3.42; coconut 4.39; and cotton 0.3. Coffee/cocoa farm size is even for all regions except for the Agni department of Abengourou, where larger farms are found, and the department of Dimbokro, where farms are, on the average, smaller. Thus, while 16.2 percent of the cocoa/coffee farmers hire permanent wage labor,

Abengourou leads with 50 percent, followed by Gagnoa's 23 percent, Dimbokro with 13 percent, and Sassandra with 4.8 percent. The east, in other words, with larger farms, has maintained its lead as a labor recipient.

123. To recapitulate: a marginal coffee region is a region which, due to use of extensive methods, increasingly becomes less productive as a result of soil exhaustion and inability of the producers to regenerate it for lack of capital.

124. The average national yield is 407 kilograms per hectare of green coffee; with proper SATMACI assistance, yields vary between 600 and 1,000 kilograms per hectare.    See Statistiques Agricoles 1973, Ivory Coast, Ministère de l'agriculture.

125. We shall not discuss the Ivory Coast's special tariff relationships with France as this is covered by her sales to quota countries, which include all the other EEC countries. For more details, see M. Lachiver, op. cit.

126. ICA-I, article 28, clause 2.

127. Fixed quantities every year for "quota" countries, unlimited quantities for nonquota countries--but such exports have to be declared to the International Coffee Organization (ICO). T. Geer, An Oligopoly: The World Coffee Economy and Stabilization Schemes (New York: Dunellon, 1971), 71-165. The Ivory Coast has had an unsteady rate of selling in the nonquota countries. Its best clients in this category have been Hungary and Senegal, both of which actually increased their demands for Ivorian coffee since 1970. Total sales to nonquota countries decreased 25,011 tons in 1970-1971 to 16,361 in 1974-1975. See "Etat récapitulatif des exportations du café vert," Caisse de Stabilisation, Abidjan.

128. Côte d'Ivoire en chiffre, op. cit., 39.

129. These materials could be obtained, on credit, from SATMACI, stored and distributed regionally according to intensity of coffee production. It was this credit system that also makes the state an exploiter of peasant labor, for the capital so advanced is repaid with a 6 percent annual interest.

130. The system of chain stores, owned by the state and private capital, is increasingly taking over petty trade in rural areas. Although the complete takeover is far from finished, the basic structure has already been laid down. See A.L. Bonnefois, "La transformation de commerce de traite en Côte d'Ivoire depuis la dernière guerre mondiale et l'indépendence," Cahiers d'Outre-Mer 84 (1968).

131. Foreign private capital investors in SERIC are Banque commerciale pour le commerce et l'industrie, Banque national de Paris, and the Société financière pour les pays d'outre-mer, all of which have majority shares in the Banque international pour le commerce et l'industrie de Côte d'Ivoire, a local SERIC shareholder. In the same way, Crédit lyonnais of France, through Société ivoirienne de banque, also has investments--hence, part ownership--in SERIC.

132. SEDES Study, 1970.

133. Interview.

134. The management of the factory was entrusted to Jean Abile Gal, an import-export firm installed in the Ivory Coast from colonial times. But Jean

Abile Gal's management was meant to be temporary. Eventually, SERIC was meant to take over the entire running of the factory and ensure the dominant intermediation of the state between the planter in Bouaflé and the consumer of Ivorian coffee in the importing countries.

135. The expression, "ils font de commerce avec nous," was commonly used by the villagers in Aboisso to describe the practice whereby those who have exchange relations with them take advantage of monopsonistic or monopolistic situations to extract greater surplus from them.

136. The Groupement à vocation cooperative (GVC), founded in 1970, handles 14 percent of the transportation of coffee/cocoa in Ivory Coast (1972/73 figures). The chief function of the GVCs is to coordinate the selling of cash crops of villagers in groups. The Centre national de promotion des entreprises cooperatives (CENAPEC), with headquarters at Bingerville, is responsible for the training of GVC field workers and planning GVC activities. By 1973, the department of Man, Guiglo, Divo, and Danané (i.e., the younger coffee-growing regions) had the highest proportions of GVCs per capita and the highest number in absolute terms.

137. "Investments in the Ivory Coast," Marchés Tropicaux 1563 (24 October 1975), 109.

138. "Reunions des exportateurs de café," Bulletin mensuel, Chambre de commerce de la Côte d'Ivoire, no. 1, January 1976.

139. F. Engels, "Origin of the Family, Private Property and the State," in Marx and Engels, Selected Works (New York: International Publishers, 1967), 532-533.

140. Ivory Coast, Ministry of Agriculture, Caisse national de crédit agricole, "Rapport d'activité, 1966-67" (BNDA Library, Abidjan).

141. From interviews with BNDA officials, 5 September 1975.

142. Interviews in Daoukro, Aboisso, Ayame, Yamassoukro, and Divo.

143. National Agricultural Census, 1974 (Ivory Coast).

144. Ministère de l'agriculture, Statistiques agricoles 1973, 62.

145. Seventy-five percent of the Aboisso coffee-growing households received the emergency fund in 1975, an unusually high proportion.

146. See for example Y.-C. Ramboz, op. cit.; and B. Lewis, op. cit.

147. Côte d'Ivoire en chiffre, op. cit., 87.

148. There were at least thirty-one coffee exporters in the Ivory Coast in January 1975.

149. See below, on Palmindustrie-Palmivoire.

150. Interview with M. Stessels, Director of Technical Operations, SATMACI, September 1975.

151. See, for example, A.-M. Pillet-Schwartz, Capitalisme d'état et développement rural en Côte d'Ivoire, La Sodepalm en pays Ebrie (Paris: Ecole pratique des hautes études, 1973).

152. Société commerciale et industrielle des produits oléagineux--Palmindustrie--has 68.5 percent state participation; Palmivoire has 60.3 percent. For this and most of the following information, see also IBRD, "Appraisal of the

Second Oil Palm and Coconut Project: Ivory Coast," Washington, 1 June 1971.

153.  Only thirty-two out of the 150 outgrowers at the Ehania estate were natives of the area; in other words, 79 percent of the outgrowers were either Voltaic or other foreigners (BNDA Divisonal Offices, Aboisso, 1975/76 figures).

154.  One of the reasons the Baoule in these areas do not stay and try cotton as an alternative to coffee and cocoa is that "cotton work is too hard.  You have to work with your back against the sun all the time.  Unlike coffee, cotton requires almost daily attention.  But, after the harvest, we do not get as much out of it as we did from coffee.  For the effort we put into it, it is not really worth it."  (Interview with a peasant in Daoukro, 1976.)

# Part 4
# The Role of the State in African Capitalism

The degree of state involvement and its consequences for economic development is a subject of intense debate among policy makers addressing the economic crisis in Africa. Although the contradictions and costs attributable to inefficient state intervention are real enough, it is ironic that these same international agencies and former colonial powers introduced the very state agencies that are now the object of scorn. If the decade of the 1970s was one of state-led economic nationalism among peripheral states, then the 1980s promise a vengeful reaction against state economic intervention and a return to the hegemony of the market and to the privatization of parastatal agencies. Just how the indigenous bourgeoisie will benefit or respond to the new conditions will be an important area for new research.

In the case of Nigeria, the petroleum boom of the 1970s was mediated by the state into civil society. Economic nationalism was a powerful integrative force among all members of the Nigerian bourgeoisie. Whatever the limits of implementation, indigenization transferred financial control of major corporations to Nigerians and increased their participation in technical and administrative positions within international firms.

Biersteker's contribution takes the reader into the boardrooms of the major actors in the Nigerian indigenization process. His insightful analysis illustrates the tension between local and international capital and the ways in which international capital still retains control, if not legal ownership. Here, the capacity of the Nigerian state to enforce its own policies again appears problematic. By comparing Nigeria with Kenya and Brazil, the strengths and limits of the dependent development perspective can be seen.  Quite perceptively, Biersteker predicts that economic nationalist interventions would decline under civilian government as they did under the Shagari administration.  The facile argument that correlates successful economic nationalist programs with authoritarian regimes fails also.  For, despite unprecedented authoritarianism, the policies of the military government of Buhari  were either insufficient or misguided mostly because of the collapse of petroleum prices.  Hence the range for state intervention remains limited.

Compared to the scale and the ambition of the Nigerianization program, the state intervention into the economy on behalf of indigenous Ivorians is, as yet, limited.  In her analysis of the role of the state in Ivorian capitalist development, Bonnie Campbell shows that even the modest program of Ivorization is essentially empty and, even then, limited to the clients of the ruling political elite.  Nonetheless, her analysis bluntly states that the failure of Ivorianization was not due to mismanagement or error but, rather, arises from the necessity of maintaining the confidence of foreign investors upon whom this model of accumulation depends.  The new policy calling for increased joint ventures does not, however, indicate movement toward strengthening indigenous private capital; rather it suggests a rationalization of state capital within an increasingly internationalized world economy.

*Paul M. Lubeck*

*Thomas J. Biersteker*

# 8 Indigenization and the Nigerian Bourgeoisie: Dependent Development in an African Context

Dependency and other contemporary critical perspectives on development share the assumption that development in peripheral economies is conditioned by their integration with the world economy. The problems of (and prospects for) development can only be understood when the history and nature of their integration is fully comprehended. In some versions of these perspectives, genuine development is not really possible within the context of the contemporary world economy.[1] Whether conceptualized as growth or capitalist accumulation, development cannot take place until the world economy is either transformed or transcended. However, dramatic changes in both the world economy and national economies located in its periphery have created a number of problems for proponents of this stagnationist thesis.

Throughout the 1970s there has been a growth of the role of the state and an assertion of economic nationalism in Africa, Asia, and Latin America. Most national states have increasingly taken on regulative, welfare, and planning functions, and the state has become a major (if not *the* major) economic actor in many countries.[2] At the same time, OPEC has succeeded in forming an effective producer cartel and has inspired attempts to form producer organizations in other commodities. The Group of Seventy-Seven has attained unprecedented levels of cooperation, policies of economic nationalism (nationalization and indigenization) have become widespread, and most host countries have levied increasingly stringent regulations on the operations of foreign firms.[3] In additional, nationally based capitalist accumulation (or apparent accumulation) has occurred in some areas of the periphery of the contemporary world economy, whether in the form of newly industrializing countries or pockets of indigenous capital accumulation in lower-growth economies.

The growth of the role of the state, the assertion of economic nationalism, and the emergence of pockets of apparent accumulation have presented formidable challenges to stagnationist versions of dependence and other critical perspectives on development. Scholars who reject simplistic stagnationist perspectives have begun to incorporate these significant changes into their analyses of international development. In Africa, this response has taken the form of the debate between Colin Leys and his critics over the nature of accumulation in Kenya.[4] In Latin America, discussion has been directed toward the formulation and elaboration of the concept of dependent development.[5] In both regions, contemporary scholarship has been directed toward a consideration of the complexity of the relationships between the state, local capital, and foreign capital. Disagreements have emerged about the relative power of these principal actors, their points of alliance and confrontation, and their capacity for autonomous accumulation. Nevertheless, their interaction has become the central focus of a great deal of the current research in international political economy.

Colin Leys provided one of the first responses to stagnationist theses in his 1978 reassessment of his earlier (1974) analysis of underdevelopment in Kenya. Leys considered the precolonial origins of the indigenous bourgeoisie in Kenya and incorporated its increasing motivations to supplant foreign capital into his analysis. According to Leys,

> the debate about dependency and underdevelopment has not shown
> either that capitalist development cannot occur at the periphery (or 'in
> the Third World'), or that it is eventually bound to. What it demon-
> strates is, rather, the need to study and theorise the conditions under
> which other periphery countries have, and others have not, experienced
> significant measures of growth.[6]

In his criticism of his earlier work, Leys contends that local capital largely controls the state and uses it to facilitate local accumulation. Rather than performing as a "register of the imbalance" between foreign capital and a much weaker local capital, the state in Kenya has become "the register of the leading edge of indigenous capital" in its assault on the barriers posed by foreign capital.[7] Accordingly, local capital is increasingly capable of constructing state policy in its interests, largely independent of the state or foreign capital. State initiatives "reflected the existing class power of the indigenous bourgeoisie, based on the accumulation of capital they had already achieved."[8]

The relationship between local and foreign capital is depicted as increasingly antagonistic. Private indigenous capital has been able to displace foreign capital in farming, service, and even in manufacturing activities. It has employed capital acquired through its commercial activities in the ivory, charcoal, and (especially in recent years) lucrative coffee trade to facilitate this displacement. The major areas of contention between local, state, and foreign capital tend, therefore, to be along national/international lines in the form of a partial state and local capital alliance against foreign capital. As a result, some local capital accumulation is taking place at present. Although further obstacles to uninterrupted local accumulation remain,

> Kenya appears, from this analysis, as a modest example of a 'systematic combination of movements' conducive to the transition to the capitalist mode of production.[9]

Capitalist development is, therefore, possible at present.

Another student of Kenyan development, Raphael Kaplinsky, has reexamined Leys's argument with detailed information he has gathered on the ownership of large-scale manufacturing and tourist farms operating in Kenya.[10] Kaplinsky diverges from Leys in a number of important respects. Although he agrees that the issue of accumulation raises "perhaps the most basic questions of all," and that local capital in Kenya has grown significantly since independence and expanded its ownership of industry, he disagrees that very much local accumulation is actually taking place.

> Insofar as the Kenyan case can be generalised, I believe it shows that the possibilities for successful accumulation in an open economy of this type are limited whatever the historical roots of the accumulating class.[11]

Although he agrees with Leys that local capital can have much influence on some state decisions, Kaplinsky does not agree that local capital is capable of directing state policy in its own interests. Rather, the relationship between local capital and the state is more ambiguous. The state is not homogeneous and can be divided between its nationalist and penetrated elements. A "national" interest is articulated within the central bank and by some middle level officers in most ministries and parastatals. However, more often than not, "the state shows little evidence of taking an antagonistic stance to foreign capital."[12]

Kaplinsky disagrees more emphatically with Leys about the relationship between local and foreign capital. Although he too has observed the trend toward the establishment of new Kenyan-owned and -controlled enterprises, Kaplinsky disagrees that local capital has begun to supplant foreign capital in certain activities. Rather, he contends that the relationship between local and foreign capital is essentially harmonious and that, for the most part, local capital is forced to rely on foreign capital for its basis of accumulation:

> More specifically in relation to Kenya, I believe that the evidence shows that although an indigenous capitalist class has managed to carve out a slice of the benefits arising from accumulating in large scale industry, this has arisen from an alliance between this class and foreign capital.[13]

Thus, Kaplinsky finds little local capital accumulation taking place and few major areas of contention between state, local, and foreign capital; he concludes that capitalist development is unlikely at the present time.[14]

Peter Evans has been concerned with many of these same issues in his recent study of dependent development in Brazil. In a context very different from that of the accumulation debate in Kenya, Evans is interested in the emergence of a complex triple alliance among elite local capital, international capital, and state capital. For Evans, these three interdependent actors form an ambivalent alliance of partners who "have a common interest in capital accumulation and in the subordination of the mass population, but whose interests are also contradictory."[15]

Evans is generally closer to Kaplinsky than to Leys with regard to the relationship between local capital and the state. Local capital is the weakest of the three partners in Brazil and is generally subordinate to the state. Rather than control the state, local capital in Brazil relies on its alliances with state enterprises for the little bargaining power it has in relation to foreign capital. The state in Brazil is described as far more autonomous and more active than in Kenya, and its enterprises have played "an increasingly central role in bringing about basic industrialization."[16]

Local capital is also generally subordinate to foreign capital in Brazil. Although it has control of certain "traditional" sectors such as leather goods, apparel and wood products, local capital generally relies on foreign capital for the basis of its accumulation. Strictly speaking, representatives of local capital are not relegated to the status of *compradores*. Rather, their possession of special abilities such as a comparative advantage in providing access to distributive contact networks and knowledge of local market conditions allows them to play an important integrative role in the emerging triple alliances:

> In the process of deciding what goes on within Brazil, their subordination to their multinational partners cannot be assumed; rather their strategies are constrained by their incorporation into a set of relations with international capital in general. They must 'play by the rules' of international capital in the same way that any capitalist must play by the rules deemed appropriate by his class.[17]

In a semiperipheral country like Brazil, complex combinations of state, local, and foreign capital provide a common form of ownership structure of the firm. In addition, there is a certain amount of division of labor between the three major actors: state capital concentrates in large, long-range return investments, local capital in retail trade and low-technology manufacturing, and foreign capital in high-technology, large-scale investments.

> But most branches of industry are not the preserves of any one kind of capital. Within these 'disputed areas' or 'buffer zones' integration on the basis of joint ventures is necessary.[18]

These divisions and disputed areas are not static, and hence points of contention develop as the terms of bargaining shift. However, like Kaplinsky, Evans sees relatively few areas of major contention between the principal actors.

Finally, with regard to the question of accumulation, Evans is generally closer to Leys than to Kaplinsky. Local capital in Brazil continues to engage in accumulation despite the erosion of its historically dominant position through denationalization in some sectors in the post-World War Two period. Not only is accumulation taking place in some of the low-technology manufacturing activities in which local capital still predominates, but Evans argues that local capital accumulation is taking place based on the share of proceeds derived from the operation of the triple alliance. Evans concludes that the collaboration among all three kinds of capital "has had the effect of deepening and diversifying Brazil's industrial capacity."[19] Because the triple alliance is a strategy for accumulation in a dependent context, the "process of accumulation in Brazil is still vulnerable to the effects of disruptions in the international economy, and that vulnerability constitutes the most obvious limitation of the triple alliance."[20]  Thus, although capitalist development is possible at present, it is an example of dependent development.

These three conceptual frameworks for describing the contemporary possibilities for capitalist development in the periphery of the world economy go well beyond the stagnationist versions of dependency and other critical perspectives on development. Each has incorporated significant developments in the world and national economies into his arguments. Leys and Kaplinsky concentrate on emerging pockets of accumulation and economic nationalism, while Evans focuses on the growth of the role of the state. For the purposes of clarification, their principal arguments and points of agreement and divergence can be summarized in a conceptual matrix. Table 8.1 is a simplification of elaborate and complex arguments and should be used only as a guide to accompany the preceding text. It captures only a portion of the accumulation and dependent development debates. However, it does help to clarify some of the issues for a comparative evaluation of developments in other, nonstagnating national economies located in the periphery of the contemporary world economy.

## Dependent Development in Nigeria

Nigeria is one of the most important semiperipheral countries in the developing world today and has one of its fastest growing internal markets. Like both Kenya and Brazil, it cannot be readily described with stagnationist versions of dependence. It too has undergone an increase in the role of the state, an assertion of economic nationalism and an emergence of local sources of accumulation. As a member of OPEC, Nigeria has been at the forefront of the confrontation with the transnational corporation. It has relied on this experience in its expansion of state involvement in the economy, notably in the petroleum and related petrochemical sectors. Direct state involvement has increased in other areas of the economy as well, notably in mining, utilities, banking, and insurance. Although Nigeria historically has offered potential investors a number of investment incentives, a basic objective of its policy since the end of the civil war in 1970 has been to increase indigenous control over economic activities. Accordingly, there have been recurring pressures for the indigenization of both personnel and share capital and for limitations on the repatriation of profits and dividends. Indigenization not only has been an important expression of economic nationalism, but also has provided a basis for local accumulation in Nigeria.

Although nonstagnationist explanations are required to incorporate many of these substantial changes, Nigeria does not appear to be a clear illustration of any one of the three conceptual frameworks discussed in the introduction. Its successive state-sponsored indigenization decrees have enabled local capital to acquire an interest (often a majority interest) in foreign capital, resembling the situation in Leys's discussion of Kenya. The relationship between local and foreign capital also appears to be essentially harmonious, similar to Kaplinsky's discussion of Kenya. And the most common forms of new enterprises in the country tend increasingly to be made up of complex combinations of state, local and foreign capital, as in Evans's Brazil.

A closer examination of one of the most important areas of state intervention in the economy, the indigenization process in Nigeria, reveals that a specific form of dependent development is emerging in the country.[21] It bears some resemblance to the Kenyan and Brazilian models, but the Nigerian version is clearly distinctive. The economy is not stagnating, but neither is a substantial amount of local capital accumulation taking place.[22] Local capital still relies on its share of the proceeds from foreign and state capital for the basis of its accumulation, but it is not subordinate to them in all areas. Rather, local capital in Nigeria is partially independent of both state and foreign capital and is able to play them off against each other for its own (nonaccumulating) interests. Local capital is engaged in a complex, dual alliance with both the state and foreign capital which, although it provides a basis for immediate individual accumulation, may not provide much of a basis for national, capitalist development.[23]

## The Sources and Objectives of Indigenization

Although Nigeria's most far-reaching and controversial indigenization decrees were promulgated during the 1970s, there is a long history of indigenization pressures in the country. Proposals for increasing Nigerianization of the economy were first incorporated in official policy statements describing investment opportunities for potential investors during the late 1950s. A national committee to promote the Nigerianization of business enterprises was created by the colonial government in 1956.[24] The 1958 Tax Relief Act required transnational corporations

TABLE 8.1: Capitalist Development

| | Relationship Between Local Capital and the State | Influence of Local Capital on State Policy | Relationship Between Local Capital and Foreign Capital | Major Areas of Contention | Accumulation by Local Capital | Capitalist Development at Present? |
|---|---|---|---|---|---|---|
| Leys (Kenya) | LC controls the state, and uses it to facilitate local accumulation. | Considerable. LC is able to construct policy in its interest (independent of the state or FC). | Antagonistic. LC has begun to supplant FC in some sectors. | Between national and international capital (LC uses the state to displace FC) | LC accumulation is taking place. | Possible. |
| Kaplinsky (Kenya) | Ambiguous. State is not homogeneous; most portions in alliance with FC (especially largest TMCs), weaker portions | Very little. Some state policies in LC interest, but not many. | Harmonious. LC must rely on and bargain with FC for its basis of accumulation. LC largely comprador in alliance with | Few areas of major contention; state shows little evidence of taking an antagonistic stance toward FC. FC and LC | Little LC accumulation taking place. | Unlikely. |

| | | | | | | |
|---|---|---|---|---|---|---|
| | in alliance with LC. | | FC. | essentially harmonious. | | Possible. |
| Evans (Brazil) | Generally subordinate to the state; LC relies on alliances with the state for its bargaining position. | Very little. Most LC in some form of alliance with FC or the state. State policy not necessarily constructed in response to LC pressure. | Symbiotic. LC subordinate to FC in most instances, but plays important role in integrating FC into local economy. LC occasionally relies on FC for basis of accumulation (but not essentially compradores.) | In buffer zones between spheres of LC, FC and state. Areas shift according to industry and over time, but generally not much contention. | Some LC accumulation is taking place based on share of proceeds from triple alliances. State is principal indigenous source of accumulation. | |

seeking "pioneer" company status both to increase Nigerian ownership and personnel and to use Nigerian materials in production; however, it was not until after independence that significant legislation was passed.   After being supported in principle in both the first national development plan and in a 1961 house of representatives resolution, provisions for increasing Nigerianization were codified into law in the 1963 Immigration Laws.   This rather stringent set of controls and regulations established quotas for newly established transnational corporations and was designed to increase Nigerian participation in the highest levels of management.

There has been a broad base of popular support for any assertion of economic nationalism in Nigeria since independence was attained in 1960.   Indigenization has been justified as a response to popular pressures, and public support has consistently been mobilized in defense of the exercise.   However, it would be misleading and inaccurate to suggest that indigenization has been pursued as a response to broad-based public pressures.   Such a response would imply a commitment to an egalitarianism that was neither a central motive nor an objective of Nigerianization.[25]

On the contrary, from the time of its inception during the 1950s, the indigenization process in Nigeria has stemmed from two primary sources, with different and occasionally contradictory purposes.   Indigenization has been instituted by an amenable military elite in response to intermittent, but recurring, pressures from an indigenous economic elite.   Nigerian businessmen had been agitating for protection against competition from foreigners in the distributive trade since the late 1950s.   This agitation became more insistent during the six years of civilian rule after independence in 1960.   It was not until after the Nigerian civil war, however, that indigenous businessmen found a Nigerian government with the willingness and ability to carry out a more comprehensive indigenization program.

The federal military government had experienced the consequences of excessive reliance on foreign governments and transnational corporations during the Nigerian civil war.   The indecision of transnational oil companies about whether to make payments to the federal government or to the Biafran government had a significant impact on the military leaders and created serious doubts about whether transnationals could be trusted.[26]   The civil war also encouraged the growth of state involvement in the economy to manage the war effort. The general strengthening of the state increased its confidence against extensive foreign involvement in the Nigerian economy.

The civil war also fostered the rise of a new bourgeoisie who accumulated "easy wealth" by supplying equipment and war material to both the Biafran and federal governments. Since this bourgeoisie did not owe its wealth to foreigners, it could afford to fan the flames of popular nationalism and put pressure on the state to Nigerianize the economy after the war.[27] There is a great deal of evidence that indigenous businessmen applied increasing pressure on the federal military government for an indigenization program during this period. Alhaji Aminu Dantata, Kano State Commissioner for Trade and Industry in 1972, commented that "by promulgating the decree the Federal Government has done what businessmen themselves wanted so badly for several years past." P.C. Asiodu, former Minister of Mines and Power, suggested that "it was in the period between 1968 and 1971 that the widest consultations were undertaken leading to the promulgation of the Enterprise Promotion Decree of 1972."

The influence of these pressures on a military elite increasingly distrustful of foreign capital led to the announcement of the Nigerian Enterprises Promotion Decree in 1972. The central objectives of the 1972 decree reflected the dual sources of support for indigenization from the government and local business community. The central objective of the federal military government was to obtain Nigerian control over the economy in general, and over strategic enterprises in particular. Former head of state Yakubu Gowon described the objective of the decree as "consolidating our political independence," and many observers have viewed it as an assertion of economic nationalism or an antidependency measure in response to the civil war experience. Paul Collins maintains that the decree was meant to give Nigerians greater involvement in economic and commercial affairs.[28] In mid-1972, the federal commissioner for trade said the goal of indigenization was to "make the country's economy truly Nigerian,"[29] and University of Ibadan professor E.O. Akeredolu-Ale later suggested that indigenization was inspired by a desire to reduce Nigeria's external dependence.[30]

At the same time, local businessmen wanted a protected niche in the economy free from foreign competition, as well as a share of the proceeds of the most successful (foreign-dominated) sectors of the economy. Both of these objectives were consistent with the federal military government's goal of increased national control over the Nigerian economy. Sule

Kolo, Nigeria's high commissioner to the United Kingdom in 1972, commented that the indigenization decree was aimed at small expatriate concerns in trade and services, which "excite resentment among rival indigenous enterprises."[31] Accordingly, much of the pressure from Nigerian businessmen in 1972 was directed mainly against the Lebanese-controlled commerce and retail sector.[32] This explains why these commercial activities were reserved for 100 percent local participation, while many of the largest European- and North American-based transnationals were not at all affected by the different schedules (or groupings of industrial activities) established in the 1972 decree.

The 1972 Nigerian Enterprise Promotion Decree stipulated that by March 1974, no person other than a Nigerian citizen could be the owner or part-owner of enterprises in twenty-two selected industries in Nigeria (called Schedule 1 industries). The industries affected included small, labor-intensive manufacturing and local service-related enterprises, many of which were already predominantly Nigerian in 1972. The 1972 decree also stipulated that aliens could not participate in thirty-three other industries (called Schedule 2 industries), where the paid-up share capital of the enterprise was less than 200,000 (Nigerian) or the turnover of the enterprise was less than 500,000 (Nigerian), whichever the Nigerian Enterprises Promotion Board (NEPB) deemed appropriate. The NEPB was granted sweeping discretionary powers to administer the decree's provisions.

Schedule 2 enterprises exempted on the basis of their size were required to make available to the Nigerian public up to 40 percent of their total equity. The businesses in this second schedule included construction firms, some large import-substitution industries, and wholesale and retail distributors. Because of the exemption of large-scale firms in these sectors, most transnational corporations were not required to make available more than 40 percent of their total equity to the Nigerian public following the 1972 decree. A great number of Nigeria's largest and most important manufacturing industries (tobacco and textiles, for example) were completely unaffected by the 1972 decree.

The release of a government white paper evaluating the implementation of the decree in 1975 revealed that only one-third of the affected enterprises had complied fully with the decree's provisions. Thereafter, pressures for increased indigenization came to a head. The new Obasanjo government responded in less than a year with an extension of the 1972 decree, first announced in June 1976 and formally promulgated in January of 1977. The Nigerian Enterprises Promotion Decree of 1977 reorganized the board responsible for implementation and increased its discretionary powers to inspect enterprises, conduct prosecutions, and seal up the premises of offending enterprises. In addition, twenty new industries were added to the list of Schedule 1 industries to be completely indigenized in ownership. Among those industries added were the wholesale distributors of local manufactures and other locally produced goods, major retail stores with an annual turnover of *less* than two million naira ($3.3 million), commercial agents such as manufacturers' representatives, and most commercial transportation companies. Thirty-three new industries were added to the second schedule, and the mandatory sale of shares was raised from 40 percent to 60 percent. Among the most significant of the new activities added were banking (commercial, merchant and development banks), insurance, shipping agencies, food manufacture, basic iron and steel manufacture, and petrochemical industries. A third schedule was added to the revised decree, which listed all remaining industries and required that they make available at least 40 percent of their equity to Nigerian subscribers. The Schedule 3 enterprises include the largest transnationals in tobacco concerns and textile firms, previously exempted from indigenization, as well as high-technology enterprises. Thus, at present, only enterprises engaged in single, nonrenewable projects are exempt from indigenization. All other enterprises are required to make at least part of their equity (a minimum of 40 percent) available to Nigerian subscribers. Clearly, the 1977 decree contains more far-reaching and stringent regulations when compared to the 1972 version, which exempted most of the largest and most important transnational corporations.

The extension of the indigenization decree in 1977 once again reflects the dual sources and changing objectives of the military and business elites in Nigeria. The Obansanjo government of the late 1970s was more strongly committed to an ideology of economic nationalism than the Gowon government.[33] Accordingly, the revised decree was quite explicit about the desire to obtain control over important aspects of production. Included among the basic objectives of the 1977 Nigerian Enterprises Promotion Decree are "to advance and promote enterprises in which citizens of Nigeria *shall participate fully* [emphasis added] and play a dominant role [and] ensuring the assumption of the control of the Nigerian economy by Nigerians in the shortest possible time."[34]

In addition to being explicit about its objectives, the Nigerian government appears to be serious about its intention to obtain control over important aspects of production. Indigenization is the most important component of Nigeria's foreign investment policy; and there is no evidence of either internal bureaucratic opposition to the decree or a tendency to trade compliance with indigenization for other (more important) concessions from transnational corporations.

Having already reserved a protected niche for commercial and low-technology activities in the 1972 decree, indigenous business modified its objectives and pressed for a larger share of the proceeds of foreign enterprises located throughout the economy with the extension of the decree in 1977. Since most of the share capital offered by transnational corporations in 1972 was heavily oversubscribed, the 1977 extension of the indigenization program offered investment opportunities for businessmen left out of the original exercise. It also provided investment opportunities for Nigeria's newest economic elite emerging from the oil boom during the mid- and late 1970s.

These objectives were broadly consistent with, but more limited than those of the federal military government in 1977. Whereas the central objective of the governmental decree was control of the economy and full participation by Nigerians, some of the strongest backers of indigenization among Nigeria's economic elite were more interested in a share of the proceeds of the economy than its control. Some indigenous businessmen began to express concern about the growth of public sector (state) acquisitions during indigenization, reflecting an uneasiness in the alliance between state and local capital in Nigeria. As we shall see below, when this divergence of objectives between the state and local capital is accompanied by a sophisticated array of transnational corporate responses to indigenization, the entire program can be effectively neutralized.

*Corporate Responses to Nigerian Indigenization:*
*Exit, Voice, or Deceit?*

Nigeria appears to be a model case of the growth of the role of the state and an assertion of economic nationalism. It is frequently cited as an illustration of these phenomena.[35] The state is gradually assuming a greater role in economic activities, the number of state corporations is growing, more stringent regulations affecting the transnational corporation have been enacted over time, and a majority of the equity of new operations is being acquired by the state and indigenous local investors. Not only has there been a marked increase in the frequency of state actions designed to control the operations of transnational corporations since 1970, but these actions give the appearance of being increasingly effective. According to official government reports, 1,858 firms have complied with indigenization requirements since 1972, selling over 500 million shares valued at more than 472 billion naira (more than $800 million). There have been very few instances of overt conflict between transnationals and the Nigerian government, and virtually every transnational operating in Nigeria has complied with the equity-sharing requirements of the recent decrees.[36]  In addition, Nigeria appears to fit the model of a gradual and incremental shift in the balance of bargaining power in the direction of a host country. Its successive indigenization decrees have required a gradual increase in the number of economic activities affected, as well as in the amount of equity that must be shared with local capital.

Despite this apparent growth of state power, transnational corporations are still quite eager to invest in Nigeria. The "gold rush" of the mid-1970s, when foreign investors could recover their investment in one or two years, is over. However, most foreign executives currently working in the country maintain that there is ample room for new firms interested not in a quick return, but in a longer-term profitable investment in one of the fastest growing markets in the world. Only two of the hundreds of large, transnational corporations operating in the country have chosen an "exit" option and pulled out of Nigeria as a result of its increasing demands on foreign operations. And at least one of them, Citibank, regrets the move and has been trying (unsuccessfully) to get back into the country. In addition, a number of the largest transnational corporations in the world not already operating in Nigeria are contemplating direct investments there. New foreign capital has continued to flow into Nigeria at an annual average of $331 million during the 1970s. It increased from $305 million to $377 million after the 1972 indigenization decree, but declined to around $200 million immediately after the 1977 decree. It has risen even further in the wake of the return to civilian rule in October 1979, to a total of nearly $600 million in 1980.[37]

Why should transnational corporations be so eager to invest in a country in which is the state is imposing increasingly stringent controls on their operations? The simple explanation is that transnational corporations are not yielding managerial control. The sharing of equity directed in Nigeria's indigenization effort is not equivalent to the sharing of control in the newly established joint ventures. Virtually every transnational corporation involved in Nigeria has found ways to neutralize the indigenization requirements. The specific strategy or combination of strategies varies from firm to firm. However, they are all designed to ensure a minimal loss of control over the operations. Transnational corporations either fight to retain a majority of the equity, or find ways to retain control with a minority share of the equity.

This conclusion is based on detailed interviews conducted during July and August of 1979 with senior executives of twenty-three of the largest transnational corporations operating in Nigeria.[38] When asked to characterize the outcome of the indigenization process, not a single one of the executives of the thirteen firms in the sample, which were reduced to a minority equity shareholding position, was concerned about having lost managerial control over their Nigerian operations. A few minor changes had taken place since indigenization (more expenditure on housing schemes and other employee benefits, for example). However, there was virtually no concern expressed when asked specifically about loss of control over day-to-day operations. Several company executives said they would not stay in Nigeria if they were to lose control over their investments. At least eight of the remaining ten firms in the sample should have yielded a majority of their equity to Nigerian subscribers according to the 1977 decree, yet have managed to obtain exemptions (or find other ways) to avoid becoming minority shareholders.

There are as many different strategies to avoid losing control as there are transnational corporations investing in Nigeria. Only a handful of the major transnational corporations have chosen "exit" or "voice" options as responses to Nigerian indigenization, often with deleterious consequences, as Citibank and American International Insurance have discovered.[39] Most have chosen a variant of a "deceit" option ranging from benignly legal strategies to blatantly illegal ones. Most of the transnational corporations choosing to remain in Nigeria have employed one or a combination of several of the following strategies to ensure that Nigeria's indigenization program will not alter control of their operations.

*Public sale of shares.* Executives of three firms explained how they encouraged the public sale of their share capital to ensure that there would be no single indigenous subscriber with a bloc of shares comparable to the 40 percent retained by the transnational corporation. As one executive advised, "Once you've made the decision to go public, spread your shares as widely as possible." Another added that "the broader the distribution, the easier it is to control the operation." In part, this strategy was unintentionally encouraged by the 1977 indigenization decree, which attempted to prevent the huge concentrations of shareholding among a small number of Nigerians that had accompanied the 1972 decree. The transnationals most likely to favor this strategy include the most visible and best known manufacturing firms with a long-term presence in Nigeria. Manufacturers of well-known consumer products are most likely to attract a broad range of shareholders necessary for the effectiveness of this strategy.

*Technical services agreements.* A second way for minority partners to retain control over their Nigerian operations is to negotiate a technical services agreement with their Nigerian partners, which provides the transnational with responsibility for technology choice, maintenance, and innovation. Agreements for the training of personnel can also ensure that the structure and standard operating procedures of the former transnational remain unchanged. As one executive confidently responded to a question about his parent firm's ability to control its Nigerian operation with only 40 percent of the equity, "It's because of our technical expertise . . . . We still train all the managers." Because of its implications for control over an enterprise, the negotiation of technical service arrangements is becoming an increasingly important aspect of the bargaining relationship between states and transnational corporations. This strategy is particularly prevalent among large transnational banks and has also been employed by two manufacturers engaged in high technology activities.

*Negotiation of exemptions.* Six of the twenty-three transnational corporations interviewed have simply tried to negotiate themselves into exemptions from certain of the requirements of the indigenization decrees. All have negotiated extensions for compliance with the provisions of the 1972 and 1977 decrees. Four have negotiated themselves into different schedules requiring less of a commitment of capital to local subscribers (40 percent as opposed to 60 percent). Two have negotiated complete exemptions from the indigenization decrees. One executive commented, "This is a beautiful place for business, because everyone keeps talking . . . everything is in flux, everything is negotiable. That's why you need a hustler, an expediter." Transnationals in the oil industry and those operating in industries with very little international competition have found it easiest to negotiate exemptions. Companies involved in one-time contractual arrangements with the government also rely on negotiating exemptions. As one executive described his negotiation with government officials, "I told them, you either want the product or you don't. Don't force the issue." He complained that indigenization would disrupt the tight schedule the government had imposed on the project and was granted an exemption from indigenization in his firm's contract. Although this strategy has worked for transnationals in oil, those with few competitors, or those receiving government contracts, it has not been successful when attempted by large, diversified manufacturing companies or by insurance companies.

*Two-company strategy.* Six of the larger, diversified manufacturing transnationals interviewed in Nigeria have responded to indigenization with a two-company formula. Since the Nigerian government has classified economic activities into categories (or schedules) requiring 40 percent, 60 percent or 100 percent local equity participation, diversified manufacturers have similarly divided their own operations. They have completely sold any subsidiaries requiring 100 percent local participation and have formed two subsidiaries for the remaining product lines or economic activities. In one subsidiary, the transnational retains 60 percent of the equity and manufactures the products assigned to this category (or schedule) by the indigenization decree. The economic activities in which transnational capital is restricted to 40 percent are organized in a second subsidiary in which local capital has 60 percent of the shares.

In this way, the transnational corporation retains uninhibited control over all of its product lines assigned to the subsidiary in which it holds 60 percent of the shares. Control is exercised over the other subsidiary in several ways. The two subsidiaries are usually established with identical organizational structures--and often they have overlapping memberships on their boards of directors. In most instances, the same indigenous partners hold the local equity in each of the subsidiary companies. It is not unusual for the subsidiary in which the transnational holds the minority equity to negotiate a technical services agreement with the subsidiary in which it holds majority equity. Often, the two companies exist almost exclusively on paper. Only one factory is constructed, with one administrative building containing two incorporated companies. The physical proximity of the two companies (usually across the hall) also facilitates control over the subsidiary in which the transnational holds only 40 percent of the equity.

In most two-company arrangements, the subsidiary in which the transnational has a minority equity position manages the distribution, sales, and servicing for the products produced by the other subsidiary. The two-company strategy can also provide other benefits in addition to retaining control for transnationals. According to one executive, "It also facilitates splitting government contracts between the two companies, thus minimizing our Nigerian tax liability in respect of such contracts."

*Fronting.* "Fronting" generally refers to the placing of Nigerians in positions of apparent ownership or responsibility, when in fact they are only operating as cosmetic "fronts" to provide legitimacy for the continued presence and dominance of foreign capital. Such overt instances of fronting are specifically prohibited by the 1977 indigenization decree and are relatively rare. Less overt forms of fronting are, however, much more common.

In their efforts to retain control over their operations in Nigeria, virtually all transnational corporations search for local partners and managers who conform to their business interests and standard procedures. This makes good business sense for the transnational corporation because it minimizes local conflicts. Critics of the transnationals describe this phenomenon as the grooming of a "*comprador* elite," whose primary allegiance is to the interests of international capital. With either interpretation, it is a modified form of fronting whenever it is deliberately employed by transnationals to retain control over the operations in which they have been reduced to a minority equity position.

Most foreign executives advise potential investors in Nigeria to take care to choose the "right" local partners. One emphasized the importance of "making the right selection," while another recommended that new ventures should look for "sensible" directors. One pragmatic American executive summed up his company's policy as one of "looking for non-controversial people with money." An oil company executive provided a more detailed recommendation:

> Make investments with the most powerful people (not so that they control operations . . . so that they can provide access). It's important to spread your risk. This [Nigeria] is the most corrupt country in the world . . . . Therefore it's necessary to buy protection.

Several foreign executives commented that they deliberately have "no management role by their board of directors." One company memorandum assigned specific weights to the contributions it expected from its local partners. The financial resources and the political clout and connections of the local partners were valued most highly and each assigned a weight of 40 percent. Within the remaining 20 percent management ability and knowledge about manufacturing were least valued, and each was assigned a weighting value of only 2 percent.

Similar procedures are employed in the selection of local managers by transnational corporations. Choosing the "right" local managers for the firm often involves grooming them in the training programs offered by transnational companies and "bringing them up through the ranks." Unlike the local partners, local managers often have to be trained to be sure they share the transnational's business objectives and conform to their standard operating procedures. To ensure that the Nigerian managers exert very little influence over company policy, they are often given virtually no management responsibilities.

Another way to ensure that local managers or partners serve as no serious threat to the control of indigenized firms is to make them personally dependent on their foreign partners. Transnational corporations can accomplish this by guaranteeing the bank loans required by their local partners to buy into the company. Some firms even go as far as to make contractual agreements with their Nigerian partners guaranteeing that commercial, financial, and technical management is the responsibility of the transnational corporation, that the managing director is appointed by the foreign partner, that the use of the transnational's trademark can be discontinued at any time by its request, and even that the company can be liquidated if the transnational loses management control.

*Changes in voting rules.* A much less subtle but still legal way to maintain control over a subsidiary is to change its voting rules. Two transnational firms have made changes in their company charters prior to indigenization, which ensure that no important policy changes can be made without their support

after they have sold a majority of the equity to local subscribers. The usual formula is to raise the number of votes
required for passage of any major motions from a simple majority to two-thirds or three-fourths. As one executive described his company's policy, "We don't want to give the control of the company to Nigeria at the present time. The company can write the voting rules any way it wants." An internal memorandum from another transnational corporation was
equally explicit. It identified a number of measures to ensure
that it would retain "a suitable measure of control over its investment." Among them were proposals to amend the articles
of association (i.e., charter) of its Nigerian subsidiary "so that
no decision can be taken without [our] consent, i.e. two-thirds
or three-fourths majority required" in the company's general
meeting. The articles were to be similarly amended for board
meetings "so that all decisions require the affirmative vote of
at least one of the nonresident . . . appointed directors, i.e.
affirmative vote of six directors."

A variant of this strategy is to change company standard
operating procedures in ways that minimize the prospects for
Nigerian influence in management. For example, one company simply began to hold fewer board meetings after indigenization and shifted many of its important decisions to other
branches of the firm.

*Division of the board.* A somewhat more malicious but still
legal strategy for maintaining control is to select board members from different ethnic groups with the hope that disputes
between them will distract them from trying to manage the
company. This strategy is not very widely employed. Only
one of the twenty-three firms interviewed suggested that it
was able to retain control by neutralizing its indigenous board
members, "playing Hausas and Yorubas against each other."
Most transnational corporations select board members from all
regions of Nigeria, but they do so in self-defense, to ensure
that they are not closely identified with a single ethnic group
in the country.

*Addition of extra expatriates.* Among the illegal strategies
occasionally employed by transnationals in their efforts to retain control is the addition of expatriate employees, without
official work permits, to key positions of the firm. The
Nigerian government specifies strict expatriate quotas for each
foreign investment and most transnationals do not exceed them
by bringing in expatriate employees on tourist or other visas

that explicitly prohibit accepting employment in the country. However, there are ways around the expatriate quotas for large, diversified investors. One transnational corporation obtained permission to sponsor what it claimed were "necessary" but were, in fact, "redundant" expatriate employees for one of its subsidiaries in Nigeria, in which it has majority control of the equity. Once these expatriates were in the country, they were simply transferred to another subsidiary of the same transnational where it held only a minority of the equity.

*Bribery.* When asked about the extensiveness of bribery in Nigeria, one senior executive replied, "Any successful business is a dirty operation." Bribery certainly is widespread in Nigeria, particularly in the granting of large, multimillion dollar contracts. Although none of the executives interviewed admitted paying any bribes themselves, one was able to quote the going rates for certain permanent secretaries, and another commented, "Personally, I don't know how we got our contracts . . . [pause] . . . I haven't asked . . . [pause] . . . I don't want to know." The senior expatriate executives of a transnational corporation are rarely directly involved in the handling of bribes. They usually provide their Nigerian managers with vague directives to "get the job done," expecting them to make use of their local connections, and don't bother to ask them how they managed to do it.

The bribing of government officials can be used to retain control in the face of indigenization pressures. Special exemptions from certain aspects of the indigenization decrees can be "negotiated," and a number of firms are keenly interested in ensuring that their new product lines are classified in the schedule of the decree that requires that they make available only 40 percent of their total equity to local subscribers. However, bribery is probably more common in the awarding of contracts than it is in the granting of exemptions from the indigenization decrees. There are simply too many other means available to maintain control.

*Unilateral violation of law.* Eight transnational corporations have retained control over their Nigerian subsidiaries by only partially complying with or by totally ignoring Nigeria's indigenization requirements. The construction industry is classified as a Schedule 2 activity, an area where foreign capital cannot exceed 40 percent. However, at least one large transnational construction company has retained a majority of the equity, selling only 40 percent to local subscribers. Its senior executives know they are in violation of the decree, but are not concerned about the consequences:

> There have been no objections raised yet with distribution requirements. We expect some in the future, but nothing much will change for a few years.

The company is fully willing to comply with the decree when confronted by the government. In the meantime, however, it is not going out of its way to raise the issue and is operating in Nigeria with a clear majority of the equity.

Another form of unilateral violation of the law is much more widespread. Seven international banking agents, shipping agents, and representatives for international airlines contend that the indigenization efforts should not apply to their activities. Since most of them have no equity in the country, there is some basis for their position. Nevertheless, several have been informed that they are in violation of Nigerian law and have chosen to ignore requests that they file papers with the Nigerian Enterprises Promotion Decree Board. As one executive confidently put it:

> We have never properly registered with the NEPB, never produced a balance sheet for them. If they pursue it, we'll pay the penalties for not filing. Or we could type up the documents later, say the NEPB lost the copy we sent them, and produce an 'original.'

It should be emphasized that this type of strategy (and arrogance) is restricted to transnational corporations with very little at stake in Nigeria.

In conclusion, the range of strategies available to transnational corporations is impressive. By employing benignly legal methods (such as encouraging a wide distribution of shares) or blatantly illegal ones (such as bribery), transnational corporations have had little difficulty retaining effective managerial control over their Nigerian operations. As well as Nigeria may appear to fit the model of a growing role of the state and an assertion of economic nationalism, transnational corporations show no signs of being held "at bay" in the country.

### Conclusions:  Indigenization and the Emergence of Dependent Development in Nigeria

The responsive and defensive capacities of transnational corporations have quite effectively neutralized the state's objectives in Nigeria.[40]  The indigenization exercise has failed to ensure that Nigerians "participate fully" or "play a dominant role" in the enterprises that have been Nigerianized. Indigenization has also done very little to increase Nigerian control over the economy in general. More than majority equity participation is required to ensure "the assumption of the control of the Nigerian economy by Nigerians." Indigenization has essentially shifted the financial risk burden of new and existing investments onto Nigerian investors without any appreciable increase in their control over the enterprises. Rather than being forced to import capital or obtain it from local sources on their own, transnational corporations have been provided with capital from Nigerian shareholders or partners.

The opportunity costs of indigenization are also very high, especially in light of the state's objective of increasing Nigerian control over the economy. Indigenization makes possible the purchase of shares from transnational corporations, enterprises with the best reputation for a safe, profitable return. Since Nigerian society is pervaded by the idea that "foreign is better," indigenization inevitably encourages investments in transnational corporations. There are no counterincentives for investments in productive, indigenously controlled enterprises, hence the program undermines the basis of accumulation by a national capitalist class. Although some pockets of local accumulation may exist, a risk-averse, profit-maximizing Nigerian investor will buy shares in foreign-owned and -dominated concerns. Indigenization thus encourages a *comprador* role for local business in a society already plagued by strong *comprador* tendencies.[41]     Accordingly, indigenization may have contributed to a decrease, rather than an increase, in Nigerian control of the economy. Additional research would be required to assess the full consequences of this decrease in Nigerian control of the economy. It could mean, however, that the process of production might be different, as well as the nature of the items produced. Many of the potential benefits of learning in locally controlled firms (about management, production, or innovation) would also be lost.

Although the state's objectives of increased Nigerian control of the economy have been effectively neutralized, the objectives of local capital have fared much better. Local businessmen have obtained state sponsorship in their bid to create a protected niche reserved for their enterprises in the distributive and commercial sectors of the economy. They have also succeeded in obtaining state sponsorship in their efforts to secure access to a share of the proceeds of the enterprises in the dynamic sectors of the economy under the control of transnational corporations.    Since they are largely satisfied with a *comprador* role and function (and never really wanted to control foreign enterprises), most indigenous businessmen have attained their essential objectives through the indigenization exercise.

Local capital has thus been engaged in a dual alliance with the state on one hand and with foreign capital on the other. At one level, local capital has been allied with the federal military government in support of a policy of indigenization. Both local capital and the state have employed the rhetoric of economic nationalism to mobilize support for the exercise, but only the state has pursued that objective with any conviction. Local capital has been able to attain its more limited objectives without going so far as to assume control over the indigenized enterprises.    At another level, local capital has been allied with foreign capital in the latter's efforts to neutralize the state's objectives.    The modified form of "fronting" taking place in Nigeria requires the active cooperation of a transnational corporation interested in maintaining control and a local partner satisfied with a largely intermediary function (providing information about local markets or important political connections).    Similarly, a change in the voting rules or unilateral violation of the law requires cooperation between local businessmen unwilling to report violations and transnational corporations willing to commit them.    It is not just "cleverness" that enables transnationals to neutralize the Nigerian indigenization program.    They also require the assistance of their local allies from the Nigerian private sector.

Although Nigerian indigenization is broadly supported as an assertion of economic nationalism, the divergent objectives of the state and local capital, combined with the responsive capacities of transnational corporations, have contributed to its neutralization as an effective policy.    Indigenization may appear to reflect a growth of the role of the state, an assertion of economic nationalism, or a potential source of accumulation in the Third World.    Under closer examination, however, these global trends appear illusory in the Nigerian case.    This becomes especially apparent when we return to consider the relationships between local capital, the state and foreign capital, and the form of dependent development emerging in Nigeria.

Indigenization does not encompass all aspects of the complex set of relationships between the state, local, and foreign capital in Nigeria.    A detailed examination of state planning, finance, or investment activities might identify different relationships.    Indigenization does, however, reveal a great deal

TABLE 8.2: The Emergence of Dependent Development in Nigeria

| Relationship between Local Capital and the State | Influence of Local Capital on State Policy | Relationship between Local Capital and Foreign Capital | Major Areas of Contention | Accumulation by Local Capital | Capitalist Development at Present |
|---|---|---|---|---|---|
| LC has allied with the state for improved access to FC in Nigeria. | LC has manipulated state policy and directed it to conform to its interests. | Harmonious. LC does not threaten FC in critical areas and has played an important role integrating FC into the local economy. | Few areas of contention, as LC manipulates the state and allies with FC, undermining the basis of national/international contention. Increasingly, triple alliances emerging. | Difficult to assess. Some potential in manufacturing, but insufficient information available. | Unlikely; especially after the return to civilian rule. |

about these relationships and about the potential for capitalist development in the country. Local capital did not "control" the state and use it to facilitate local accumulation during the 1970s. Successive military governments were sufficiently autonomous to have their own agendas and policy objectives in the indigenization exercise. Local capital could also not be described as having been generally subordinate to the state, as Evans has observed in Brazil. Rather, local capital has been manipulative and able to direct state policy to conform to its interests. It has been nearly autonomous in this regard but has used its alliance with economic nationalist elements in the state for its improved access to foreign capital operating in Nigeria.[42]

The relationship between local and foreign capital, however, has not been entirely antagonistic. Local capital has forced itself into joint ventures with foreign capital, but it has made no concerted effort to control the enterprises.[43] Hence, foreign capital has not been seriously threatened by the indigenization exercise. Local capital has not begun to supplant it in areas foreign capital deems critical to its control, such as finance, technology, or production. Rather, local capital has provided risk capital and played an important role in integrating foreign capital into the Nigerian economy, closer to the Brazilian than the Kenyan experience.

There have been few areas of major contention between state, local, and foreign capital in Nigeria. Transnationals and their local allies have effectively neutralized the state's objectives, hence contention has not developed between allied national actors and foreign capital, as in Leys's description of Kenya. The state has singled out a few transnational corporations for special attention, particularly when they resist the equity-sharing requirements of indigenization (as American-International Insurance or Citibank did) or when they can be used to make an important foreign policy statement (as with the nationalization of British Petroleum in 1979). However, there is generally not much contention between the three principal actors, especially since indigenization has mandated joint ventures for virtually every transnational corporation operating in Nigeria. Increasingly, these joint ventures have taken the form of a complex variety of triple alliances among the state, local capital and foreign capital, once again vaguely resembling Brazil.

It is very difficult to say whether very much accumulation by local capital is taking place in Nigeria as a result of its indigenization program. Most observers of Nigerian political economy dismiss local capital as *comprador* or intermediary, largely engaged in commerce, services, and other nonproductive activities. However, there is some investment by local capital in productive manufacturing enterprises controlled by indigenous entrepreneurs. Local capital is already important in food processing, furniture, printing, publishing, metal fabrication, and electronic assembly. And there are some signs that it is moving into the production of chemicals and pharmaceuticals as well.[44] Additional information on savings and investment at an individual level *after indigenization* would be required to assess accurately the amount of local capital accumulation taking place at present in Nigeria. For it is also apparent that there is a great deal of conspicuous consumption taking place, a considerable acquisition of land, a great deal of construction and substantial reinvestment in other transnational corporations in the wake of indigenization.

Thus although capitalist development in Nigeria remains a theoretical possibility at present, it does not appear exceedingly likely. This is particularly true since the return to civilian rule in October of 1979. Although more research on this question is needed, it appears that the Nigerian state may be more penetrated by representatives of local capital (with very little interest in accumulation) than were the preceding military regimes. This would imply that it is now less autonomous, less nationalistic, and accordingly less concerned with increasing local control of the economy and establishing a basis for national capitalist development.

## NOTES

The assistance of Marc R. Cohen with the research, conduct of interviews in Nigeria, and conceptualization of this paper was indispensable and is gratefully acknowledged. Nancy Gilgosch provided valuable assistance with the computer analysis and general organization of the argument. Vicki Igel assisted with editorial suggestions and, along with Paul Lubeck, made a number of substantive comments which improved the clarity of the argument. Financial assistance was provided by the Department of Political Science, Yale University, and the International Peace Research Institute, Oslo. This chapter is a theoretical and empirical extension of the argument presented in "The Illusion of State Power" in the Journal of Peace Research, vol. 17, no. 3 (1980).

1. See the discussion of two variants of this stagnationist thesis in Latin America (within the work of Frank, Dos Santos, and Furtado, and within the ECLA school) described in Gabriel Palma, "Dependency: A Formal Theory of Underdevelopment or a Methodology for the Analysis of Concrete Situations of Underdevelopment?" World Development, vol. 6 (1978): 899-909.

2. Alfred Stepan, The State and Society: Peru in Comparative Perspective (Princeton: Princeton University Press, 1978). By describing a "growth of the role of the state," I am referring to a growth in the intensity of its involvement in planning, in regulation, in finance, and in accumulation.

3. C. Fred Bergsten, Thomas Horst and Theodore H. Moran, American Multinationals and American Interests (Washington, D.C.: The Brookings Institution, 1978).

4. For exemplary statements see especially Colin Leys, "Capital Accumulation, Class Formation and Dependency: The Significance of the Kenyan Case," Socialist Register (1978); Raphael Kaplinsky, "Capitalist Accumulation in the Periphery--The Kenyan Case Re-examined," Review of African Political Economy, no. 17 (1980); and Leys's response, "Kenya: What Does 'Dependency' Explain?" in the same issue.

5. See, especially, Fernando Henrique Cardoso and Enzo Faletto, Dependency and Development in Latin America (Berkeley: University of California Press, 1978); Peter Evans, Dependent Development: The Alliance of Multinational, State and Local Capital in Brazil (Princeton: Princeton University Press, 1979).

6. Leys, "Capital Accumulation," op. cit., 244.

7. Ibid., 251-53.

8. Ibid., 251.

9. Ibid., 261.

10. Kaplinsky has updated the National Christian Council of Kenya 1968 survey of Who Controls Industry in Kenya? and has drawn on the revised survey for his empirical discussion of Leys.

11. Kaplinsky, op. cit., 103.

12. Ibid., 99.

13. Ibid., 104.

14. At least part of their disagreement can be traced to the fact that Leys and Kaplinsky differ in their definitions of accumulation. The implications of their definitional and methodological differences will be discussed more fully in the conclusion.

15. Evans, op. cit., 52.

16. Ibid., 214.

17. Ibid., 282.

18. Ibid., 286.

19. Ibid., 287.

20. Ibid., 290.

21. It should be noted that this paper examines in detail only one of the four principal state functions described earlier in the introduction. Indigeniza-

tion is an example of state regulatory policy and can be separated from state planning, finance and accumulation activities.

22. Capital accumulation is defined broadly to refer to revenues or earnings transferred from consumption to investable savings. It can be indicated by a combination of growth, a shift to production, productivity gains, and/or concentration.

23. As we shall see later, precisely what local capital chooses to do with its earnings is critical for an assessment of both accumulation and national capitalist development.

24. Ankie Hoogvelt, "Indigenisation and Foreign Capital: Industrialisation in Nigeria," Review of African Political Economy, no. 14 (1979).

25. O. Aboyade, "Closing Remarks," in Nigeria's Indigenisation Policy, Proceedings of the Symposium organized by the Nigerian Economic Society (Ibadan: University of Ibadan, 1974). See also P.C. Asiodu's closing remarks in the same volume.

26. Paul Collins, "The Policy of Indigenization: An Overall View," Quarterly Journal of Administration (January 1975).

27. Omafume F. Onoge, "The Indigenisation Decree and Economic Independence: Another Case of Bourgeois Utopianism," in Nigeria's Indigenisation Policy, Proceedings of the Symposium organized by the Nigerian Economic Society, op. cit.

28. Collins, op. cit.

29. Quoted in West Africa (23 June 1972).

30. E.O. Akeredolu-Ale, "Private Foreign Investment and the Underdevelopment of Indigenous Entrepreneurship in Nigeria," in Gavin Williams, ed., Nigeria: Economy and Society (London: Rex Collings, 1976).

31. Sule Kolo. Quoted in West Africa (23 June 1972).

32. Gavin Williams, "A Political Economy," in Gavin Williams, ed., Nigeria: Economy and Society, op. cit.

33. The ideology of economic nationalism was also useful for providing legitimacy and broad-based support for a regime in power less than two years and already shaken by the assassination of its head of state, General Murtala Muhammed, in February 1976.

34. Federal Government of Nigeria, "Nigerian Enterprises Promotion Decree, 1977," Supplement to Official Gazette, vol. 64, no. 2, part A (Lagos: Ministry of Information, Printing Division, 1977).

35. For example, C. Fred Bergsten cites Nigeria's indigenization program as an illustration of growing economic nationalism in the Third World in "Coming Investment Wars?", Foreign Affairs, vol. 53, no. 1 (1974). Peter Evans devotes a section of his concluding chapter of Dependent Development to apply his triple alliance ideas to Nigeria; Evans, op. cit., 209-314.

36. The well-publicized experience of the American-International Insurance Group seems to be an exception.

37. These data are obtained from the IMF's annual Balance of Payments Yearbook (IMF, 1981).

38. The interviews were conducted with the most senior foreign executives in twenty-three of the largest transnational corporations in Nigeria. Eighteen of the firms interviewed are included in the UN Center on Transnational Corporations lists of the 200 largest enterprises in the world. Seven of the firms were engaged in banking activities, seven in manufacturing, four in petroleum or petrochemical activities, three in consulting firms, two in services, two in construction, and one in insurance. The total number of activities in this itemized breakdown exceeds twenty-three because a number of transnational corporations have established diversified investments in Nigeria and therefore operate in more than one sector.

39. Citibank pulled out in 1975 and has been unable to return to banking operations in Nigeria, despite repeated attempts. American-International Insurance complained publicly about the valuation of its indigenized shares and, for this (and several other reasons), had one of its senior expatriates charged with currency law violations and imprisoned in 1977.

40. The "state" is not defined here solely in terms of its relationship to a dominant class. Rather, it is considered an analytically separable entity, composed of the principal institutions of the governmental apparatus (the military, police, civil service, and administrative bureaucracies). The state has a monopoly on the legitimate use of force within a given territory and also has a financial basis of support through taxation.

41. Although Nigerians have historically played an intermediary role in West African trade and commerce, it would be a mistake to suggest that their present approaches to transnational corporations simply reflect an inability or an unwillingness to play any other role today. See, especially, E.O. Akeredolu-Ale, The Underdevelopment of Indigenous Entrepreneurship in Nigeria (Ibadan: Ibadan University Press, 1975); Thomas J. Biersteker, Distortion or Development? Contending Perspectives on the Multinational Corporation (Cambridge, Mass.: The MIT Press, 1978) for examples of Nigerian capabilities in the performance of productive and nonintermediary functions in economic activities.

42. Some of the strongest support has come from economic nationalists in the Ministry of Finance and the central bank.

43. Effective control requires more than a holding of a simple majority of the equity share capital. It requires the ability to use equity or other means to determine with regularity the outcomes of decisions on the most important questions confronting the management of the firm (i.e., questions concerning production output, technology choice, reinvestment, local-content use, export promotion, profits and dividends, local research and development, etc.). Thus, control should be defined in terms of managerial responsibility for financial, technical, and commercial aspects of production, rather than in terms of responsibility for noncritical functions such as labor relations, product distribution and advertising.

44. I am currently undertaking a research project examining the scope and significance of local capital accumulation in Nigeria.

*Bonnie Campbell*

# 9 The State and Capitalist Development in the Ivory Coast

The debate concerning the postcolonial state is important not merely as an academic exercise but, above all, as an aid in clarifying the more fundamental questions to which the analysis of the postcolonial state is inextricably linked. As applied to the Ivory Coast, these questions are:

1.  What is the nature of the process of accumulation that exists at present in the Ivory Coast? Under what specific conditions does it occur?
2.  In favor of what social groups, both internal and external, does this process take place, or in other words, what interests does it promote?
3.  Under what circumstances might the orientation of the present process be redefined?
4.  What does this analysis tell us about the socioeconomic and political basis of the local state and the way in which the state intervenes to reproduce the conditions for the process of accumulation and the social forces on which it itself is based?

Since there does not exist an accepted "theory of the postcolonial capitalist state," the first problem one must address is how to approach the question of the postcolonial state's role in the process of accumulation.

In a volume on the impact of multinational companies on the economic development of the Ivory Coast--a study of Nestlé (agro-business), Air Liquide (the chemical industry), and Carnaud SA (the mechanical and electrical industry)--the authors adopt the following hypothesis:

> In contrast to other peripheral areas such as Latin America, the passage to this second stage [industrial production directed to the internal

281

market] is not a consequence of a crisis in the international economic system, but a strategy formulated by the political power which has as its objective the industrialisation of the country.[1] [Our translation]

While never made explicit, this approach is based on a very definite view of the state, one which (a) inevitably implies a particular view of the scope for local state initiative, and (b) presupposes important degrees of autonomy and voluntarism concerning state actions. The methodology that follows is to describe the industrial policies of the state and, on this basis, to assess the implication of these policies for industrial development. Posed in this manner, the study considers Ivorian accumulation on a national scale. This assumes that the coherence of the "national economy" either came into existence simultaneously with the granting of political independence or, alternatively, that it has been created since, by the local state. Moreover, it assumes that the local state can play an interventionist role, which implies that local structures have a considerable degree of autonomy and margin of maneuver. The model that seems implicitly to have been adopted is that of the European state, one which has radically different social origins. Although the premises on which the concept of the state is based are not clarified, they inevitably help determine the conclusions that are drawn.

In contrast, one may take a much broader historical and dialectical perspective in approaching the question of the postcolonial state. One might start from the specificity of the area that became the Ivory Coast and then proceed to study the interaction of changes in that area and the former metropolitan power during the colonial period, in an attempt to explain the political economy of the Ivory Coast in the postindependence period. On the basis of this perspective, one would then attempt to define more specifically how, under what conditions, and in what historically determined structures the process of surplus appropriation has taken place in the Ivory Coast. In this way, we begin to define the essential characteristics of the Ivorian social formation and, more importantly, the nature of the postcolonial state.

By focusing on the state's role within the organization of production and appropriation of the social surplus and, conversely, on the way in which the state is itself determined by this process, we inquire directly into the identity of the interests on whose behalf the state defines and performs its tasks. We may attempt to clarify in this manner the social and economic basis of state power.

Our analysis of those who manage the state, or, more broadly, of those who are in control of production and of those who are in opposition to their control, must be undertaken in relation to a specific set of social relations, a specific mode of production. In a postcolonial situation, this attempt is made far more difficult because social relations have not crystallized but are in the full process of mutation. Therefore, one must turn to the analysis of the actions of the state to see whether they throw some light on the class character of this entity. Such an approach, however, must be seen as part of, and not as an alternative to, an overall analysis of emerging social relations. Moreover, given such a perspective, our analysis of the postcolonial Ivorian state must be placed in the context of an analysis of the process of accumulation not only at a national level but on a regional and an international scale as well.

If one adopts such an approach, the Ivory Coast presents a particularly clear example of a historical experience which led to the emergence, in the postwar period, of a local group who took over the leadership of the nationalist movement and simultaneously consolidated its position of internal control over the local process of capital accumulation. I refer here to the emergent planter group whose consolidation of control over the production of the major export crops and direction of local political activities took place during the postwar period known as "decolonization."[2]

In spite of the extensive and persisting discrimination in their favor, the European planters, who in 1942 produced approximately 55 percent of the coffee and 8 percent of the cocoa, by 1952 produced only 6 percent of the coffee and 4 percent of the cocoa. By 1947 African planters produced 90 percent or more of the coffee and cocoa exported from the Ivory Coast.[3]

Significantly, it was the producer organization of the larger African planters, the Syndicat agricole africain (SAA), which was to become the basis of the Parti démocratique de la Côte d'Ivoire (PDCI). After the war, the SAA's membership lists were used to draw up electoral registers, and, during the first campaign, the organization served as an admirable machine to promote the candidacy of its president, Houphouët-Boigny, who by this time was one of the richest planters in the country. Houphouët-Boigny not only symbolized the achievements of the emerging planter bourgeoisie but personally possessed the means to finance a political campaign.[4] To summarize this critical period, it was the African planters, with their additional and very immediate interest in the struggle against the discriminatory effects of colonialism (notably its labor policies), who were to supply the political leadership of the anticolonialist movement in the Ivory Coast. The mixture of particularistic and nationalist interests in the leadership was to have far-reaching implications for the outcome of the movement and for the orientation of political and economic changes in the Ivory Coast after independence.[5]

It is important here to recognize the historically specific conditions which made possible (1) the existence of a local process of capital accumulation sufficiently advanced at the moment of "decolonization"; (2) the emergence of and key role assumed by a particular group formed out of the local process of capital accumulation; and (3) the reproduction of their control as a group or class over that process.

Concerning the local process of capital accumulation, one may note the following factors. The withdrawal of settler capital from the production of export crops at the time of political independence left the local planter group to deal directly with international capital, and it became the crucial link responsible for the organization of labor relations with peasant commodity producers. Certain factors were to reinforce the internal position of the local planter group: for example, the relatively late start of the process of accumulation in relation to other West African countries; the availability of labor from neighboring countries; the importance of French investment in infrastructure and port facilities in the preindependence period. However, these and other local factors must be seen within the larger framework of the continuing dominance of the metropole. This domination was perpetrated through the very hierarchical structure of French metropolitan monetary and commercial regulations (the franc zone, for example), stabilization and military schemes, and through aid and defense agreements favorable to the perpetuation of a particular orientation to economic growth and, to this end, the reinforcement of a certain group of local interests.[6] Given this framework, the question that must be raised is, to what extent was the local emergent group able to exercise control over the local process of accumulation at the time of political independence, with regards not only to production but also to commercialization, price fixing, interest rates, etc.? And, in view of the continuing export orientation to the process of accumulation-- in 1980, two crops, coffee and cocoa, remained responsible for 60 percent of export earnings--to what extent can the control of the local group be said to have evolved?

Concerning the emergence of a particular local group in the process of accumulation, one may draw attention to the origins of the planter class in the traditional elite. Traditional power became a means during the colonial regime to appropriate land for private use. Moreover, the cohesion of this class made it easier for them to reach agreements with northern chiefs, who supplied workers at a time when labor was normally reserved for European planters. The relative homogeneity of the planter class as a group became a factor in their accession to power. Their rapid enrichment was due in part to the relatively late development of export crops in the Ivory Coast and, in part, to the abundant supplies of migrant labor, arable land, and colonial investments in infrastructure. These internal factors were reinforced by external conditions. During the 1950s, flows of French public and private capital into the territory and the stimulus of the Korean war enriched the emerging Ivorian bourgeoisie and consolidated their relations with the metropolitan power.

Concerning the reproduction of their control as a group and class over the process of accumulation, the social and economic interests of the Ivorian planter class, who favored the continuation of close economic ties with the metropolitan power, must be analyzed, once again within the broader context of the redefinition of French colonial interests. This redefinition included (and still includes) an elaborate and critically important network of development plans, aid, price and stabilization funds, etc., oriented in a certain manner.

The importance of the emergence of this local group from the standpoint of metropolitan interests has led certain analysts to describe conservative planter nationalism not as a sign of "alienation" vis-à-vis the metropole, but rather as a condition and a reflection of the "convergence" of interests between the Elysée and representatives of the Ivorian elite.[7] In terms of the role of the dominant local group itself in the reproduction of the local accumulation process, existing studies have placed more emphasis on the nature of state intervention in the economy, whether in the urban or rural sector. This reflects a view of the state which attributes it with considerable autonomy and sees it as playing a "balancing" role between foreign and local interests. It is not difficult to see how such a perspective, by polarizing these two sets of interests, has failed to recognize that in the postindependence period it may also be in the interest of foreign capital to encourage certain "nationalist" policies in order to be able to associate domestic capital to its schemes.[8] This point is crucial to the conclusions drawn in the analysis presented below.

Since political independence, one aspect of local state intervention has been the creation of the conditions necessary for a specific orientation to the process of accumulation. In pursuing its objectives, the Ivorian state has put forward with remarkable consistency its adherence to the doctrine of economic liberalism. More concretely, as has been well documented elsewhere, this has meant intervening in order to perpetuate a pattern of export-oriented growth, which depends heavily on foreign factors--labor, capital, and technology.

The manner in which those in control of the state reproduce and enlarge their own social basis is another crucial aspect resulting from the nature of state intervention in the economy. For in the perspective proposed here, the state is not only seen as a determinant factor in the process of accumulation but is itself determined by this process. More often than not, this area of state policies, Ivorization, has been treated as a distinct area of intervention. Consequently, the slowness and difficulties of this process have been presented as the "dysfunctioning" of state policies, rather than as a reflection of the conditions in which these policies are forged or, more generally, as a reflection of the very nature of a specific set of social relations and forms of accumulation.

It is in this broader context that we propose to reexamine the question of Ivorization as it took place over the period 1960-1980. In raising this problem, we are in fact raising the question of the conditions for the position of strategic control exercised by those who hold state power over the process of postcolonial political alignment, a condition necessary for the next phase of accumulation. In other words, in analyzing the question of Ivorization, we are inquiring into the conditions and manner in which those who control state power reproduce its social, economic, and political basis.

Subsequent to this period, certain important changes have taken place, notably in the rapidity of the process of Ivorization. For example, according to the Ivorian statistical service, the Centrale des bilans, whereas Ivorian *encadrement* (management, administrative, or technical supervisory positions) represented 58.6 percent of total encadrement in 1979, this figure had increased to 69.1 percent in 1984. However, this trend was not the result of a fundamental change in government policy. It resulted, on the one hand, from the slowing of economic activity, which has led to the departure of many expatriates and their replacement by nationals. On the other, it has been the policy of international lenders to associate nationals with policies of strucutral readjustment introduced in order to overcome the obstacles to past patterns of growth and to meet obligations of foreign payments, which have resulted from the country's massive indebtedness. Consequently, more recent changes which have come about in the area of Ivorization which, while important, reflect a new set of structural and international conditions, rather than changes in the manner in which those who continue to control state power have attempted to reproduce its social, economic, and political basis.

In order to introduce the subject of Ivorization, it may be useful to view the specificity of this experience in general terms by contrasting it in three ways with interpretations of Kenya, which have attributed a key role to the domestic bourgeoisie in the transition to capitalism.[9] First, in contrast to such interpretations of the Kenyan experience, it cannot be said of the Ivory Coast that there has been a significant degree of penetration by local private capital or a new phase of African entry into manufacturing in the late 1970s. Second, the Ivory Coast does not seem to have played the same role as the Kenyan state in the above interpretation in facilitating the movement of African private capital out of circulation and into production; on the contrary, the emphasis of Ivorian state intervention appears to remain the promotion of speculative outlets. And third, the Ivory Coast state has not undertaken any measures that would displace monopolies enjoyed by foreign capital and substitute monopolies for African capital.

In contrast to the Kenyan interpretation and to summarize the argument that will be developed below, the Ivorian state appears to have played the role of an intermediary, creating quite specific places to be ceded in time and only under certain circumstances to local interests. This permits the emergence of local capital but only at such a time and in such a manner as to be in subordinate association and, therefore, compatible with foreign capital. If the exercise of state power may be seen as the means by which those who achieved power set about reproducing the conditions of accumulation, then what is most striking in the case of the Ivory Coast is the continuity of the manner in which this has been done and the success, defined solely in terms of the reproduction of these conditions, with which it has met so far.

The ideological formulation of the liberal option of Ivorian growth, although incapable of attenuating the contradictions that it entails, has nonetheless been an important component of its success.[10] Stated at the time of independence, it has been reiterated over the last twenty years and appeared plainly in the Plan quinquennal du développement économique social et culturel, 1976-1980:

> The most fundamental option is that of planned, contractual, and controlled liberalism. Private initiative and profitability must remain the essential motor of economic activity particularly concerning industrial development. The management of enterprises must therefore be private and the model of private management must be applied as well in statal and parastatal bodies.[11] [Our translation]

As industrial growth is to be left to private initiative, the same document goes on to define the circumscribed areas of state economic intervention. The state is to intervene directly only under the following conditions: (1) where economic activities are considered to be of a strategic nature (transport, energy); (2) so as to promote certain activities which private initiative neglects; (3) or, as to favor the creation of regional poles of development.[12] [Our translation]

The consistent commitment to the encouragement of private initiative has meant in the Ivorian context, in the immediate postindependence period, reliance on foreign private initiative. In this regard, the absence of the creation of institutions capable of effectively tapping Ivorian domestic savings and ensuring their reinvestment contrasts strikingly with other non-franc zone West African nations--notably Nigeria, where institutions were established for the "Nigerianization" of the economy before 1967.

Easy access to the French capital market through the Caisse autonome d'amortissement (which handles the central government's debt) has permitted the Ivory Coast to sell bonds guaranteed by the French government. Privileged access to metropolitan funds has thus inevitably stifled local initiatives. These external factors provide part of the framework for understanding the particular orientation of internal policies in the area of Ivorization.

The lateness of the creation of institutions in favor of local participation may be considered a first indication of the Ivorian leadership's attitude to the emergence of a local entrepreneurial group. The performance and mediocre results of the institutions created after 1968 are even more revealing.

The decision to establish such institutions in the late 1960s was prompted by several factors. By this time, the early phase of easy import-substitution activities was drawing to a close. Moreover, it was suggested in certain reports, such as that of

BIDI (Banque ivoirienne de développement industriel), that in order for a new phase of industrialization to become more permanent, it must involve Ivorian entrepreneurs and the mobilization of Ivorian capital. One may presume that a further motive for the creation of such institutions was the simple wish to placate opposition discontent in the 1960s over the foreign dominance of the economy. The institutions created were, in any case, in little danger of realizing the stated aims of the BIDI report. In 1962 and 1963 two organizations had been created, the Fonds national d'investissements (FNI) and the Société nationale de financement (SONAFI) respectively, in order to give financial backing to local enterprise. Their weakness is suggested in part by their limited role--in 1974, for example, SONAFI's participation in share capital represented only 7 percent of the total--but more particularly by the lack of promotion of entrepreneurial skills.[13]

In July 1968, the Office for the Promotion of Ivorian Enterprise (Office de promotion de l'entreprise ivoirienne, OPEI) was created to encourage enterprises of an artisanal nature (bakeries, joiners shops, and service trades such as plumbing and tailoring). But such institutions can scarcely provide the material for top industrial management positions--a prerequisite for the Ivorization of local industrial activity. If one looks closely at the activities of promotion agencies such as the OPEI, one must seriously question whether they were not created more to mitigate pressures for greater Ivorian participation in the productive sectors of the economy than as serious efforts to transform the structure of production.

As a result of the recommendations put forward in the 1971-1975 Economic Plan, the Office de la main-d'oeuvre de Côte d'Ivoire (OMOCI) was established. In 1973, the National Commission on Ivorization was set up, and it began to elaborate a series of measures to encourage "voluntary" Ivorization of top posts in the economy. As may be documented, these measures have so far made little impact. Regardless of the source cited, the various evaluations of the promotion of Ivorians to decision-making posts still fall short of nationalist expectations. At the beginning of 1978, Ivorians held 22 percent of senior management posts, 52.2 percent of junior management posts and 72 percent of supervisory personnel posts.[14] In 1979, according to the central statistical unit of the Ivory Coast, the Centrale des bilans, the figures for all enterprises, including the private, public and semi-private sectors were:

*Direction* (management)--22.97 percent
*Cadres* ("junior" mgmt.)--44.15 percent

*Maîtrise* (supervisors)--72.76 percent

The overall average (*encadrement global*) given by the same source was 58.6 percent. According to the Service autonome de l'ivoirisation de l'emploi, the unit created in September 1978 and made responsible for this question within the Ministry of Labor, the figures were slightly lower. Of a total of 26,076 higher staff (*cadres*) in 1979, 14,478 or 55.5 percent were estimated to be Ivorian. Moreover, the breakdown between *cadres* and *maîtrise* was as follows:

Of the 26,076 higher staff, there were 11,845 *cadres*--38.8 percent Ivorian, 61.2 percent foreign
Of the 26,076 higher staff, there were 14,231 *maîtrises*-- 69.4 percent Ivorian, 30.6 percent foreign

Thus the available figures for the period to 1980 reveal that considerable progress remained to be made, particularly in the areas of higher management and technical skills. Paradoxically, while the number of salaried workers who fell under the jurisdiction of the Ministry of Labor continued to increase, and as the question of Ivorization became all the more glaring, the means at the disposal of the services responsible remained totally inadequate to accomplish their task.

If one reviews the period 1977-1979, the very period when energetic initiatives were to be undertaken within the new structures of the Ministry of Labor and the *ivoirisation* of *cadres*, one must recognize the discrepancy between the policies announced and the means effected. While the overall administrative budget of the Ivorian state increased by 67 percent during this period, that of the Ministry did so by 46 percent and that of the OMOCI by only 34.5 percent. If one takes into account the effects of inflation, this amounted to the stagnation of the budget of the former and a regression in the budget of the latter body responsible for the Ivorization of personnel.

Moreover, since 1977, although the work of the Ministry of Labor and the *ivoirisation* of *cadres* has increased, its technical personnel or *inspecteurs du travail* (who are paid about one-third of what they would receive in the private sector) remain totally insufficient in number. The settlement of individual litigation is by far the largest responsibility of the technical staff, and it is increasing. Significantly, for those who claim that skilled Ivorians are not available, more than 6,000 cases were examined in 1977 and 6,500 in 1978. In addition, in view of the lack of means at its disposal, it is impossible for the specialized services of the ministry to undertake their periodic visits to the 2,000 firms where, theoretically, they are supposed to be supervising the process of Ivorization. At a time when controls might be expected to be on the increase, the number of firms visited by the personnel of the ministry actually decreased from 429 in 1977 to 376 in 1978. There appears little doubt that the services responsible for Ivorization do not have nor do they appear to be meant to have the necessary means to exercise control over this process or the labor market in general.

The consequence of persistent dependence on foreign skills, whether technical or managerial, may be seen in the persistent imbalances in salary distribution. An official document, the *Five Year Plan, 1976-1980*, drew attention to the slowness of the process of Ivorization:

> The principal characteristic of employment in the Ivory Coast today remains the low degree of participation of Ivorians. In 1974, Ivorians occupied less than half of salaried positions and received only approximately one-third of the wage bill distributed by the private and semi-public sectors.[15] [Our translation]

The same source documented the situation in 1974:

TABLE 9.1: Ivorian Employment, 1974

|  | Percent of Salaried Employment | Percent of Wage Bill |
|---|---|---|
| Ivorians | 49.6 | 43.6 |
| Non-Ivorians (Europeans) | 5.5 | 35.2 |

The figures obtained for 1971 were:[16]

TABLE 9.2: Ivorian Employment, 1971

|  | Percent of Salaried Employment | Percent of Wage Bill |
|---|---|---|
| Ivorians | 48.0 | 36.4 |
| Non-Ivorians (Europeans) | 6.0 | 32.2 |

The comparison of the two situations (1971 and 1974) suggests that although Europeans represented in employment decreased, the proportion of the wage bill that they received increased to the detriment of non-Ivorian Africans rather than Ivorians. This reflects a crucial point about the Ivorian economy, the fact that its work force consists of over two million non-Ivorian African workers--mostly from the Sahelian countries (Burkina Faso and Mali)--who supply 78 percent of the unskilled labor force in the plantation sector, and who are very often remunerated at a rate less than the minimum wage. This "regional" character of the Ivorian labor force underlines, from another standpoint, the difficulty raised earlier of placing the analysis on a national scale, which assumes the existence of a coherent "national economy." Similarly, the regional organization of the labor force suggests the shortsightedness of attempts to speak of an improving or more egalitarian distribution of resources within the Ivory Coast.

Alternate figures concerning salary distribution confirm the persistence of past patterns. According to the central statistical unit of the Ivory Coast, in 1979 30 percent of the wage bill in the modern sector went to non-Africans. The definition of the modern sector used here, however, excludes the administration and banks. More revealing is the distribution of the wage bill within the category of "skilled labor." In 1979, according to the same source, the wage bill was divided as follows:

| | |
|---|---|
| Ivorians | 32.80 percent |
| Non-Ivorian Africans | 3.84 percent |
| Europeans | 63.36 percent |

The official figures for average monthly salaries of skilled workers for the same year were:

| | |
|---|---|
| Ivorians | 183.166 francs *cfa* |
| Non-Ivorian Africans | 159.005 francs *cfa* |
| Europeans[17] | 618.575 francs *cfa* |

The process of Ivorization remained particularly weak in the commercial sector during the 1970s. According to the *Five Year Plan, 1976-1980*, in this sector only 26 percent of the heads of enterprises in 1974 were Ivorian; 18 percent of middle cadres and only 10 percent of senior cadres were Ivorian.[18]

These figures reflect a more fundamental issue--that of control. The persistance throughout the 1970s of the marginal place of nationals in the commercial sector is suggested by the fact that in 1978 national capital amounted to only 18.5 percent of the share capital of the Ivorian Syndicat des commerçants importateurs-exportateurs (Scimpex).[19]    A study published in August 1979, for 1978, revealed that 53 percent of equity of commercial ventures was controlled by French capital and 30 percent of the industrial sector then belonged to French nationalists.[20]    According to 1979 estimates of the Banque ivoirienne des données financières, the above figures reveal only part of the reality, as French equity holdings in the Ivory Coast are strategically placed.    This explains that French interests handled 45 percent of business turnover in the modern sector of the economy.    And even more important, French interests were estimated to make 81 percent of all profits.[21]   This last figure becomes all the more significant in view of the fact that it has been shown that, at least between 1967 and 1974, the value of repatriated profits resulting from direct investment was far greater than the value of new direct investment entering the Ivory Coast.[22]    "It is this trend which, among other things, explains the balance of payments deficits beginning in 1971."[23]

Contrary to what one might conclude in light of these various trends and apparent contradictions (whether with regard to the slowness in the Ivorization of skilled personnel or the marginal place occupied by nationals in ownership of enterprises in the industrial and commercial sectors), there does appear to have existed in the Ivory Coast a systematic pattern by which nationals are integrated into the local economic activities.    Central to an understanding of this pattern is the analysis of the role of the Ivorian state in the process of accumulation.    Several indicators may serve to illustrate the importance of its role in this regard:    first, in terms of national participation in share capital, of a total seven billion francs *cfa* in 1974 5.9 billion or 84 percent was held by the state; second, in 1978, depending on the source used, Ivorian private capital represented only 7.32 percent (according to the National Accounts) or 11.65 percent (according to *Fraternité Matin Industrie* 80) of total investment; and third, of a total of 67.9 billion francs *cfa* invested by the national sector in 1978, 59.8 billion came from public funds and only 8.1 billion (or approximately 12 percent) came from the private sector.

The central role of the state, both in the area of public funds invested in share capital and as the primary investor, underlines the importance of the analysis of state policies vis-à-vis those social groups--most notably the rural sector--responsible for the production of surplus value.    In the Ivory

Coast, this perspective is crucial. It is estimated that over one-third of public participation in the industrial sector in 1973/74 came from the rural sector.[24] In more recent years, with the severe indebtedness of the country, the revenue of the Caisse de stabilisation et de soutien des prix agricoles (the national marketing board, which draws its surplus from the rural sector) has decreased substantially, and the portion of the investment budget attributable to loans has increased accordingly. In the 1980 investment budget (Budget spécial d'investissement et d'equipement, BSIE), the caisse's contribution represented 121 billion francs *cfa* or approximately 26 percent of the total budget of 467 billion. In view of the country's worsening position in 1981, it was anticipated that of a proposed budget of 423 billion francs *cfa*, the caisse's contribution would be reduced to 23.6 billion and that 304.9 billion would be funded through government borrowing.[25]

State intervention in local industry is also the starting point for understanding the means by which those who hold power have successfully managed to reproduce the conditions of accumulation. The interdependence between the role of the state and Ivorian participation in the economy may be viewed from several angles. First, there exists a link between private Ivorian investors and the state apparatus. In terms of the origins of Ivorian investors, the 1975 ORSTOM study, carried out by Chevassu and Valette in 1971, suggests that the twenty most important Ivorian investors of a sample of approximately 300 (i.e., those who were involved in several enterprises) may be divided in three numerically equal categories:[26] (a) *hommes politiques*, ministers at the national level; mayors, deputies, etc., at the local level; (b) high-ranking civil servants who were already in public corporations, *sociétés d'état ou organismes publics*, rather than the central administration; (c) *hommes d'affaires*, merchants, planters, etc.

Second, there exists a link between private Ivorian investors and public participation. In terms of the official explanation of the Ivorian government, public corporations have been created in the case of specific activities where administrative or private intervention alone would not have produced the necessary encouragement or permitted a sufficiently rapid development. In terms of the nature of state involvement, the active role of the state is illustrated by the fact that in one third of the firms where there was private Ivorian participation, according to the 1975 ORSTOM study, there was also state participation. Three reasons are given for this: (a) public organizations such as SONAFI have transferred part of their holdings to individuals;[27] (b) the state has helped Ivorian firms by buying in share; and (c) there exist close and frequent links between private Ivorian investors on the one hand and the political and administrative apparatus on the other. This last factor may be considered key.  Apart from the official reasons for the creation of public and semipublic corporations, other factors have plainly contributed to the rapid expansion of these bodies, openly criticized by the World Bank mission in 1971.

Third and finally, there exists a link between those who hold political power and the management of Ivorian enterprises, whether public or private.  The state-owned corporations are managed by leading members of the government, often deputies of the National Assembly.  Although they may intervene in economic activity in a wide variety of sectors, they do so under the direction of ministries of planning and economic affairs, a consideration that is crucial because it ensures that their activities will be compatible with the role played by the foreign capital in very profitable sectors.  As one study suggests:

> The growth of state capitalism, through the many sociétés d'état and the departments of government, provided opportunities for economic activity to complement what had previously been only political and administrative roles. A study of the Ivorian membership of the conseils d'administration shows that 129 individuals hold the 287 seats involved.[28]

Perhaps even more significant than the concentration of this control is its political nature, as revealed by the findings of the same study:  62 percent of the positions in the eighty-eight Ivorian enterprises or associations were held by members of government.[29]  In 1981, the same pattern remained prevalent. Together the forty-eight Ivorians who sat on the administrative councils of the twenty-seven companies quoted at the Abidjan Stock Exchange accumulated approximately thirty political positions, including three seats on the political bureau, two on the executive committee and fourteen on the comité directeur of the PDCI.

If one turns to official recommendations concerning the Ivorization of the industrial and commercial sectors, one is struck by the remarkable continuity of proposed measures as compared with those of the past.  In the industrial sector, the 1976-1980 plan suggested that in order to promote the Ivorization of industrial management the state should:    (1) systematically encourage the passage of civil servants to the private sector by putting forward advantages and even limiting the duration of office in the public service; (2) mobilize national savings; (3) favor the association of national and foreign capital through studies, which will evolve new forms of mixed financing; (4) favor the promotion of small and medium-sized industries.[30]

In order to promote the Ivorization of industrial and commercial capital, the 1976-1980 plan proposed: (1) to reactivate the Fonds de rachat des actifs industriels et commerciaux created under the 1971-1975 plan, as well as the OPEI and Programme d'action commercial, PAC; (2) to draw up and apply a program of *ivoirisation* of former, already existing small and medium enterprises; (3) to draw up and apply new regulations concerning the process of *ivoirisation* of new enterprises.[31]

More specifically concerning the commercial sector:

> Un programme de sélection et de formation de 'managers' commerciaux sera conçu et mis en oeuvre en vue de l'ivoirisation du management des grands maisons de commerce.

> Concurrement à ce moyen stratégique, des dispositions appropriées seront introduites dans la loi-cadre sur le commerce en particulier en ce qui concerne le droit d'établissement des étrangers dans les professions commerciales et la possibilité de restrictions temporaires de la concurrence vis-à-vis des nationaux créant des entreprises commerciales dans des professions et des lieux déterminés (secteurs réservés).[32]

There is nothing here which would indicate the least discontinuity with or redefinition of past orientations. New local, small or medium-sized enterprises were to be established in commerce and industry in well-defined sectors (*secteurs réservés*) in such a manner as to be compatible with existing interests and structures. As has been pointed out, these enterprises were above all to have the responsibility as subcontractors in forward or backward linkages associated to large projects created by the state.[33] Local participation in share capital continued to be initiated by the state, which was to continue to purchase shares and then transfer them progressively to Ivorians. If one studies the measures in favor of the investment of local private savings, it is abundantly clear that local participation was to remain of a speculative rather than a productive nature.[34]

Before concluding, it is important to consider one final point that helps to clarify the meaning of state capitalism in the Ivory Coast and that concerns the far-reaching decisions announced in June 1980 to suppress or redefine the vast majority of state corporations.[35] By these measures, of the thirty-six state corporations only seven were to continue: Air Ivoire, Caisse de stabilisation, Palmindustrie, Petroci, Sitram, Sodesucre and Sodemi. The others were either to be attached to the civil service, discontinued, or given over to private enterprise. While the main reasons for this important reshuffle have to do with mismanagement and the fact that these corporations had become too onerous a burden for the country to support, given the worsening economic situation, their suppression gave rise to an extremely clear formulation of the Ivorian doctrine concerning the role of the state.

> Liberalism is the basis of our concept of the state and all institutions must see that they contribute to the safeguarding of the right to free enterprise. The state is not a speculative entrepreneur nor an industrialist nor a merchant.

> The government will proceed, as it has already begun to do, to dissolve all state corporations of a speculative nature that come into direct competition with private initiative, unless the latter [private enterprises] associate themselves with state corporations and take over full responsibility for their management.[36] [Our translation]

The above analysis leads to the following very tentative conclusions. Until more empirical work is done, these conclusions may only be seen as preliminary formulations in the ongoing debate concerning the postcolonial state and its role in the process of local accumulation.

In spite of the considerable resources at its disposal, the postcolonial Ivorian state has not assumed nor has it claimed to assume the dynamic role of a true entrepreneurial state in initiating and directing the local process of accumulation. Contrary to the suggestions of some that it has been responsible for putting forward determinant industrial strategies, its role might more correctly be seen as supplying the conditions for growth--not only economic but social, political, and ideological conditions as well. The initiative for economic growth has been left very much to private interests, and in the case of the Ivory Coast, this has meant foreign private interests. Moreover, as regards the promotion of local Ivorian interests, the Ivorian state has assumed a crucial role in channeling, mediating and, if necessary, delaying their emergence in order that they be compatible with existing foreign interests.

The state's economic intervention, through the creation of public and semipublic corporations, through public investments, and through participation in local firms, etc., has indeed been an important element in the perpetuation of a certain orientation to the process of accumulation. It has provided, as well, a crucial means of accommodating national urges with foreign initiatives. Given the dominant position that foreign interests can be shown to have retained within the local economy, the emergence of national interests, in order to take place at all, has been mediated by the local state. This mediation has resulted in the interdependence and continuity of interests between the bureaucracy and local *hommes d'affaires* on the one hand, and between the bureaucracy and *hommes politiques* on the other. The state may be seen as the means and political loyalty as the condition for access to Ivorian participation in the economy.

Presented at the time as a means to prevent class differentiation in the Ivory Coast, the centrality of the role of the state was foreseen many years ago, as is revealed by President Houphouët-Boigny's address to the National Assembly on 3 January 1961:

> Nous accepterons chez nous, la coopération avec n'importe quels capitalistes étrangers . . . mais parce que ce capitalisme constituerait les germes d'une lutte des classes dont nous ne voulons pas, nous ferons en sorte que toutes les participations soient faites par l'Etat, et par l'Etat seul.[37]

The reasons for the restricted sphere of action of the state, whether it be in the orientation of the process of accumulation or in the promotion of national control and participation, must be sought in the historical analysis of the origins and the specificity of the process itself. Central to the explanation appears to be the conditions under which a local group extended its control over those productive activities responsible for the supply of social surplus.

The Ivorian experience of the last twenty years illustrates the success of those who came to power at the time of political independence in reproducing and enlarging a particular alignment of class forces on which state power has been based. In this regard, the question of Ivorization throws some light on the social basis or class character of the local state. The mediations, delays, and apparent contradictions involved in the process of Ivorization should not be seen as dysfunctions, deceptions, or errors, but rather as a reflection of the conditions under which these policies have been forged and, more generally, of the specificity of the nature of the accumulation process in the Ivory Coast.

Concerning the nature of the process of accumulation the question remains, just as at the time of the anticolonial struggle, of the degree to which the local dominant group actually exercises control over this process. Experiences such as the sugar fiasco, which resulted in the loss of tens of billions of francs *cfa* due to overpricing and mismanagement on the part of foreign promoters and was denounced by the president himself, suggest that the problem of control remains extremely acute.[38] To what extent can the "joint-venture" formula, which the government has officially privileged as a new prototype for relations with foreign investors, guarantee under present conditions a decisive place for nationals in the control over local activities? Or, on the contrary, as certain analysts of the same phenomenon in Latin America suggest, might the joint-venture formula represent not a new strategy on the part of certain states but, rather, a pragmatic compromise at the present stage of the redefining of the international capitalist system?[39]

If, in Latin America, the failure of the import-substitution phase of industrialization points to the historical failure of the national bourgeoisies due to their relative lack of control over that phase of the local process of accumulation, then certain more recent African experiences appear to suggest even more strikingly that it is only through association as the subordinate adjunct of transnational corporations that the local bureaucracy can justify the entrepreneurial role that it assumes or permits other nationals to assume.

Moreover, in the present phase of development characterized by the fiscal crisis of the state, massive indebtedness, and the imposition of programs of structural adjustment, etc., the intervention of international lending organizations has led to short-term attempts to overcome the obstacles created by past patterns of accumulation.

This new phase of capital penetration would seem to require both changes in the mode of accumulation and finance and, increasingly, changes in the organization of production as well. To this end there is an important need for associating nationals with the objectives and projects that previously have been held almost exclusively by foreigners. It is within this context that one can see the fuller significance of policies recommending the acceleration of Ivorization, whether it be, for instance, the promotion of local capital formation or the training of nationals according to the norms of the new suppliers of loans and foreign capital, etc. Moreover, a proposed strategy for changes in the mode of accumulation is made explicit in the 1981 IMF report that recommends a process of "financial deepening and the spread of the capital market," notably through the creation of a domestic market in government securities. Just as at the time of political decolonization, when a particular phase of capital penetration had as its counterpart an internal process of differentiation, with the emergence of a dominant planter group closely linked to metropolitan markets and resources, current attempts to restructure the process of accumulation call for the consolidation of new local forces as economic partners and political allies. In terms of control of state power, it will be important to analyze the impact of foreign interventions, whether they be those of international financial organizations, public or private capital, or the constellation of forces within the ruling alliances. More fundamentally, and underlying the political process, is the question of the emergence of new social relations and new contradictions within the dominant local groups and between them and new categories of producers and other social and economic groups.

It is this internal process that will determine, in the context of the reorganization of accumulation on an international scale, to what extent the role of the Ivorian state will be closer to that of the internationalization of local initiatives, as opposed to that of the promotion of a national bourgeoisie.

## Notes

1. J. Masini, M. Ikonicoff, C. Jedlecki, M. Lanzarotti, Les multinationales et le développement:   Trois enterprises et la Côte d'Ivoire (Paris:   Presses universitaires de France; Brussels:  Centre européen d'étude et d'information sur les sociétés multinationales, CEEIM, 1979).

2. This process is described in greater detail, in B. Campbell, "The Ivory Coast," ch. 4 in John Dunn, ed., West African States: Failure and Promise. A Study in Comparative Politics (Cambridge: University Press, 1978). See also the chapter on the Ivory Coast in Ruth Schachter Morgenthau, Political Parties in French-speaking West Africa (Oxford: Clarendon Press, 1964).

3. John Dunn, ed., op. cit., 72.

4. Ibid., 73.

5. Ibid., 70.

6. For further details concerning this framework, see Georges H. Lawson, "La Côte d'Ivoire: 1960-1970. Croissance et diversification sans africainisation," in L'Afrique de l'indépendance politique à l'indépendance économique, John A. Esseks, ed., (F. Maspéro et Presses universitaires de Grenoble, 1975). See especially 207-210.

7.  Jacques Baulin, La politique africaine d'Houphouët-Boigny (Paris: Editions Eurafor-Press, 1980), 17.

8.  Björn Beckman has pointed out in this respect how a structuralist view of capital accumulation, which he associates with dependency theory, denies the contradictory nature of this process and has consequently obscured the degree to which foreign capital depends on domestic class forces for its own penetration. "Imperialism and Capitalist Transformation:  Critique of a Kenyan Debate," Review of African Political Economy 19 (September-December 1980):  59.

9.  This position, illustrated by Colin Leys, Underdevelopment in Kenya: The Political Economy of Neocolonialism (1975), has become the center of an ongoing debate.  While it has come under criticism, it has forced a clarification not only of the "dependency" debate, but also of the relative autonomy of the domestic bourgeoisie supported by the state, and for this reason, it is of considerable relevance to the study presented here.

10.  This point is developed in Bonnie Campbell, "The Fiscal Crisis of the State:  the Case of the Ivory Coast," in Contradictions of Accumulation:  Studies in Economy and State, H. Bernstein and B. Campbell, eds. (Beverly Hills:  Sage, 1985), and in Bonnie Campbell, "L'idéologie de la croissance:  une analyse du plan quinquennal de développement, 1971-1975 de la Côte d'Ivoire," in Revue canadienne des études africaines, vol. 10, no. 1 (1975):  211-233.

11.  République de la Côte d'Ivoire, Plan quinquennal de développement économique, social et culturel, vol. 1 (Abidjan:  Ministère du plan, 1977), 31.

12.  Ibid., 33.

13.  J. Masini et al., op. cit., 28.

14.  Africa Confidential, vol. 20, no. 16 (1 August 1979).

15.  Plan quinquennal de développement, 1976-1980, op. cit., vol. 3, 560.

16.  J. Dunn, ed., op. cit., 28.

17.  It must be remembered that these figures for European salaries do not include added subsidies for housing; expatriation allowance of 30 percent of the basic salary (prime d'expatriation); an automobile (voiture de fonction); air tickets; one month paid holiday; social security at European rates, etc.  This explains that the real cost of an expatriate for a local firm or for the administration is between one and 2.2 times more than the cost of a national of equivalent qualifications.

18.  Plan quinquennal de développement, 1976-1980, op. cit., vol. 1, 109.

19.  Marchés tropicaux et méditerrannéens, 34[e] année, no. 1697 (19 May 1979):  1320.

20.  Africa Confidential, op. cit. (1 August 1979).

21.  Ibid.

22.  J. Masini et al., op. cit., 64.

23.  République de la Côte d'Ivoire, La Côte d'Ivoire en chiffre, ed. 1976, Ministère du plan, n.d., 57.

24.  Jean Chevassu and Alain Valette, Les industriels de la Côte d'Ivoire. Qui et pourquoi? (Ivory Coast:  Office de la recherche scientifique et technique outre-mer.  Ministère du plan ORSTOM 1975, Série d'études industrielles, no.

13), 12.

25. The above figures are those of the Ministère de l'économie et des finances. They give a slightly different picture than those published in the official daily, Fraternité Matin, which incorporates into the 1981 budget contributions based on different fiscal years in comparison to those of the Ministry of Economy and Finance, and consequently lessen the degree of indebtedness. According to the former, in the 1981 investment budget, 109 billion francs cfa or 40.1 percent of the total budget of 272 billion francs cfa was provided by the Caisse de stabilisation. Fraternité Matin (Ivory Coast, 2 April 1981): 17.

26. Chevassu and Valette, op. cit., 16.

27. In 1972, SONAFI sold part of the shares it held in the Société ivoirienne des tabacs, SITAB, to private Ivorian interests, just as it sold shares for purchase by individuals when the Bourse de valeurs (the Abidjan Stock Exchange) was created in April 1976. One may note that the same movement in favor of private share holders with the measures announced in June 1980 to withdraw state participation from public corporations.

28. Michael A. Cohen, Urban Policy and Political Conflict in Africa--A Study of the Ivory Coast (Chicago: University of Chicago Press, 1974), 62.

29. Ibid.

30. Plan quinquennal de développement, 1976-1980, op. cit., vol. 1, 33.

31. Ibid., 65.

32. Ibid., 109. (Editor's translation: A program of selection and training of commercial managers will be devised and put into operation with a view to the Ivorization of management of large commerce houses.

Jointly with this strategy, appropriate provisions will be introduced into the legal framework regarding commerce, in particular as concerns the foreigner's right of establishment in commercial professions and the possibility of temporary restrictions on competition with nationals [who are] establishing commercial enterprises in the professions and [other] designated areas [reserved sectors].)

33. J. Masini et al., op. cit., 13.

34. The section entitled "Politique d'orientation de l'épargne privée" reads:

L'orientation de l'épargne privée nationale vers l'investissement dans le capital industriel et commercial sera recherchés par:

--la détaxation à l'interieur de certaines limites de placements industriels et commerciaux ayant fait l'objet d'un agrément.

--la garantie par l'Etat d'un revenu minimum de ces placements pendant une période initiale.

--la création avec la participation de l'épargne institutionelle (Caisse nationale de prévoyance sociale, Caisse de stabilisation, Caisse nationale d'épargne, compagnies d'assurances, etc.) d'une ou plusiers sociétés d'investissements à capital variable bénéficiant en ce qui concerne les revenus distribués des avantages énoncés au paragraphe précédent.

--l'étude de dispositions obligeant les entreprises à distribuer à leur personnel des titres représentatifs d'une part de leurs résultats, ces titres pouvent ensuite faire l'objet de négotiations entre nationaux.

--l'étude de la possibilité d'imposer aux entreprises existantes la possession d'une partie de leur capital par des nationaux.

--le développement du marché de valeurs mobilières et de mécanismes aptes à assurer à ce marché une régulation adéquate.

Plan quinquennal de développement, 1976-1980, op. cit., vol. 3, 565-566.

35. Fraternité Hebdo, no. 1105 (20 June 1980).

36. Ibid., 10.

37. J. Baulin, op. cit., 17. Editor's translation: "We will accept [in the Ivory Coast] cooperation with any and all foreign capitalists, but because this capitalism would plant the seeds of a class struggle that we do not desire, we will ensure that all [foreign] participation is handled through the state, and only through the state."

38. "Complexes 'good idea in theory'," Financial Times Survey (15 December 1980): 6.

39. Luciano Martins, "La 'joint-venture,' Etat-Firme transnationale--entrepreneurs locaux au Brésil," in Sociologie et Sociétés, vol. 11, no. 2 (Montreal, October 1979): 169-190.

# Part 5

# The Transition to Industrial Capitalism

The industrial manufacturing sector in African economies remains largely outside the control of indigenous capital. The appropriate question concerns its relative growth over the past three decades and the technical development of productive forces controlled by indigenous accumulators. Both state and private bourgeois interests are engaged in the expansion of the industrial sector, but both must, in the intermediate term, rely on the technical expertise of international firms. This is a structural and historical determination that constrains indigenous accumulators, but does not prevent them from benefitting from competition among international firms. Coordinated action by private and state capital, however, is capable of reducing the degree of imported raw materials and inputs from the international economy by developing small and intermediate industries and by strengthening linkages to the agricultural sector.

There is no shortage of first-generation industrialists in the Nigerian case. The names of Ibru, Lawson, Dantata, and Rabiu are associated with industrial investment. But the Nigerian state's control over petroleum rents enabled it to commence an ambitious basic industrial strategy and to control the distribution of capital to aspiring industrialists. Tom Forrest evaluates the role of the Nigerian state in industrialization by reviewing the available evidence and by arguing that the state serves the general interest of Nigerian capital in spite of factional disputes. Although the thrust of capitalist penetration into new areas of accumulation was borne by the Nigerian state, private capital may soon gain control over such areas of accumulation during subsequent periods during which private capital is dominant (i.e., privatization).

Forrest takes issue with dependency theorists who focus on the sectional share of capital, e.g., international or national, rather than the generalized process of industrial capitalist development. Like the share of state capital versus private indigenous capital, the proportions shared by indigenous versus international capital will vary according to the dictates of the conjuncture. In contrast to Kitching's emphasis on the wage bill for stimulating indigenous accumulation, Forrest argues that Nigeria's vast natural resources and the size of its internal market will, in the longer term, provide the stimulation for indigenous accumulation by unifying regional and ethnic sections of the bourgeoisie as reflected in the indigenization policy.

In the final essay, Steven Langdon offers a carefully documented response to Swainson and Leys regarding the capacity and potential growth of indigenous industrialists in Kenya. Rather than concluding that a social transformation toward capitalist development is in progress, Langdon's analysis of indigenous industrial enterprises argues that industrialization is having only limited effects due to restricted employment and restricted linkages to small and intermediate-scale industries. Prospects for export-oriented industrialization also appear grim, because more lucrative opportunities for European transnationals already exist in more dependent capitalist states such as the Ivory Coast. The income redistribution strategy for stimulating the internal market, as advocated by the ILO mission, he points out, contradicts the export orientation strategy. His final comment argues that the crisis of accumulation will generate a political crisis--one that will threaten control of the state now held by the indigenous accumulating bourgeoisie. As the coup attempt and subsequent political repression by the Arap Moi government indicate, Langdon's final comment is prescient indeed.

*Paul M. Lubeck*

*Tom Forrest*

# 10 State Capital, Capitalist Development, and Class Formation in Nigeria

Over the last thirty years, the capitalist development of Nigeria has seen the formation of a bourgeois class. This class spans the public sector and the large-scale, foreign-controlled capitalist sector. Its dominant elements are administrative, managerial, and supervisory; local private capital and professional groups are included as well. State institutions, state capital, and state policies have all been involved in the formation of this bourgeoisie which has, to a large extent, emerged in and through the state. In the 1950s, local groups and classes at the regional level progressively came to exercise state power and acquire control over state resources. Access to state funds provided the means to acquire property and the money capital for private accumulation. Gradually, the administrative colonial state, which supported the operations of merchant capitalists in Nigeria, gave way to a state that actively promoted the arrival of foreign monopoly capital in industry. Marketing board funds, appropriated from the peasantry, were used for infrastructure, for subsidies and loans for industry, and for the expansion of the bureaucracy. Later, the state underwent a process of centralization, and state power increased. The federal state assumed new responsibilities for the support and regulation of national capital accumulation. State power was also used to strengthen the national bases for capital accumulation through the expansion of state capital and measures that involved nationalization, indigenization, and Nigerianization. Critical to these more recent developments in the centralization of the state and the localization of capital accumulation on Nigerian territory has been the expansion of centralized oil revenues. The arrival of large oil revenues sustained state accumulation at a time when the marketing board system was in crisis and the agrarian basis of the economy was in danger of being undermined by the exactions placed on it by the state.[1]

As Beckman has emphasized, these processes of class and state formation have taken place under imperialist domination.[2] As Cardoso puts it, the external system of domination reappears as an "internal" force through the practices of local groups and classes who try to enforce the interests of capital.[3] The rise of the capitalist state and domestic class formation in Nigeria are directly linked to the integration and creation of a national economy within the international capitalist system. International capital creates the conditions for the internal expansion of capitalist enterprise in collaboration with the Nigerian state and local capital.

It should be clear from the foregoing that we do not accept perspectives where the state is subordinate to international capital, where the state apparatus is merely an extension of international capital, and domestic classes act as intermediaries. Nor do we think that the role of the state in capitalist development can be adequately understood in terms of a fractional approach where foreign, state, and local private capitals and their respective class fractions compete, ally, or dominate according to their relative strength through time. Biersteker,[4] like Evans[5] on Brazil, has adopted this approach in his work on indigenization in Nigeria. Williams provides another view of the state, presenting a picture of the Nigerian state and bureaucracy under military rule, incapable of establishing the conditions for capitalist production, of creating stable long-term relations with international capital, or of establishing the conditions for bourgeois rule.[6] Here, the state becomes an arena where a mass of private conflicts and political struggles over access to state resources and their allocation effectively prevents the state bureaucracy from pursuing a capitalist path and disrupts the functions of the state. Such a perspective, however, fails to appreciate the long-term involvement of state institutions, state capital, and the bureaucracy in the promotion of capitalist development, class formation, and creation of a national base for capital accumulation.

This chapter is about the role of state capital in the processes we have outlined, concentrating especially on the period since 1970, when state expenditures increased rapidly. In this period, heavy federal expenditures began to lay the administrative, infrastructural, industrial, financial, and educational groundwork for national capitalist development.[7] New state corporations and companies were established in the oil, mining, and manufacturing sectors; state ownership was extended, often in response to the indigenization decrees that required the partial divestment or dilution of foreign capital over a wide range of industry; and federal finance capital increased in commercial, merchant, and development banking. A number of questions arise here. How is state capital related to private accumulation, both foreign and local? What are the consequences of greatly increased state expenditures for local private accumulation? What are the nature and capacity of the state sector and the bureaucracy?

The scope of state economic activity is, of course, much wider than that of state capital. A more comprehensive treatment of the political economy of the state needs to consider the totality of state revenues and expenditures in the context of national accumulation. Industrial and agricultural policies also have to be examined. Externally, the various ways in which the state manages and regulates domestic accumulation within the context of international capital accumulation have to be considered.

There has been little systematic study of the state sector in Nigeria; the empirical study of state capital and the bureaucracy lags well behind generalizations about the nature and functions of the state. Early study of the regional development institutions included work by Helleiner[8] and Teriba.[9] Schatz studied the loans boards.[10] More recently, Turner[11] has worked on the oil industry, and the Nigerian Economic Society published a symposium on the public sector.[12] One object of this work is to bring together some of the scattered information that exists and document the expansion of the state sector, hence the empirical and descriptive tone of much of the chapter. In our concluding section, we take up some of the issues raised in this introduction.


## 1940-1970

Before 1940, public-sector enterprises were limited to a few isolated concerns such as the coal mines at Enugu, the furniture and saw mills at Ijora, and the stone quarry at Aro.[13] The war period saw the origin of the marketing board system based on the export of peasant commodity production. This system was to play a central role in the funding and growth of state capital in Nigeria in the 1950s and early 1960s. It allowed a regional concentration of finance capital in the hands of the bureaucracy and the political class at a time when

Nigerian private capital was small-scale, largely commercial in orientation, fragmented, and regional in outlook. Helleiner estimated that fully 96 percent of the funds for publicly owned development institutions came, directly or indirectly, from the marketing boards.[14] At this time too, large-scale manufacturing enterprises were established, protected, and subsidized by the state. They were dominated by foreign capital, which was supplemented by state capital. These industries were heavily concentrated in Lagos, with secondary concentrations in the Kaduna and Port Harcourt zones.

The earliest vehicles for the expansion of state capital were the Regional Production Development Boards, which concentrated on plantations and agricultural processing industries. After 1954, when the marketing board system was regionalized and the inherited trading surpluses of the system were run down, the regional development corporations, led by the Western Region Development Corporation, broadened their activities to include manufacturing. This brought the first extensive contact between foreign and state capital in capitalist production. Banks, finance and insurance companies, property and housing corporations, and hotels were also established. In the case of the banks, substantial regional state funds were injected into securing indigenous banks, thereby ultimately converting them into regional state banks. Most of these institutions were controlled by the political class and became a source of funds for private and party use.[15]

Table 10.1 shows that capital expenditure by development institutions in the Nigerian west was equal to the combined expenditure of the east and north. The west experienced the strongest tendency to state capitalism. This was primarily the result of the large cocoa revenues at the disposal of the regional government, but it also stemmed from a stronger business community, eager to take advantage of Awolowo's ideological commitment to state intervention and the oligarchic character of Yoruba society. In the east, the regional premier was open to competitive pressures from professionals, bureaucrats, and businessmen to sell off state investments to individuals, once a class of investors had emerged. In the north, which had no plantations, public investments were mainly undertaken by Northern Nigeria Investment Ltd., a joint venture of the Northern Nigerian Development Corporation and the Commonwealth Development Corporation. As a report on the Northern Nigeria Development Corporation makes clear, the corporation was beset by weak management subject to political

TABLE 10.1: Major Uses of Capital Regional Development Institutions, March 1962--£N million

|  | East | North | West | Total |
|---|---|---|---|---|
| Total grants | 839.9 | 4,294.6 | 2,842.2 | 7,976.7 |
| Investment in commercial schemes | 4,943.2 | 436.7 | 8,353.1 | 13,733.0 |
| Small loans and loans outstanding to official bodies | 935.2 | 1,828.8 | 1,484.5 | 4,248.5 |
| Equity investment and loans to private companies | 2,992.3 | 3,345.4 | 7,152.6 | 13,490.3 |
| Total | 9,710.6 | 9,905.5 | 19,832.4 | 39,448.5 |

Note: In 1972, the Nigerian currency changed from the Nigerian pound (£N) to the naira (N); the exchange rate was 1£N=2N.

Source: Adapted from G.K. Helleiner, Peasant Agriculture, Government and Economic Growth in Nigeria (Irwin, 1966), 255.

pressures and spent much of its resources buying into existing enterprises on unfavorable terms.

Investment expenditures in the regions were equally divided between commercial schemes (mainly plantations) and equity and long-term loans. The latter investment occurred after 1957, when import-substituting industrialization got underway, and it was concentrated in the textile, cement, and construction industries. A list of state investments in the east in 1963 shows a variety of investments--ceramics, glass, beer, soft drinks, tires, steel rolling, paper, cement, asbestos, enamelware, textiles, plastics, flour milling, gas, and construction. Wholly state-owned industries in all three regions were generally unsuccessful. Most industries were foreign-owned, with state capital playing a supplementary and supporting role, especially for new entrants to the Nigerian market. A breakdown of the capital structure for the first eight textile plants in Nigeria shows that state agencies provided much of the loan capital, thereby shifting the risk of investment away from the foreign equity investors.

TABLE 10.2: Capital Structure of Eight Textile Mills in Nigeria (1958-1965)-- £N000s.

|         | Equity | Loan |
|---------|--------|------|
| Private | 4565   | 3134 |
| Public  | 1606   | 5045 |
| Total   | 6171   | 8179 |

Source: Adapted from Kilby, Industrialisation in an Open Economy: Nigeria 1945-1966 (Cambridge, 1969), 120-121.

Although state agencies at both the federal and regional levels were often charged with support for private Nigerian enterprise, they were not generally successful in promoting a productive bourgeoisie. State patronage favored the contractors, produce buyers, importers, agents, and real estate dealers who were actively engaged in primitive accumulation. Those political notables who secured bank loans used them to build up an urban property base.

In 1959, the Commonwealth Development Corporation (CDC), anxious to maintain an institutional presence after independence, took up the invitation of the eastern and northern governments to establish investment companies as joint ventures with the regional development corporations. The involvement of the CDC brought additional funds and strengthened management. It was particularly successful in the case of the Northern Nigeria Investments Ltd. (NNIL), whose main interests were in the profitable Kaduna textile industry. Textile distributorships, based on this industry, became an important avenue for private accumulation by Kano businessmen. In 1970, NNIL had investments worth £N8.6 million. In the east, the growth of the Development Finance Company was interrupted by the war; by 1970, it held investments worth £N3.4 million, spread over fifteen enterprises. Apart from its investment in finance companies the CDC, by 1970, also had interests in the Nigerian Cement Company, Dunlop, four textile firms, and two plantation joint ventures, as well as a stake in the Nigerian Building Society, Nigerian Hotels, and Northern Hotels. Invariably, these activities involved investment with federal or state agencies.

The year 1959 also saw the establishment of the Investment Company of Nigeria in Lagos by British banking interests and the CDFC. In 1964, the bank was reorganized as the Nigerian Industrial Development Bank (NIDB) with the following shareholders: Central Bank of Nigeria, 25 percent; International Finance Corporation (IFC), 25 percent; and private foreign banks, 49 percent. Through the IFC, the World Bank secured a presence and subjected the bank to discipline in its capital structure and lending procedures. Until 1970, the bank's lending was largely to foreign-owned companies; the bank then switched its loans to Nigerian companies as a deliberate policy.[16]

Until the war period, the political and financial strength of the federal center, relative to that of the regions, was limited. A number of unitary economic institutions were established (Central Bank, Planning Board, NIDB), but the federal plan was essentially a collection of regional plans; plans for a steel plant, for example, first proposed in 1958, foundered upon regional rivalry over location. Direct federal investment in agriculture and manufacture was limited to a sugar estate, a paper mill, the Port Harcourt oil refinery, and a mint.

Federal activity was more important in the provision of infrastructure and public utilities. The first statutory corporations were created from government departments in the 1950s, and included the Electricity Corporation of Nigeria (1951), the Nigerian Coal Corporation (1951), Railway Corporation (1955), Nigerian Ports Authority (1955), and Nigerian Broadcasting (1955). There followed the Nigerian National Shipping Line (1958), Nigerian Airways (1959), and Nigerian External Telecommunications (1962), each of which involved the purchase of existing foreign assets. These bodies did not accumulate capital and usually relied on transfers from the federal government. In the 1960s, only the Nigerian Ports Authority made a significant operating surplus (see table 10.3). In 1967-1968, the level of foreign borrowing by statutory corporations (guaranteed by the federal government) was £N28.5 million, amounting to 30 percent of the total external debt.[17]

As the commissions of inquiry that followed the end of the first republic made clear, the corporations were beset by numerous problems, including nepotism and favoritism, ethnic rivalry over board membership and employment, ministerial interference, and poor management and administration. These weaknesses should not obscure the fact that the corporations did increase their output and that the diversion of public funds was not as large as that at the regional level. Debate

TABLE 10.3:  Current Operating Performance of Public Corporations, 1960-1970
(£N million)

| | |
|---|---|
| Nigerian Railway Corporation | -35.2 |
| Electricity Corporation of Nigeria | -8.8 |
| Nigerian Ports Authority | +18.8 |
| Nigerian Airways | -0.9 |
| Nigerian Broadcasting | +1.7 |
| Posts & Telegraph | -5.4 |

Source:  Derived from Nigeria--Options for Long-Term Development, IBRD
(Johns Hopkins University, 1974), 167-168.

and criticism of the corporations did not stop with the in-
quiries or the Ani report that followed them.[18]  There are four
perennial topics for debate--efficiency (relative to a private
sector that is itself supported by the public sector?), degree of
autonomy, salary relativities, and pricing and subsidy.   The
Ani recommendation, that a central unit for the accounting
and financial control of public corporations be set up, was not
acted on; statutory Corporation Service commissions for staff
matters were established for a number of years in two states
and at the federal level.
    The years following the civil war saw an upsurge in state
intervention with new state institutions, a consolidation and
extension of state ownership, and new policies designed to
strengthen Nigerian control of the economy and promote
structural changes in it.   Behind these moves lay a more powerful federal bureaucracy with experience in centralized decision making, a nationalist desire for more control in the aftermath of the civil war experience, and the arrival of large oil
revenues, which allowed a measure of autonomy from flows of
foreign capital and "aid."
    Before we examine the various elements in the growth of
state capital in the 1970s, there are a number of matters that
need to be borne in mind.   First, there is the practical difficulty of measuring the size of the state sector and its significance for capital accumulation in the Nigerian economy.   To
say that this is a problem is not, of course, to miss the point
that the absence of detailed public accounts is an integral part
of the political economy.   Ideally, we would like to set out the
evolution of individual and consolidated accounts for public
corporations, state enterprise, and other organizations in which
the state has a substantial interest.   This is not possible, how-

ever, even at the federal level. The situation is compounded in Nigeria by the existence of three tiers of government and the creation of new states on two occasions.

The other issues that we need to consider briefly, relevant to the expansion of state capital, are the changes in federal-state relations and the impact of large oil revenues on state finances. From a weak position, relative to the regions in the 1950s and 1960s, the federal center became stronger under military rule.[19] Backed by the army, the power of the federal bureaucracy increased. Following the creation of states in 1967 (twelve in all) and changes in the system of federal revenue allocation, the distributable pool at the center was enlarged. The increased importance of oil as a source of revenue ensured the absolute dominance of federal expenditures and made the state governments increasingly dependent on transfers from the federal center. The share of federal expenditures (including transfers to the states) in GDP rose from 12 percent in 1966 to 36 percent in 1977. It was against this background of increased federal financial and political strength that the second and third plans launched an expanded role for the public sector. Table 10.4 shows the growth of federal expenditures and the overall budget position.

The growth in state expenditure was rapid following windfall oil revenues. For four years, state revenues comfortably exceeded expenditures. There followed budget deficits, inflation and, later, external deficits that led to external borrowing, cuts in government spending, and a severe recession. Since capital accumulation depends on the growth of state expenditures, the pressures to expand state expenditures are very great; they are reinforced in Nigeria by a federal system in which the state and local governments rely on transfers from the federal center.

To stress the growth of federal expenditure is not to suggest that there was a parallel increase in the organizational capacity of the state or in the ability to plan and control on the part of the bureaucracy. It was the very combination of an upsurge in the centralized oil revenues and a weak administration that undermined the Gowon regime. Budgetary control was lax, and economic policy retreated passively in the face of commercial pressures and a consumption boom that was thinly disguised as an anti-inflation strategy. Large wage and salary awards and payment of arrears fueled a monetary expansion that had begun with increases in foreign exchange reserves. Financial transfers to the states accelerated to cover growing

TABLE 10.4: The Federal Budget Position, 1970/71--1978/79, naira million.

| | 70/71 | 71/72 | 72/73 | 73/74 | 74/75 | 75/76 | 76/77 | 77/78 | 78/79 |
|---|---|---|---|---|---|---|---|---|---|
| Revenue | 756 | 1411 | 1390 | 2172 | 5177 | 5856 | 7070 | 8359 | 7252 |
| Current Expenditures [a] | 774 | 849 | 1021 | 1120 | 1912 | 3402 | 3574 | 4425 | 3853 |
| Current Surplus | -18 | 562 | 378 | 1051 | 3265 | 2454 | 3496 | 3934 | 3399 |
| Capital Expenditures [b] | 99 | 214 | 311 | 529 | 1684 | 3823 | 4913 | 5627 | 3742 |
| Overall Surplus/Deficit | -117 | 348 | 67 | 522 | 1581 | -1369 | -1417 | -1693 | -3437 |

Notes: [a] Excludes contributions to development fund
[b] Excludes loans out to states

Source: Federal Current and Capital Estimates and Official Gazettes.

deficits, and there was a rushing of contracts by state governors when their demise appeared imminent.

The failure of the regime to act decisively on the question of the new states and the failure to redeploy state governors allowed full reign to the personal predilections of the governors. The new regime of Murtala Mohammed promptly created new states--nineteen in all. This further segmented the former regional blocs and created new foci for state expenditure in areas that had been relatively deprived of national resources and where, consequently, the demand for state creation was strong.

We now consider, in turn, the following forms of state capital:

1. Public corporations, including oil, mining, and steel
2. Direct federal investment in manufacture and agriculture
3. Federal finance capital, including the industrial development banks
4. Investments by state governments


## Public Corporations

In the 1970s, the range of public corporations and companies was extended with the addition of the Nigerian National Oil Corporation (1971), the Nigerian Steel Development Authority (1971), the Nigerian Mining Corporation (1972), the Nigerian National Supply Company (1972), the National Freight Company (1976), the National Cargo Handling Company (1977), Central Water Transportation Company (1977), and the Nigerian Airports Authority (1978). Heavy capital expenditures by public corporations, especially on electricity and ports, were funded by oil revenues, and the importance of external borrowing declined. The underlying financial weakness of the corporations remained. The External Telecommunications and the Electricity Authority made consistent small operating surpluses; the Ports Authority ran operating deficits for the first time, as a result of inflation and rigid tariffs; the Railway Corporation continued to run large deficits. Little investment was made in the railways, and transport policy was heavily biased toward private car ownership. This policy included heavy expenditure on roads (especially in the vicinity of the capitals of the nineteen states), subsidized petrol prices, cheap vehicle credit and car allowances for senior members of the public service, and the arrival of car assembly plants that linked the demand for local "production" to state credit policies.

For public enterprise as a whole, there was no evidence of increased financial planning and control--rather, the reverse. If the plan documents are an accurate guide, progressively less attention was given to planning public sector enterprise in the period from the first to the third plan. An irrelevant attempt was made by the Udoji commission[20] to infuse the public sector with the jargon of U.S. corporate management (management by objectives, and program performance budgeting) at a time when the basic budget and accounting functions of the state were weak.[21] Throughout this period, the public sector was weakened by a flow of senior civil servants and technocrats to the private sector.[22]

Although the state had taken a generally passive role in the oil industry until the late 1960s, a number of measures were aimed at increasing Nigeria's share of the oil revenues: state income per barrel of oil was raised from $0.295 in 1966 to $1.87 in 1972.[23] Nigerianization of the oil sector also began to receive attention as civil servants began to link Nigerianization to national control of the industry in line with developments in the OPEC countries. In 1970, at the end of the war, concessions were open to private companies, and one Nigerian company took up a concession. The following year, the state took a 100 percent interest in new concessions, with private operators getting a share of the output. The state also took a 35 percent undivided participation interest in all existing oil producing companies. This share was later raised to 55 percent (1974) and subsequently to 60 percent. The state participation interest was vested in the Nigerian National Oil Corporation (NNOC), which was set up in 1971, the year Nigeria became a member of OPEC.

The responsibilities of the NNOC were the subject of controversy between technocrats in the corporation and the controlling Ministry of Mines and Power. The issue of the appropriate organization for the oil industry did not end with the merger of the Ministry of Petroleum and the NNOC in 1976 to form the Nigerian National Petroleum Corporation. It has been argued that the reorganization was responsible for the lack of coordination between macroeconomic policy and oil-pricing and incentive policies that became evident in 1977.[24] More recently, the corporation, which had not published audited accounts since 1973, was involved in an inquiry, following allegations that large sums of oil money were missing. The corporation has been slow to get involved in oil production and exploration, and the buildup of a cadre of oil experts has been delayed; the state has taken a controlling interest in three oil marketing companies. With regard to downstream projects, two new oil refineries and a pipeline system have materialized--little associated gas from the oil fields is used in industry. Other projects--like the petrochemicals industry, the huge liquefied natural gas plant and a nitrogenous fertilizer plant--have all been subject to delay and reorganization after their initial conception and planning.

The Nigerian Mining Corporation was set up in 1972; it has taken a majority share in existing tin mines, including the Associated Tin Mines of Nigeria, the largest of the alluvial tin mining companies and producer of about half of Nigeria's output. In an attempt to mobilize local resources, the corporation has promoted eight clay brick plants with state governments; the corporation also operates quarries and holds equity in marble and ceramics projects. Recently, the formation of the Nigerian Uranium Mining Company was announced as a joint venture with French interests to exploit uranium deposits near Bauchi.

In the steel sector, the large projects have yet to materialize. Plans for a steel industry, in its present form, were put forward in 1970. After a search for iron ore and coal deposits, the location of a blast furnace plant at Ajaokuta was decided in 1975; the plant is due to start production in 1985. A turnkey direct-production plant at Warri started production in 1981, and three steel rolling mills are to be constructed at Oshogbo, Katsina, and Jos.

## Manufacture and Agriculture

Direct state investments by the federal government are aimed at accelerating changes in industrial structure, speeding up technology transfer, and dispersing industry more widely. Table 10.5 lists federal capital expenditures on industry from 1970 to 1977/78. Projects begun in the 1970s include cement (four), car and truck assembly (six), pulp and paper (two), fertilizer (one), wood and furniture (two), machine tools (one), electric meters (one), transformers (one), distilling (one), yeast and alcohol (one), and sugar refining (one).[25] This gives the state a monopoly in some areas (fertilizer, pulp and paper, and salt) and a substantial presence in others, but it does not constitute a dominant force in manufacturing as a whole. Many of the projects are joint ventures with the state performing a

TABLE 10.5:  Federal Capital Expenditure on Industry 1970-1977/78 (naira millions)

1. Oil ................................................................... 1329.1
   Joint Ventures ...................................................... (514.6)
   Refineries ........................................................... (506.0)
   Other .................................................................. (308.5)
2. Industrial Development Banks ........................... 282.2
3. Cement ............................................................. 169.5
4. Iron & Steel ....................................................... 161.4
5. Sugar ................................................................. 97.5
6. Pulp & Paper ...................................................... 96.6
7. Mining ............................................................... 38.6
8. Car Assembly ...................................................... 26.9
9. Fertilizer ........................................................... 17.8
10. Small-scale Industries ...................................... 10.9
11. Salt .................................................................. 8.3
12. Industrial Development Centers ......................... 3.7
    Other ............................................................... 44.3

TOTAL ............................................................... 2286.8

passive role, providing security, funds, and a protected market. For reasons of scale and profitability, some of these projects would not be attractive to foreign capital. In the case of the car and truck assembly plants, which are highly subsidized joint ventures aimed at eventual manufacture, state participation may have preempted some private investment. The component industry and the small commercial vehicle sector are open to private investment and have attracted some capital. Dr. Adeboye has argued forcefully that the record of the federal government to date in manufacturing projects shows a weak entrepreneur with a negative impact on the transfer of technology and high costs.[26]

Since the late colonial period, when the regional development corporation established a number of plantations, few large-scale agricultural schemes have materialized in Nigeria. A number of state governments promoted food projects in the 1970s, notably Bendel State, Cross River State, and the Agricultural Development Authority in East Central State; these expensive schemes made little or no contribution to output. Potentially more important is the federal government policy of promoting large-scale production schemes with foreign management and/or equity participation. These schemes include: (a) sugar estates in Nigeria and abroad; (b)the mechanized food farms of the National Grains Production Company, which are scheduled as joint ventures with foreign companies and state governments; (c) the cassava plantations of the National Roots Production Company; (d) three oil palm plantations; (e) the Nigerian Beverages Production Company (tea); (f) a ranching joint venture; and (g) three large-scale irrigation projects in Bornu, Kano, and Sokoto states. The latter schemes, which make a leap into untried technologies, are explicable only in terms of oil wealth, interstate competition, and the benefits which accrue to the bureaucracy, machinery merchants, and foreign consultants.

Large-scale production schemes account for only a small part of the activities of the federal bureaucracy in agriculture.[27] These now include eleven river basin development authorities, six commodity boards, the Nigerian Agricultural and Cooperative Bank, and the very important World Bank projects, which are gradually being extended throughout the country to include a high proportion of the peasantry and the best agricultural land. The Nigerian Agricultural and Cooperative Bank, which has been funded by federal transfers, lends to cooperatives, parastatals, companies, and individuals at subsidized rates. Gross cumulative disbursements over 1974-1979 amounted to N169 million.

## Federal Finance Capital

Local ownership and control of finance capital, which originated with the repatriation of marketing board funds from London and the setting up of regional banks and a central bank, has been further extended by majority Nigerian ownership of commercial and merchant banks, the establishment of new federal banks, and the Nigerianization of management. Other measures include the extension of federal ownership in the Nigerian Industrial Development Bank and the insurance companies, and disinvestment by the Commonwealth Development Corporation. Table 10.6 sets out the institutions, their ownership, and their asset position.

There are two federal industrial development banks: the Nigerian Industrial Development Bank (NIDB) and the Nigerian Bank for Commerce and Industry (NBCI). In terms of asset size, table 10.6 shows that these banks are dwarfed by the commercial banks and are roughly equivalent to the lead-

TABLE 10.6:  Federal Finance Capital

| | Equity | | Total Assets N million | |
|---|---|---|---|---|
| | Federal | Other | | |
| 1. Nigerian Industrial Development Bank | 100% | | 213 | Dec. '79 |
| 2. Nigerian Bank for Commerce and Industry | 100% | | 118 | Mar. '79 |
| 3. Nigerian Agricultural and Cooperative Bank | 100% | | 140 | Mar. '79 |
| 4. Federal Mortgage Bank | 100% | | 99 | Mar. '78 |
| 5. Federal Savings Bank | 100% | | NA | |
| 6. National Provident Fund | 100% | | 390 | Dec. '79 |
| 7. National Insurance Corporation | 100% | | 92 | Dec. '78 |
| 8. Nigerian Reinsurance Corporation | 100% | | NA | |
| 9. United Bank for Africa Ltd. | 49% | BNP 30%, BT 5%, Public 11%, Italian Banks 5% | 2488 | Mar. '80 |
| 10. First Bank of Nigeria Ltd. | 45% | Standard Chartered 38%, Public 17% | 2084 | Mar. '80 |
| 11. Union Bank of Nigeria Ltd. | 52% | Barclays Int'l 20%, | 1208 | Sep. '79 |

| | | | | |
|---|---|---|---|---|
| 12. | International Bank for West Africa Ltd. | 60% | Public 28% BIAO (Paris) 40% | 542 | Dec. '78 |
| 13. | Savannah Bank of Nigeria Ltd. | 60% | Bank of America 40% | 284 | Mar. '80 |
| 14. | Nigerian Arab Bank Ltd. | 60% | Arab Bank (Jordan) 40% | 68 | Dec. '79 |
| 15. | Allied Bank of Nigeria Ltd. | 60% | Bank of India 40% | 56 | Dec. '78 |
| 16. | ICON (Merchant Bank) | 45% | (NIDB), 15% (NICON), Morgan Guaranty 25%, Barings 15% | 206 | Dec. '79 |
| 17. | ICON (stockbrokers) | 100% | (NIDB) | NA | |
| 18. | Nigerian Acceptances Ltd. | 20% | (NICON) 25%, (NNDC) 10%, Continental Illionis 40%, Individuals 5% | 146 | Mar. '80 |
| 19. | Chase Merchant Bank Nigeria Ltd. | 60% | Chase 40% | 70 | Dec. '78 |
| 20. | International Merchant Bank | 60% | First Chicago 40% | 80 | Dec. '78 |
| 21. | Nigerian Merchant Bank | 60% | UBA 40% | 68 | Mar. '80 |
| 22. | Commonwealth Development Corporation (Nigeria) | 60% | (NIDB) CDC 40% | NA | |
| 23. | African Development Bank, Abidjan | 12% | Others 88% | NA | |

Sources: Annual reports and interviews

TABLE 10.7: <u>NIDB and NBCI: Cumulative Net Disbursements, N million</u>

| | NIDB | | | NBCI | | | TOTAL | | |
|---|---|---|---|---|---|---|---|---|---|
| | Equity | Loan | Total | Equity | Loan | Total | Equity | Loan | Total |
| 1969 | 2.1 | 5.4 | 7.5 | | | | | | |
| 1970 | 2.2 | 6.9 | 9.1 | | | | | | |
| 1971 | 2.7 | 9.7 | 12.1 | | | | | | |
| 1972 | 3.5 | 14.1 | 17.6 | | | | | | |
| 1973 | 3.6 | 16.4 | 20.0 | | | | | | |
| 1974 | 5.0 | 20.7 | 25.7 | | | | | | |
| 1975 | 6.5 | 29.2 | 35.7 | 0.6 | 1.7 | 2.3 | 7.1 | 30.9 | 38.0 |
| 1976 | 10.7 | 53.7 | 64.4 | 1.6 | 4.6 | 6.2 | 12.3 | 58.3 | 70.6 |
| 1977 | 13.0 | 90.1 | 103.1 | 3.6 | 24.4 | 28.0 | 16.6 | 114.5 | 131.1 |
| 1978 | 18.0 | 122.2 | 140.2 | 7.9 | 36.7 | 44.6 | 25.9 | 158.9 | 184.8 |
| 1979 | 22.5 | 159.0 | 181.5 | 8.8 | 57.6 | 66.4 | 31.3 | 216.6 | 247.9 |

Note: Figures are end-of-year for NIDB and end-of-March for NBCI

Sources: Annual reports and accounts of NIDB and NBCI

ing merchant banks. The banks are not the main vehicle for federal industrial investment, which is undertaken by the Ministry of Industries, nor are they the only source of loans to industry, since the Federal Ministry of Finance both lends directly and guarantees loans. Both the NIDB and the NBCI have had access to federal funds, and the NIDB has also obtained funds from the World Bank and the European Industrial Bank. Since 1975, the activities of both banks have expanded rapidly (see table 10.7). By 1979, the NIDB had investments (equity and loan) of N181 million and had sanctioned 297 projects. The NBCI had investments of N66 million in seventy-six projects with 142 projects sanctioned. Unfortunately, it is not possible to give an accurate picture of the capital and ownership structure of these projects or their share of total industrial investment. There is little doubt, however, that since 1970, when the proportion of foreign-owned companies financed by the NIDB dropped dramatically, the banks have financed many of the large-scale projects owned, publicly or privately, by Nigerians. The activities of the two banks are not coordinated, though they have cofinanced some large projects at the federal and state levels.

A product breakdown of the value of NIDB sanctions shows that food and beverages (especially beer), textiles and cement dominate the lending (see table 10.8). The NIDB has taken a small equity share in about half the projects as a source of income; the ratio of equity to loan is only 0.14. The bank has financed projects promoted by federal and state agencies and was assigned the responsibility of public industrial investment by the Okigbo Commission.[28] The bank has

TABLE 10.8: Allocation of NIDB Gross Sanctions by Industry, December 1979, N million

| | |
|---|---|
| 1. Textiles | 49.0 |
| 2. Food & Beverages | 96.7 |
| 3. Metal | 13.5 |
| 4. Wood | 16.3 |
| 5. Chemicals | 58.1 |
| 6. Hotel & Tourism | 30.7 |
| 7. Other | 73.4 |
| | 337.7 |

Source: NIDB 1979 annual report

recently refinanced two state-level investment institutions. Ironically, the NIDB has taken a 60 percent share in the Commonwealth Development Corporation, after the CDC failed to gain exemption from the provisions of the Nigerian Enterprises Promotion Decree (NEPD).

The geographical location of cumulative gross disbursements shows a concentration of NIDB financing in Lagos and Western States.[29] This concentration does not accurately reflect the dispersion of the bank's recent lending, however. This dispersion can be partly explained by new state-level investment companies, which attract federal funds, and by NIDB support of federal projects.

The Nigerian Bank for Commerce and Industry (NBCI) was set up in 1973, partly as a result of dissatisfaction with the performance of NIDB, which was felt to be heavily committed to foreign-owned companies in the Lagos area, and partly to increase Nigerian control of the economy by providing loans for the takeover of companies that were affected by the NEPD. Although NBCI did initially give loans for the acquisition of indigenized enterprises, its main activity has been the funding of new enterprises and the expansion of existing ones. Unlike the NIDB, the NBCI is authorized to engage in all merchant banking activities.

In 1971, the federal government acquired a 40 percent interest in the three foreign-owned commercial banks which dominated the financial system: Barclays, Standard, and UBA. Nigerian participation was later raised to 60 percent. The Okigbo Commission on the financial system (1976) agreed with the decision to raise Nigerian participation, but argued against a public sector majority interest because

> the most critical sector of the financial system would then be exposed to risks and dangers that the economy could ill afford at this stage . . . it would be anomalous to take 51 percent and then enter into a management agreement with these foreign partners . . . it would be more prudent policy for government not to contemplate majority ownership by the public sector until and unless it is in a position to take over the management.

In the event the federal government did secure a majority interest in a number of commercial and merchant banks (see table 10.6), it found itself in the anomalous position of penalizing Barclays for its South African connections after it had done so. These changes in the ownership of banks have been accompanied by a rapid Nigerianization of management. For example, in the United Bank for Africa, Nigerians hold the posts of chairman and chief executive, as well as three of the four executive directorships. The federal government holds a majority share in five merchant banks, either directly or indirectly through the NIDB and the National Insurance Company of Nigeria, thus extending collaboration with international finance capital. These foreign banks have accepted their minority position and Nigerian management. Together with the commercial banks, they have been active in funding local syndicate loans for industry of up to N60 million.

The federal government has also extended its ownership and control in the insurance industry. Until 1969, when the National Insurance Company of Nigeria (NICON) was set up, insurance was dominated by foreign companies (in 1964, they were required to invest 40 percent of their income in Nigerian securities). NICON was given a monopoly of government business, and insurance companies were required to reinvest 10 percent of their income with the corporation. In the early 1970s, the government began to acquire shares in foreign companies, the Nigerian share eventually rising to 60 percent. In 1977, the Nigerian Reinsurance Corporation was formed, and companies were required to cede 20 percent of their business to the corporation. An African Reinsurance Corporation was also set up with the head office in Lagos. It is currently estimated that foreign-associated companies account for 30 percent of the N300 million Nigerian insurance market, state-owned companies for 50 percent and private Nigerian companies for the remaining 20 percent.[30]

The Federal Mortgage Bank (1977) is an expanded version of the former Nigerian Building Society whose loans policy was directed at middle- and high-income groups. It is the third strand in federal housing policy, which includes the provision of funds for "low cost" housing schemes in the states and the untouched colonial heritage of heavily subsidized housing for all senior public employees. The slow growth of the bank has recently been attributed to inadequate capitalization, unrealistic interest rate structures, and a lack of control in asset management.[31]

The National Provident Funds is financed by employer and employee contributions at 5 percent of the wage bill. It acts as a forced savings mechanism for the state, and funds are used to finance federal bond issues. Contributors get cash benefits in the event of retirement, invalidity or loss of earnings for more than a year.

## The Nineteen States

No comprehensive picture of state capital in the nineteen states of Nigeria is attempted in this chapter. After an introduction, we look briefly at parastatals in Bendel State, the relation of state expenditures to private accumulation in Cross River State, and the activities of the New Nigeria Development Company in Kaduna. We end with some observations on the links between the federal center and the states.

Like the old regions, many of the states have a great variety of state agencies involved in industry, agriculture, banking, insurance, trade, transport, construction, hotels, property, housing, and publishing. The creation of parastatal bodies and the growth of the bureaucracy were given a great boost by the creation of new states and the transfer of large federal funds to them. A number of older regional institutions and companies still survive; in particular, two development corporations have been refashioned to form the Odu'a Investment Company and the New Nigeria Development Company.[32]  Many states have created their own investment agencies alongside the ministries, although the extent to which either body actually promotes industries varies widely.  State-promoted projects tend to be light consumer goods industries like breweries, but projects underway include particle board, glass, machine tools and batteries, and iron and steel projects.

The record of state agencies is a mixed one, and it is hazardous to generalize for the federation as a whole.  Reports of commissions of inquiry in some states, in the aftermath of the Gowon regime, revealed weaknesses similar to those seen in the federal corporations in the 1960s.  In addition, the personal involvement of military governors in the affairs of various parastatals is amply recorded, as are the opportunities for corruption provided by the sale of enterprises under the Nigerian Enterprises Promotions Decree.[33]  Board membership and distributorships attached to government-owned companies are a long-standing means of patronage.  Research in Kwara State confirms the rapid turnover of board members and the general unimportance of experience and knowledge, as against ethnic balancing and political influence, in the appointment to boards.[34]

In Bendel State, the Odje Commission of Inquiry reported on no less than seventy-four state boards, corporations and companies.[35]  The luxuriant and indiscriminate growth of parastatal bodies in Bendel State is made possible, and perhaps explained, by the fact that the state has received very high revenues per capita due to the operation of the derivation principle in revenue allocation (20 percent of on-shore mining revenues and royalties go to the state of origin).  The creation of parastatals may well be an efficient way of absorbing and containing additional revenues within the bureaucracy and political class.  In the period 1974/75 to 1978/79, over half of the recurrent expenditures in Bendel State were classified as grants and subventions to state boards and corporations.[36] Loans outstanding to the private sector at N53 million (March 1978) exceeded those to the state boards and corporations at N28 million, indicating that state funds were also being used to support private accumulation on a large scale.[37]

Direct state intervention in industry and agriculture has had a checkered history in Bendel State.  Three older turnkey projects (glass, cement, and textiles) were resuscitated after the war but have performed erratically.  Under the energetic leadership of Governor Ogbemudia, a number of enterprises were purchased from aliens, and new industries were speedily promoted (soap, pharmaceuticals and medical supplies, plastics, beer, and food farms).[38]  Large-scale mechanized food farms have a disastrous record--over N13 million was spent in two years; these farms have recently been placed under federal management.[39]

Two states that have an active record of industrial promotion are Cross River and Ondo.  Both areas were physically isolated under the former regional governments and attracted little by way of state investment or industry.  Among the projects completed or in the pipeline in Ondo State are soft drinks, corrugated iron, paper conversion, medical products, soap and detergents, and glass.

We now pursue the case of Cross River State for the light it sheds on how local classes establish a base for capital accumulation.  The creation of the state and the arrival of large oil revenues brought heavy state expenditures and a construction boom.  This opened up new avenues for private accumulation in an area where wealth had previously been associated with commerce, palm oil, and the professions.  Individuals connected with the construction industry (builders, contractors, consultants, architects, engineers, and quantity surveyors) have built up considerable wealth from inflated contracts which are, in effect, direct transfers from the state.  An urban property base is then established, which can be used as security for bank loans and, in a few cases, the promotion of industry. These individuals account for most of those who have taken shares in industries promoted by the state investment company.

Investigations in other states confirm the importance of the construction industry and state contracts as sources of finance for the promotion of large-scale manufacture.

The Investment Trust Company in Cross River was formed in 1973 and currently holds investments (equity and loans) of about N20 million, the largest of which are in asbestos, beer, flour milling, cement, fishing, the wood industry, oil palm estates, and insurance. The company has actively promoted projects attracting foreign partners and capital from the federal banks in Lagos (including projects in beer, plastics, matches, paints, biscuits, and batteries). The company takes a residual share of the equity after attracting funds from individuals. Typically, groups of shareholders take some 30 percent of the equity, with individuals investing up to N250,000.

The origins of the New Nigeria Development Company go back to the Northern Region Production Development Board, established in 1949, which was superseded by the Northern Nigerian Development Corporation in 1960. As a result of an inquiry by the new military rulers in 1967, the corporation was reorganized into a group holding company with four main operating subsidies covering property, industrial investment (NNIL), hotels, and agriculture. The NNDC is now owned by the ten northern states, with Kano holding 19 percent, Kaduna 14 percent, Sokoto 12.35 percent, Bornu 9.28 percent, Plateau 8.62 percent, Bauchi 8.43 percent, Gongola 8.29 percent, Kwara 8.0 percent, Niger 6.65 percent, and Benue 5.38 percent. Table 10.9 shows that the NNDC, which has not received any grants or subventions from state governments, grew rapidly after 1976. In 1978 the NNDC held an investment portfolio (equity) larger than that of NIDB and NBCI combined. Investments were diversified, with interests in textiles (twelve), hotels (eight), finance (nine), mining and metals (nine), tanneries (five), agro-allied projects (seven), and real estate and construction (seven). In 1979, it had interests in 120 companies, and a number of these investments are in Lagos-based companies. Recently, the company has been recapitalized with total assets of about N120 million, and the property division has been merged to give the company a stronger borrowing base. In 1978, the Commonwealth Development Corporation sold its 40 percent share holding in the NNIL after nineteen years of association.

The NNDC has provided regional support for the penetration of foreign capital and was, until recently, involved in most large-scale projects in the north. This regional role persists, but the arrival of active state investment companies in

TABLE 10.9:  New Nigeria Development Company, N million

| | Total Investment[a] | Total Assets | Number of Companies with NNDC Interests | Rate of Return |
|---|---|---|---|---|
| 1970 | 17.6 | 20.0 | | 5.3% |
| 1971 | 18.5 | 21.4 | | 5.5% |
| 1972 | 18.9 | 22.5 | | 5.0% |
| 1973 | 19.1 | 22.3 | | 6.1% |
| 1974 | 21.0 | 22.6 | | 5.8% |
| 1975 | 21.8 | 23.3 | | 8.1% |
| 1976 | 22.8 | 25.0 | | 16.7% |
| 1977 | 24.5 | 26.9 | 65 | 16.5% |
| 1978[b] | 33.8 | 46.8 | 80 | 14.1% |
| 1979[c] | | 60.1 | 120.(October) | |
| 1980 | | 120.0 (estimate) | | |

Notes:  [a] Total investment is unconsolidated.
   [b] About N4 million of the N33.8 million investment in 1978 was loan.
   [c] In 1979, assets included N10 million paid-up share capital,
      N26 million reserves, and N24 million in loan capital.

Source:  Annual reports

Kano, Kaduna, and Jos, the higher levels of private Nigerian accumulation, and Federal investment have eroded its position. The company attracts capital from and cofinances projects with the NIDB and NBCI in federal, state and privately promoted projects. Recent examples include the salvaged Sokoto cement company (Federal GT 31 percent, NNDC 25 percent, Sokoto 22 percent, Kano 12 percent, and Kaduna 10 percent) and the Nigerian Asbestos Industries (Bauchi State 33 percent, Hydrabad Asbestos 33 percent, Nigerian businessmen 13 percent, NIDB 11 percent, NNIL 5 percent, and NBCI 5 percent). Since 1976, the company has actively sought out and concentrated capital from groups of Nigerian businessmen, warehousing the equity if necessary. A common pattern is a group of individuals taking 10-30 percent of the equity (or more, if the project is privately promoted). Our preoccupation with state capital in this chapter should not blind us to the fact that private Nigerian investment in manufacturing in the northern states also occurs without state participation (e.g., in motor parts, ceramics, television assembly, biscuits, gases, textiles, plastic pipes, and aluminum). Like other investment companies, the NNDC bought shares in publicly quoted companies.[40] As the 1978 annual report explained, "Although such refinancing activities do not form a normal feature of our operations, the Board is convinced that an institutional presence in such companies is in the national interest, particularly in view of the diffused ownership structures." The purchase of shares by state agencies was clearly one way of attempting to offset the bias of share applications toward Lagos and the western states, which was the product of uneven development and the civil war.    Finally, the NNDC encouraged the opening of a branch of the Nigerian Stock Exchange in Kaduna.

The NNDC has provided an important training ground for managers and technocrats, acting as a conduit to state and federal appointments. The company has been steadily Nigerianized. In the early 1970s, managing agency agreements were replaced by secondments and consultancy agreements. Also, the representation of NNDC interests on boards of subsidiary companies and, in some cases, associated companies was no longer restricted to NNDC staff. The NNDC has been an important element in the power and patronage available to the would-be successors of the northern establishment, otherwise known as the Kaduna "mafia." Under the military, little direct control was exercised by state governments.

We end this section by bringing together a number of strands in economic relations between the center and the states. Some of these are relatively minor, but together they amount to a substantial change compared to the early 1960s.

We have already stressed the increase in federal political and financial power, the breakup of the old regions and the erosion of their independent sources of finance. State creation has brought a wider dispersal of industry, as has federal direct investment in the states. Host states usually take a minimum 10 percent share in federal projects, as well as contributing to infrastructure and services.[41] Federal institutions such as the NIDB, NBCI, NACB, and FMB lend directly to projects in the states, in some cases refinancing the activities of state-level institutions. The spread of share ownership in many of the largest companies increased with the public sale of shares under the NEPD. The United Africa Company set aside blocks of shares for each state government in order to ensure its "federal character" under the first phase of the indigenization decree.[42] Over 30 percent of the shares of the UAC are held by state governments or their agencies.[43] In 1979, the total number of shareholders in the company was 135,543.[44] Many other companies also have a substantial state ownership. For example, Julius Berger, the largest construction company, is 40 percent-owned by Lagos, Plateau, and Benue States. During the second phase of indigenization, I estimated on the basis of eleven major public issues that state governments and their agencies obtained over 16 percent of the shares on offer. Finally, we note that some state-based companies, especially in the construction industry, have extended their operations to cover the whole country.

## Conclusion

In the 1950s, as power shifted from the colonial regime, so political, bureaucratic, and professional groups who otherwise lacked independent sources of wealth obtained access to state funds that had been appropriated from the peasantry through the marketing board system. Urban property was the prime target for these groups. Private capital was small in scale, fragmented, and regional in outlook. It was engaged mainly in commerce, transporting, and contracting, and played very little part in the development of medium- or large-scale industry. State capital was used to support the initial advance of foreign monopoly capital into industry. The Commonwealth Development Corporation joined with state capital to provide management, organization, and finance for the start-up of large-scale capitalist enterprise. This enterprise was heavily concentrated in the Lagos area, with secondary concentrations in the Kano/Kaduna and Port Harcourt/Aba zones and minor pockets in Ibadan, Benin, and Enugu. After independence, federal institutions and policies were weakened by regional struggles for central control; and, at the regional level, the privatization of state funds sometimes degenerated into a kleptocracy that gnawed into the fabric of the state.

The accelerated growth, greater national cohesion, and consolidation of the bourgeoisie in the 1970s owe much to the timely arrival of large centralized oil revenues, which sustained state accumulation. Oil permitted the expansion and spread of capitalist enterprise and a second phase in the expansion of state capital. This expansion built on and extended the earlier regional development of state capital. It also involved a much stronger federal drive at the center, led by the federal bureaucracy, and, as we have seen, the creation of new linkages between the center and the states. The creation of new states, on two occasions, altered the pattern of state economic activity and the spatial organization of the state; it also widened the opportunities for access to money capital and increased the dispersion of capitalist enterprise. The state has also been instrumental in creating a national base for capital accumulation through the extension of infrastructure, the development of a local financial system, the expansion of state capital in industry and agriculture, and measures to increase local ownership and control.

The Nigerian bourgeoisie is predominantly a managerial and supervisory class that includes elements of large-scale local capital. Leading elements include bureaucrats, technocrats, and state managers in the public sector and the managerial cadre and directors associated with capitalist enterprise in the private sector. Though distinct, these groups share common interests and a common bureaucratic development ideology-- many heads of service and senior civil servants retire from the public service at a relatively young age to take executive positions in the private sector. Nigerian private capital has increased rapidly in scale since the 1960s. Primarily commercial in orientation, it has moved into large-scale industry where joint ventures with foreign capital and management have been set up. The relative strengths of the various groups that comprise the bourgeoisie, and the cohesion of the class as a whole, change through time. Under the military, federal bureaucrats had a powerful influence on state policy. Though often obscured and weakened by sectional and distributive conflict, these class elements have, nevertheless, exercised a general influence on the character of state policy. Recent specific class actions include the indigenization decrees, the entrenchment of private property under the new constitution, and the exclusion of organized labor from electoral politics.

In the current phase of capitalist development in Nigeria, state capital has begun to assume a more direct responsibility for directing and structuring the accumulation of capital. Here, the role of state capital goes well beyond the provision of infrastructure, finance, and protection that supported the early penetration of foreign capital into large-scale manufacture. The state has initiated and promoted a series of large-scale industrial projects (steel, petrochemicals, pulp and paper, vehicle assembly, machine tools, and other capital goods) and a series of important projects in agriculture in collaboration with the World Bank. Industrial projects, where the state has taken full or part ownership, are concentrated in higher technology areas, often under monopoly conditions. Internally, these developments reflect the centralization of the state, the growth of state capital and the bureaucracy, and the internal expansion and deepening of the domestic market. Externally, they involve new forms of collaboration between international capital and the state, as well as more comprehensive integration of the Nigerian economy within the international capitalist system. Here, the Nigerian state is not passive or entirely subordinate; it may exercise considerable leverage or bargaining power by virtue of the large domestic market, competition between foreign capitals, and imperialist rivalry. In the case of collaboration with the World Bank, we find that international finance capital has come to play a very direct part in shaping agricultural policies in Nigeria. Industry and agriculture do not exhaust the areas of collaboration between the state and international capital: as we have seen, the extension of state ownership in the financial sector has brought extensive participation alongside foreign banks. In summary, state capital has started to play a central role in directing the future pattern of domestic accumulation in alliance with international capital.

The indigenization decrees, which enforced the divestment or dilution of foreign capital through the sale of shares and new share subscriptions in large-scale, foreign-controlled enterprises, might appear to run counter to the collaborative trends we have just outlined. This is not the case. Indigenization reflected some of the same forces, including bourgeois national aspirations for a stronger local base for capital accumulation and the rise of a stronger state apparatus. Biersteker, who adopts a fractional approach to indigenization, has argued that local capital has been involved in a dual alliance with the state on the one hand and foreign capital on the other.[45] Local capital, while supporting the objectives of the state, combined with foreign capital to effectively neutralize the outcome of indigenization. It is questionable how far state objectives, or the aspirations of the bourgeois elements that underlie them, were in any sense really neutralized. It is true that the first stage of indigenization lost much of its nationalist legitimacy because of the obvious private and sectional advantages it entailed. When the second phase of the decree was under discussion, groups that spanned the private and public sectors combined to ensure a decree that did not challenge the position of foreign capital and that arrived at a more legitimate national outcome for those bourgeois elements in a position to take advantage of the decree. Portfolio investment by public agencies at the state level performed the function of broadening the geographical basis of share ownership and giving foreign companies a national identity. The decrees strengthened local class formation through the increase in local share ownership and by the impetus given to local managerial classes in the longer term.

How have the growth of state capital and, more generally, the expansion of state expenditures affected Nigerian private accumulation and the acquisition of property? Official policies designed to support local capital, including indigenization, have generally been much less significant than the general expansion of state expenditures in creating channels for the buildup of money capital and in influencing the scale and direction of any subsequent private capital accumulation. Perhaps the major exception here has been the activity of the various state investment bodies that have acted to centralize private capital and direct it into manufacture. Other much less important state measures include the small-scale industries credit scheme, guidelines for commercial bank credit, the raising of minimum thresholds for expatriate tenders for building and construction contracts, and the breaking up of sole distribution agencies.

The inflation of state contracts has provided an important means of access to money capital for all those associated with the building and construction industry. Our investigations suggest that this has also been an important route to investment in manufacture by Nigerian entrepreneurs; the construction boom throughout the country has meant that this source of capital has been widely spread. Other channels to wealth, private property, and private accumulation deriving from state expenditure include various kinds of intermediary activity (commissioning, contracting, and consultancy), commerce, savings out of state employment, and corruption. In some states, the expansion of state agencies and the bureaucracy approximates the privatization of state resources.

Kitching, in his work on Kenya, has placed great emphasis on the importance of savings out of the state wage bill by petit bourgeois elements for investment and capital accumulation in industry and agriculture.[46] He argues that there is a major contradiction in the fact that this route to a capitalist transformation is blocked by constraints on the growth of the state wage bill, which is, in turn, constrained by the expansion of real output in the economy. Whatever the merits of this analysis for Kenya, it is not appropriate for Nigeria. In Nigeria, in the last twenty years, there have been other avenues to money capital and private accumulation more important than the state wage bill. Moreover, the prospects for capitalist development in Nigeria do not depend crucially on the investment propensities of a petite bourgeoisie. They rest, rather, with the Nigerian bourgeoisie and state policies that actively support large-scale foreign, state, and private capital, and that attempt to ensure a basis for national accumulation once oil revenues diminish.

What is the nature of the state sector and the bureaucracy? The adoption of stronger nationalist measures by the federal government has not led to a state capitalism where a state bourgeoisie plans and manages capital accumulation. Nor, on the other hand, has it led to reliance upon local private capital. The weakness of local private capital effectively ruled out this "ideal" path and also weakened the state drive because the bureaucracy could expect no support from this quarter. Rather, the state has continued to support and sustain private accumulation while taking measures to localize and structure accumulation. This is not to suggest that these policies have been particularly effective or efficient. For example, the expansion of the state sector has involved much waste, and the high cost of infrastructure, lack of security, overvaluation of the naira, and smuggling have all diluted the attractions of Nigeria as a base for capital accumulation as distinct from a market for foreign goods and technology.

Within the state sector, there is little evidence of capital accumulation apart from the exceptional case of the state oil corporation and a number of state-owned breweries. State corporations and companies have been funded by transfers from the Ministry of Finance, and state capital is generally used to finance private accumulation. In the 1970s, the state sector generally demonstrated a weak entrepreneurial capacity in initiating, planning, and managing state projects. The accounting and budgeting functions of the state were also poorly developed. The expansion of the state sector led to little conflict or debate over the limits or content of state investment; there was more concern over implementation, organization, location, and timing of state projects. The main debates occurred in three areas where local merchant interests were affected by the monopoly of agricultural exports by the commodity boards, by the operations of the Nigerian National Supply Company, and by crude oil sales that excluded local buyers.

What reasons can be advanced for the nature of the state drive? First, although military rule provided cover for the federal bureaucracy and allowed scope for more nationalist policies, it did not result in a strong military-bureaucratic alliance; only in a few isolated instances did the military take leading positions in the ministries or parastatals.  After the Gowon regime fell, the civil service was purged, and the military then made preparations for its own withdrawal.  Second, although technocratic elements within the public sector increased, they did not establish strong bases within public corporations and enterprises:  ministerial control of federal enterprises was jealously guarded, and state bodies developed very little autonomy over policy or conditions of service.  Technocrats also lacked experience, and there was a constant drain of personnel to more lucrative opportunities in the private sector.  Third, the existence of the federal system and the need to balance sectional and communal pressures and struggles over the distribution of federal largesse could dilute the federal drive and lead to conflict within the state apparatus.  Against this, however, it should be remembered that the creation of new states and the greater equality of access to federal funds did reduce the potential for intense social antagonism among representatives of the old regional blocs.  It created lower levels of rivalry among the states and reduced the opportunity for regional gain from the exercise of federal power.

With the return to civilian rule, it is tempting to argue that a shift in power from the center to the states and the rise to power of the National Party of Nigeria, in which business and propertied interests are well represented, will check the expansion of state responsibilities and result in policies that are more favorable to international capital.  However, the class content of state power has not altered significantly, and more continuity than change can be expected.  There has been a more concerted attempt to attract foreign capital, as well as some relaxation of the indigenization decree to allow greater foreign equity participation in areas where local capital is weak.

The central role of state capital in promoting private accumulation on a national basis and creating opportunities for private gain can be identified in a pervasive bureaucratic developmentalism and the rhetoric of the mixed economy. Here, the state is seen as the main agent of development, capable of clearing away the obstacles on the path to an industrial, capitalist future.  It can, for example, overcome the manpower shortage and the constraint of inadequate executive capacity by providing higher education, management courses, and technical training.  State ideology in Nigeria is notable for the absence of any strong ideological currents or any attempt to identify and promote a particularly Nigerian path or "model." Occasionally this ideological vacuum at the top leads to attempts to create ideology from above:   under the Gowon regime, there was an attempt to create a set of national goals using liberal democratic principles; later, the Udoji commission tried to infuse the public sector with the ideology of corporate management.   The absence of ideological antagonism does not indicate the presence of a strong bourgeois class hegemony.   Rather, it reflects the dependence of private property and capital accumulation upon the expansion of state expenditures and various mechanisms of privatization, together with the fact that, under imperialism, monopoly capital requires access to the state for its profitable operation.   A final factor is the nature of the bourgeoisie that has emerged across the public-private divide and the manner of its formation in and through the state.

## Notes

1. T.G. Forrest, "Agricultural Policies in Nigeria, 1900-1978," in J. Heyer, P. Roberts and G. Williams, eds., Rural Development in Tropical Africa (New York: Macmillan, 1981).

2. B. Beckman, "Whose State?  State and Capitalist Development in Nigeria" (Paper presented to the Conference of the Nordic Association of Political Scientists, Turku, Finland, August 1981).

3. F.H. Cardoso and E. Faletto, Dependency and Development in Latin America (Berkeley: University of California Press, 1979), preface, 16.

4. T. Biersteker, "Indigenization and the Nigerian Bourgeoisie:  Dependent Development in an African Context" (in this volume).

5. P. Evans, Dependent Development:  The Alliance of Multinationals, State and Local Capital in Brazil (Princeton: Princeton University Press, 1979).

6. G. Williams, "Nigeria:  A Political Economy" and "Politics in Nigeria," both reprinted in State and Society in Nigeria (Nigeria: Afrografika, 1980).

7. T.G. Forrest, "Federal State and Capitalist Transformation" (Unpublished paper, Department of Economics, Ahmadu Bello University, Zaria, June 1979).

8. G.K. Helleiner, Peasant Agriculture, Government and Economic Growth in Nigeria (Homewood, Ill.: Irwin, Inc., 1966).

9. O. Teriba, "Development Strategy, Investment Decisions and Expenditure Patterns of a Public Development Institution:  The Case of the Western Nigeria Development Corporation, 1949-1962", Nigerian Journal of Economic and Social Studies 8, 2 (1966).

10. S.P. Schatz, Development Bank Lending in Nigeria:  The Federal Loans Board (Nigerian Institute of Social and Economic Research Series, Oxford

University Press, 1964); Economics, Politics and Administration in Government Lending, The Regional Loans Boards of Nigeria (NISER Series, Oxford University Press, 1970).

11. T. Turner, "The Transfer of Oil Technology and the Nigerian State," Development and Change, 7, 4; "The Working of the Nigerian National Oil Corporation," in P. Collins, ed., Administration for Development in Nigeria (Lagos: African Education Press, 1980).

12. Nigerian Economic Society, Public Enterprises in Nigeria: Proceedings of the 1973 Annual Conference of the Nigerian Economic Society (Ibadan, 1974).

13. O. Aboyade, "Nigerian Public Enterprises as an Organizational Dilemma," in Public Enterprises in Nigeria, ibid.

14. G.K. Helleiner, op. cit., 248.

15. A white paper on the military government policy for the reorganisation of the Northern Nigeria Development Corporation (Kaduna, 1966).

16. I. Diaku, "The Capital Structure, Financing Practices and Profit Performance of the Nigerian Industrial Development Bank, 1964-1972," Nigerian Journal of Economic and Social Studies, vol. 18, no. 1 (1976).

17. Report of the Interim Revenue Allocation Committee (The Dina Report), (Lagos, 1969).

18. Report of the Working Party on Statutory Corporations and State-owned Companies (Lagos: Federal Ministry of Information, 1967).

19. This paragraph draws on my "Recent Developments in Nigerian Industrialisation," in M. Fransman, ed., Industry and Accumulation in Africa (London: Heinemann, 1982).

20. Federal Republic of Nigeria, Public Service Review Commission, Main Report (Lagos, 1974).

21. See A Review of the Federal Budgetary System, Final Report (Nigerian Institute of Social and Economic Research, and Federal Ministry of Finance, 1977).

22. Among the most well known are Ade John, Ayida, Damcida, Joda, Katugum, and Udoji.

23. T. Turner, "The Working of the Nigerian National Oil Corporation," op. cit.

24. P.C. Asiodu, "Nigeria and the Oil Question," Nigerian Economic Society (1979).

25. A full list of federal industrial investments would also include beer (one), textiles (two), fishing (two), construction (three). A shipbuilding project has been announced.

26. T.O. Adeboye, "Public Sector Participation in Manufacturing" (Paper delivered to the 1978 Annual Conference of the Nigerian Economic Society, Lagos, 1979).

27. For further discussion of agricultural policy, see T.G. Forrest, "Agricultural Policies in Nigeria, 1900-1978," op. cit.

28. Report of the Committee on the Financial System (Lagos, 1977).

29. The distribution of cumulative gross disbursements for 1964-1979 was

Lagos 28.5 percent, Ogun 16.1 percent, Oyo 7.3 percent, Bauchi 7.1 percent, Bendel 6.6 percent, Cross River 6.4 percent, Benue 4.6 percent, Kaduna 4.2 percent, Imo 4.0 percent, Anambra 3.9 percent, Kano 3.9 percent, and other states 7.2 percent. Business Times (Lagos, 3 June 1980).

30. Financial Times (London, 29 September 1980).

31. Business Times (Lagos, 26 August 1980).

32. The Odu'a Investment Company owned by Oyo, Ogun, and Ondo states is not discussed in this paper.

33. See: (a) the Panel to Investigate into the Benue-Plateau State Houses and Contract Procedure and also to Investigate Whether Some Persons have made improper gains. Government Decisions on the Panel's Report of the Investigations (Jos, 1975); (b) Conclusions of the Government on the Report and Recommendations of the Commission of Inquiry into the Rivers State Transport Corporation under the Chairmanship of Justice A. Alagoa (Port Harcourt, n.d.); (c) Report of the Kano State-owned Organisations and Companies Commission of Inquiry, Main Report (Kano, December 1975); (d) Report of the Commission of Inquiry into the Kano State Tenders Board and Ministries of Agriculture and Natural Resources, Finance, Health and Social Welfare, and Education for the period 1 January 1970--29th July 1975 (Kano state, n.d.); (e) Conclusions of the Government of Cross River State on the Report and Recommendations of the Commission of Inquiry into the Southeastern State Loans Board (Cross River State, 1977).

34. S.S. Lawal, "The Politics of Board Membership of Public Enterprises in Kwara State" (M.P.A. thesis, University of Ife, 1979).

35. Government Views on Decisions of Odje Commission of Inquiry. Findings and Recommendations on some Government owned Companies, Boards and Corporations, Official Document no. 1 of 1977, Bendel State. See also Official Document no. 4 of 1977.

36. "N20 million 7 percent First Bendel State of Nigeria Loan Stock 1988," prospectus issued in Lagos, 1978.

37. Ibid.

38. Governor Ogbemudia stated that "the Government will be only too pleased to withdraw from this area and confine itself to its more traditional field as soon as indigenous private capital is forthcoming to relieve it of its present commitments in these ares." Bendel State Budget Speech, 1972-73.

39. See Bendel State of Nigeria Estimates 1978-79, 392.

40. The market value of quoted shares held by the New Nigeria Development Company was N5.9 million (1978); Kano State Investment and Properties Ltd., N6.1 million (1979); Kaduna Investment Company Ltd., N4.3 million (1980).

41. Oyo State contributed N0.5 million for infrastructure and services for the Leyland plant in Ibadan.

42. P. Collins, "Public Policy and the Development of Indigenous Capitalism; the Nigerian Experience," Journal of Commonwealth and Comparative Politics, 15, 2 (1977).

43. Supplement on Federated Motor Industries (New Nigeria, Kaduna, 6 June 1979).

44. United Africa Company of Nigeria Ltd., Annual Report, 1979.

45. Biersteker, op. cit.

46. G. Kitching, Class and Economic Change in Kenya: The Making of an African Petite Bourgeoisie (New Haven, Conn.: Yale University Press, 1980), ch. 13.

Steven Langdon

# 11 Industry and Capitalism in Kenya: Contributions to a Debate

"The 1980s," according to a key Kenyan government document published at the start of the decade, "will be a time of perpetual crisis in the world economy."[1] This essay examines the progress of a country on the periphery of the world economy in such a difficult context. Kenya has been identified in recent analysis as an example of relatively successful economic growth and capital accumulation despite its peripheral position. The evidence reviewed here questions this analysis and points to the continued vulnerability and limitations imposed on the Kenyan economy by its peripheral role in the world economy. Despite industrial growth and the emergence of important African industrialists, it is argued, Kenya is not experiencing dynamic capitalist development; the country is seen to be dependent on external changes in the world capitalist economy and in the strategies of transnational corporations. The result is an economic crisis in Kenya that mirrors that at the world level.

This chapter begins with a detailed analysis of the continuing theoretical debate regarding Kenyan capitalism. It then reviews the character of recent industrialization and the rise of new African industrialists in the country. The third section analyzes the broad patterns of Kenyan economic indicators and foreign exchange flows, before focusing on the policy effort to expand export manufacturing in response to foreign exchange and employment problems. Finally, the conclusion suggests how the economic difficulties traced in the two previous sections may lead to political change within Kenya.

## The Debate on Kenyan Capitalism

A rather important debate has been underway regarding Kenya's postcolonial economic growth. Certain analysts have interpreted the country's performance in terms of a "dependency" framework, stressing widening inequalities and structural segmentation, and relating these to the growing links with foreign capital that have marked postcolonial Kenya.[2] Others have challenged this view, stressing instead the role of an increasingly powerful indigenous class--a class in effective control of the Kenyan state and leading a relatively dynamic capitalist transformation in the country, resulting in faster expansion of production at a lower social cost than any possible alternative pattern or strategy.[3] The debate has been a confusing one, because a lack of clarity in defining the points at issue has meant that the same evidence has sometimes been held by each side to support its view. It is a significant debate, however, because of its relevance to more general theoretical and strategic concerns regarding the economic prospects of "periphery capitalism" and the usefulness of a "dependency" perspective.[4] It is, moreover, a debate particularly relevant to assessing industrialization patterns, in that the industrial sector has been the focus of much of the research and analysis that has shaped differing interpretations.

There are certain areas in which both sides in this debate would concede agreement. These can be summarized as follows:

1. It is agreed that Kenya exhibited rapid growth in gross national product after 1965, relative to other African countries; data show an average annual rate of increase in real GNP of 5.7 percent between 1964 and 1977[5]

2. It is agreed that a class of indigenous African capitalists has grown significantly since independence and has expanded its ownership of capital into industry in recent years

3. It is agreed that the state has played an important role in the growth of this bourgeoisie, and that there are important and intimate interlinkages giving this African bourgeoisie much influence on state decisions

4. It is agreed that foreign capital plays a large role in Kenyan industry, and that the state has also played an important supporting role in the continuing predominance of transnational corporations in the country[6]

5. It is agreed that the growing indigenous bourgeoisie is presently in close alliance with foreign capital, with the

state playing a role in managing or mediating this alliance

6. And, it is agreed that "uneven development" or "internal polarization" means that increased inequalities have characterized this postindependence pattern of economic growth.

Where, then, do the differences in perspectives emerge?

Perhaps the most critical difference revolves around the character and potential of the African capitalist class that has been expanding in Kenya. Both Leys and Swainson see this class as rooted in the preindependence past (rather than newly formed through the actions of the state and foreign capital), and they see it as playing what can fairly be described as a dynamic and leading role in accelerating capitalist development in Kenya--that is, in "the progressive transformation of relations of production into capitalist ones through the expanded reproduction of industrial capital."[7]    Kenya, says Leys, is "a country undergoing a comparatively rapid transition to capitalist relations of production, due in large part to the political strength of an indigenous class of capital."[8]    Both Leys and Swainson recognize that this class is weaker than foreign transnationals in its capacity to accumulate, particularly in the industrial sector, but both see "tendencies"[9] and a "trajectory"[10] indicating that indigenous capitalists are strengthening themselves through takeovers and moves into manufacturing at the expense of foreign capital.    For Leys at least, this African bourgeoisie is a "progressive" class, as compared to "the petty bourgeoisie which seeks to defend, in general, relations of production . . . in which the exploitation of the workers does not expand the forces of production."[11]    Swainson seems to agree, although both recognize the oppressive character of this bourgeoisie's relations with workers.    Both also recognize this class's alliance with foreign capital, but suggest that "connections of this sort are the essence of modern industrial production everywhere" (Leys)[12] and that there is "no reason to assume that these alliances will remain stable" (Swainson).[13]    In short, Leys and Swainson seem to believe that, in alliance with foreign capital, the indigenous bourgeoisie in Kenya has the capacity to carry forward capitalist development in the country.

It is this very point on which the counterperspective is most skeptical.    Dependency analysts recognize that industrial capitalism did fundamentally transform social relations of production in Western Europe, but they view it as extremely unlikely that similar capitalist transformation will occur in periphery countries like Kenya. This is because the indigenous bourgeoisie is "dependent" on foreign capital (in the sense of relying heavily on alliance with transnationals to accumulate capital) and because the character of industrial production under the control of transnationals does not generate the employment and linkage effects necessary to widely expand capitalist production relations in the periphery. In this framework, thus, the Kenyan bourgeoisie's alliance with foreign capital is not necessarily seen as a weakness (Leys is surely correct in seeing such ties as natural); rather, it is seen as an inevitable reality in the present international context and as a critical factor that, in consequence, means that the indigenous bourgeoisie *cannot* carry forward a broad capitalist transformation of social relations.[14] Thus the Kenyan bourgeoisie is seen as undynamic and unable to play its traditional role in capitalist development because it is dependent on foreign capital.

This is not to say that such capitalist transformation is therefore impossible in Kenya. One could foresee circumstances in which Kenya was strongly linked to Western Europe, for example, as a source of processed food, or in which foreign capital, for whatever reasons, heavily concentrated new investments in the country. Extensive capital accumulation might then broadly transform social relations and fully establish capitalist ties within the society, but the critical point is that this transformation would itself be dependent on external developments over which Kenya (and the Kenyan bourgeoisie) has very little control.

A second, and related, difference between the two perspectives concerns the role of the state in Kenya and its relationship with both local and foreign capital. Leys and Swainson are both quite clear in their view that the indigenous bourgeoisie controls the Kenyan state. As Swainson puts it

> The postcolonial state in Kenya has been dominated by the hegemonic fraction of indigenous capital and the apparatuses and functions of the state have been realigned since 1963 to foster the development of this class.[15]

And Leys agrees that[16]

> the indigenous capitalist class assumed the hegemonic place in a new "power bloc" (i.e., alongside international capital and elements of nonindigenous local capital).

This, says Swainson, determines the outcome of conflicts between local and foreign capital "where domestic and foreign capital compete, the state will invariably . . . act in support of national capital."[17] And, while Leys is more qualified in his view, he stresses that "it would be difficult to deny that the state's interventions over time have expressed the *growing* strength of indigenous capital."[18]

Just as the counterview is skeptical about the dynamism of the indigenous bourgeoisie, so does it strongly question their evaluation of the strength of that class in relations with the Kenyan state and with foreign capital. Kaplinsky, for instance, argues that the state "is not a homogeneous entity" and identifies the central bank and middle-level officers in various ministries and parastatals as those most critical and independent of foreign capital, with support for this position coming from small-scale local industrialists.[19] Foreign capital is, in fact, quite likely to win out in disputes in which the state is involved with local capital. And the state role, it is argued, demonstrates a relative autonomy from both local and foreign capital, based on a symbiosis (or mutual dependence) among the senior state bureaucracy and political leadership, indigenous capital, and foreign capital.[20] This symbiosis is seen to involve state support for local capital in its embourgeoisement process and, as well, a disciplining or restraining of local capital when disputes with foreign capital are sufficiently serious to concern large transnationals and their key interests.

Both sides in the debate would recognize the movement toward tighter state controls on foreign capital in Kenya, through the Capital Issues Committee and other agencies. But their analyses of this development reflect differing views of the state and class relations within Kenya. Swainson, for instance, clearly sees the increased application of such controls as a function of the indigenous bourgeoisie's moving into industrial production and using its dominance over the state to facilitate this by restricting foreign capital.[21] Kaplinsky, who has been directly involved in some of the new regulative moves in Kenya, sees the roots of such efforts very differently--as attempts to deal with the growing foreign exchange gaps inevitably shaped by a transnational-dominated import-substitution industrialization strategy, and as reflections of concern by middle-level and other state functionaries, who have shared little in the considerable benefits of symbiosis in Kenya.[22] Given the somewhat autonomous role that the state is seen as playing, it may be valid to recognize a technocratic stratum in the bureaucracy and elsewhere, similar to that which emerged in various Latin American countries in the 1965-1975 period and with a similarly critical role in articulating and partially implementing nationalist controls on foreign capital.[23]

A different analysis of class formation and structure in Africa may be perceived in this counterview. Traditional notions of bourgeoisie and petite bourgeoisie are not emphasized as the fundamental categories in analyzing Kenyan class formation (contrary to Leys's and Swainson's approach); the role of an indigenous bourgeoisie is seen to be weaker, and class divisions more directly based on access to state institutions are stressed. This view reflects Cohen's work on class formation in Africa, with its emphasis on a ruling "political class" and a separate "intendant class" of state functionaries and middle-level bureaucrats, as well as a working class and peasantry.[24] "The intendant class," says Cohen, "owes its social character to its training . . . acquired in Western educational institutions or local institutions heavily influenced by Western standards"; it is potentially in conflict with the "political class," in large part because of the latter's "unfair expropriation of wealth." The significance of such a division in Kenya seems considerable and helps to clarify some of the otherwise inexplicable evidence in Swainson's book. Analyzing the control mechanism established to screen foreign firm entries into Kenya, she notes several cases in which projects were turned down, but "powerful local interests" had the decision reversed; this would suggest that it is elements of the "political class," in particular, which are allied with foreign capital (and larger-scale local capital), while an "intendant" or "technocratic" class organizes certain of the control mechanisms that constrain foreign (and large-scale local) capital.[25]

Finally, there is an important difference in assessment of the recent and future performance of the Kenyan economy. Although neither Leys nor Swainson supports the view that the Kenyan case demonstrates "the notion of an autonomous capitalist path that is free from contradictions," both seem impressed by the economic growth that is occurring.[26] Leys has been most explicit in this regard, stressing that much accumulation has been taking place, that the potential of this continuing in the future remains, and that no alternative pattern is historically possible that would expand productive forces faster, with fewer social costs for the masses of the Kenyan population.[27] Kaplinsky questions this view strongly, suggesting that Kenya's growth, since 1973, has been unstable and limited; he sees dim prospects for the future. The high import-protection underwriting accumulation in the industrial sector is seen as a source of growing inefficiency, foreign exchange problems are seen to be accelerating, and the agricultural productivity that sparked much Kenyan growth from 1964 to 1973 is seen to be reaching its limits. Thus, says Kaplinsky,

> it is difficult to envisage continued and successful accumulation in Kenya. Almost the only way out, barring a further protracted squeeze on rural and urban working class incomes, is for a rapid growth in manufactured exports.[28]

This, in his view, is most unlikely to occur.

Leys's challenge regarding alternatives remains. Is he correct in his argument that dependency analysts are contrasting Kenya's performance with some wholly utopian alternative? He suggests, in fact, that the real choice is between the Kenyan model and what he refers to as

> a strategic labelled 'nationalist' and 'socialist', put forward by the petty bourgeoisie, involving 'state socialism' in industry and trade along lines already broadly charted in Ghana under Nkumrah, Uganda under Obote, and in Tanzania.[29]

Any other alternative--such as the reformist "redistribution with growth" formulations of the 1972 ILO Kenya Report and subsequent World Bank theorizing--is considered politically improbable, while a socialist alternative is considered historically improbable.[30]

Surely, however, what is "improbable" depends in some part upon the contradictions emerging within the present strategy. And if Kaplinsky is correct in his assessments of the prospects for continued accumulation, then the improbable may become the possible, given the conjuncture of class developments and international pressures that many Third World countries confront in an international capitalist economy increasingly in crisis. Kenya is faced with unstable export earnings, a growing trade deficit (which high interest rates make crippling to finance on the international capital market), stagnation in international public capital transfers, and concurrent decreases in real income per capita. It is possible that, in response a reform coalition of urban workers, state technocrats, small-scale industrialists, and peasants in less prosperous regions could push Kenya significantly in the direction of a redistribution strategy similar to that outlined in the ILO Kenya Report, with its emphasis on land redistribution, tax reform to squeeze the local bourgeoisie, support for small-scale local industry, and a decreased role for foreign transnationals. It is less probable, but still possible, that a radical coalition of urban workers and intellectuals, supported by many peasants and the growing number of landless in the countryside, could push Kenya toward a more socialist strategy of large-scale nationalization, extensive land reform, and egalitarian wage and salary policies. Whereas detailed analysis would be required to evaluate the implications of either of these directions in comparison to the present Kenyan strategy, it does seem that Leys has sketched the choices in Kenya too narrowly.

Overall, then, three basic issues are the focus of the debate regarding Kenya: the nature of the emerging Kenyan bourgeoisie, the relations within the political economy that shape the state role in Kenya, and the current pace and future prospects of capital accumulation in the country. One view suggests (to oversimplify the argument) that the indigenous bourgeoisie is dynamic and autonomous; it is in control of the Kenyan state and, consequently, is leading relatively successful capitalist development in the country. The other side argues that the indigenous bourgeoisie is dependent on foreign capital and, therefore (given the nature of industrial growth under transnational control), is unable to carry forward a broad transformation to capitalist social relations; the indigenous bourgeoisie is only one element shaping state activity in interaction with foreign capital and state technocrats. The present development pattern in Kenya is also seen, in this view, to be subject to growing limitations and blockages and to be increasingly dependent on external economic events.

Evidence on the state role in Kenya, and on relations among the state, local capital, and the transnationals, has been presented and analyzed in detail elsewhere.[31] In the remainder of this chapter, therefore, the other two focuses of the Kenyan debate are explored. In the next section, evidence is reviewed on the character of postindependence industrialization in Kenya, so as to test the extent of transformation to capitalist social relations that it is generating and to probe the spread effects associated with the sector; the overall economic performance and prospects are analyzed. This analysis tests the differing interpretations of the viability of continuing Kenyan capital accumulation and looks particularly at the recent record of export manufacturing in the country. Serious problems in such export expansion efforts, combined with evidence of growing trade deficits for the country, would support Kaplinsky's view of growing limitations on Kenyan capitalist development. In the conclusion, the analysis returns to an overall evaluation of the differing perspectives that have been reviewed in this section.

## Industrialization in Kenya

In his detailed analysis of capitalist transformation in Western Europe, Karl Polanyi concentrates, above all, on the emergence of national labor markets in the framework of which the vast majority of the population must sell its labor power, for a wage, in order to live.[32] Although such social change was not the sole defining characteristic of capitalism, this growth of wage employment was at the heart of the new capitalist relations of production that emerged in Western Europe. In analyzing capitalist transformation in Kenya, then, it is essential to focus on the growth of wage employment in the country.

Table 11.1 provides an overview on this question. Several points illustrated by the data deserve underlining. First, there has been a distinct slowdown in wage employment growth since 1974: the average annual increase in the 1975-1979 period has been 3.4 percent, compared to 6.4 percent in the 1971-1974 period. The increase in 1979, it should also be

TABLE 11.1:  Wage Employment and Output Growth in Kenya, 1971-1979

| Year | Percentage Change in Total Wage Employment | Percentage Change in Real Gross Domestic Product | Percentage Change in Manufacturing Employment | Percentage Change in Real Manufacturing Output |
|------|------|------|------|------|
| 1971 | 7.2% | 7.0% | 12.8% | 10.5% |
| 1972 | 4.1 | 6.8 | 2.7 | 5.0 |
| 1973 | 5.8 | 4.3 | 11.4 | 9.7 |
| 1974 | 8.5 | 1.1 | 7.2 | 9.7 |
| 1975 | -0.9 | 4.1 | -0.6 | 0 |
| 1976 | 4.7 | 2.4 | 8.0 | 18.2 |
| 1977 | 5.3 | 8.8 | 8.4 | 15.9 |
| 1978 | 1.0 | 6.6 | 10.3 | 12.6 |
| 1979 | 6.7 | 3.3 | 6.3 | 7.1 |
| Average 1971-1979 | 4.7 | 4.9 | 7.1 | 9.9 |

Source:  Statistical Abstracts, 1973, 1977, 1979; Economic Surveys, 1974, 1978, 1980.

noted, was due to exceptional intervention by the government --a decree by the president that modern sector employment was to be increased by 10 percent. If the pattern of the earlier government intervention of this sort, in 1970-1971, is reproduced, then the 1979 increase will simply represent an *acceleration* of hiring intentions, to be followed by a significantly lower-than-average increase in the 1980 data (as was the case for 1972). Second, it is significant that, although there has not been a great divergence between rates of change in overall wage employment and in GDP in the country, there has been, in recent years, much more divergence in the manufacturing sector itself, in the direction of lower rates of employment growth. Taking the 1971-1979 period, average annual growth in total employment has been 4.7 percent and in GDP 4.9 percent, while in manufacturing employment growth has averaged 7.4 percent, compared to 9.9 percent for manufacturing output; that is, expanding production has been matched significantly less by expanding employment in the manufacturing sector. Third, it should be stressed that manufacturing employment has proved to be relatively limited in its growth in recent years, despite very dramatic increases in output in the manufacturing sector--18 percent, 16 percent and 13 percent in 1976, 1977 and 1978, respectively.

An approach to evaluating these trends is suggested by Stewart in her work on technology and underdevelopment. The basic question she asks is under what conditions the "modern" sector, with its more advanced technology and wage employment relations, will expand sufficiently to at least begin to reduce the absolute number of persons not in such wage employment (although in the labor force). As such, this is a question about the transformation of social relations of production, and it provides useful insight for our analysis. Stewart shows that the trends involved can be summarized in terms of the following equation:

$$(Qf)\left[\frac{1+f}{1+p}\right]^n = \frac{p}{f}$$

where $Qf$ = the proportion of the total labor force employed in the enumerated wage sector

$f$ = annual rate of increase in employment in that sector

$p$ = annual rate of increase in population (or in labor force)

and n = number of years until
the absolute total of those in the
labor force but outside enumerated wage employment ceases to
grow

Calculating for Kenya, on the basis of data from 1966-1971 and using labor force growth estimates of 2.8 percent annually, Stewart demonstrated that n = 201--that is, it would take over 200 years to begin to reduce the number of those in the labor force but outside enumerated wage employment in Kenya.[33] This same kind of calculation can be done on the basis of more recent data. Taking 1976 statistics on numbers in enumerated wage employment as a percentage of the overall labor force,[34] 1976-1979 data on average growth in wage employment (4.4 percent) and 1980 revised estimates of annual population and labor force growth (3.9 percent), the solution of "n" suggests 363 years before numbers begin to fall outside enumerated wage employment![35] The detailed numbers in such calculations should not be taken too seriously, since they are very sensitive to small changes in the data inputs, and there are, of course, changes in wage-employment relations that are not caught in the official enumeration of government.[36] Nevertheless, the magnitude of the calculated figures above and the increase in their size between 1966-1971 and 1975-1979 do illustrate the very limited dynamism that marks recent Kenyan employment growth.

Import reliance for inputs to the industrial sector can be examined from a similar perspective. A marked decrease in the import share of goods used by Kenyan industry would suggest growing linkage effects to the rest of the country and an increased impact on social and economic transformation throughout the country. However, the evidence reported in table 11.2 does not indicate such tendencies. On the contrary, the latest year for which data was available (1974) showed the highest import dependency of any year in the table.

The limited employment and linkage effects of Kenyan industry can be understood in the context of the considerable role of transnational corporations in this sector of the economy. Such corporations accounted for more than half of Kenyan manufacturing output in the early 1970s and were especially predominant in footwear, leather, rubber, petroleum, industrial chemicals, paint, soap, cement, and metal products subsectors. Existing transnationals have continued to expand considerably in the country since that period, while new

TABLE 11.2: Intermediate Consumption Imports in Kenyan
Manufacturing, 1966-1974

| Year | Current Value of Manufacturing Output (a) (K£ 000) | Intermediate Consumption Imports (b) (K£ 000) | (b) as a percentage of (a) |
|---|---|---|---|
| 1966 | 136,899 | 50,422 | 36.8% |
| 1967 | 164,936 | 53,896 | 34.8 |
| 1968 | 163,852 | 57,982 | 35.4 |
| 1969 | 186,893 | 60,839 | 32.6 |
| 1970 | 200,682 | 72,823 | 36.3 |
| 1971 | 251,146 | 95,022 | 37.8 |
| 1972 | 301,862 | 85,098 | 28.2 |
| 1973 | 368,340 | 112,086 | 30.4 |
| 1974 | 550,592 | 209,106 | 38.0 |

Source: Kenya, Development Plan 1979-1983, 330.

transnational entries have occurred in such industries as vehicle assembly.[37]

The employment and linkage limitations of transnational-dominated manufacturing in Kenya are based particularly on the product transfer strategy of parent firms.  Most Kenyan subsidiaries, earlier research showed, rely for over 95 percent of their sales on products they manufacture locally which were first developed and manufactured *by the parent company* to meet *developed-country* demand.  When these products are transferred to Kenyan facilities to manufacture, the companies involved engage in heavy advertising to promote and extend local demand for precisely those brand-name items; thus, earlier research also showed over 80 percent of radio advertising and 75 percent of newspaper advertising being accounted for by such taste transfer efforts by transnationals.[38]

The resulting developed-country product choice of Kenyan manufacturing subsidiaries has had a profound impact on their employment effects, because most parent firms have wanted to use capital-intensive, labor-saving technology in their subsidiaries; that is how they have produced their specific products at home, and they wish these products to be virtually identical when produced abroad.  Thus, of subsidiaries undertaking such exclusive product transfer in 1973, 56 percent showed capital employed per employee of over K£3000, with only 4 percent showing a figure of under K£1000; for those *not* exclusively making parent products, the percentage with the higher capital employed was only 8.3, and 75 percent were in the lower category.[39] The variable of product choice was by far the most significant evident in statistical testing of factors influencing subsidiary technology levels.

However, other factors were present. The size of subsidiaries was significant: when established, some subsidiaries were serving very small markets and consequently could not use the high-volume, capital-intensive technology employed in the parent firm; instead, they often used an earlier generation of low-volume machinery, with greater employment effects. Thus, 63 percent of larger subsidiaries had capital employed of over K£3000, compared to only 17 percent of smaller subsidiaries interviewed.[40] In addition, a majority of subsidiaries reported that parent companies had some direct say in machinery choices by subsidiaries, and this tended to lead to the choice of more capital-intensive techniques. This was particularly likely where the transnationals involved had machinery-manufacturing subsidiaries elsewhere from which they supplied the whole corporation.

Over time, further considerations came into play that tended to accelerate the labor-saving trends in subsidiary choice of technique. As small, low-volume subsidiaries grew, they often became able to afford higher volume and automated equipment--and shifted accordingly. Product-differentiation efforts, too, often led subsidiaries to try to distinguish their brand with new imported packaging or through improved quality standardization. Both trends tended to encourage use of the most recent automated packaging or production equipment possible. In addition, some subsidiaries indicated more strategic reasons for automating: reducing a labor force to ease managerial control or cutting back numbers while it was still legally possible, in anticipation of future government controls in Kenya prohibiting this.

The overall result was low-employment effects from subsidiaries, relative to those generated by their local alternatives in cases where comparison was possible. In soap manufacturing, for instance, an alternative industrialization pattern could have been based on the expansion of existing firms owned by resident Asian industrialists. A survey of most of these firms in 1973 found their average capital employed per workplace to range between KShs28,400 for less mechanized factories and Kshs94,500 for mechanized firms; the equivalent figure for the large transnational soap subsidiary was KShs140,000. In shoe manufacturing, expanded production could have relied on small-scale African shoe manufacturers scattered across the country; these were very labor-intensive, compared to the large shoe subsidiary. In practice, however, the subsidiaries were the accumulating and expanding elements in each of these industries--in significant part because of the way government tax policy was structured to favor them--and the result was limited employment effects in the country.[41]

The same basic pattern was evident in analyzing linkage effects; most subsidiaries interviewed imported over 70 percent of their intermediate inputs. Once again, transnational product and taste transfer was at the root of these limitations. Of those subsidiaries that produced parent-company, developed-country products, 78 percent imported over three-quarters of their material inputs, while only 47 percent of less imitative subsidiaries did likewise.[42]

Interviews with subsidiaries suggested additional factors that shaped these limited linkages. Capital-intensive choice of technique itself worked to reduce the possibilities of local input production; it required highly exact specifications that were often more difficult to meet in a less developed economy than were those for more labor-intensive production. Many subsidiaries also reported that their integration into parent company networks limited local input purchase both because parent firms often insisted on rigorous quality controls that encouraged home supply and because head offices often wished to supply Kenyan subsidiaries from affiliated manufacturing sources abroad. Taking forty-one subsidiaries for which answers were provided, some 23 percent of corporate imports, on average, were produced by the parent or associate companies; thus, this pressure for intrafirm sales reached notable dimensions. The impact both of greater capital-intensity and of integration into parent company networks emerged as statistically significant in testing of overall subsidiary import levels.[43]

The result was limited linkage effects, relative to local alternatives, that might have been emphasized instead. In the case of soap manufacturing, the subsidiaries imported 75 percent to 90 percent of their material inputs, while the less mechanized local Asian firms imported 40 percent to 50 percent. In shoes, the subsidiary imported 50 percent to 60 percent (by value) of its inputs, while the local small-scale manufacturers purchased virtually all of their inputs locally. Moreover, for subsidiaries as a whole, there was very little evidence of potential improvements in local linkage effects in the future; the vast majority of subsidiaries interviewed (all but six out of forty-eight in domestic market manufacturing) saw no prospects for future subcontracting to local manufacturers.

Overall, then, the character of transnational subsidiary manufacturing can be seen to have restricted significantly the transformative impact on social relations from expanded industrialization in Kenya. The retarded employment growth that marked rapid industrial expansion in 1976-1978 and the continued import dependence noted above for all Kenyan manufacturing must both be traced to the central role of transnationals in the country, given the pressures seen to be working on subsidiaries to limit their employment and linkage effects.

But what are the "trends" and "tendencies" in Kenya (to recall the arguments of Leys and Swainson)?  Might it not be suggested that transnational subsidiaries are losing their central role, if powerful local African capitalists are emerging at their expense?  These questions can be explored on two levels-- through an analysis of the continuing presence of transnationals in Kena and through a discussion of the orientation of activity of those large-scale African capitalists who are emerging.

Although table 11.3 deals only with public corporations in Kenya, it provides some rough indication of the recent patterns of subsidiary expansion.  As such, it points to a very healthy profitability for subsidiaries in Kenya.  This is particularly true for such giant subsidiaries as Lonrho-controlled Motor Mart, East African Industries, Kenya Canners, and Socfinaf; each of these firms had capital employed in excess of K£5,000,000 by 1978.  Other large subsidiaries have also maintained very healthy levels of profitability after tax--as with BAT, East African Oxygen, and Metal Box.  Such smaller subsidiaries in manufacturing as East African Cables, Kenya Paper Mills, and Raymond Woollen Mills have enjoyed good profitability, while new subsidiaries such as Pan-African Paper also have established themselves as solidly profitable.  The two cement companies have faced some squeeze on their profit levels as huge expansions have taken place, and East African Packaging Industries experienced a difficult period in 1976-1977 as export markets were lost, but only Kenyan Orchards Ltd. in manufacturing showed serious problems--it had always been a marginal operation, and was sold to local capital in 1976.  In short, the evidence overall shows the transnational

TABLE 11.3: Profitability in Public Kenyan Corporations

| Firm | After Tax Profits (Loss) as Percentage of Capital Employed[a] | | | | | |
|---|---|---|---|---|---|---|
| | 1974 | 1975 | 1976 | 1977 | 1978 | 1979 |
| **Benchmark Nontransnational Public Corporations** | | | | | | |
| Ecta (Kenya) Ltd. | -26.3 | 1.9 | 4.9 | n.a. | n.a. | n.a. |
| Eslon Plastics of Kenya | 7.7 | 10.5 | 7.8 | 6.0 | 6.4 | n.a. |
| Ndume Ltd. | 4.1 | 1.1 | 1.8 | 2.6 | n.a. | n.a. |
| Kamyn Industries Ltd.[b] | 12.3 | 15.7 | 10.0 | 7.5 | 8.8 | 8.0 |
| Average: | -0.5 | 7.3 | 6.1 | 5.4 | 7.6 | 8.0 |
| **Transnational Subsidiaries: Commercial and Holding Companies** | | | | | | |
| Baumann's | 11.9 | 9.4 | 9.3 | n.a. | n.a. | n.a. |
| Consolidated Holdings | 11.8 | 6.3 | 15.1 | 12.1 | n.a. | n.a. |
| Marshalls E.A. | 23.2 | 26.1 | 24.0 | 18.7 | n.a. | n.a. |
| Motor Mart | 18.4 | 17.3 | 13.3 | 19.0 | n.a. | n.a. |
| Average: | 16.3 | 14.8 | 15.4 | 16.3 | n.a. | n.a. |
| **Manufacturing Companies** | | | | | | |
| African Radio Manufacturing | n.a. | n.a. | 9.0 | 18.1 | 16.2 | 14.5 |
| Bamburi Cement | 8.5 | 10.7 | 9.6 | 3.4 | 3.9 | n.a. |
| BAT Kenya | 19.4 | 17.3 | 18.0 | 15.6 | 30.5 | n.a. |
| East African Cables | 23.4 | 17.4 | 26.4 | 18.6 | 19.0 | n.a. |
| East African Industries | 37.7 | 46.7 | 49.8 | 42.2 | 26.2 | n.a. |
| East African Oxygen | 13.2 | 22.7 | 17.9 | 24.6 | 15.2 | 8.4 |
| East African Packaging | 45.1 | 19.1 | 2.1 | 9.7 | 11.0 | n.a. |
| East African Portland Cement | 15.2 | 7.6 | 9.2 | 5.5 | 6.5 | n.a. |
| Finlay Industries | 8.9 | 3.2 | n.a. | n.a. | n.a. | n.a. |
| Kenya Orchards Ltd. | 1.2 | -4.9 | -4.3 | n.a. | n.a. | n.a. |
| Kenya Paper Mills | 98.6 | 31.2 | 19.9 | 5.3 | 21.0 | n.a. |
| Metal Box | 18.0 | n.a. | 13.9 | 22.4 | 14.7 | 13.5 |
| Pan African Paper | -8.9 | -19.4 | 9.2 | 6.5 | 10.7 | 8.6 |
| Raymond Woollen Mills | 14.9 | 8.8 | 18.8 | 16.0 | 6.6 | n.a. |
| Average: | 22.7 | 13.4 | 15.4 | 15.7 | 17.1 | 11.3 |
| **Agricultural Companies** | | | | | | |
| Brooke Bond | n.a. | n.a. | n.a. | n.a. | 17.4 | 10.8 |
| Kenya Canners | 2.8 | 3.4 | -3.0 | 18.9 | 28.6 | 8.8 |
| Socfinaf | 11.9 | 3.1 | 24.0 | 38.3 | 12.0 | 5.9 |
| Average: | 7.4 | 4.3 | 10.5 | 28.6 | 20.8 | 8.5 |

[a] Capital employed = fixed assets + net current assets

[b] This firm is a subsidiary of the holding company formerly controlled by the Shah of Iran

n.a. Not available

Source: Data collected from the Companies Registry, Nairobi, 1980.

sector in Kenya growing from strength to strength and demonstrating considerably higher profitability than the benchmark nontransnationals included in the table. The group-by-group results in the table bring this out especially clearly. Profitability, on average, in the years for which a reasonable base of data is available, has been more than twice as high in all of the transnational groups in the table as in the benchmark firms.

Just as important in analyzing trends in the character of Kenyan industrialization is an examination of the orientation of emerging large-scale African capitalists. Drawing on the detailed research on company directorships of Kaplinsky and on the discussions of emerging industrial entrepreneurs in Swainson, it is possible to identify a number of interesting cases of either important African industrialists or significant industrial enterprises in which Africans exercise ownership control.[44] These cases can be examined to assess the degree to which emerging African industrialists are likely to shape industrialization patterns that differ from the limitations of subsidiary enterprise.

### Chui Soap Factory

This firm is mentioned by Swainson as a direct competitor with the large soap multinationals in Kenya[45] and is owned by two Africans--one a public servant, the other an executive in a large subsidiary. The firm expanded with strong state support but moved quickly from labor-intensive to highly mechanized production, using machinery imported from Italy (with consequent lower employment effects and much greater import dependence for raw materials). The company also intended to begin advertising to promote its own brands and to move into higher-quality toilet soap and detergent manufacturing, rather than simple laundry soap.[46] In short, unlike some of the local Asian capitalists in the industry, this firm was moving very much in the direction of the employment-minimizing, linkage-limiting style of the transnational subsidiaries in Kenya.

### Tiger Shoes and Njenga Karume

The latter is cited by Swainson as a prominent example of emerging African industrialists, and the former is analyzed as one of his firms that is in direct competition with the giant

Bata subsidiary. Again, however, unlike the small-scale African shoe manufacturers noted above, this firm is very much moving in the highly mechanized, import-intensive direction of the transnationals, as Swainson herself recognizes.[47] Karume's other activities demonstrate a similar orientation; his large Gema Holdings enterprise attempted, in the later 1970s, to establish with Fiat a joint-venture assembly plant, which would have been precisely in the style of import-reproduction industry that already characterized Kenyan manufacturing.

### African Radio Manufacturing Company (ARMCO)

This firm was originally established by Africans, with an African general manager (J. Murimi) holding a sizeable share in the firm; it has often been held up as an example of successful African industrial enterprise. Again, the state has played an important role in this firm's progress, providing share capital from the Industrial and Commercial Development Corporation (ICDC) and using its ICDC shares in another subsidiary to push the latter into distributing ARMCO products. However, this firm also is engaged in import-intensive import reproduction, buying all of its inputs from its Japanese shareholder (Sanyo), transferring a wide range of imported Sanyo products to Kenya, and advertising heavily to promote the Sanyo brand name.[48]

### J.K. Industries and Justus Kalinga

The latter is identified by Kaplinsky as one of a number of entrepreneurs with multiple directorships and significant involvement in industry. His firm, however, as Kaplinsky notes, produces plastic articles under license from foreign firms. Kaplinsky details one such license, for toothbrushes with a Norwegian firm, in which the latter retains comprehensive control over production and inputs, receives high royalty fees, and enforces minimum levels of advertising.[49]  Clearly, J.K. Industries is engaged in transnational product-transfer, despite its ownership structure.

## Kenneth Matiba

Matiba is another entrepreneur listed in Kaplinsky's survey of directorships. His activities in manufacturing, however, are very limited, comprising two flower nurseries and a share in a construction firm.[50]

## J. Maina Wanjigi

Wanjigi is also identified by Kaplinsky's survey. As a former executive director of ICDC and then an assistant minister, Wanjigi used his access to state loans to build up a sizable business empire in the early 1970s, including shares in a number of industrial enterprises (in concrete pipes and in printing).[51] By 1979, his shareholdings in these industrial firms had increased somewhat, but there was no evidence of his having launched any new industrial enterprises, and his directorships as of that year suggested an increasing involvement with foreign capital as a director of Bata, George Williamson (Kenya) Ltd., Leyland Paints and others.[52]

## Udi Gecaga and Ngengi Muigai

These are two very prominent African entrepreneurs discussed by both Swainson and Kaplinsky. They represent important and interesting cases that can be examined together. Both used their key positions in large transnational subsidiaries to develop their own business empires--in the case of Gecaga by investing individually in joint ventures with Lonrho, the subsidiary of which he was Kenyan managing director, and in the case of Muigai by engineering the takeover of a majority share in the Inchcape subsidiary (Mackenzie Dalgety) of which he was managing director. This latter takeover was done in partnership with Gecaga, and both extended their manufacturing interests therefore. What was particularly significant about both men, however, was their complete orientation toward the transnational sector of the economy. Granted that both Lonrho and Inchcape are unusual in the extent of their industrial diversification in Kenya, they are nevertheless transnationals, and Gecaga and Muigai were their chief executive officers in Kenya.[53] Thus, it was not surprising that the major industrial enterprise in which both men were involved recently was a classic import-reproduction vehicle assembly plant in Mom-

basa, highly import-intensive and subject to all the inefficien-
cies of wide product differentiation, involving Lonrho, Inchcape, and the two African industrialists in a joint venture with
the ICDC.

What is also striking about these cases is the way they
show the vulnerability of the emerging African industrialists,
because of their combined dependence on the state and on
transnationals.    After Kenyatta's death, Muigai's takeover of
Mackenzie Dalgety was challenged by Inchcape and reversed
in the Kenyan courts; Gecaga lost his position as chief executive of Lonrho in Kenya.

Overall, this evidence suggests a clear conclusion.  Unlike
some Asian industrial enterprise, which has been relatively labor-intensive and active in developing local linkages,[54] and
unlike the locally oriented small-scale African industry evident
in shoes and some other product areas,[55] the orientation of industrial activity undertaken by the emerging large-scale
African capitalists is very much toward the style of capital-
intensive, import-dependent product transfer, which has
characterized subsidiary manufacturing in Kenya.    African
entrepreneurs, like Karume for instance, may well achieve
their initial capital accumulation in industry in activities that
are locally oriented and labor-intensive (e.g., sawmilling), but
the "trends" and "tendencies" among large-scale African capitalists certainly seem to be toward the transnational style of
enterprise, with its built-in blockages to broad social transformation in Kenya.  This is not surprising, of course, for as the
company data reported earlier indicated, that form of enter-
prise--with a degree of monopoly power based on the differentiated and specific products being transferred from abroad--
can be remarkably profitable in the highly unequal framework
of income distribution that marks contemporary Kenya.

The review in this section, then, does not support the Leys
and Swainson interpretation of Kenyan development.    The
evidence suggests that growing industrialization is having only
limited effects on social transformation in Kenya, because of
restricted employment and linkage effects.    These restricted
effects, in turn, are seen to be associated with the character of
subsidiary manufacturing enterprise, with product-transfer
strategies and head-office controls establishing capital-intensive choice of technique and import dependency in Kenyan
subsidiaries.  Evidence shows that such subsidiaries retain their
central role in the Kenyan industrial sector and, more important, that those large-scale African industrialists who are
emerging are oriented to the transnational style of industrial

enterprise--with all its limitations on widespread effects and social transformation.


## The Kenyan Economy and Export Manufacturing

This section begins with a review of the varied performance of the Kenyan economy during the 1970s. Then it discusses the development of export-manufacturing policies as a response to the significant problems evident in that performance. Finally, the progress of such export manufacturing is reviewed and assessed.

Tables 11.4 and 11.5 present summary data on key economic indicators and on the balance of payments, permitting analysis of recent patterns of change in Kenya. Most important to stress, perhaps, is the appearance of a series of interrelated signs of difficulty in the economy in the post-1973 period: a slowdown in the high and sustained growth rates of the postindependence period; relatively limited employment growth; a falloff (except for 1978) in investment shares in GDP; and the common occurrence of very large merchandise trade deficits. These signs should be read in conjunction with the 3.9 percent rate of increase in population in the country, which means the 3.3 percent increase in 1979 represented a decrease in real per capita income. Equally clear from the data is the profound impact of external change on the Kenyan economy. The dramatic rise in international terms of trade in 1976 and 1977 (from an index of 86 to 131), which is mirrored in the increase in agricultural prices (from an index of 69 to 148.6), set off high GDP growth in 1977 and 1978, increased investment (to 24 percent and 30 percent of GDP respectively), sparked real wage increases and even generated a current account surplus in the balance of payments (in 1977). All of this served to mask briefly the fundamental problems that emerged again in later 1978 and 1979 as coffee and tea prices (the main elements in the upsurge in Kenya's terms of trade) fell once more.

The Kenyan economy seems to be subject to a stop-and-go cycle that makes sustained capital accumulation very difficult. When international terms of trade improve for the economy, as they did in 1970 (rising by over 4 percent)[56] and again in 1976-1977, this raises growth rates (witness the 7 percent and 8.8 percent levels in 1971 and 1977), and sets off an investment boom (especially clear in 1977-1978). But this growth and investment then spark a balance-of-payments crisis, as

TABLE 11.4: Key Indicators in the Kenyan Economy, 1971-1979

| Year | Change in Real GDP | Change in Enumerated Employment | International Terms of Trade for Kenya 1976 = 100 | Share of GDP Spent on Investment | Quantity Index of Agricultural Production 1976=100 | Index of Current Agricultural Prices 1976=100 | Rural-Urban Terms of Trade 1976=100 | Change in Real Wages | Debt Service Charges as a Share of Exports |
|------|------|------|------|------|------|------|------|------|------|
| 1971 | +7.0% | +7.2% | 112 | 25.2% | n.a. | n.a. | n.a. | +0.4% | n.a. |
| 1972 | +6.8 | +4.1 | 110 | 22.7 | 90.0 | 47.2 | 83 | +0.1 | n.a. |
| 1973 | +4.3 | +5.8 | 112 | 28.8 | 91.9 | 52.8 | 79 | -4.9 | 3.5% |
| 1974 | +1.1 | +8.5 | 94 | 28.4 | 92.2 | 64.4 | 76 | -5.6 | 2.4 |
| 1975 | +4.1 | -0.9 | 86 | 18.2 | 94.0 | 69.0 | 73 | -2.5 | 2.8 |
| 1976 | +2.4 | +4.7 | 100 | 20.2 | 100.0 | 100.0 | 100 | +5.6 | 2.5 |
| 1977 | +8.8 | +5.3 | 131 | 23.7 | 111.6 | 148.6 | 126 | +3.4 | 2.3 |
| 1978 | +6.6 | +1.0 | 105 | 29.7 | 107.7 | 126.1 | 101 | -1.2 | 5.5 |
| 1979 | +3.3 | +6.7 | 97 | 22.4 | 105.8 | 121.1 | 95 | +0.9 | 4.4 |

Source: Kenya, Statistical Abstracts and Economic Surveys, annual.

TABLE 11.5: Summary of Kenyan Balance of Payments, 1971–1979

(Kf million--deficits are in brackets)

| | 1971 | 1972 | 1973 | 1974 | 1975 | 1976 | 1977 | 1978 | 1979 |
|---|---|---|---|---|---|---|---|---|---|
| Merchandise account balance | (91) | (66) | (55) | (158) | (125) | (77) | (61) | (357) | (285) |
| Investment income transfers | (9) | (12) | (36) | (36) | (35) | (58) | (66) | (55) | (49) |
| Total current account balance | (40) | (24) | (47) | (122) | (84) | (52) | 11 | (253) | (178) |
| Private long-term capital movements | 17 | 15 | 31 | 42 | 15 | 62 | 48 | 76 | 81 |
| Government long-term capital movements | (4) | 15 | 17 | 22 | 31 | 30 | 36 | 84 | 104 |
| Total capital account balance | 15 | 35 | 53 | 86 | 69 | 89 | 102 | 171 | 251 |
| Total current and capital account balance | (25) | 11 | 6 | (36) | (15) | 37 | 113 | (82) | 73 |

Source: Kenya, Statistical Abstracts and Economic Surveys, annual.

imports explode and the merchandise trade deficit balloons. Faced with shrinking foreign exchange reserves (given an overall deficit on current *and* capital account), the government is then forced into strongly restrictive import policies (as in both 1972 and 1979) and retrenchment in its own activities (especially in 1979). This, in turn, results in lower rates of investment and lower growth rates. The economy, in short, does not have the export capacity to sustain the high level of imports set off by accelerated growth and investment, and this regularly chokes off the accumulation process. At the same time, when international terms of trade *decline* significantly for Kenya (as they did in 1974 and 1975), this sharply hits growth rates (which fell to 1.1 percent in 1974) and spurs balance-of-payments problems (with a large merchandise trade deficit in 1974); in turn, employment levels are affected (falling 0.9 percent in 1975), and investment declines (to 18 percent of GDP in 1975).

What all of this points to is the fundamental fact that Kenya has *not* developed its own autonomous capacity to sustain capital accumulation through internal interaction among sectors of the economy (e.g., industry and agriculture). As Kenyan vice-president and minister of finance Mwai Kibaki frankly conceded in mid-1979:

> This is an agricultural economy dependent for its export earnings on a few exports which bring us the bulk of those earnings, and we are totally dependent on what happens to the price of those exports. The prices of those exports are subject to fluctuations over which we have no control at all.[57]

This reality, in turn, has severely damaged the capacity to plan structural change in the Kenyan economy in order to improve export capacities or reduce import intensity. Again, government sources are explicit about this--as in the 1980 Economic Survey:

> The turbulent nature of Kenya's export earnings over the last few years with a high dependence on coffee and tea which fluctuate markedly in price from year to year has made it difficult to plan ahead or even to expect forecasts of earnings to be met.[58]

The basis of this endemic structural crisis in Kenya deserves more probing. What shapes the continuing emergence of excessive foreign exchange outflows to which the government must respond through retrenchment and recession that limit accumulation?[59]   Variation in flows related to direct foreign investment has *not* been a notable factor in this; table

11.5 shows a sharp drop in inflows in 1975 but, aside from that, inflows relative to investment income outflows have remained fairly healthy. Serious problems in the Kenyan agricultural sector seem the critical factor. As the index of marketed agricultural output in table 11.4 shows, production in Kenyan agriculture has been relatively limited in its growth during the 1970s and has indeed declined in the two most recent years. This is in marked contrast to the experience of the 1960s, during which dramatic expansion in peasant production drove the Kenyan economy ahead and rapidly expanded export volumes.[60]    Export volumes are now falling in Kenyan agriculture:  coffee down 17 percent between 1977 and 1979, sisal down 40 percent between 1975 and 1979, and cotton down 37 percent between 1975 and 1979, with only tea providing sustained increases in volume.[61]  At the same time, domestic food supplies of basic cereal crops have also become inadequate, and Kenya has been forced to move to *imports* of such grains.[62]    The Kenyan government has conceded that "agricultural production must more than double over the next twenty years in order to provide sufficient food and make reasonable contribution to the foreign exchange needs of a growing economy."[63]  But the record of the 1970s shows that this is extremely unlikely.

In the face of this combination of volatile export earnings and recurrent foreign exchange problems, Kenya has had to rely increasingly on external government borrowing.   This shows up in table 11.5 in the considerable jump in government long-term capital movements in 1978 and 1979 (exceeding private movements in both years); but this indicator does not include all foreign borrowings and, in fact, understates the situation, as the government has stressed in its most recent analysis:

> In 1978 and 1979 total external loans which were used to finance 41 percent of total capital formation amounted to Kf455.2 million compared with Kf350 million for the eight years 1970 to 1977.[64]

The consequence is a growing debt service burden for the economy, as indicated in table 11.4. This burden, the government's own analysis suggests, will worsen sharply in the next few years.[65]

This is all a familiar pattern, previewed for Africa by many Latin American countries:  the interplay of dependence on a few export crops, agricultural stagnation, growing balance-of-payments pressures, rising external indebtedness, and slow growth except in a highly protected, inefficient, and capital-intensive industrial sector. The result in Latin America has been explosive inequalities and imbalances, and the evidence suggests that Kenya continues in that same direction. The most detailed studies available suggest that, by the beginning of the 1970s, Kenya was already extremely unequal in its size distribution of income--with the bottom 50 percent of the population receiving 12 percent of national income, the top 5 percent receiving 44 percent, and the top 1 percent receiving over 18 percent.[66] And there is no significant evidence of an improvement in this situation during the 1970s. Kaplinsky has reviewed the available data in detail and concludes that some elements of distribution have even become more unequal, with coffee producers in the already richer regions widening the gap between themselves and the poorer Kenyans, and with wage earners facing real declines in income while local and foreign company profits were maintained.[67] Between 1970 and 1979, real wages per employee in Kenya fell at an average rate of 1.2 percent per year, and real incomes of small-scale farmers rose at an annual 2 percent rate; but both these groups saw their share of GDP *fall* significantly, as table 11.6 shows, from 32.3 percent to 28.5 percent for wage earners and from 24.7 percent to 22.8 percent for small-scale farmers.

The large gains went to those receiving rental and profit income. Clearly the inequalities of the early 1970s have continued or worsened, contributing to the weakness of internal markets in Kenya on which a more autonomous process of capital accumulation otherwise might conceivably have been based.

As early as 1973, prior to the oil price hikes of the fall, the Kenyan government began to point to export manufacturing as its strategic response to the country's economic difficulties. This theme was underlined in the 1974-1978 Development Plan:

> International firms with production facilities in Kenya will be encouraged to regard Kenya as a supply point and to seek foreign markets for their output. The Government also strives to induce local firms to think more about export markets and will continue to do so during the current plan period. An export compensation scheme will be introduced by the Government to encourage producers of manufacturers to become more export minded in their outlook.[68]

Chemicals, processed and tinned foodstuffs, and textiles were all mentioned explicitly as industries where import-substitution was expected to lead to export manufacturing.

TABLE 11.6:  Distribution of GDP, 1970 and 1979

|  | 1970 | 1979 |
|---|---|---|
|  | (Percentage of Total) | |
| Remuneration of employees | 42.7% | 40.4% |
| -- of wage earners | 32.3 | 28.5 |
| -- of others | 10.5 | 11.8 |
| Operating surplus of small-scale farmers | 24.7% | 22.8% |
| Profits and Rental Income | 32.5% | 36.8% |

Source:  Calculated from Economic Survey, 1980, 25-26.

With the 1974 and 1975 slowdown in the economy, this export-manufacturing policy priority became more insistent and urgent in government economic statements.  As Finance Minister Kibaki argued in 1977,

> The European Economic Community . . . are being encouraged to invest abroad.  We want to encourage them to invest in Kenya.  There are many lines of industry which, by their nature, are becoming expensive in Europe, particularly where they require a lot of labour.  They would be the right industries for Africa.[69]

The 1979-1983 development plan outlined intentions to reduce import protection in manufacturing, standardize levels of such protection, phase out nontariff protection, and improve export compensation and promotion:

> Future industrial growth must be based increasingly on the penetration of export markets.  This plan period will be used to effect the transition from an industrial sector primarily serving the domestic market to one that is actively and competitively engaged in export sales.[70]

The bleak entrenchment of government activity early in 1980 was announced with the same threat:

> The manufacturing sector requires substantial imported raw materials, intermediate inputs and machinery, making it a net consumer of foreign exchange to the detriment of our balance of payments position . . . . Thus, in order to sustain industrial growth and to turn industry into a net contributor of foreign exchange, industrial production must be increasingly oriented toward export markets.[71]

The 1972 ILO-sponsored report on Kenya articulated what were in fact two separate and alternative strategy priorities. The one (noted earlier) was a redistribution strategy, involving significant land reform, tax levies on the well-off, investment in small-scale rural and urban activities of benefit to the working poor, and moves away from reliance on foreign firms and technology and from concessions to large-scale capital. The second was an export-oriented strategy, in both manufacturing and agriculture, which focused mainly on a transition from import-substituting industrialization and, in fact, involved *continuing concessions to large-scale capital and increased reliance on foreign firms and technology* (so long as they were export-oriented).

In practice, the Kenyan government made policy statements favoring both strategies, following these through in the 1974-1979 plan (despite obvious contradictions between the two thrusts, which analysts like Killick have pointed out.)[72] But the redistribution strategy was not, in fact, seriously implemented, as the distributional data reviewed above indicate so clearly.[73] And the export-manufacturing strategy was only implemented in such a way as to not threaten the fundamental interests in import protection of large-scale foreign and local capital, as evidenced by the unblinking decision to establish such classic import-substitution excesses as *three* separate vehicle assembly subsidiaries (at least one involving higher foreign exchange costs for knocked-down kits than for the finished vehicle).[74] As the statements above from 1974 and 1977 show, the essence of Kenya's export-manufacturing strategy was to draw new export-manufacturing subsidiaries into Kenya, especially from Europe, and to encourage firms in Kenya to consider exports via new concessions to large-scale capital.

The results of the early moves toward export manufacturing seemed promising. As table 11.7 shows, most manufactured exports grew in 1973-1975, relative to their quantity in 1972. But the same table shows that this early promise was soon eroded, and a dramatic fall in Kenyan manufactured exports accelerated over the 1976-1979 period. By 1979, all categories of such exports were less than two-thirds of what they had been in 1972, even though total export quantities had made at least a marginal advance. This was a devastating result after seven years of policy statements advocating emphasis on export manufacturing. The situation was, in part, a reflection of the loss of important export markets in Tanzania in 1977 and thereafter, as the East African community broke

TABLE 11.7:  Manufactured Exports from Kenya, 1972-1979

(Quantum Index, 1972 = 100)

| Year | Chemicals | Manu-<br>factured<br>Goods | Machinery<br>and<br>Transport<br>Equipment | Miscellaneous<br>Manu-<br>factured<br>Articles | Total<br>Exports |
|------|-----------|----------|-----------|-----------|--------|
| 1972 | 100 | 100 | 100 | 100 | 100 |
| 1973 | 123 | 121 | 170 | 120 | 117 |
| 1974 | 130 | 105 | 176 | 106 | 111 |
| 1975 | 91 | 103 | 143 | 90 | 101 |
| 1976 | 87 | 102 | 147 | 69 | 107 |
| 1977 | 74 | 75 | 78 | 54 | 111 |
| 1978 | 77 | 69 | 68 | 52 | 103 |
| 1979 | 65 | 65 | 61 | 55 | 101 |

Source:  Statistical Abstracts, 1977, 1979; Economic Survey, 1980, 85.

TABLE 11.8:  Selected Manufactured Exports from Kenya, 1972-1978

(Current values - K£ 000,000)

| Product | 1972 | 1973 | 1974 | 1975 | 1976 | 1977 | 1978 |
|---------|------|------|------|------|------|------|------|
| Leather | .3 | .5 | .4 | .5 | 1.6 | 1.8 | 2.1 |
| Textile yarns & fabric | 1.7 | 2.4 | 3.0 | 2.6 | 1.7 | 1.5 | 1.7 |
| Wood products | .2 | .2 | .6 | .7 | .6 | 1.1 | .7 |
| Cement | 2.7 | 2.7 | 4.5 | 6.0 | 8.1 | 8.6 | 9.0 |
| Glassware | .4 | .7 | .6 | .8 | .9 | .8 | .6 |
| Paper products | 2.5 | 3.5 | 4.6 | 4.9 | 5.0 | 4.4 | 3.8 |
| Steel doors & windows | .1 | - | .1 | .2 | .2 | .1 | 1.0 |
| Aluminum ware | .1 | .1 | .1 | .2 | .5 | .2. | .5 |
| Metal containers | .7 | .7 | 1.3 | .8 | .7 | .5 | .7 |
| Footwear | .8 | .6 | .4 | .3 | .5 | .3 | .4 |
| Printed matter | .7 | 1.0 | 1.3 | 1.6 | 1.2 | 1.0 | .4 |
| Tinned pineapple | .9 | 1.5 | 1.4 | 3.6 | 7.0 | 10.5 | 9.6 |

Source: Statistical Abstract, 1979, 60.

TABLE 11.9: <u>Destinations of Kenyan Exports, 1970-1979</u>

Percentage of Total Exports to:

| Year | Western Europe | North and South America | Africa | Far East and Australia |
|------|----------------|-------------------------|--------|------------------------|
| 1970 | 34.9% | 8.4% | 39.4% | 6.9% |
| 1971 | 31.1 | 5.8 | 42.6 | 7.6 |
| 1972 | 39.4 | 6.0 | 36.3 | 7.6 |
| 1973 | 38.4 | 7.5 | 34.5 | 10.2 |
| 1974 | 36.0 | 5.5 | 34.8 | 10.3 |
| 1975 | 33.4 | 7.7 | 34.4 | 9.1 |
| 1976 | 46.4 | 8.8 | 26.3 | 8.2 |
| 1977 | 55.4 | 7.1 | 19.8 | 5.4 |
| 1978 | 51.2 | 6.0 | 21.0 | 6.8 |
| 1979 | 48.3 | n.a. | 24.0 | 7.6 |

Source: Calculated from <u>Statistical Abstract</u>, 1979, 64; and <u>Economic Survey</u>, 1980 (for 1979), 93.

down completely and Tanzania shut its borders with Kenya; some 23 percent of the value of Kenya's 1976 manufactured goods had gone to Tanzania. But this could not explain all the decline noted in table 11.7; indeed, there were many product categories where Kenyan exports dropped in which the Tanzanian market had played little role in 1976, including textile products, footwear, and aluminum ware.[75] Table 11.8 provides a more detailed review of manufactured exports, measuring these in current value (so that merely the maintenance of existing quantity levels would show up as significantly increasing values, given price increases in the world economy). In fact, with a few exceptions (cement, tinned pineapple, and leather), the failure of export manufacturing in Kenya is evident in *lower* values by the 1977-1978 period.

The causes of the failure of Kenyan export manufacturing can be analyzed on a number of levels. As already suggested above, the import substitution thrust of the 1960s was emphasized in the shape of high protection, import bans, proliferation of projects in the same industry, and capital-intensive product reproduction during the 1970s: this meant that the high cost structure of most Kenyan manufacturing endured and made many potential exports uncompetitive on the unprotected world market. Another factor was implicit in the continuing dominance of transnational enterprise in Kenya, as reviewed in the second section of this chapter: subsidiaries of such enterprises were subject to the export strategies of their parent companies and were therefore restricted in where they could export; this was true of over 60 percent of subsidiaries interviewed in earlier research.[76] An even more critical factor, however, was that the European Community multinationals to which Kibaki had explicitly addressed himself in pronouncing the new export strategy by and large did not respond to the Kenyan invitation. As table 11.9 makes clear, with the coming of the Lomé Convention in 1975, and the closing of Tanzania's borders, Kenya's trade decisively oriented itself toward Western Europe (giving it twice the share of exports of Africa by 1977-1979, a massive turnaround from 1970-1971). Kenya's trade thus became increasingly subject to the forces at work in the Western European political economies.

When the Lomé Convention was first instituted, there was evidence that its provisions for duty-free EEC import of African industrial goods were aimed at least in part at facilitating European multinationals' relocation of some of their production to lower-wage African bases from which to export back to Europe.[77] Some export-oriented manufacturing investment in Africa accordingly took place. In the Dutch wood industry, for instance, as part of its restructuring strategy in the Netherlands (moving out of standard plywoods where import competition was strong, and concentrating instead on specialty, marine, and construction plywoods), the large Dutch wood multinational, Bruynzeel, located a new facility for veneer production in the Congo. The Dutch government helped finance this, through the FMO (a state-private sector venture providing financing to Third World industrial projects). In addition, another Dutch firm with investments throughout Africa, CCHA, established new plywood manufacturing in Liberia in 1977 explicitly to export back to the more open European market after the Lomé Convention.[78] In the French textile industry, also (although not in the Dutch textile industry), some firms identified new exporting facilities in Africa as part of their efforts to maintain corporate profitability and restructure their activities in the face of rising low-cost textile imports from Southeast Asia and elsewhere. These new export investments were concentrated especially in the Ivory Coast and Cameroon and had financial support from French government sources.[79]

Kenya did receive some investment by multinationals aiming to use the country as a base to export to Western Europe--and, where this happened, there was a significant increase possible in exports of the product. In table 11.8, for instance, the rise of tinned pineapple exports reflected a decision by the U.S. food multinational, Del Monte, to use Kenya as its source of supply for the Western European market (which is, hence, where virtually all such exports from Kenya go).[80] But on the whole, Kenya was ignored by those multinationals that were restructuring in Europe, in favor of French-speaking West Africa--where the tax benefits for subsidiaries were potentially greater (witness the tax holidays that would be negotiated in Ivory Coast industry), and where those companies, which were coming to consider Africa as a potential export base in their new strategies, were already active (e.g., the French textile and Dutch wood firms).[81] The fact was that export-manufacturing growth, given the approach that was being taken toward it in Kenya, was made functionally dependent on developments in Western European industry and on consequent moves by European transnationals; and these moves were not made into Kenya.[82]

In contrast, textile expansion in the Ivory Coast was led by European textile interests from early on. Dollfus-Mieg, France's second largest textile manufacturer, was involved in the largest textile enterprise in the country; Schaeffer, with small French textile-printing, dyeing, and engineering interests, managed another of the four largest Ivorian textile enterprises; and Gamma Holdings, the largest Dutch textile conglomerate, owned the third.[83]

These differing relationships with Western European capital meant that the Ivory Coast textile industry *was* reshaped as a function of European textile restructuring, while the Kenyan industry was not. In the Ivorian case, the changing strategies of both Dollfus-Mieg and Schaeffer did lead to new export facilities being set up in the mid-1970s, although Gamma, faced with different forces at work in the Dutch political economy, reached different strategic conclusions and rejected such African export options.[84] The result of these European moves can be seen in table 11.10, which measures 1979 ACP imports into the EEC in certain textile and clothing categories. The Ivory Coast accounts for the majority of all ACP cotton yarn imports and, for a large portion of the most important area (by value), cotton cloth imports; Kenya's role, except in garments, is virtually nil. These opportunities shaped for the Ivory Coast turned out to be seriously constrained by their de-

TABLE 11.10: Imports of Sensitive Manufactured Textile Products into the European Community from ACP Countries, 1979

| Product | From Total ACP (Quantity) | From Kenya | From Ivory Coast |
| --- | --- | --- | --- |
| | | (Percent of ACP Total) | |
| Cotton yarn | 1,993.tons | - | 57% |
| Cotton cloth | 10,509.tons | 0.1% | 35 |
| Synthetic cloth | - | - | - |
| T-shirts | 3,423,000 | 28 | 1 |
| Sweaters | 7,977,000 | - | - |
| Pants | 1,458,000 | - | 52 |
| Blouses | 1,411,000 | - | 1 |
| Shirts | 1,445,000 | 5 | 1 |

Source: Unpublished data, European Community, Brussels, 1980. Collected by M. Dolan.

pendent character; the European Community imposed explicit guidelines to limit Ivorian textile exports to itself (despite the supposedly free access for ACP-manufactured goods under the Lomé Convention). But the key point, for the purposes of this analysis, is how export manufacturing success in this industry, in two economically open, European-oriented African countries, differed dramatically depending on the level of involvement of European transnationals in each case and on the forces at work in Europe shaping the changing corporate strategies of specific firms.

Thus, Kenya's new export-manufacturing strategy had failed badly by 1980--not least because of the terms in which it had been conceived, emphasizing reliance on European transnationals to build up new exports to Western Europe. In only a few cases (especially in food processing) did such transnationals become interested in this option in Kenya. Meanwhile, given their sense of long-term insecurity in Kenya, some resident Asian enterprises preferred to *invest* in manufacturing in Europe rather than to export there (as with the Chandarias who, by 1976, had 15 manufacturing subsidiaries in Western Europe).[85] Large-scale African capital, as discussed earlier, remained firmly oriented to lucrative joint ventures in import reproduction. And small-scale African capital remained without the institutions or financial strength to undertake much exporting.

Overall, then, the evidence of the 1970s does seem to call into question the optimistic view of Kenyan capital accumulation taken by Leys and Swainson. It would appear that their views were overly shaped by the temporary 1976-1977 boom in coffee and tea prices, which briefly obscured the longer term structural problems that provoke balance-of-payments crises and recurrent retrenchments in Kenya. The export capacity of the Kenyan economy is clearly weak, based on the very limited dynamism of agriculture since the early 1970s and on the failure of the transnational-dependent, export-manufacturing strategy. This means that the Kenyan economy is becoming increasingly dependent on external factors (i.e., price increases for its two major exports--coffee and tea, as well as sources of international financing such as the IMF) to determine its capacity to accumulate in the face of foreign exchange pressures.

### Conclusion--From Economic to Political Crises?

The debate on Kenyan development patterns and prospects has focused on three major questions. Is a dynamic indigenous African bourgeoisie leading a rapid transition to capitalist social relations in Kenya? Is the state firmly under the control of that bourgeoisie? And, are there consequently good prospects of sustained capital accumulation in at least this example of a peripheral capitalist economy?

This work has reviewed evidence relevant to the first and third of these questions. The import-reproduction form of industrialization, led by transnationals in Kenya, was seen to have limited employment and linkage effects and thus to have retarded the rapid growth of capitalist employment. At the same time, the emerging larger-scale African industrialists were seen to be strongly oriented toward that restrictive and inefficient style of enterprise because of their growing relationship with transnational firms. Thus, a negative answer is suggested to the first question: a powerful class of African industrialists may be emerging in Kenya, but they seem most unlikely to lead a dynamic transformation of social relations in the country because of the import- and capital-intensive character of transnational-run industrialization. Similarly, the detailed evidence of national economic indicators from the 1970s questions the potential to sustain capital accumulation in Kenya. A built-in structural constraint appears to choke off growth through the mechanism of large foreign exchange outflows when investment accelerates. Serious problems are evident in agricultural production, explaining part of the weak export capacity of the country. And the endurance of import-reproduction industrialization (now benefitting both transnationals and large-scale African capital) has guaranteed the failure of Kenya's export-manufacturing strategy. Throughout the 1970s, that strategy relied on European transnationals to set up new export facilities to serve EEC markets, but the restructuring strategies of those firms in Europe pushed them elsewhere. By 1980, then, Kenya was experiencing decreases in per capita income, serious foreign exchange gaps, forced cutbacks in government development expenditures, major food imports, and dim prospects for any kind of sustained capital accumulation.

The effects of this economic crisis in Kenya could spur important political conflict. Relatively slow employment growth and widening inequalities feed this; so do falling real wages and cuts in government social expenditure. But perhaps the main impact of economic crisis, in the short run, is to strengthen those forces in the state structure, referred to earlier as technocrats or an "intendant class," who are able to use the seriousness of the situation to advance reform strategies to counter import-reproduction privileges. Such strategies, however, could be deeply threatening to both large-scale African capital and transnational subsidiaries in Kenya. This could open up a more serious split within the state structure than anything Kenya has experienced since the late 1960s. It would also demonstrate clearly that the state structure is not directly dominated by that rising African bourgeoisie.

In such circumstances, the dynamics of political crisis are hard to anticipate. But it is not inconceivable that leaders of those technocrats would be forced to try to widen their base of support by introducing redistribution policies that respond to urban workers and small-scale entrepreneurs, to peasants in less prosperous regions and to the growing number of landless and unemployed in Kenya. Such a strategy alone could not break the structural blockages to Kenyan capital accumulation; Kenya would remain dependent on developments at the international level in commodity prices and in transnational corporate strategies, and there would be major transitional problems in Kenyan industry, including job dislocation, that could quickly weaken the political resolve behind the new thrust. Nevertheless, it is possible that such a strategy might well accelerate capitalist transformation in Kenya. Redistribution would build a broader internal market that could support more sustained local capital accumulation, and a well-organized land reform in agriculture might improve output and exports from that sector. Ironically, though, in view of the arguments of Leys and Swainson, the most powerful social forces opposing this new thrust would be the same emerging African industrialists who have been described as the leaders in Kenyan capitalist transformation.

In the years ahead, then, political conflict spurred by the present economic crisis in Kenya could well resolve in practice what has been at issue theoretically in the debate over capitalism in Kenya. The dynamism of the new African industrialists will be tested; their control over the state will be at issue; and the seriousness of the limitations to sustained capital accumulation in Kenya will be more easily evaluated.

## NOTES

1. Republic of Kenya, Sessional Paper No. 4 of 1980 on Economic Prospects and Policies (1980), 31.

2. See M. Godfrey and S. Langdon, "Partners in Underdevelopment? The Transnationalisation Theses in a Kenyan Context," Journal of Commonwealth and Comparative Politics, vol. 14, no. 1 (1976): 42-63; R. Kaplinsky, "Capitalist Accumulation in the Periphery--the Kenyan Case Reexamined" (Mimeograph, IDS, University of Sussex, 1979); F. Stewart, "Kenya:    Strategies for Development," in U. Damachi et al., eds., Development Paths in Africa and China (New York: Westview, 1976).

3. See C. Leys, "Capital Accumulation, Class Formation and Dependency--the Significance of the Kenyan Case," Socialist Register (1978): 241-266; C. Leys, "'State Capitalism' in Kenya" (Paper presented to the annual meeting of the Canadian Political Science Association, Saskatoon, 1979); N. Swainson, The Development of Corporate Capitalism in Kenya, 1918-1977 (Berkeley: University of California Press, 1980).

4. See Leys, Socialist Register, op. cit.; also, S. Lall, "Is 'Dependence' a Useful Concept in Analysing Underdevelopment?" World Development vol. 3, nos. 11 and 12 (1975).

5. S.P. 4 (1980), 6

6. Swainson goes so far as to say: "In comparison with large multinational firms in Kenya, indigenous capital is small and insignificant." op. cit., 289.

7. Leys, 1978, op. cit., 243.

8. C. Leys, "State Capital in Kenya: A Research Note," Canadian Journal of African Studies, vol. 14, no. 2 (1980): 317.

9. Swainson, op. cit., 203.

10. Leys, 1979, op. cit., 17.

11. Leys, 1978, op. cit., 262.

12. Leys, 1979, op. cit., 17.

13. Swainson, op. cit., 273.

14. For reasons why the technology choices of foreign capital make this so, see F. Stewart, Technology and Underdevelopment (London: MacMillan, 1977).

15. Swainson, op. cit., 18.

16. Leys, 1978, op. cit., 260.

17. Swainson, op. cit., 18.

18. Leys, 1979, op. cit., 18.

19. Kaplinsky, op. cit., 31, 39.

20. S. Langdon, "Multinational Corporations and the State in Africa," in J. Villamil, ed., Transnational Capitalism and National Development (Sussex: Harvester Press, 1979), 223-240.

21. Swainson, op. cit., 211.

22. Kaplinsky, op. cit., 31, 39.

23. S. Langdon, Multinational Corporations in the Political Economy of Kenya (London: MacMillan, 1981), 199-200.

24. R. Cohen, "Class in Africa:  Analytical Problems and Perspectives," Socialist Register (1972): 248-249.

25. Swainson, op. cit., 210-211.

26. Ibid., 288.

27. Leys, 1979, op. cit., 19-21.

28. Kaplinsky, op. cit., 36-37.

29. Leys, 1979, op. cit., 21.

30. Employment, Incomes and Reality:  A Strategy for Increasing Productive Employment in Kenya, Report of an Inter-Agency Team Organized by the International Labor Office (Geneva, 1972); H. Chenery et al., Redistribution with Growth (London: Oxford University Press, 1974).

31. Langdon, op. cit.; also S. Langdon, "Multinational Corporations in the Kenyan Political Economy," in R. Kaplinsky, ed., Readings on the Multinational Corporation in Kenya (Nairobi:  Oxford University Press, 1978), 134-200; S. Langdon, "The State and Capitalism in Kenya," Review of African Political Economy vol. 8 (1977): 90-98.

32. K. Polanyi, The Great Transformation (Boston: Beacon Press, 1958).

33. F. Stewart, Technology and Underdevelopment, 52-55.

34. Some 16.3 percent--Republic of Kenya, Development Plan, 1979-1983, 34.

35. S.P. no. 4, 1980, op. cit., 6.

36. The 1979-1983 development plan, for instance, suggested that rural, nonfarm, nonenumerated employment was 990,000 in 1976, well above the total for enumerated wage employment.

37. This judgment is based on data collection in the Companies Registry in Nairobi 1980-present, reported in more detail below. See, also, Langdon, 1978, op. cit., 142-144.

38. Langdon, 1981, op. cit., 55-56, 62-63.

39. Ibid., 99-101.

40. Dividing subsidiaries on the basis of having more or less than K£300,000 in capital employed. Ibid., 100-102.

41. For details of the cases referred to here, see ibid., ch. 4.

42. Ibid., 110.

43. For details, see ibid., 111-118.

44. I am particularly indebted to Kaplinksy, 1979, op. cit.

45. Swainson, op. cit., 209.

46. Interview with company manager, Nairobi, July 1973.

47. Swainson, op. cit., 272.

48. Langdon, 1978, op. cit., 197.

49. Kaplinsky, 1979, op. cit., 19.

50. Ibid., 19.

51. See Langdon, 1981, op. cit., 26.

52. Evidence from Companies Registry, Nairobi, collected August 1980.

53. As is true of some other commercially based holding companies active in Kenya; see Langdon, 1981, op. cit., ch. 6.

54. See, for instance, the soap case in ibid., 70; also the detailed analysis of the Chandaria family empire in R. Murray, "The Chandarias," in Kaplinsky, 1978, op. cit.

55. For additional evidence, see K. King, "Kenya's Informal Machine-makers: A Study of Small-scale Industry in Kenya's Emergent Artisan Society," World Development vol 2., nos. 4 and 5 (1974).

56. Republic of Kenya, Development Plan, 1974-78, Nairobi (1974), 54.

57. Speech to the Kenya Association of Manufacturers, reprinted in East African Report on Trade and Industry (June 1979): 19.

58. Republic of Kenya, Economic Survey, 1980, Nairobi (1980), 33.

59. The 1980 retrenchments have involved cuts of over K£550 million in planned departmental and development expenditure over the 1979/80-1982/83 plan period--much of this by the ministries of agriculture and water development. S.P. no. 4 (1980), op. cit., 5, 34-35.

60. B. Van Arkadie, "Dependence in Kenya," in Development Trends in Kenya (University of Edinburgh Center for African Studies, 1972), 332ff.

61. Economic Survey, 1980, 90.

62. S.P. 4 (1980), op. cit., 4.

63. Ibid., 26.

64. Economic Survey, 1980, 19.

65. S.P. 4 (1980), op. cit., 10.

66. T. Killick, "Strengthening Kenya's Development Strategy: Opportunities and Constraints," Discussion Paper No. 239, Institute for Development Studies, University of Nairobi (October 1976): 11.

67. R. Kaplinsky, "Trends in the Distribution of Income in Kenya, 1966-76," Training Course on the Appraisal and Monitoring of Foreign Investment, Nairobi (1978).

68. Development Plan, 1974-78, 19.

69. Reported in the East African Report on Trade and Industry (June

# Bibliography

Abdullahi, M. "The Modernization of Elites in North Western State, Nigeria" (Ph.D. diss., University of Chicago, 1977).

Aboyade, O. "Closing Remarks," in Nigeria's Indigenisation Policy, Proceedings of the Symposium organized by the Nigerian Economic Society (Ibadan: University of Ibadan, 1974).

Aboyade, O. "Nigerian Public Enterprises as an Organizational Dilemma," in Public Enterprises in Nigeria,Proceedings of the 1973 Annual Conference of the Nigerian Economic Society (Ibadan, 1974).

Adeboye, T.O. "Public Sector Participation in Manufacturing" (Paper delivered to the 1978 Annual Conference of the Nigerian Economic Society, Lagos, 1979).

Adeleye, R.A. Power and Diplomacy and Northern Nigeria 1804-1906 (New York: Humanities Press, 1971).

Africa Confidential, vol. 20, no. 16 (1 August 1979).

Africa South of the Sahara (London: Europa Publications, 1986).

African Business, November 1985, 19.

African Contemporary Record 1983/84 (New York: Africana Publishers, 1985).

Agboola, S.A. An Agricultural Atlas of Nigeria (Oxford: Oxford University Press, 1979)

Akeredolu-Ale, E.O. "Private Foreign Investment and the Underdevelopment of Indigenous Entrepreneurship in Nigeria," in Gavin Williams, ed., Nigeria: Economy and Society (London: Rex Collings, 1976).

Akeredolu-Ale, E.O. The Underdevelopment of Indigenous Entrepreneurship in Nigeria (Ibadan: Ibadan University Press, 1975).

Alavi, H., quoted in John Saul, The State and Revolution in Eastern Africa (London: Heinemann, 1979).

Allen, G.C. A Short Economic History of Modern Japan 1867-1970 (London: Allen & Unwin, 1972).

Amin, S. "Accumulation and Development: A theoretical model," Review of African Political Economy, no. 1 (1974).

Amin, S. Class and Nation, Historically and in Crisis (London: Heinemann Ed., 1980).

Amin, S. Imperialism and Unequal Development (Sussex: Harvester, 1978).

Amin, S. Unequal Development: An Essay on the Social Formations of Peripheral Capitalism, translated by Brian Pearce (Sussex: Harvester, 1976).

Amin, S.,ed. Modern Migrations in West Africa (London: Oxford University Press, 1974).

Amin, S. Neo-Colonialism in West Africa (New York: Monthly Review Press, 1973).

Amin, S. Le développement du capitalisme en Côte d'Ivoire (Paris: Editions de Minuit, 1967).

Amon d'Aby, F.  Croyances religieuses et coutumes juridiques des Agni de la Côte d'Ivoire (Paris:  Larose, 1960).

Andrae, G. and B. Beckman.  The Wheat Trap (London:  Zed Press, 1985).

Anouma, R.  "L'impôt de capitation en Côte d'Ivoire de 1901 à 1908:  modalités et implications d'un instrument de politique et d'économie coloniales," Annales de l'universite d'Abidjan, série I, 3 (1975).

Asiodu, P.C.  New Nigerian, 22 November 1980.

Asiodu, P.C.  "The Impact of Petroleum on Nigerian Economy," New Nigerian, 21 November 1980.

Asiodu, P.C.  "Closing Remarks," Nigeria's Indigenisation Policy, Proceedings of the Symposium organized by the Nigerian Economic Society (Ibadan:  University of Ibadan, 1974).

Audru to the Chief of the Agriculture Service of the Ivory Coast, 8 July 1934 (ANCI XI-42-313).

Baldwin,J.  Groundnut Marketing Survey (Kaduna:  Ministry of Agriculture, Northern Region, Nigeria, 1956).

Bassett, T.  "Food, Peasantry and the State in the Northern Ivory Coast" (Ph.D. diss., University of California, Berkeley, 1984).

Baulin, J.  La politique africaine d'Houphouët-Boigny (Paris:  Editions Eurafor-Press, 1980).

Beckford, G.L. et al., Agribusiness Structures and Adjustments (Boston:  Harvard University GSBA, 1966).

Beckman, B.  "Whose State?  State and Capitalist Development in Nigeria" (Paper presented to the Conference of the Nordic Association of Political Scientists, Turku, Finland, August 1981).

Beckman, B. "Imperialism and Capitalist Transformation:  Critique of a Kenyan Debate," in Review of African Political Economy 19 (September-December 1980):  59.

Berg, E.  "The Economics of the Migrant Labor System," in H. Kuper, ed., Urbanization and Migration in West Africa (Berkeley:  University of California Press, 1965).

Berg, E.  "Recruitment of Labour Force in Sub-Saharan Africa" (Ph.D. diss., Harvard University, 1960).

Bergsten, C.F., Thomas Horst, and Theodore H. Moran.  American Multinationals and American Interests (Washington, D.C.:  The Brookings Institution, 1978).

Bergsten, C.F.  "Coming Investment Wars?", Foreign Affairs, vol. 53, no. 1 (1974).

Berman, B., and J. Lonsdale.  "Crises of Accumulation, Coercion and the Colonial State," Canadian Journal of African Studies, vol. 14, no. 1 (1980).

Bernstein, H.  "African Peasantries:  A Theoretical Framework," Journal of Peasant Studies, vol. 6 (1979).

Bernstein, H.  "Sociology of Underdevelopment vs. Sociology of Development?" in D. Lehmann, Development Theory:  Four Critical Studies (Totowa, N.J.:  Biblio Distributors, 1979).

Bernstein, H.  "Capital and Peasantry in the Epoch of Imperialism," memo, University of Dar es Salaam, 1976.

Berry, S.  Cocoa, Custom and Socio-economic Change in Rural Western Nigeria (Oxford: Clarendon Press, 1975).

Berry, S.  "Cocoa and Economic Development in Western Nigeria," in C. Eicher and C. Liedholm, eds., Growth and Development of the Nigerian Economy (Lansing: Michigan State University Press, 1970).

Bienen, H. and V. Diejomaoh, editors.  The Political Economy of Income Distribution in Nigeria (New York: Holmes and Meier, 1981).

Biersteker, T.  "Indigenization and the Nigerian Bourgeoisie:  Dependent Development in an African Context" (in this volume).

Biersteker, T.  Distortion or Development?  Contending Perspectives on the Multinational Corporation (Cambridge, Mass.: The MIT Press, 1978).

Binger, L.  Rapport sur la commission de délimitation de la Côte d'Ivoire, 20 October 1892, ANF-OM: Côte d'Ivoire III 3.

Bluestone, B., and B. Harrison.  Corporate Flight: the Causes and Consequences of Economic Dislocation (Massachusetts:  Washington Progress Alliance, 1981).

Bonnefois, A.L.  "La transformation de commerce de traite en Côte d'Ivoire depuis la dernière guerre mondiale et l'indépendence," Cahiers d'Outre-Mer 84 (1968).

Boutillier, J.  "Les captifs en AOF (1903-1905)," Bulletin de IFAN 30, série B, no. 2 (1968).

Braithwaite, T. in The Nigeria Standard, 1 November 1980.

Braverman, H.  Labour and Monopoly Capital:  The Degradation of World in the Twentieth Century (New York: Monthly Review Press, 1974).

Brenner, R.  "The Origins of Capitalist Development:  A Critique of Neo-Smithian Marxism," New Left Review, no. 104 (1977).

Brett, E.A.  Colonialism and Underdevelopment in East Africa (New York: Nok, 1973).

Business Times, Lagos, 3 June 1980.

Business Times, Lagos, 26 August 1980.

Campbell, B.  "The Ivory Coast," ch. 4 in John Dunn, ed., West African States: Failure and Promise.  A Study in Comparative Politics (Cambridge: University Press, 1978).

Campbell, B.  "L'idéologie de la croissance:  une analyse du Plan quinquennal de développement 1971-1975 de la Côte d'Ivoire," in Revue canadienne des études africaines, vol. 10, no. 1 (1975).

Campbell, B.  "Neo-Colonialism, Economic Dependence and Political Change: Cotton Textile production in the Ivory Coast," Review of African Political Economy, vol. 2 (1975).

Campbell, B.  "The Social, Political and Economic Consequences of French Private Investment in the Ivory Coast, 1960-70" (Ph.D. diss., University of Sussex, 1973).

Capet, M.  Traite d'économie tropicale (Paris: Pichon et Burand-Auzias, 1958).

Captain Braulot, Rapport de mission, 1893; ANF-OM: Côte d'Ivoire III 3.

Cardoso, F. "Associated-dependent Development: Theoretical and Political Implications," in A. Stephan, Authoritarian Brazil (New Haven: Yale University Press, 1973).

Cardoso, F. and Enzo Faletto. Dependency and Development in Latin America (Berkeley: University of California Press, 1978).

Cercle d'Abengourou, Rapport politique et social, 1941 (ANCI VI-44/17).

Cercle d'Indénié, Poste d'Assikasso. Rapport mensuel, August 1904, ANCI IEE 43 (4).

Cercle de l'Indénié, Rapport sur la situation agricole et zootechnique, second trimester, 1932 (ANCI XI-43-426).

Cercle de l'Indénié, Service de l'agriculture, Rapports trimestriels, 1930 (ANCI XI-43-426).

Cercle de l'Indénié, Service de l'agriculture, Rapports 1912-1930 (ANCI XI-43-426).

Chambre de commerce de la Côte d'Ivoire "Réunions des exportateurs de café," Bulletin mensuel, no. 1, January 1976.

Chauveau, J.P. "Agricultural Production and Social Formation: The Baule Region of Toumodi-Kokumbo in Historical Perspective," in M. Klein, ed., Peasants in Africa (Beverly Hills: Sage, 1980).

Chauveau, J.P., and J. Richard. "Une 'périphérie recentrée': à propos d'un système local d'économie de plantation en Côte d'Ivoire," Cahiers d'études africaines 17: 485-523.

Chauveau, J.P., and J. Richard. Bodiba en Côte d'Ivoire (Abidjan: ORSTOM, 1976).

Chenery, H. et al. Redistribution with Growth (London: Oxford University Press, 1974).

Chevassu, J., and Alain Valette. Les industriels de la Côte d'Ivoire. Qui et pourquoi? (Ivory Coast: Office de la recherche scientifique et technique outre-mer. Ministère du plan ORSTOM 1975, Série d'études industrielles, no. 13).

Clerc, L. Cercle de l'Indénié, Rapport agricole, second semester, 1919 (ANCI XI-43-426).

Clerc, L. Rapport politique du cercle de l'Indénié, 3e trimestre, 1921 (ANCI 1EE 59, 1/2).

Cliffe, L. "Rural Class Formation in East Africa," Journal of Peasant Studies 4 (January 1977).

Cohen, G. Karl Marx's Theory of History: A Defence (London: Oxford University Press, 1979).

Cohen, M.A. Urban Policy and Political Conflict in Africa--A Study of the Ivory Coast (Chicago: University of Chicago Press, 1974).

Cohen, R. "Class in Africa: Analytical Problems and Perspectives," Socialist Register (1972).

Collins, P. "Public Policy and the Development of Indigenous Capitalism; the Nigerian Experience," Journal of Commonwealth and Comparative Politics, 15/2 (1977).

Collins, P. "The Policy of Indigenization: An Overall View," Quarterly Journal of Administration (January 1975).

Côte d'Ivoire, Circulaire sur l'intensification de la production agricole et pastorale en Côte d'Ivoire, 4 April 1931 (ANCI VI-8-203).

Côte d'Ivoire en chiffre (Abidjan: Imprimerie de gouvernement, 1976).

Cowen, M. "The British State, State Enterprise and an Indigenous Bourgeoisie in Kenya after 1945" (Unpublished manuscript, London, 1981).

Cowen, M. "Capital and Peasant Households" (Mimeo, Department of Economics, University of Nairobi, July 1976).

Cowen, M. and K. Kinyananjui, "Some Problems of Capital and Class in Kenya," Institute of Development Studies Paper (Nairobi: University of Nairobi, 1977).

Chronique Coloniale, 30 June 1931.

Crowder, West Africa Under Colonial Rule (London: Hutchison, 1968).

Dellabonin to the Director of the Agricultural Service, 6 April 1925 (ANCI XI-43-426).

de Groot, J. "The Iranian Revolution: What's Happening," Marxism Today (February 1980).

de Groot, J. "Iran: What Past? What Future?" Marxism Today (April 1979).

de Janvry, A. The Agrarian Question and Reformism in Latin America (Baltimore: Johns Hopkins, 1981).

Delafosse, M. "Les sociétés indigènes de prévoyance en Afrique de l'Ouest française," Revue indigène (July-October 1919).

de la Rochere, J.D. "L'état et le développement économique de la Côte d'Ivoire," Série Afrique Noire 6 (1976).

den Tuinder, B. The Ivory Coast: The Challenge of Success (Baltimore: Johns Hopkins, 1978).

Diaku, I. "The Capital Structure, Financing Practices and Profit Performance of the Nigerian Industrial Development Bank, 1964-1972," Nigerian Journal of Economic and Social Studies, vol. 18, no. 1 (1976).

Dickson, K. A Historical Geography of Ghana (Cambridge: University Press, 1971).

Dore, R.P. Land Reform in Japan (London: Oxford University Press, 1959).

D'Silva, B.C., Yahaya A. Abdullahi, and M.R. Raza. "Policies Affecting Rural Development in Nigeria" (Paper prepared for presentation at the 5th World Congress of Rural Sociology, Mexico City, 7-12 August, 1980).

Dumett, R. "The Rubber Trade of the Gold Coast and Ashanti in the Nineteenth Century," Journal of African History 12 (1971): 79-101.

Ekuerhare, B.U. "The Impact and Lessons of Nigeria's Industrial Policy under the Military Government, 1966-1979" (Paper presented at Department of Economics Seminar, Ahmadu Bello University, 23 January 1980).

Emmanuel, A.  "White Settler Colonialism and the Myth of Investment Imperialism," New Left Review, no. 73 (1972).

Engels, F.  "Origin of the Family, Private Property and the State," in Marx and Engels, Selected Works (New York: International Publishers, 1967).

Etienne, P. and M. Etienne, "L'émigration Baoule actuelle," Cahiers d'Outre-Mer 82 (April-May 1968).

Evans, P.  Dependent Development: The Alliance of Multinational, State and Local Capital in Brazil (Princeton: Princeton University Press, 1979).

Falola, T. and J. Ihonvbere, The Rise and Fall of Nigeria's Second Republic (London: Zed Press, 1985).

Federal Republic of Nigeria, Joint-Ventures Enterprises, Federal Republic of Nigeria, Public Service Review Commission, Main Report (Lagos, 1974).

Financial Times, London, 29 September 1980.

Financial Times Survey, United Kingdom, 15 December, 1980.

Forkosch, M.  "Henry George," American Journal of Economics and Sociology, vol. 38 (1979).

Forlacroix, C.  "La pénétration française dans l'Indénié (1887-1901)," Annales de l'université d'Abidjan, série F (Ethnosociologie), 1 (1969).

Forrest, T.G.  "Recent Developments in Nigerian Industrialisation," in M. Fransman, ed., Industry and Accumulation in Africa (London: Heinemann, 1982).

Forrest, T.G.  "Agricultural Policies in Nigeria, 1900-1978," in J. Heyer, P. Roberts, and G. Williams, eds., Rural Development in Tropical Africa (New York: Macmillan, 1981).

Forrest, T.G.  "Federal State and Capitalist Transformation" (Unpublished paper, Department of Economics, Ahmadu Bello University, Zaria, June 1979).

Fourneau, L.  Cercle de l'Indénié, Service de l'agriculture, Rapport annuel (1927).

Frank, A.G.  "The Development of Underdevelopment," Monthly Review, vol. 18, no. 4 (1966).

Frankel, S.H.  Capital Investment in Africa: Its Course and Effects (New York: Oxford University Press, 1938).

Fraternité Hebdo, no. 1105, 20 June 1980.

Fraternité Matin, Ivory Coast, 2 April 1981, 17.

Frechou, H.  "Les plantations européenes en Côte d'Ivoire" (Ph.D. diss., University of Bordeaux, 1956).

Frischmann, A.  "The Spatial Growth and Residential Location Pattern of Kano" (Ph.D. diss., Northwestern University, 1977).

Geer, T.  An Oligopoly: The World Coffee Economy and Stabilization Schemes (New York: Dunellon, 1971).

Gerschenkron, A.  Economic Backwardness in Historical Perspective (Cambridge, Mass.: Harvard University Press, 1966).

Godfrey, M.  "Kenya: African Capitalism or Simple Dependency?" in M. Bienefeld and M. Godfrey, eds., The Struggle for Development, National

Strategies in an International Context (M. Phil. textbook, Sussex, forthcoming).

Godfrey, M. "Prospects for a Basic Needs Strategy: The Case of Kenya," Institute of Development Studies Bulletin (June 1978).

Godfrey, M., and S. Langdon. "Partners in Underdevelopment? The Transnationalisation Theses in a Kenyan Context," Journal of Commonwealth and Comparative Politics, vol. 14, no. 1 (1976).

Goody, J. The Developmental Cycle in Domestic Groups (Cambridge: Cambridge University Press, 1971).

Governor Antonetti, Rapport politique, second trimestre, 1923 (ANCI 2EE 9, 13).

Groff, D. "The Development of Capitalism in the Ivory Coast: The Case of Assikasso, 1880-1940" (Ph.D. diss., Stanford University, 1980).

Helleiner, G.K. Peasant Agriculture, Government and Economic Growth in Nigeria (Homewood, Ill.: Irwin, Inc., 1966).

Heyer, J. "A Survey of Agricultural Development in the Small Farm Areas of Kenya since the 1920s" (I.D.S. Nairobi Working Paper No. 194, October 1974).

Hiernaux, C.R. "Les aspects géographiques de la production bananière de la Côte d'Ivoire," Cahiers d'Outre-Mer 1, January-March 1948.

Hill, P. Rural Hausa: A Village and a Setting (London: Cambridge University Press, 1972).

Hill, P. Studies in Rural Capitalism in West Africa (Cambridge: Cambridge University Press, 1970).

Hill, P. Migrant Cocoa Farmers of Southern Ghana (Cambridge: Cambridge University Press, 1963).

Hobsbawm, E.J. Industry and Empire (New York: Penguin, 1968).

Hodges, M. Multinational Corporations and National Government: A Case Study of the United Kingdom's Experience 1964-1970 (Lexington, Mass.: Lexington Books, 1974).

Hogendorn, J. Nigerian Groundnut Exports (Zaria: Ahmadu Bello University Press, 1978).

Hogendorn, J. "The Origins of the Groundnut Trade in Northern Nigeria" (Ph.D. diss., University of London, 1966).

Hoogvelt, A. "Indigenisation and Foreign Capital: Industrialisation in Nigeria," Review of African Political Economy, no. 14 (1979).

Hopkins, A.G. An Economic History of West Africa (New York: Columbia University Press, 1973).

Hopkins, A.G. Inventaire économique.

House, W. and T. Killick, "Social Justice and Development Policy in Kenya's Rural Economy," in D. Ghai and S. Radwan, editors, Agrarian Policies and Rural Poverty in Africa (Geneva: ILO, 1983), 31-33.

Hull, H.M. Report on the Rubber Industry, enclosure in Maxwell to Chamberlain, 27 May 1897. (PRO CP96 293 5269).

Huxley, F.A. "Colonies in a Changing World," The Political Quarterly 13 (October-December 1942).

Hyden, G. Beyond Ujamaa in Tanzania: Underdevelopment and an Uncaptured Peasantry (Berkeley: University of California Press, 1980).

Jörberg, L. "The Industrial Revolution in the Nordic Countries 1850-1914," in C.M. Cipolla, ed., The Fontana Economic History of Europe, vol. 4, part 2 (New York: Fontana/Collins, 1973).

Journal officiel, Documents parlementaires Assemblée Nationale, Session de 1951, Séance de 15 février, 1959.

Kaplinsky, R. "Capitalist Accumulation in the Periphery: Kenya," in M. Fransman, Industry and Accumulation in Africa (London: Heinemann, 1982).

Kaplinsky, R. "Capitalist Accumulation in the Periphery--The Kenyan Case Re-Examined," Review of African Political Economy, no. 17 (1980).

Kaplinsky, R. Readings on the Multinational Corporation in Kenya (Nairobi: Oxford University Press, 1978).

Kaplinsky, R. "Trends in the Distribution of Income in Kenya, 1966-76," Training Course on the Appraisal and Monitoring of Foreign Investment, Nairobi (1978).

Kay, G. Development and Underdevelopment: A Marxist Analysis (New York: St. Martin's Press, 1975).

Killick, T. "Strengthening Kenya's Development Strategy: Opportunities and Constraints" (Discussion Paper No. 239, Institute for Development Studies, University of Nairobi, October 1976).

King, A. An Economic History of Kenya and Uganda (Nairobi: EAPH, 1975).

King, K. "Kenya's Informal Machine-Makers: A Study of Small-scale Industry in Kenya's Emergent Artisan Society," World Development vol 2., nos. 4 and 5 (1974).

Kitching, G. Class and Economic Change in Kenya: The Makings of an African Petite Bourgeoisie, 1905-1970 (New Haven: Yale University Press, 1980).

Köbben, A.J. "Le planteur noir," Etudes éburnéennes 5 (1956).

Köbben, A.J. "L'Héritage chez les Agni: l'influence de l'économie de profit," Africa 24 (1954).

Labaye, Rapport sur la captivité dans le cercle de l'Indénié (ANCI 1M: 63, K21).

Labouret, H. Paysans d'Afrique Occidentale (Paris: Gallimard, 1941).

Lachiver, M. "Le marché du café dans l'Europe des six," Cahiers d'Outre-Mer 60 (October-December 1962).

"L'Agriculture à la Côte d'Ivoire--conférence faite devant la chambre de commerce de Grand Bassam par professeur Perrot," 11 April 1914 (ANS R16).

Lall, S. "Is 'Dependence' a Useful Concept in Analysing Underdevelopment?" World Development vol. 3, nos. 11 and 12 (1975).

Landes, D.S. The Unbound Prometheus: Technological Change and Industrial Development in Western Europe from 1750 to the Present (New York: Cambridge University Press, 1969).

Lang, J.E.    Report on the Mission to Delimit the Gold Coast-Ivory Coast Frontier, 13 July 1892 (PRO CO96 225).

Langdon, S.    "Industry and Capitalism in Kenya: Contributions to a Debate" (in this volume).

Langdon, S.    "Industrial Dependence and Export Manufacturing in Kenya" (Paper presented at the International Seminar on Alternative Futures for Africa, Dalhousie University, Halifax, May 1981).

Langdon, S.    Multinational Corporations in the Political Economy of Kenya (London: MacMillan, 1981).

Langdon, S.    "Industrial Restructuring and the Third World: The Case of Dutch Textile Manufacturing, 1965-79" (Mimeo, Carleton University, April 1980).

Langdon, S.    "Multinational Corporations and the State in Africa," in J. Villamil, ed., Transnational Capitalism and National Development (Sussex: Harvester Press, 1979).

Langdon, S.    "Multinational Corporations in the Kenyan Political Economy," in R. Kaplinsky, ed., Readings on the Multinational Corporation in Kenya (Nairobi: Oxford University Press, 1978).

Langdon, S.    "The State and Capitalism in Kenya," in Review of African Political Economy no. 8 (1977).

Langdon, S.    and M. Godfrey, "Partners in Underdevelopment, The Transnationalisation Thesis in the Kenya Context," Journal of Commonwealth and Comparative Politics, no. 14, 1 (1976).

Lansberg, M.    "Export-led Industrialisation in the Third World: Manufacturing Imperialism," URPE, vol. 11, no. 4 (1979).

Last, M.    "Aspects of Administration and Dissent in Hausaland, 1800-1968," Africa, vol. 40 (1970).

Lauer, J.J.    "Economic Innovations Among the Dou of Western Ivory Coast, 1900-1960" (Ph.D. diss., University of Wisconsin, Madison, 1973).

Lawal, S.S.    "The Politics of Board Membership of Public Enterprises in Kwara State" (M.P.A. thesis, University of Ife, 1979).

Lawson, G.H.    "La Côte d'Ivoire: 1960-1970. Croissance et diversification sans africanisation," in L'Afrique de l'indépendance politique à l'indépendance économique, John A. Esseks, ed. (F. Maspéro et Presses universitaires de Grenoble, 1975).

"Le Développement de la culture du cacaoyer," JOCI, 15 March 1916.

Leduc, G.    Les Institutions monetaires africaines:    pays francophones (Paris: Editions A. Pedone, 1965).

Lee, E.    "Export-led Development:    The Ivory Coast," in D. Ghai and S. Radwan, editors, Agrarian Policies and Rural Poverty in Africa (Geneva: ILO, 1983).

Lenin, V.I.    The Development of Capitalism in Russia (Moscow:    Progress Publishers, and London: Lawrence, 1956).

Lewis, A.    Reflections on Nigeria's Economic Growth (Paris, 1967).

Lewis, B.  "Ethnicity, Occupational Specialisation and Interest Groups:  The Transporters' Association of the Ivory Coast," (Ph.D. diss., Northwestern University, 1971).

Leys, C.  "Kenya:  What Does 'Dependency' Explain?," Review of African Political Economy, no. 17 (1980).

Leys, C.  "'State Capitalism' in Kenya" (Paper presented to the Annual Meeting of the Canadian Political Science Association, Saskatoon, 1979).

Leys, C.  "Capital Accumulation, Class Formation and Dependency:  The Significance of the Kenyan Case," Socialist Register (1978).

Leys, C.  Underdevelopment in Kenya:  The Political Economy of Neo-Colonialism (Berkeley and Los Angeles:  University of California Press, 1974).

Lt. Governor Angoulvant's 1915 circular to cercle administrators (ANCI XI-39-407).

Lt. Governor to the Governor-General of AOF, 5 September 1929 (ANCI IV-35-124); and the decree of 26 July 1932, Journel officiel (1933).

Lt. Governor's Political Report, Second Trimester, 1919 (ANS 2G 19-7).

Lt. Governor Angoulvant, circular of 29 July 1910, ANCI XVII-41-22 and the Journel officiel for July 1910.

Lt. Governor of the Ivory Coast, Political Report for the Second Trimester, 1919 (ANS 2G 19-17).

Lt. Governor Bourgine's Arrête local of 29 December 1931 (ANCI IV-43/20).

Lipietz, A.  "Toward Global Fordism," New Left Review no. 132 (March-April 1982): 33-47.

Lissner, W.  "On the Centenary of Progress and Poverty," American Journal of Economics and Sociology, vol. 38, no. 4 (1979).

Lloyd Prichard, M.F.  An Economic History of New Zealand to 1939 (Auckland: Collins, 1970).

Lubeck, P.  "Islam and Resistance in Northern Nigeria," in W. Goldfrank, ed., The World-System of Capitalism (London: Sage, 1979).

Lugard, F.  cited in F. Okedji, "An Economic History of the Hausa-Fulani Emirates" (Ph.D. diss., Indiana University, 1972).

Lugard, F.  Political Memoranda (London:  Waterlow, 1906; 1970 edition, Cass).

MacWilliam, S.  "Commerce, Class and Ethnicity:  The Case of Kenya's Luo Thrift and Trading Corporation, 1945-1972" (Conference paper for the Australasian Political Studies Association, Sydney, 1976).

Mamdani, M.  Politics and Class Formation in Uganda (New York:  Monthly Review Press, 1976).

Marchés coloniaux 34 (July 1946).

Marchés coloniaux 2 (1947), 761; vol. 3 (1948), 468; vol. 4 (1949).

Marchés tropicaux et méditerrannéens, 34e année, no. 1697 (19 May 1979).

Marcussen, H. and J. Torp.  The Internationalisation of Capital (London:  Zed Press, 1982).

Martins, L.   "La 'joint-venture,' Etat-Firme transnationale--entrepreneurs locaux au Brésil," in Sociologie et sociétés, vol. XI, no. 2 (Montreal, October 1979).

Marx, K.  Capital, vol. I (New York: International Publishers, 1973).

Masini, J., M. Ikonicoff, C. Jedlecki, M. Lanzarotti.  Les multinationales et le développement.  Trois enterprises et la Côte d'Ivoire (Paris:  Presses universitaires de France, and Brussels:  Centre européen d'étude et d'information sur les sociétés multinationales, CEEIM, 1979).

McKenzie, K. E.  Comintern and World Revolution, 1928-1943:  The Shaping of Doctrine (New York:  Columbia University Press, 1964).

Meddick, H.  "The Protoindustrial Family Economy," Social History, no. 3 (October 1976).

Meillassoux, C.  "Introduction," in C. Meillassoux, ed., Esclavage en Afrique précoloniale (Paris:  Maspéro, 1975).

Meillassoux, C.  "Introduction," in C. Meillassoux, ed., The Development of Indigenous Trade and Markets in West Africa (London:  Oxford University Press, 1971).

Mendels, F.F.  "Proto-Industrialisation:  The First Phase of the Industrialisation Process," Journal of Economic History, vol. 32 (1972).

Ministère de l'agriculture, Statistiques agricoles (1973).

Ministère de la France d'Outre-Mer, L'équipement des territoires français d'Outre-Mer, 1947-50.

Ministère du Plan, Inventaire économique et social de la Côte d'Ivoire, 1947-58 (Abidjan:  Imprimerie du gouvernement, 1960).

Ministry of Information, Federal Government of Nigeria, "Nigerian Enterprises Promotion Decree, 1977," Supplement to Official Gazette, vol. 64, no. 2, part A (Lagos:  Printing Division, 1977).

Ministry of Overseas Development, Overseas Research Publication No. 21, (London, 1976).

Mohammed, Y.  New Nigerian, 1 November 1980.

Morgenthau, R.S.  Political Parties in French-Speaking West Africa (Oxford:  Clarendon Press, 1964).

Mytelka, L.K.  "Crisis and Adjustment in the French Textile Industry," in H. Jacobsen and D. Sidjanksi, eds., The Emerging Economic Order:  Dynamics, Constraints and Possibilities, (Beverly Hills:  Sage, forthcoming).

Mytelka, L.K.  "Direct Foreign Investment and Technology Transfer in the Ivorian Textile and Wood Industries" (Mimeo, Carleton University, October 1980).

Mytelka, L.K. and M. Dolan, "The Political Economy of EEC-ACP Relations in a Changing International Division of Labour," in C. Vaitsos and D. Seers, eds., European Integration and Unequal Development (London:  MacMillan, 1980).

National Agricultural Census, Ivory Coast (1974).

National Concord, 20 November 1980.

Naylor, R.T.  "The Rise and Fall of the Third Commercial Empire of the St. Lawrence," in Gary Teople, ed., Capitalism and the National Question in Canada (Toronto:  University of Toronto Press, 1972).

New Nigerian, 21 November 1980.

New Nigerian, 20 November 1980.

Newbury, C.  "The Government General and Political Change in FWA," St. Anthony's Papers 10 (London:  Chatto and Windus, 1961).

Nigerian Economic Society, Public Enterprises in Nigeria:  Proceedings of the 1973 Annual Conference of the Nigerian Economic Society (Ibadan, 1974).

Nigerian Institute of Social and Economic Research, and Federal Ministry of Finance, A Review of the Federal Budgetary System, Final Report (1977).

Nigerian National Archives at Kaduna (NAK) SNP 6 C 162/1907:68.

The Nigeria Standard, 31 October 1980.

The Nigeria Standard, 8 August 1980.

Njonjo, A.  The Africanisation of the White Highlands:  A Study in Agrarian Class Struggles in Kenya, 1950-1974 (Ph.D. diss., Princeton University, December 1977).

Njonjo, A.  "The Kenyan Peasantry:  A Reassessment," Review of African Political Economy no. 20 (April-June 1981):  39.

Okonjo, I.M.  British Administration in Nigeria, 1900-1950:  A Nigerian View (New York: Nok, 1974).

Onoge, O.F.  "The Indigenisation Decree and Economic Independence: Another Case of Bourgeois Utopianism," in Nigeria's Indigenisation Policy, Proceedings of the Symposium organized by the Nigerian Economic Society.

Oyediran, O.  Nigerian Government and Politics under Military Rule (New York: St. Martin's Press, 1979).

Pack, H.  "Employment and Productivity in Kenyan Manufacturing," East African Economics Review (new series), vol. 4, no. 2 (1972).

Palma, G.  "Dependency:  A Formal Theory of Underdevelopment or a Methodology for the Analysis of Concrete Situations of Underdevelopment?" World Development, vol. 6 (1978).

Park, S.S.  Growth and Development:  A Physical Output and Employment Strategy (New York:  St. Martin Press, 1977).

Peemans, J.P.  "The Social and Economic Development of Zaire Since Independence:  An Historical Outline," African Affairs 295 (London), April 1975.

Perrot, C.H.  "Les captifs dans le royaume Anyi de N'Dényé," in C. Meillassoux, ed., Esclavage en Afrique précoloniale (Paris:  Maspéro, 1975).

Phillips, A.  "The Meaning of Development," in Review of African Political Economy, no. 8 (January-April, 1977).

Pillet-Schwartz, A.M.  Capitalisme d'état et développement rural en Côte d'Ivoire, La Sodepalm en pays Ebrie (Paris:  Ecole pratique des hautes études, 1973).

Piquemal, M.  "Exportation des capitaux aux colonies," Economie et Politique (August-Sept. 1957).

Polanyi, K.  The Great Transformation (Boston:  Beacon Press, 1958).

Post, K.  "'Peasantization' and Rural Political Movements in Western Africa," Archives européenes de sociologie 13 (1972).

Poste d'Assikasso, Rapport mensuel, March 1902 (ANCI 1EE 43, 2).  Post of Assikasso, monthly reports, March 1908, July 1909 (ANCI 1EE 45).

Poulantzas, N.  Political Power and Social Classes (London:  New Left Books, 1973).

Poulantzas, N.  Classes in Contemporary Capitalism (London:  New Left Books, 1975).

Preobrazhensky, E.  The New Economics (London:  Oxford University Press, 1965).

Prothero, R.  Migrant Labor from Sokoto Province (Kaduna:  Government Printer, 1957).

Ramboz, Y.C.  "La politique cafeière de Côte d'Ivoire et la reforme de la caisse de stabilisation des prix du café et du cacao," Revue juridique et politique 2 (April-June 1965).

Rapport politique et social, 1941 (ANCI VI-44/11).

Rapport de l'Inspecteur de l'agriculture Bervas sur le cercle de l'Indénié, 30 November 1918 (ANCI XI-43-426).

Raynault, C.  "Circulation monetaire et evolution des structures socio-économiques chez les Hausa du Niger," Africa, vol. 47 (1977).

Report of the Auditor-General on the Accounts of the Government of the Western State of Nigeria for the year ended 31st March, 1974, no. 2 (1976).

Report of the Committee on the Financial System (Lagos, 1977).

Report of the Interim Revenue Allocation Committee (The Dina Report), (Lagos, 1969).

Report of the Northern Nigeria Lands Committee (London:  HMSO, Cd 5101, 5102, 1910).

Report of the Working Party on Statutory Corporations and State-Owned Companies (Lagos:  Federal Ministry of Information, 1967).

Report of the Working Party on Statutory Corporations and State-Owned Corporations, 1968, Nigeria.

Report on the Territory Explored by the English Commissioner for the Delimitation of the Frontier on the West of the Gold Coast Colony, 17 November 1892 (PRO CO96 229 5269).

Republic of Kenya, Sessional Paper No. 4 of 1980 on Economic Prospects and Policies (1980).

Republic of Kenya, Development Plan, 1979-1983.

Republic of Kenya, Development Plan, 1974-78, Nairobi (1974).

Republic of Kenya, Economic Survey, 1980, Nairobi (1980).

Republic of Kenya, Statistical Abstract, 1979, Nairobi, 1979.

République de Côte d'Ivoire, Plan quinquennal de développement économique, social et culturel, vol. 1 (Abidjan:  Ministère du plan, 1977)

République de Côte d'Ivoire, La Côte d'Ivoire en chiffre, ed. 1976, Ministère du plan.

Rey, P.P. Alliances de classes (Paris: Maspéro, 1976).

Richards, A. "The Political Economy of Commercial Estate Labor Systems: A Comparative Analysis of Prussia, Egypt, and Chile," Comparative Studies in Society and History 21 (October 1979): 4.

Richards, A. "The Political Economy of Gutwirtschaft: A Comparative Analysis of East Elbian Germany, Egypt and Chile," CSSH 21 (1979): 483-518.

Rodney, W. How Europe Underdeveloped Africa (Tanzania: Tanzanian Publishing House, 1972).

"The Roosevelt-Churchill Eight Points and Africa's Future," The Atlantic Charter.

Rouch, J. "Migrations au Ghana," Journal de la Société des africanistes 26 (1956).

Rougerie, G. "Le pays Agni du sud-est de la Côte d'Ivoire forestière," Etudes éburnéennes 6 (Abidjan, 1957).

Rowling, G. Report on Land Tenure, Kano Province (Kaduna: Government Printer, 1949).

Schachter Morgenthau, R. Political Parties in French-Speaking West Africa (Oxford: Clarendon Press, 1964).

Schatz, S.P. Nigerian Capitalism (Berkeley: University of California Press, 1977).

Schatz, S.P. Economics, Politics and Administration in Government Lending, The Regional Loans Boards of Nigeria (NISER Series, Oxford University Press, 1970).

Schatz, S.P. Development Bank Lending in Nigeria: The Federal Loans Board (Nigerian Institute of Social and Economic Research Series, Oxford University Press, 1964).

Scott, J. "Hegemony and Peasantry," Politics and Society, vol. 7, no. 3 (1977).

SEDES Study, 1967.

SEDES Study, 1970.

Semi-Bi, Z. "La politique coloniale des travaux publics en Côte d'Ivoire (1900-1940)," thèse de troisième cycle, University of Paris VII (1973).

Service de l'agriculture, cercle d'Abengourou, subdivision d'Agnibilekrou, Fiches cadastrales (1957).

Shanin, T. The Awkward Class (Oxford: Clarendon Press, 1972).

Shenton, "The Political Economy of Northern Nigeria" (Ph.D. diss., University of Toronto, 1981).

Simkin, C. G. F. The Instability of a Dependent Economy: Economic Fluctuations in New Zealand, 1890-1914 (London: Oxford University Press, 1951).

Skinner, E.P. The Mossi of the Upper Volta (Stanford: Stanford University Press, 1964).

Skocpol, T. States and Social Revolutions (New York: Cambridge University Press, 1979).

Smith, M. "Historical and Cultural Conditions of Political Corruption among the Hausa," Comparative Studies in Society and History, vol. 6 (1964).

Smith, M.G.   The Economy of Hausa Communities in Zaria, Colonial Research Series no. 16 (London: HMSO, 1955).

Solichon, A.   Adjoint des affaires indigènes, "La Côte d'Ivoire et ses produits," 30 April 1905 (ANCI R8, microfilm).

Stavenhagen, R.   Social Classes in Agrarian Societies (Garden City, N.Y.: Anchor, 1975).

Stepan, A.   The State and Society:  Peru in Comparative Perspective (Princeton: Princeton University Press, 1978).

Stewart, F.   "Kenya:  Strategies for Development," in U. Damachi et al., eds., Development Paths in Africa and China (New York:  Westview, 1976).

Suret-Canale, Afrique Noire occidentale et centrale:   de la colonisation aux indépendances (Paris:  Editions Sociales, 1961).

Suret-Canale, French Colonialism in Tropical Africa (London:  C. Hurst, 1971).

Sutcliffe, B.   "Imperialism and Industrialisation in the Third World" in R. Owen and B. Sutcliffe, eds., Studies in the Theory of Imperialism (New York: Longman, 1972).

Swainson, N.   The Development of Corporate Capitalism in Kenya, 1918-1977 (London:  Heinemann Ed., 1980).

Tahir, I.   "Scholars, Sufis, Saints, and Capitalists in Kano, 1904-74" (Ph.D. diss., Cambridge University, 1974).

Taméchon, M.   Rapport d'inspection, cercle de l'Indénié, 6 October 1932 (ANCI IV-44/15).

Tauxier, L.   Religion, moeurs et coutumes des Agni de la Côte d'Ivoire (Paris:  P. Geuthner, 1932).

Tauxier, L.   Nègres Gouro et Gagou (Paris:  Librairie Orientaliste, 1926).

Tauxier, L.   Le Noir de Bondoukou (Paris:  Payot, 1921).

Tauxier, L.   Le Noir de Soudan--Pays Mossi et Gourounsi (Paris:   Editions Earnest Laroux, 1917).

Taylor, J.   From Modernization to Modes of Production (New York:  Humanities Press, 1979).

Temple, C.   Native Races and Their Rulers (London:   Cass, 1918, reprinted 1968).

Teriba, O.   "Development Strategy, Investment Decisions and Expenditure Patterns of a Public Development Institution:  The Case of the Western Nigeria Development Corporation, 1949-1962", Nigerian Journal of Economic and Social Studies 8/2 (1966).

Terray, E.   "Classes and Class Consciousness in the Abron Kingdom of Gyaman," in M. Bloch, ed., Marxist Analysis and Social Anthropology (New York: John Wiley and Sons, 1975).

Terray, E.   "Relations de domination et d'exploitation dans le royaume du Gyaman" (Paper presented at the seminar of GRASP, 1970/71, Centre d'études africaines, Ecole pratique des hautes études, Paris).

Thomas, C.   Dependence and Transformation:  The Economics of the Transition to Socialism (New York:  Monthly Review Press, 1974).

Thompson, E.P.   "Eighteenth-Century English Society:  Class Struggle Without Class," Social History, vol. 3 (1978).

Thompson, E.P. "Time, Work, Discipline and Industrial Capitalism," Past and Present, no. 38 (1967).

Thompson, V., and R. Adloff. French West Africa (Palo Alto:  Stanford University Press, 1958).

Tiffen, M. The Enterprising Peasant:  Economic Development in Gombe Emirate North Eastern State, Nigeria, 1900-1968, Overseas Research Publication No. 21, Ministry of Overseas Development (London, 1976).

Tomlinson, G. and G. Lethem. History of Islamic Propaganda in Nigeria (London:  Waterlow, 1927).

Tricart, J. "Les exchanges entre la zone forestière de Côte d'Ivoire et les savanes soudaniennes," Cahiers d'Outre-Mer 35 (July-September 1956).

Turner, T. "The Transfer of Oil Technology and the Nigerian State," Development and Change, 7/4; "The Working of the Nigerian National Oil Corporation," in P. Collins, ed., Administration for Development in Nigeria (Lagos: African Education Press, 1980).

United Africa Company of Nigeria Ltd., Annual Report, 1979.

Usman, Y.B. "The Transformation of Katsina ca. 1796-1903" (Ph.D. diss., Ahmadu Bello University, 1974).

Van Arkadie, B. "Dependence in Kenya," in Development Trends in Kenya (University of Edinburgh Centre for African Studies, 1972).

Von Freyhold, M. "The Post Colonial State in its Tanzania Version," Review of African Political Economy, no. 8 (1977).

Walicki, A. The Controversy over Capitalism:  Studies in the Social Philosophy of the Russian Populists (London:  Oxford University Press, 1969), 122.

Wallace, T. "Agricultural Projects and Land" (February 1980).

Wallace, T. "Planning for Agricultural Development:  A Consideration of Some of the Theoretical and Practical Issues Involved" (Revised version of a paper presented at the 9th World Congress of Sociology, Uppsala, Sweden, August 1978).

Wallerstein, I. "Semiperipheral Countries and the Contemporary World Crisis," Theory and Society, 3, 4 (1976):  461-484.

Wallerstein, I. "Dependence in an Interdependent World," African Studies Review 17, 1 (1974): 1-26.

Wallerstein, I. The Modern World-System:  Capitalist Agriculture and the Origins of the European World-Economy in the Sixteenth Century (New York: Academic Press, 1974).

Wallerstein, I. "The Rise and Future Demise of the World Capitalist System: Concepts for Comparative Analysis," Comparative Studies in Society and History, vol. 16 (1974).

Warren, B. Imperialism:  Pioneer of Capitalism (London:  New Left Books, 1980).

Watts, Michael J. Silent Violence (Berkeley:  University of California Press, 1983).

Weekly Review, Nairobi, 24 November 1978.

Weekly Review, Nairobi, 5 January 1979.

Weekly Review, 2 February 1979.

West Africa, 7 January 1985.

West Africa, 28 October 1985.

Wilks, I. Asante in the Nineteenth Century (Cambridge: Cambridge University Press, 1975).

Williams, E. Capitalism and Slavery (Chapel Hill: University of North Carolina Press, 1944).

Williams, G. "A Political Economy," in Gavin Williams, ed., Nigeria: Economy and Society.

Williams, G. "Nigeria: A Political Economy" and "Politics in Nigeria," both reprinted in State and Society in Nigeria (Nigeria: Afrografika, 1980).

Williams, G. Nigeria: Economy and Society (Oxford: Oxford University Press, 1976).

Williams, G. "Taking the Part of Peasants," in P. Gutkind and I. Wallerstein, eds., The Political Economy of Contemporary Africa (Beverly Hills: Sage, 1976).

World Bank, World Development Report 1980 (World Bank and Oxford University Press, 1980).

Youngson, A.J. "Sweden, 1850-1880" and "Denmark 1865-1900" in A.J. Youngson, Possibilities of Economic Progress (London: Cambridge University Press, 1959).

Zeitlin, M. et al. "Class Segments: Agrarian Property and Political Leadership in the Capitalist Class of Chile," American Sociological Review 41 (1976): 1006-1029.

Zolberg, A. One-Party Government in the Ivory Coast (Princeton: Princeton University Press, 1969).

## Sources Abbreviations:

ANCI:  Archives nationales de la Côte d'Ivoire

ANS:  Archives nationales du Sénégal

ANF-OM:  Archives nationales de France, section Outre-Mer

PRO:  Public Record Office, London

# The Contributors

*Paul M. Lubeck* is associate professor of sociology and history at the University of California, Santa Cruz. He is the author of *Islam and Urban Labor in Northern Nigeria.*

*Gavin Kitching* teaches development studies at the Polytechnic of North London. He is the author of several books on development. In 1981, his major work, *Class and Economic Change in Kenya,* received the Herskovits Award, a prize awarded annually by the African Studies Association.

*Michael J. Watts* teaches geography and development studies at the University of California, Berkeley. His field work and historical analysis of famine in northern Nigeria provided the material for his book, *Silent Violence: Food, Famine, and Peasantry in Northern Nigeria.* He is a member of the Joint Committee on African Studies.

*David H. Groff* teaches African history at Reed College. His doctoral dissertation for Stanford University was based on extensive field work in the Ivory Coast. He also conducted research and practiced agricultural development in the Republic of Niger.

*Okello Oculi* teaches politics at Ahmadu Bello University and received his doctorate from the University of Wisconsin. He has written extensively for both scholars and the popular media on the agrarian transformation of northern Nigeria.

*Peter Anyang' Nyong'o* received his doctorate from the University of Chicago and has taught at the Universities of Nairobi and Addis Ababa as well as El Colegio de México. His most recent work is entitled *State and Society in Africa.* He is currently with the Economic Commission for Africa.

*Thomas J. Biersteker* teaches international relations at the University of Southern California. His dissertation received the Helen Dwight Reid award from the American Political Science Association and was published as *Distortion or Development: Contending Perspectives on the Multinational Corporation.* His current research assesses the long-term impact of indigenization programs in developing countries.

*Bonnie Campbell* teaches political science at the University of Quebec at Montreal. Her doctoral work was conducted at the Institute for Development Studies, University of Sussex. It examines the impact of French investment in cotton and textiles on the economic development of the Ivory Coast. Her most recent work examines the capacity of the state to direct linkages between industry and agriculture.

*Tom Forrest* is a research associate at the Institute for Commonwealth Studies, Oxford University. He taught economics at Ahmadu Bello University and has written extensively on Nigerian agriculture and industry.

*Nicola Swainson* is a research fellow at the Institute for Development Studies, University of Sussex, and the author of *The Development of Corporate Capitalism in Kenya, 1918-1977*. She has taught political science at the University of California, Los Angeles, the University of Nairobi, and the University of Canterbury (New Zealand). Her current research focuses on the national economic response to the internationalization of corporate capital.

*Steven Langdon* is the author of *Multinational Corporations in the Political Economy of Kenya*. He has taught economics at Carleton University and at the University of Nairobi. Currently, he is director of the Regional Office for East and Southern Africa for the Canadian development agency, the International Development Research Centre.

# Index

# DATE DUE

DEMCO NO. 38-298